Sir Robert Walpole's
Poets

Sir Robert Walpole's Poets

The Use of Literature as Pro-Government Propaganda, 1721–1742

Tone Sundt Urstad

DELAWARE

Newark: University of Delaware Press
London: Associated University Presses

Associated University Presses
440 Forsgate Drive
Cranbury, NJ 08512

Associated University Presses
16 Barter Street
London WC1A 2AH, England

Associated University Presses
P.O. Box 338, Port Credit
Mississauga, Ontario
Canada L5G 4L8

The paper used in this publication meets the requirements of the American National Standard for Permanence of Paper for Printed Library Materials Z39.48-1984.

Library of Congress Cataloging-in-Publication Data

Urstad, Tone Sundt, 1952–
    Sir Robert Walpole's poets : the use of literature as pro-
government propaganda, 1721–1742 / Tone Sundt Urstad.
        p.   cm.
Includes bibliographical references and index.
    ISBN 0-87413-690-3 (alk. paper)
    1. English poetry—18th century—History and criticism.
    2. Walpole, Robert, Earl of Orford, 1676–1745—Relations with poets.
    3. Politics and literature—Great Britain—History—18th century.
    4. Literature and state—Great Britain—History—18th century.
    5. Poets, English—18th century—Political and social views.
    6. Political poetry, English—History and criticism.   7. Great
Britain—Politics and government—1714–1760.   8. Propaganda,
British—History—18th century.   I. Title.
PR555.H5U75   1999
821'.509358—dc21   99-26940
                                                                CIP

The Verse, tho grac'd with Fashion's prize,
On Party built, with Party dies.

"A Familiar Epistle to the Author of the Heroic Epistle."

Contents

Preface and Acknowledgments

Subsequent to Sir Robert Walpole's enforced resignation in 1742, after more than twenty years as "Prime Minister," the parliamentary committee appointed to investigate the last ten years of his administration discovered that he had dispensed more than £50,000 during that period for the purpose of organizing propaganda in support of his administration.[1] Although this was an exorbitant sum by eighteenth-century standards, the findings of the committee nevertheless represented only the tip of the proverbial iceberg.

The rate at which Walpole was prepared to spend money on propaganda is, in itself, an indication of the importance he attached to this activity. It is all the more surprising, therefore, that although historians have devoted much attention to the measures by which Walpole sought to restrict the opposition press, they have shown little interest in the organization of pro-government propaganda, or in the contents of publications, whether literary or journalistic, subsidized by the government during this period. One partial exception to this general rule, however, is Michael Harris, who, in his book on the London newspaper press in the age of Walpole, does offer valuable information about the overall structure of newspapers of all political denominations, and describes the framework within which government control of the subsidized newspapers was exercised. However, he neither examines the propaganda content of pro-government newspapers, nor defines the nature of the censorship to which they were exposed.[2] The two studies that do deal specifically with government propaganda in the first half of the eighteenth century are restricted to periods before and after Walpole's term of office.[3]

Literary critics too have been little concerned with writers associated with—or employed by—Walpole's government. In large measure, of course, this can be explained by the political polarization of the literary community during his term of office. Nearly all the major writers of the period (Swift, Pope, Dr. Johnson, Fielding for most of his career, etc.)—with Defoe a notable exception—adopted an antigovernment stance, reflected in their works. Literary critics

9

have therefore tended to concentrate their attention on these writers, and on the particular political sphere with which they were associated. That is understandable; but it has, I think, in some ways distorted our view of the literary history of the period.

For one thing, ever since Walpole's days it has been an accepted truth that pro-government propaganda was uniformly dull and uninteresting. Pope, Swift, Fielding, and other major authors said so repeatedly, and there has been a tendency among literary critics to take their word for it. Indeed the neglect of Old Corps Whig writers—both collectively and individually—is hardly surprising when seen against the opposition's success in promoting an image of Sir Robert Walpole as "Bob, the Poet's Foe," surrounded by mercenary Grub-street hacks, whose willingness to write according to political dictation compensated for their lack of scruples and ability;[4] but the truth is that a reexamination of Old Corps Whig writings is long overdue.

I was awakened to this myself through what was originally an interest just in the life and works of one figure of the times, Sir Charles Hanbury Williams, on whom I wrote my Cambridge doctoral thesis. The best of Hanbury Williams's political satires were highly effective as propaganda. Although far too rich and independent to be considered a party scribbler, he was remarkable for the consistency with which he attempted to use his satire as a weapon in the political power struggle, and for his willingness to adjust his writings so as to fit in with party policy by, for instance, changing their implied political provenance. In this he was aided by friends who were prominent members of his party. Not only did they suggest appropriate themes and provide criticism and encouragement, but they can also be found advising Hanbury Williams to suppress a given work altogether, suggesting changes that would bring it more into line with party requirements, or arranging for publication through various channels—all according to their estimate of readers' likely responses. This seems to reflect a highly sophisticated awareness of the potential of literary works used as political propaganda and automatically raised the question whether Hanbury Williams's case should be seen as an isolated phenomenon, or as part of a larger context within which other writers played similar roles.[5] I thus became curious to read other Old Corps Whig writers, and found that the quality of their work—although seldom first-rate— was sometimes surprisingly high. That led me to question the opposition myth that talent and ability were all on their side, and that only the very worst Grub Street hacks were prepared to support Walpole with their feeble efforts: this book is the result.

The case it presents is not, I hope, an unnuanced one. It is certainly true that Walpole never commanded the services of a writer of the same stature as—say—Swift or Pope. It is also true that much pro-Walpole propaganda does range from bad to mediocre, just as on the *opposition* side of the political divide, works by Swift, Fielding, and Pope with an opposition slant stand out against a general background of dull grinding anti-Walpole propaganda.[6]

Although much interesting pro-government material has also been uncovered, I feel strongly that even if Walpole's propaganda had been every bit as inept as it has been made out to be, a study of the literature created by writers associated with the government would still be of value. The full extent and richness of political allusion in the works of the major writers of the period can never be *fully* recognized until it can be seen in detail how the fund of politically sensitive themes, imagery, and symbols on which authors more or less loosely associated with the opposition to Walpole could draw, developed not in a vacuum but in an agon between these writers and their pro-government counterparts.

More formally stated, then, the aim of this book is to try to explain what the Old Corps Whig leadership hoped to achieve by spending so lavishly on propaganda, how Walpole's propaganda network was organized, what sort of propaganda was issued through government channels, and so to show how opposition and pro-government propaganda interacted to create a climate of extreme sensitivity to the political nuances of literary works.

After a short introduction, devoted largely to a description of the image created by contemporary opposition writers of Walpole and of the authors prepared to write in his service, the book is divided into three main sections corresponding to three main areas of interest.

The first section provides an outline of how propaganda was organized under Walpole, which will be concerned with the following questions: What was the relationship between leaders of the party on the one hand and editors, writers, printers, and booksellers on the other? Who formulated polemical strategy at any given time, and how were editorial decisions made? In essence, then, this first section will be concerned with the political pressures brought to bear on individuals active within the sphere of pro-government propaganda, as well as with the incentives and encouragement the government had to offer in return. It is important, here, to explore the extent of Walpole's influence in the world of publishing. After all, newspapers and journals represented only part of the publishing network available to authors willing to write in support of the administration. Miscellanies were another outlet, while a great number of politically sensitive poems and other works were issued separately as broadsheets and other productions.

The second section will be concerned with what the government hoped to achieve by spending so massively on propaganda, concentrating on the theories pro-government writers and politicians developed as to how best to influence certain target groups. One interesting question that will be discussed in this section pertains to the reasons why certain literary forms, preponderant in the political literature of the day, were considered as better suited for propaganda purposes than other literary forms.

The third section contains an analysis of the most important themes contained in the literary productions that were used as pro-government propaganda, concentrating on the works of writers associated with Walpole and on anonymous literary works contained in government-sponsored newspapers and other publications. The Old Corps Whig writers had far more in common than just a political ideology. Over the years they developed a fund of themes, symbols, and imagery distinctly their own, but they also tried to diffuse opposition propaganda by reinterpreting opposition themes and so on in order to hit back at their opponents.

Underlying the whole work is an interest in the development of what might be called literary-political "languages." The pro-government press developed under Walpole from a primarily defensive weapon, merely responding to attacks on the government by opposition writers, into being also a first-strike force involved in its own aggressive mythmaking.[7] The pattern of attacks and counterattacks, whether initiated by the government or the opposition, created a climate within which certain words and phrases acquired distinct political overtones. The study of this process at work sheds light on the literary productions of authors on both sides of the political divide.

※

In the search for the underlying structure of Walpole's propaganda network, extensive use has been made of manuscript sources. The papers of writers, politicians, printers, booksellers, etc. have been consulted, together with the official records of the Treasury, when necessary. I have consequently spent many happy hours reading manuscripts in various libraries and record repositories. The greater part of the research for this book was carried out at the Cambridge University Library and at the British Library and I am greatly indebted to the librarians of both these institutions, especially to Mr. Godfrey Waller, Superintendent of the Manuscripts Department, for help with the Cholmondeley (Houghton) archives at Cambridge and to Assistant Keeper Robert A. H. Smith for information concerning the Wolterton manuscripts which have only recently been deposited in the British Library and are in the process of being catalogued. At the Lewis Walpole Library, Yale University, I have been fortunate to receive help from Mrs. Joan Sussler, Curator of Prints (including those reproduced in this book) and the Assistant Librarian, Mrs. Anna Malicka, especially with the Sir Charles Hanbury Williams archives deposited there.

I am also most grateful for all the assistance I have received from librarians and archivists during visits to the Bodleian Library in Oxford, the National Register of Archives, the National Art Library and the Guildhall Library in London, the National Library of Scotland, the Newport Public Library in Gwent, the university libraries of Oslo, Edinburgh, San Francisco, and California (at Stanford and Berkeley), and the Public Record Office in London.

At one time or another I have received photocopies or microfilm of manuscript material from all the above mentioned institutions as well as from the Beinecke Rare Book and Manuscript Library at Yale University, the West Sussex Record Office, the Dumfries and Galloway Regional Library Service, and the Centre for Kentish Studies (a document belonging to the Trustees of the Knole Estate), and for this I am most grateful. I should also like to thank the archivists of the following record repositories for clearing up details in the biographies of minor literary figures and for responding to my queries about the possible location of manuscript material by offering suggestions which in many cases led to discoveries: the record offices of Dorset, Wiltshire, Essex, Shropshire, Hertfordshire, Buckinghamshire, and Northumberland, the Lambeth Archives Department, the Hackney Archives Department, and the Dumphries Archive Centre.

The work for this book was carried out while I held a four-year Research Fellowship at the Institute for British and American Studies at Oslo University. During that time I was fortunate to receive a number of generous grants from the institute, the university, and the Norwegian Research Council that made it possible for me to spend my summers doing research in England. I am most grateful to the fellows and staff of my old college New Hall at Cambridge University for allowing me back every year as Visiting Scholar.

While working on this book I have received invaluable help from a number of people. Professor Keith Brown and Professor Stein

Haugom Olsen of Oslo University both read the manuscript and suggested changes, as did Dr. Howard Erskine-Hill of Pembroke College, Cambridge University. In expressing my deep gratitude to them for their many helpful suggestions, I must emphasize that any mistakes contained in this book are of course entirely my own.

I should also like to thank my husband, our son, my parents and the rest of my family for their support and encouragement, as well as Dr. Kari Anne Rand Schmidt and Professor Bjørn Tysdahl of Oslo University, Dr. Donald C. Mell of the University of Delaware Press, Mr. Julien Yoseloff and Mrs. Christine A. Retz of the Associated University Presses, and Val and John Galpin, who over the years have taken me to see some truly wonderful eighteenth-century houses and gardens.

My greatest debts are—as always—due to Dr. Penelope Wilson of New Hall, Cambridge University and to Professor Keith Brown of Oslo University for their unwavering support and generosity with their time.

Introduction

In the early 1730s Lord Hervey—a strong supporter of Sir Robert Walpole—went to the theater in Goodman's Fields to see James Ralph's adaptation of a Restoration play, *The Fall of the Earl of Essex*. When the actor who played the main part delivered his lines:

> Abhor all Courts if thou art brave or wise,
> For then thou never shalt be sure to rise,
> Think not by doing well a Fame to get,
> But be a Villain & thou shalt be great,

"Her Grace of Marlborough cry'd charming; & clapt her Hands so loud that we heard her cross the theatre into the King's Box."[1]

This simple story illustrates just how sensitive people were to political allusions in literary works during the Walpole era. As a violent opposition supporter the Duchess seized the opportunity to demonstrate her contempt not only for the king and his court, but also for the man at the head of the government, Sir Robert Walpole. Although the "Prime Minister" is not mentioned by name in the passage quoted above, contemporaries would have had very little difficulty in reading an allusion to Walpole into the last line. First of all, the word "Courts" in the first line suggested more than simply the entourage of kings and queens; it evoked the whole range of Old Corps Whig supporters who kept Walpole in power. At the time opposition spokesmen were insisting that the old party labels of Whig and Tory were obsolete and should be replaced by the new nomenclature of Court and Country. This they did partly for ideological reasons, and partly to slur over the political differences between the Tories and the dissident Whigs who were cooperating in the opposition. Consequently, for the Duchess of Marlborough and her contemporaries the first line read as an injunction to avoid, not only King George II's court but also all contact with the Old Corps Whig party, which the opposition sometimes insisted on calling the Court and Treasury Party. In the last line the mere mention of the adjective "great" would have been enough to conjure up the image of Sir Robert Walpole as the corrupt statesman. Opposition writers habitually and ironically referred to Walpole as "the Great Man," to the point where the word "great" carried very negative overtones. To be a "great" man in the state implied that this position had been acquired through lack of scruples and was based on ill-gotten gains of one sort or another. "Great" and "good," used within this context, had in fact almost become antonyms, just as in the little passage from Ralph's play an opposition is established between "brave," "wise" and "doing well"—qualifications that *ought* to lead to high office—and words that express social success ("Courts," "rise," "Fame," and "great"), all in this context linked with the unambiguously negative word "Villain."

Just how sensitive governments were to this kind of political satire is shown by the sort of passages that were censured after the introduction of the Licensing Act of 1737:

> The Statesman's skill, like mine, is all deceit.
> What's policy in him—in me's a cheat.
> Titles and wealth reward his noble art,
> Cudgels and bruises mine—sometimes a cart.
> 'Twas, is, and will be, to the end of time,
> That poverty, not fraud, creates the crime.[2]

This sensitivity to language is perhaps only possible at times of extreme political polarization. It is generally accepted that the Whig/Tory dichotomy was less violent during Walpole's era than it had been during the reign of Queen Anne, but this does not mean that party divides were not acute. Few contemporaries were as intransigent as Lady Wigtown who as a Jacobite, "would not speak to any one she thought a Whig."[3] But this was, after all, a time when Walpole had one of the King's chaplains removed for preaching on the bible text "Take away the wicked from before the king, and his throne shall be established in righteousness,"[4] when Whigs and Tories frequented different coffeehouses, and when garden art could express political convictions: in his garden at Stowe Lord Cobham, in accordance with his opposition principles, erected a ruined Temple of Modern Virtues to offset the Temple of Ancient Virtues which was whole and intact.[5] Alluding primarily to the theater, Sir Richard Steele wrote in 1721 to the Lord Chamberlain, "the Crowd Assemble themselves, even in their Pleasures, according to their inclinations in Politicall [sic] Affairs."[6]

Unless critics keep in mind this substratum of political allusion omnipresent in literature of the first half of the eighteenth century they can very easily be led astray. Dr. Johnson's definition: "Patriotism is the last refuge of a scoundrel," for example, is often quoted as a comment on patriotism as a phenomenon, whereas it should be seen for what it was: a Tory's indirect, disgruntled comment on the "Patriots"—the dissident Whig faction who after years in opposition to Walpole, flaunting their "patriotic" disinterestedness, abandoned their Tory and opposition Whig allies and were bought off by places and pensions for themselves at Walpole's resignation.[7]

Textual analysis combined with a close study of the political situation at the time has in recent years brought out the undercurrent of political allusion present in many works by major authors of the eighteenth century. Literary critics have also shown increasing awareness of what Bertrand Goldgar has termed an opposition "argot," in which certain words acquired layer upon layer of political connotations to the point where the mere mention of "screen" or "brass" conjured up the image of Walpole as the corrupt political leader.[8]

It is hardly unusual, of course, for politicians to be criticized for the policies carried out under their administration. Walpole's era was remarkable, however, for the degree to which this criticism was voiced through literary works, and for the extent to which writers hostile to the government were prepared to contribute towards the myths that the opposition was creating of Walpole as a character by referring constantly to him in their works. It is no exaggeration to say that Walpole was an obsession with writers more or less loosely associated with the opposition. He was a man whom contemporaries loved to hate, reviled both as a private and a public figure. Allegedly morally corrupt in every way—avaricious, lecherous, above all self-serving—he was portrayed as the corrupt statesman whose ever-increasing private fortune was based on the ruin of the state. The word "corruption" carried with it connotations of a spreading contagion, and as a man who had the financial means to corrupt others, Walpole came to symbolize in his own person a perceived threat to public virtue and morality. Through the systematic and extensive use of patronage he was thought to have ensured a permanent majority in Parliament. By insinuating himself into the king's favor and ruthlessly eliminating all rivals, he had made himself a "Prime Minister"—a term of disapprobation at the time.[9] By these actions he had allegedly endangered that fine balance between king, lords and the commons on which the unwritten Constitution was based.

Because of the libel laws, criticism of Walpole had to be veiled and tortuous, however. In contemporary fiction he had innumerable aliases such as Sir Blue String, King Bob, Quidam, Sir Positive

Screenall, Sir Robert Brass. Opposition writers "combed the history books, discovering parallel cases of evil ministers, overgrown in power, who met a tragic end" (Buckingham, Cardinal Wolsey, Sejanus, etc.).[10] Older plays that portrayed the downfall of corrupt and self-seeking politicians could within the contemporary political context be interpreted as attacks on Walpole, and were consequently revived.

All the major writers alluded to Walpole in their works. We are all familiar with the way Fielding's attacks on Walpole and the Royal family in his deliriously funny plays supposedly occasioned the Licensing Act, and how Gay in *The Beggar's Opera* made an implied comparison between the criminal world and the world of politics, in terms of the subjection of all moral values to commercial considerations. Every student of the Neoclassical period is taught to recognize an allusion to Walpole in Swift's description of how "Flimnap, the Treasurer" does "a Dance on the Rope" to prove to the Emperor of Lilliput that he has not lost his touch and is still worthy of the high office he holds by cutting "a Caper on the straight Rope, at least an Inch higher than any other Lord in the whole Empire." This image is rendered doubly grotesque when we recall—as many contemporaries could not help but do—Walpole's tubby, well-nourished frame, and try to imagine him performing an act that demands physical dexterity and subtlety of motion.[11] Not only is the exercise of rope dancing an apt metaphor both for the contortions contemporary politicians went through to obtain and retain power, and for the inappropriate nature of their qualifications for high office, there is also an implied comment on Walpole's unfitness for the post he held even within these defined terms, since the physical stature of the real man helps to render the image of Flimnap dancing on the rope doubly incongruous.

Such allusions are not only to be found in the works of major writers of the period: Walpole was the theme of countless broadsheet ballads, one more scurrilous than the other. A critic who has studied prose satires in the general manner of *Gulliver's Travels* during Walpole's term of office, found that with one exception, all were antigovernment, and that Walpole himself was alluded to with obsessive frequency. In contradiction to Vincent Carretta's claim that "Walpole's enemies couched their assault on his rule in constitutional terms," the aim of these stories was:

> to portray the prime minister as a grotesque, even bestial figure, a creature of enormous excesses: he is variously a wicked Eastern vizier, a dastardly criminal, an evil magician or avaricious usurer, a rapist of vir-

gins, a disease-ridden whoremonger. His machinations are revealed to be the natural result of his appetites for power, personal wealth, and succulent female flesh.[12]

The numerous prints that satirize Walpole also conform to this basic pattern. A typical example is *Idol-Worship or the Way to Preferment* in which Walpole is represented as a gigantic figure blocking the door to St James's Palace. By his control over the entrance that leads to the king and therefore to high office within the state, he reduces the other figures to moral pygmies; without debasing themselves to him they cannot embark on the road that leads to preferment. Scurrilous as it is, this print is moderate in comparison with certain other attacks on the "Prime Minister" published in what was basically a rumbustious age. In one print he was depicted as having incestuous relations with his daughter, for instance.[13]

One might well ask why Walpole himself was such an obsession with so many of his contemporaries. One obvious explanation is the basic principle behind all mudslinging: it is normally easier and more effective to discredit somebody by attacking their person than their policies. In addition, historians have tried to explain this phenomenon by referring to the longevity of Walpole's administration, and to the fact that he was "Prime Minister" at a time when important changes—social and political—were taking place in Britain. For all these developments, whether he could influence them or not, Walpole was held directly responsible, since opposition writers needed a symbol that could embody their disapproval of the changes that were taking place.

One such development was the expansion of the book trade following the lapsing of the Licensing Act in 1695. It has been calculated, for instance, that by 1704 about forty-four thousand copies of newspapers were being printed in London every week.[14] Minor authors proliferated in a way that must have seemed threatening to anyone concerned about upholding standards, and it is understandable that major authors should have felt crowded by their less competent brethren.

Connected with this trend and perhaps in some measure dependent on it was a changing attitude in government circles to the patronage of major authors, whatever their political convictions. The best writers of the age felt excluded from what they considered their rightful place in society. Earlier administrations had—it was claimed—patronized writers for their ability, not for their politics; but Walpole, with his alleged indifference to the arts, was not fulfilling his obligations. It is true that Walpole was reluctant to pro-

IDOL-WORSHIP
or
The Way to Preferment.

And Henry the KING *made unto himself a great* IDOL, *the likeness of which was not in Heaven above, nor in the Earth beneath; and he reared up his Head unto ỹ Clouds, & extended his Arm over all ỹ Land: His Legs also were as ỹ Posts of a Gate, or as an Arch stretched forth over ỹ Doors of all ỹ Publick Offices in ỹ Land, & whosoever went out or whosoever came in, passed beneath, & with Idolatrous Reverence lift up their Eyes, & kissed ỹ Cheeks of ỹ Postern.*

Pub. 1740   Chronicle of the Kings, page 51

Idol-Worship or The Way to Preferment. **Courtesy of the Lewis Walpole Library, Yale University.**

mote literary figures to positions in the state, which in his view
demanded quite other qualities than they were masters of. According to his late-eighteenth-century biographer William Coxe he was
"often heard to say, that they were fitter for speculation than for
action, that they trusted to theory, rather than to experience, and
were guided by principles inadmissible in practical life" (on making Congreve a Commissioner of Taxes, he observed, "You will
find he has no head for business").[15] However, this was not an entirely new trend. In 1715 Sir Richard Steele had complained to the
Duke of Newcastle, about lacking patronage from the government:
"I know I am reckoned, in Generall [sic], an ill manager, and know
also that it is made a Bar against doing for Me."[16]

Walpole also expected rather more gratitude—expressed in political loyalty—than many authors were prepared to offer. The anger
that the major writers felt at being thus excluded was intensified by
their belief that other less deserving writers were occupying the
places that should, as they saw it, be theirs by right. It has been
suggested that this explains the venom with which they attacked all
pro-government writers as inept and corrupt, slowly creating a
myth that still has not lost its force today.

Even so, certain gaps between the myth and the reality have always been plain for all who choose to see. There are grounds for
thinking that Defoe's *A Journal of the Plague Year* was written as
part of the government's public health policies.[17] Henry Fielding
seems to have deserted to Walpole's camp in 1741, and with the
recent discoveries of early unpublished material it is no longer self-
evident—as it was to his early biographers—that he was an opposition Whig writer born.[18] Samuel Richardson too, in his capacity of
printer, worked for Walpole.[19]

One reason why the image of the pro-government writer as invariably incompetent and dull has survived is of course the underlying assumption of many modern critics that commissioned writing
will *automatically* be inferior. Only this can explain why a writer
like Thomas Gordon of "Cato's Letters" fame is lauded by critics
as an excellent polemicist for his opposition writing, only to become a nonperson to them the moment he made his peace with the
government.[20]

Yet, ironically, recent research has proved that there was a very
good market for literary works with an opposition bias and that this
may help to account for the overwhelming quantity of hostile allusions to Walpole and his administration in contemporary literary
works.[21] "No one is so ignorant as not to know that the Temple of
Fame, according to the modern Structure of it, has but two Gates,

which are *Faction* and *Infidelity*," stated the pro-government news-paper the *Senator*. An opposition slant quite simply ensured good sales. When the Lord Chamberlain prohibited the play *Gustavus Vasa* from being acted, it was brought out in book form and promptly pirated, an indication that it was selling very well. As a press spy explained, government attempts to suppress scurrilous opposition literature "Serves but for an advertisement to the Libel & helps to mend the Sale & consequently encreases [sic] their Profit."[22] Edward Cave correspondingly used the image of the river Thames to explain the disadvantages that pro-government writers labored under in the competition to attract readers since "the People are not taken with Truth so much as Novelty, and less with Order than Confusion":

> Yet such is the case of the writers for the Government. They maintain that the Current of the Government flows undisturbed within its Channel, to the great benefit of every Subject.[23]

Sir Robert Walpole's
Poets

I

The Organization of Pro-Government Propaganda Under Walpole

1

The Political Climate

When prepublication censorship in England came to an end in 1695 with the lapsing of the Licensing Act, there was an immediate upsurge in the publication of political works of every description, and politicians soon started to look for ways in which to curb the press.

By the time Walpole came to power in 1721 a thriving trade in newspapers, books, pamphlets, separately published poems, and broadsheets bore witness to the fact that politicians—both Whigs and Tories—had been incapable of devising effective means to control the press. The introduction in 1712 of the Stamp Duty on printed matter had only temporarily reduced the total output of published material. Soon the trade—and especially its more unscrupulous members—had worked out how to circumvent or make the best of the new regulations.[1]

But if the politicians had singularly failed to regulate the press with its unwelcome intrusion into political life, they had certainly learned to exploit it for their own advantage. Whigs and Tories alike had seen the need to present their parties' points of view outside Parliament to a wide readership, and over the years each party had acquired extensive contacts within the publishing trade. While Robert Harley was at the head of the Tory ministry during the last four years of the reign of Queen Anne, he created a comprehensive network designed to promote his particular brand of Tory government propaganda. With someone like Jonathan Swift willing to write and to act as middleman between other writers and the politicians, Harley has become famous for the quality of some of the propaganda produced in support of his administration. The Whigs in opposition organized their own propaganda effort in much the same way by influencing and employing writers, printers, newspaper-proprietors, booksellers, etc. In those days the Whig side could muster writers of the caliber of Addison and Steele, while Daniel Defoe wrote alternately—and sometimes simultaneously—for both sides.

Robert Downie, who has documented the organization of political propaganda in the early years of the eighteenth century, claims that the Whigs maintained an active interest in propaganda whilst in opposition, but became "notoriously lax" about such matters the moment they gained political power. The research carried out for this book indicates that Walpole in this respect conformed to the pattern established by his predecessors. Although there was clearly a propaganda effort on foot in the early 1720s—with Steele, for instance, referring to the writing he was doing under Walpole's "Observation and Patronage"—it would not seem to have been nearly as extensive as it was later to become under pressure from the opposition propaganda campaign. There is certainly no evidence of any overwhelming interest in press matters on Walpole's part during the first years of his administration, before he had consolidated his position as "Prime Minister."

It is true that when Walpole came to power he did not stand in the same need of defence as he was later to do. Naturally he was derided in pamphlets and newspapers for the role he had played in shielding prominent politicians against public rage and scrutiny over financial malpractice in connection with the South Sea Company scandal (his sobriquet "the Screen" dates from this time). However, as C. B. Realey has shown, this first opposition against Walpole soon folded, and was followed by a period of relative calm.[2]

In these first years the ministry had at its disposal the services of a number of Whig writers, but there seems to have been little group feeling among these authors. This may reflect a lack of political leadership, but could also be explained by divisions created between them during the Whig Schism prior to Walpole's rise to power. Some writers, like Steele and Cibber, had been on Walpole's side in opposition, while others, like Eusden and Welsted, had been the protégés of politicians such as the Duke of Newcastle, who supported Stanhope and Sunderland's government. It seems likely that such a rift would take time to heal. Steele who had been forced out of his patent at Drury Lane by Newcastle, was promptly reinstated 2 May 1721 by Walpole who compelled the other patentees to readmit Steele.[3] Ambrose Philips, on the other hand, although a committed Whig who during the Whig Schism had written the *Freethinker* "by the Direction of the Government," only joined (or was allowed to join) the Walpole side in 1724.[4]

It was really only about the year 1725 that satirists and others started to concern themselves wholeheartedly with Walpole. By then he and Lord Townshend had succeeded in ousting all Sunderland's ministerial supporters from office (Roxburgh, Macclesfield,

Cadogan, and Carteret who was exiled in Ireland as Lord Lieutenant) and were firmly in control.[5] When the *Craftsman* was launched at the end of 1726 and joined *Mist's Weekly Journal* as the most important vehicle for opposition propaganda, Walpole's period of grace was definitely over. With prominent contributors like Lord Bolingbroke and William Pulteney, the *Craftsman* became a formidable weapon that brought energy to the new opposition.

Perhaps contemporaries only really started to wake up to how impregnable Walpole had succeeded in making his position, when George II ascended to the throne. Everyone, Walpole included, believed that Sir Spencer Compton would succeed him in office. When the new king failed to dismiss Walpole, Swift wrote to Gay: "he has held the longest hand at hazard that ever fell to any Sharpers [sic] Share and keepe [sic] his run when the dice are changed." With the realization of Walpole's entrenched position as virtual head of the government, attacks upon him started to increase in frequency and virulence, especially—as Quentin Skinner has pointed out—with the opening in 1728 of the first session of the new parliament.[6] For years Walpole was slightly overshadowed in the ministry by his brother-in-law, Lord Townshend. When the latter resigned in 1730 Walpole truly became the "Prime Minister" and thus the main focus of opposition attention. The London theater does not seem to have been remarkably hostile to Walpole before 1728 when the first performance of John Gay's *The Beggar's Opera*, ushered in a period when the theater became increasingly politicized.[7]

As the opposition against Walpole grew, because of defections from his own camp, the Tories and the dissident Whigs intent on forcing Walpole out of office, acquired an impressive number of outlets for material sympathetic to their cause. Political themes became ever more important in the literature of the day.

There is clearly a parallel development in the world of prints. For the first years of Walpole's reign few cartoons were published, and fewer still were concerned with politics, Paul Langford going as far as to suggest that the engravers and their publishers "seem studiously to have avoided politics as a theme as well as Walpole's own growing stature." Between 1727 and 1730 this situation was transformed, as the theme of general corruption in society and government which had been so prevalent in the early years of the century was translated into personal attacks on Walpole.[8]

At the outset, then, the propaganda initiative was taken by the opposition. Under the onslaught of increasingly virulent attacks Walpole was forced to retaliate. It would seem that in the early 1720s he was largely content to employ defensive tactics. As shown below, he tried to limit the damage the opposition could cause, by intermittently restricting their access to a wide readership, and by discouraging individuals from producing or promoting opposition propaganda through various means.

However, as the years went by, the paper war against Walpole reached truly formidable proportions. Under the smart of a mud-slinging campaign that makes most subsequent campaigns of that nature pale into insignificance, Walpole seems to have decided that decisive action was necessary. Defensive measures were no longer adequate, and so Walpole set to work to improve and expand the pro-government propaganda network, extending the influence that the ministry already had in the world of publishing. As a result of these activities pro-government propaganda became increasingly assertive. No longer were the people behind Walpole's propaganda effort content to merely counter opposition moves; they had become capable of taking the initiative in the propaganda war.

The intensification of Walpole's propaganda offensive led to an increased polarization of the literary community. Soon we find writers routinely being divided along political lines, although there was certainly nothing new about this. In a poem called "Cloe to Mr. Tickell, Occasion'd by his *Avignon* Letter" published in 1729 but written before Addison's death in 1719, the persona claims to have been changed from "a Woman-Bigot" into a supporter of Tickell's "glorious Cause" by reading his works. She pours scorn on Pope and Gay, reserving all her praise for a string of Whig writers: Addison (who is urged to "Convince the wond'ring World, that GEORGE's Reign | Is not condemn'd to Folly, and to Gain"), Garth, Philips, Congreve ("silent long"), Vanbrugh, and Welsted. Throughout the period it was generally recognized that literary works were—in the words of William King regarding one of his own compositions—"extolled or condemned according to the prejudice of party." Colley Cibber, for instance, was said to have had a great number of "undeserved enemies," because his "steady attachment to those revolution principles which he first set out with in life, though not pursued by him with violence or offence to any one, created a party against him, which almost constantly prevented his receiving those advantages from his writings, or that applause for his acting, which both justly merited."[9]

Theater audiences frequently divided along political lines, and for this and other reasons writers often packed first-night audiences with as many of their friends as possible. When Benjamin Martyn, who was Examiner of the out-ports in the Custom-house, produced his one and only play, it was acted "with some success." So much so that the opposition writer James Miller claimed that "when *Timoleon* was represented for the first time, the author's friends were so very zealous in doing it justice, that not a scene was drawn without a clap, the very candle-snuffers received their share of approbation, and a couch made its entrance with universal applause." A play about the just overthrow of a tyrannical ruler in Corinth, its relevance to a British theater audience less than half a century after the Glorious Revolution was obvious (Benjamin Martyn left a manuscript life of the first Earl of Shaftesbury). The prologue "Written by a FRIEND" subtly hinted at such a connection: "*His Hero burns with Liberty, and Love. | With Liberty, each manly* Briton's *care.*" In his dedication to the king in the printed version, Benjamin Martyn spelled out the political implications of the play. *Timoleon* had been "written with an Ambition to render Your People easy under Your Government, to make them æmulous [sic] only for Virtue, and to shew them the Value of that Liberty, which is so eminently Your MAJESTY's Care." He also claimed to have drawn his description of perfect kingship "by copying from Your MAJESTY the Virtues of a King, who is a Blessing to his People."[10]

2

Dealing with the Opposition

Walpole had two main objectives: firstly, to diffuse and render harmless, propaganda produced or abetted by the opposition, and to thwart all efforts on their part to circulate their more extreme material to a nationwide readership; secondly, to explain government policies and promote a positive image of government activities and personalities.

The government kept a strict eye on everything that appeared in print. In 1721 a suggestion that a "general Libell-Committee" be appointed had been overruled for fear it might prove too heavy-handed.[1] Instead, from 1722 onwards Nicholas Paxton—then acting as an assistant to the Treasury Solicitor—was paid £200 a year for "Perusing and observing on pamphlets published." He was also expected to keep an eye on newspapers and report on unacceptable material.[2] Consequently a pamphletseller (latterly a Mrs. Winbish) was paid regularly every quarter for providing the Secretary of State's office with newspapers. And from 1726 onward all the provincial newspapers were provided by Joseph Bell, the Comptroller of the post office. The Messengers of the press were also involved in "buying up and getting marked for evidence, by their Lordships' order" all pamphlets and newspapers published in London. Walpole also tried to keep himself informed of antigovernment pamphlets being printed abroad and on occasion attempts were made to have such material suppressed before copies were smuggled into England.[3]

From the point of view of the government it was important that certain works should be prevented from circulating freely, especially in the provinces. For this reason employees at the post office routinely received orders from the Secretaries of State to stop material considered libelous or seditious. In this way the post office functioned efficiently as an organ of censorship.[4]

Exceptionally outrageous material could, of course, be prosecuted in the courts of law, but government officials were reluctant to do so for several reasons. Firstly, the seditious material was nearly always disguised in some way or other. A Jacobite attack on the king, for example, could be presented in the form of an allegory or an historical essay (complete with pointed italics) about a usurper in the past who had supplanted the rightful monarch of some country or other. To prove a work such as this seditious, the government would have to demonstrate that it was really intended as a comment on the Hanoverian Succession, a thing that could prove not only difficult but embarrassing.

Secondly, the most experienced of the opposition printers and publishers knew precisely how to play the legal game so as to make it difficult to prove their complicity in the publishing of seditious material, even if their names were on the imprint. Writing to the Attorney General on the subject of Richard Francklin, in charge of producing the *Craftsman*, who had been examined about an issue held to be seditious, one of the officials—clearly exasperated—wrote ironically, "He, poor Innocent, knows not who that Francklin is that puts his Name to ye Craftsmen, & has no manner of Concern with that Paper; however by accidental Conversation he has learnt who is ye Author, & if I will give him my Word of honour that he, Francklin, shall not be put to give in Bail or brought into any further trouble, he will discover ye Author, who he believes will own it." The "reputed Author" of the *Craftsman*, Nicholas Amhurst, had been overheard "directing Francklin to give such an Answer."[5] Faced with opponents who were receiving expert legal advice, the government found it increasingly difficult to persuade juries to return the wished-for verdict.

Thirdly, even if the prosecution against a printer, publisher, or bookseller were successful, the inevitable adverse publicity had to be taken into account. Members of the government were acutely conscious that any attempts to curb the opposition press only gave the opposition papers the chance to complain in their next issues about unwarranted government interference, increasing their sales significantly in the process. "There was never a Mist or any other Person taken up or tryed, but double the number of papers were sold upon it, besides ye irritating the people from ye Notion of persecution," wrote a press informer who used the pseudonym of "John Smith."[6] On another occasion he argued that,

'tis the Reception Libels meet with rather than the Arguments contained in them which make them dangerous & sometimes this Reception is actually owing to apprehending the Publishers & Authors. This makes both known to the Publick and the Voice of the Populace from that time forward Sanctifies all the Trash which comes from the same Quarter establishing it on the foolish Maxim that A thing must be very extraordinary in its kind w.ch is taken notice off [sic] by those in Power.[7]

"John Smith" did not disapprove of all prosecutions, however. His advice was that such treatment should be reserved for the major characters behind opposition propaganda, except in cases where "the treating a new Setter up in that way roughly" might have a salubrious effect.[8] Similar views were voiced by many government supporters. Bishop Hoadley wrote to the queen's Mistress of the Robes:

> . . . what can be proposed by the Administration from the prosecution of printers and publishers now again, after so many disappointments, set on foot? I defy them to name any one instance (excepting the case of high treason) in which a prosecution of this sort did not end to the prejudice of the Administration, even where they succeeded in the sentence for punishment; much less where they perhaps can never succeed, but must go on still to disappointment, as they have done already. I wish they would consider this experience, instead of consulting their present anger.[9]

It was left to the government lawyers to counsel the Secretaries of State as to whether a prosecution was possible or desirable. Lord Chancellor Hardwicke regularly advised against prosecutions on the grounds that the outcome would be uncertain. After 1731 the policy of consistent legal pressure was abandoned (although there was another surge of activity in 1737). In the provinces there was a corresponding spate of activity in terms of prosecutions between 1728 and 1731, after which the central government was content to leave the problem of the country newspapers to the local authorities, which, with notable exceptions like Exeter, Norwich, and Nottingham, were "noticeably reluctant to take action."[10]

However, it should be emphasized that in exercising their right to prosecute libels on private individuals, government officials may at times have had vicarious political motives. When in 1733 the *London Evening Post* carried "the grossest libel" on Sir Charles Gunter Nicholl, deceased, the Treasury Solicitor, Nicholas Paxton, immediately started legal proceedings against two of the publishers, expressing delight that "this Opportunity . . . might have a Tendency to suppress a villainous Paper." Only afterwards was he approached by the dead man's executors and asked to prosecute. This lends credence to the conclusions reached later by the committee investigating Walpole's last ten years in power, that the court case had been paid for by the government, and only served as a pretext to harass an opposition paper.[11]

Despite the assertion in one pro-government production that to "weary them with perpetual *Prosecutions*" would be a strategy below the dignity of the administration, it seems quite clear that this is precisely the policy adopted by the government with respect to tiresome opponents, such as Nathaniel Mist, the printer of *Mist's Weekly Journal*, and the printer and one of the proprietors behind the main opposition newspaper the *Craftsman*, Henry Haines and Richard Francklin. Given the legal hazards involved, however, government officials seem to have preferred unofficial harassment to wholesale prosecution, and to have used their informal powers "with shrewdness and determination." Printers, publishers, booksellers, or others involved in the production or dispersal of objectionable works could be arrested, kept in prison, and then released without charges being pressed against them. This would not only disrupt their work but could cause considerable economic hardship. Nathaniel Mist, for instance, was arrested and/or fined and/or imprisoned every year between 1721–1727, except 1726.[12] In response to an article by William Arnall on the subject of the freedom of the press in the *Free Briton* of 1 July 1733, the opposition writer Paul Chamberlayne exclaimed:

Alas! poor innocent Gentleman, is he alone ignorant of what all the World knows? Does not he know, that taking up the *Printers* and *Publishers*, and harrassing [sic] their *Persons* and *Pockets* with *Imprisonments* and *Prosecutions*, will as effectually restrain the Press, as any *Grand Committee* in *England*.[13]

The government also seems to have been willing—at least certain contemporaries were persuaded of this—to pay to have offensive material suppressed. At one point Henry Giffard, manager of Goodman's Fields Theatre, wrote to Walpole, clearly offering to suppress a play in return for a suitable reward:

'Tis with the greatest Difficulty, I have prevail'd with my self to entertain a Thought of reviving any thing for the Stage, w:ch might carry in it the remotest Construction against any part of the Conduct of the present happy Administration & I entreat your Honour, to believe, I do a Violence to my Inclination, in being oblig'd to receive a Premium, for what my Principle disclaims, & on that Score shou'd reject, were I not bound by fatal Necessity, And give me leave to assure you, Sir, if any thing in my little Power, cou'd contribute to the Welfare of this Government . . .[14]

To what extent Walpole was prepared to buy off adverse criticism is not known, although rumors of such transactions were rife during the period. Tom Davies claimed that Walpole was extremely sensitive to criticism, and would have a friend invite an offending author to dinner so that he might "be of the party, as if by chance" and effect the "conversion of the patriotic author, by the powerful eloquence of a bank note." This was after all not an unknown practice in the eighteenth century. It is well known that Pope supposedly received "a favor" from the Duchess of Marlborough to suppress his description of her under the character of Atossa (that this constituted £1000 may be "apocrypha"). And Lord Bute is said to have bought an entire unauthorized edition of one thousand copies of some of his mother-in-law Lady Mary Wortley Montagu's letters, with the editor quoted as saying "I know not what I should have done to make both ends meet, in my old age, if it had not been for the *repeated kindnesses* of my enemies."[15]

Henry Fielding was prepared to be unusually candid on the subject. In the preface to *Of True Greatness*, addressed to George Bubb Dodington in 1741, he wrote: "tho' I have been obliged with Money to silence my Productions, professedly and by Way of Bargain given me for that Purpose, tho' I have been offered my own Terms to exert my Talent of Ridicule (as it was called) against some Persons (dead and living) whom I shall never mention but with Honour. . . ." If we are to believe him then, Fielding could not suffer the indignity of writing by dictation, as it were, but could somehow justify to himself accepting money for suppressing works (a fact which probably explains the withdrawal of *The Grub Street Opera* and the postponed publications of *Jonathan Wild*).[16]

The evidence seems to suggest that in their efforts to curb the worst excesses of the opposition press, the Old Corps Whig leadership was prepared to employ some very insidious methods. Before Walpole came to power Daniel Defoe had for a time been paid by the government to "remove the sting" from the bothersome opposition newspaper *Mist's Daily Journal* and other publications by writing in such a manner that his contributions would "pass as Tory papers and yet be disabled and enervated so as to do no mischief or give any offence to the government" ("it was proposed by my Lord Townshend that I should still appear as if I were, as before, under the displeasure of the Government and separated from the Whigs").[17] And Defoe's son Benjamin Norton Defoe seems to have had something similar in mind when he, who was in his own words "a Servant of the Administration," was caught writing for the *Craftsman*:

> I had no Sooner Embraced the offer, but I made it my Study, how I might make it turn to the Service of the Government; which Service, if it might be Accepted of, I assure myself, is now many ways more in my power to promote, than ever it was before.[18]

3

The Pro-Government Publishing Network

Michael Harris has described Walpole's move into the area of propaganda as an "apparently reluctant decision" on his part. However, once Walpole put his mind to organizing propaganda on a grand scale, he did so with characteristic efficiency. Adopting and extending the system created to combat Harley's Tory government, he organized a comprehensive system for providing, printing, and distributing propaganda material intended to defend his administration and propagate the Old Corps version of Whiggery to which he and his associates subscribed. This was a task for which Walpole was eminently suited. His administrative ability has never been called into question. Nor has anyone ever doubted his ability—by hook or by crook—to make people do his bidding. Lord Chesterfield, who deserted Walpole to join the opposition in 1733, referred to his "most extraordinary talent of persuading and working men up to his purpose." The result was—in Allan Downie's words— "an increase at least in quantity, if not in quality, over the efforts of earlier administrations."[1]

Not surprisingly, Walpole based his propaganda network firmly on patronage, simply extending a system which was at the root of contemporary political life. This made the Old Corps propaganda effort into an enormous and complicated web, in which politicians, writers, and people concerned with the publication and distribution of propaganda were inextricably linked through bonds of obligations and gratitude. "Men who are to do one a service must be gained by something particular. No one thinks it an obligation to be lumped with a crowd," wrote a worldly Irish bishop.[2]

Within such a system, political considerations entered into even the most minor decisions. For the job of supplying the Secretary of State's office with newspapers, for instance, a woman—probably Mrs. Winbish—whose family had been "ruined . . . for selling Whig papers" under the Tory government was recommended because she "was always in the Whig interest & very carefull in what

She sells."[3] More important decisions were subject to the same considerations. When Laurence Eusden died in 1730, it was obvious that the new Poet Laureate would be an Old Corps Whig supporter. Likely contenders approached the leadership just like any other candidates for promotion in church and state. Lewis Theobald went with Lord Gage to Sir Robert Walpole, who recommended him warmly (though unsuccessfully) to the Duke of Grafton, then Lord Chamberlain, and "procured those recommendations to be seconded even by his Royal Highness Frederick Prince of Wales." Other writers had other backers, all of them stressing the literary worth and impeccable political credentials of their protégés. Lord Tyrconnel recommended Richard Savage, whom both the king, the queen, and even Alexander Pope seem to have favored, and spoke incorrectly but in good faith of Savage's "loyalty and good affection to the Government."[4] In the end of course Colley Cibber won.

Where patronage was concerned few could beat Walpole, but he naturally had the help of other Whig grandees. One such was Thomas Holles Pelham, Duke of Newcastle. At the beginning of the Walpole period Newcastle had been an aggressive Lord Chamberlain, intent on controlling the London stage. Later, as Secretary of State for the Southern Department, he became partially responsible for domestic affairs. Newcastle, with his obsessive attention to detail—what one Whig politician called his "true frippery scrap-mongering qualities"—is recognized as one of the great wielders of political patronage, especially in connection with elections. This in conjunction with the responsibilities of his office made him an important figure in organizing pro-government propaganda.[5]

BOOKSELLERS, PRINTERS, AND PUBLISHERS

The eighteenth-century book trade was a cutthroat business, in which market forces prevailed and the profit motive ruled supreme. Nonetheless, the political polarization of contemporary society was manifest even in the world of publishing. As early as 1724 the printer Francis Negus—seemingly acting on his own initiative—had drawn up a list for one of the Secretaries of State, in which he attempted to define the political sympathies of the main London printers. Although many printers, publishers, and booksellers were prepared to handle any material that came their way, others were clearly considered to be working either for the opposition or for the government. Of the handful of individuals referred to as "publishers" by contemporaries—men and women whose names were on the imprints of works in which they had invested no money but were selling for a fee on behalf of booksellers, printers, or authors—John Nutt was "always very closely associated with the Tory interest" whereas James Roberts, publisher and printer, was his "major Whig rival." According to Michael Harris, editorial policy was so clearly defined in the politically backed essay-papers, that "the printers seem generally to have been sympathetic to the party line."[6]

It was only natural that many members of the book trade should seek refuge with either the opposition or the government. The price to pay for publishing libelous or seditious material was high: in certain cases the protection of prominent politicians could be essential, especially, of course, for people working in the opposition interest. Common prudence dictated that printers and others should take such precautions, but members of the trade must also have found it financially to their advantage to come out in favor of one or the other political group, since they could then expect to be patronized by that group. In this respect they were in the same situation as other tradesmen: in order to maintain their election interest in the boroughs, for instance, Old Corps Whig adherents tended to restrict their custom to shopkeepers who were politically well-inclined.

In return for increased trade, a more regular income, and some degree of protection, such booksellers, printers, and publishers naturally had to give up some of their independence. For those who worked for the government this is very clear. Among Sir Robert Walpole's personal papers there is a memorandum stating that Chrichley ought not to be employed in supplying "the Secretary's Office with News" since he had been "a Confederate with Rayner in printing his Scandalous Pamphlets, & was taken up for publishing the Pamphlet for w.ch Rayner was convicted," but since this paper is undated, it is not known whether Walpole acted on this information.[7]

A familiar pattern was displayed when a printer "not ill look'd upon by the Ministry" was handed some documents submitted to Nathaniel Mist who was known to be a Jacobite. Understandably worried about what he might be letting himself in for, the printer "consulted Sr Robert." As a consequence Walpole "forbid the Publication of it" which rendered Mist "apprehensious of being troubled, under some pretext or other for the sake of this Affair." The publisher John Peele, to take another example, lost an annual income of £35 when he allegedly "threw up the Publication of ye Daily Post (after having published it thirteen years) because he could not prevail upon the Proprietors to continue it a neutral Paper, as it always had been." He also claimed to have foregone a yearly income of £80 by refusing offers to publish other newspapers: the *Daily Post-Boy* ("because it was a Paper ag.st the Administration"), the *Whitehall Evening Post* ("because they occasionally inserted Letters & Paragraphs against ye Administration, though more frequently for it"), and the *Political State of Great Britain* published monthly ("because against ye Administration"). In 1723 William Wilkins, known as "the favourite printer of the Whig Party," whose imprint was on the *London Journal*, the *Daily Courant* and other pro-government newspapers, got into trouble over the *London Journal* of which he was part proprietor. He was ordered to correct an account of a riot at Gloucester. Secretary of State Lord Townshend was informed that Wilkins had "on several occasions received favours from the government which ought to have made him not so ready to put into his paper a story of so malicious a tendency towards the government." After this single episode, the newspaper gave no further cause for complaint and—in Laurence Hanson's words—"maintained a tone of uncritical adulation of the ministry."[8]

Clearly publishers, printers, and booksellers who wished to do business with the government had to be very careful about what they published. Not only was their freedom to handle opposition material that might come their way severely restricted, in addition, they must not be seen to be acting against the interests of the government in any way. Michael Harris tells the story of how William Wilkins was reported in the opposition press to have been present at the anti-Excise demonstrations in the City in 1733. Wilkins replied—in print—that "*from the first opening of the Late Project about Excises, he at all Times, and in all Companies, gave his Opinion freely against it . . . and that tho' he prints the said Papers, he is no way the Author or Director of either; always disapprov'd every Thing unbecoming in them; and consequently, ought no more justly to be charg'd with Blame in this Case, than he ought to have had the Merit given him of Writing the Learned and Ingenious* Mr. Bayle's Works, *if he should have happened to be the Printer thereof.*" Six months later the printing of the *Daily Courant* was "remov'd from Mr. Wilkins," as a result of which he offered several shares in the newspaper for sale, perhaps as a result of political pressure.[9]

Of course the ministry were most likely to trust members of the trade who could be seen to have suffered in the Whig cause. Samuel Buckley had been summoned to the House of Commons under

Queen Anne's Tory government for publishing antigovernment material, and seems to have been a Whig by persuasion and not merely convenience. The printer of the original *Spectator* essays, and a friend of Pope's, Buckley was regarded by John Nichols as "a man of excellent understanding and great learning, very sincere where he professed friendship; a pleasant companion, and greatly esteemed by all who knew him." When the Whigs regained power in 1714 Buckley was put in charge of the official government newspaper the *Gazette*, and in 1717 made "Gazetteer for life." In this capacity he worked closely with officials in the offices of the Secretaries of State on a regular basis.[10] James Roberts was another very important contact for Walpole in the publishing community. Considered "a Printer of great Eminence," he owned "by far the largest trade publishing shop in London." Roberts was Master of the Stationers' Company for "an almost unprecedented four-year term," from 1729.[11]

However, other printers and publishers who had originally handled opposition material, decided at some point or other to restrict their publishing activities to pro-government material, and with time they were given positions of trust. At the beginning of Walpole's time in office, for instance, John Peele had been the publisher and William Wilkins the printer of the *London Journal* in which "Cato's Letters" and other opposition Whig material appeared. During the government clampdown on the *London Journal* in 1721, John Peele who was "a very considerable Bookseller in paternoster-row," actually absconded. When next year the *London Journal* became subsidized by the government, Peele and Wilkins seem to have come over to the government side, and to have remained loyal (except for Wilkins's revolt during the Excise crisis) to the Walpole line.[12]

These men all had extensive contacts in the publishing community, and were therefore very useful to Walpole. Not only did they provide an outlet for pro-government material, they were clearly active in other ways. Over the years Samuel Buckley, for instance, received substantial sums from the government "for printing and delivering several Pamphlets for his Majesty's Service" (£ 786.17.6 in 1739), and "for printing several Things for the Use of the Publick" (£ 460.8.8 in 1740), but there are also oblique references to "Disbursements on his Majesty's Service" (£ 980.14.0 in 1735), which may or may not refer to similar activities.[13]

Walpole would also seem to have made use of far less respectable members of the book trade, at least if Eustace Budgell's testimony can be believed. Budgell, whose mental stability was already in question, claimed to have met the notorious bookseller Edmund Curll by chance at a friend's house. In an effort to impress Budgell, Curll had affirmed that "Sir Robert Walpole sent to him for his assistance, and to desire his judgement and opinion, in whatever related to printing, pamphlets and libels. That for a very extraordinary job, of which he gave him with his own hands a bank bill for 50 l; that he afterwards sent him to his brother Townshend, who gave him another bank bill for 50 l for the very same job: that Sir Robert was the best custom he had; that he owed him a bill at that very time; that he could see him whenever he pleased, and could persuade him to almost any thing." Publishing this story in an open letter to Walpole in *The Bee*, Budgell described himself as disenchanted with the "Prime Minister" ("I have for some years past declined waiting upon you, as I used to do formerly"), but willing to recount to him personally all the details concerning "the very extraordinary job" that Curll boasted of, if Walpole were to apply to him in order to clear his name:

> Curll . . . adds so many circumstances to this story as woud induce any man to believe it, who was not thoroughly acquainted with this fellow's infamous character. I do think, Sir, that I have conversed (familiarly conversed) with wiser men and abler statesmen than either yourself or the Lord Townshend; and yet I must own I cannot think you would be so very weak as to put yourselves in the power of Curll the Bookseller.

Walpole took no notice of this, but the author was set on by Curll's son who "gathered the mob about Mr. Budgell, and told them, that was the Rogue who was the Scribbler of the BEE, the Villain that wrote against the Government, and the Fellow that had forged the Will [Dr. Tindal's]."[14]

Since some printers, publishers, and booksellers were known to be either Whig or Tory, or at least to publish in one or the other interest, writers who were in the know would have had little difficulty in finding the right bookseller to approach with the intent of publishing political material of whatever description. Each political party had its familiar channels through which material submitted to prominent politicians for approval could pass. The opposition satire *Verres and his Scribblers* describes the pro-government writers as "P[eele], W[ilford']s, R[oberts']s, dull loquacious Train," and it is certainly true that a sizeable amount of pro-government propaganda was issued under the imprints of John Peele, John Wilford, and especially James Roberts.[15]

The result is that one can often tell just by looking at the imprint

of an eighteenth-century pamphlet whether it is likely to be an opposition or a pro-government production. This assertion needs to be
modified, however, since the eighteenth-century book trade was far
too complex—even chaotic—for such conclusions to be drawn confidently. Newspapers of similar political persuasions would sometimes attacked each other in order to generate interest and ensure
higher sales figures.[16] Many works with a pro-government slant
carry the imprint of Thomas Cooper who often published on both
sides of political controversies, a practice which could be of advantage to all groups since it ensured that the political provenance of
specific works was less immediately obvious. Even James Roberts
published the *Grub-Street Journal*, which, although it devoted little
space to politics, had an antigovernment stance. (It is noteworthy in
this connection that he was criticized for not selling enough copies,
a normal enough source of friction between owners and publishers,
but a fact that raises the question whether Roberts on occasion
could have exercised a politically motivated inertia. In 1735 he was
replaced by John Wilford.)[17]

More research into publishing history is needed before it will be
possible to give a proper picture of Walpole's propaganda network.
What is clear, however, is that many channels were automatically
open to a writer whose works could be seen as defending the government, especially if he contacted prominent politicians close to
Walpole. Different outlets were designed to cater for different
works. Pamphlets, poems, and other works could be published separately through the agency of booksellers, printers, and publishers
who, out of self-interest or persuasion, were prepared to work in the
Old Corps Whig interest. And poems and essays could be published
in any number of pro-government newspapers.

NEWSPAPERS

"A paper writ on the Minister's side,—I never read one of them
before, knowing they are either nonsense or false" wrote Lady
Marlborough, whose opinion of Walpole's government was that
"there never was any instance in any government of so much bru-
tality, ill principles, and folly."[18]

Even at the time, it must have been impossible to determine what
sort of effect the pro-government newspapers had on contemporary
popular opinion. It is certain, however, that Walpole and other
members of the Old Corps would never have used so much money
and energy on propaganda, had they not been convinced of the ne-

cessity and efficacy of such expense. Oldmixon had no doubts about the results of his own efforts on behalf of the Whig party before and after the death of Queen Anne:

> . . . tho' the Nature of such Things do not admit of Proof of the Good they do, yet we may lay it down as a necessary Consequence of the Dispersing.[19]

Since the market rendered it more lucrative to write against the government than for it, very many London newspapers had an opposition slant, although few of them seem to have had direct financial links with opposition politicians. As provincial newspapers tended to copy from what Samuel Negus called "the rankest papers in London," this material was spread throughout the country. The provincial newspapers that supported Walpole's government were few and far between, and generally kept a low political profile, their policy often restricted to suppressing awkward truths. Walpole had, however, an ally in "Wye's Newsletter," the most important of the manuscript newsletters sent regularly to subscribers in the country and used by editors of newspapers of all political persuasions all over the country.[20]

As time went by, Walpole found it necessary to support several newspapers to ensure that they carried his message. In 1722 the opposition vehicle the *London Journal* had been bought and made into a pro-government newspaper.[21] During the negotiations the proprietor computed his profits at £960 a year on the basis of 15,000 copies per issue, and asked for a compensation of £800 a year over a ten-year period, since "by turning off the strength of expression & thereby lessening the sale to about 7 or 8,000 there would be little, or, no profitt [sic] att all." Subject to these conditions, the government was to "have the power to order the Journal in such a manner as they shall think fit & as if it was their own." In September 1722 Lord Townshend ordered that 650 free copies of each issue should be distributed by the post office to readers in the provinces. Performing a political volte-face, Daniel Norton Defoe continued to write for the newspaper, but was joined by other Whig controversialists, such as Bishop Benjamin Hoadly who became an occasional contributor.[22]

Once the *Craftsman* was launched at the end of 1726, Walpole really had no choice but to organize a more comprehensive propaganda campaign. The first significant signs of a more concerted effort to present the government's point of view became apparent when the *British Journal* in 1728 started to publish William Arnall's essays under the pseudonym of "the Censor." Soon after, the *Free Briton* was launched. For years the *Daily Courant* had been faithfully pro-government, with contributors like Dr. Bland, Dean of Durham, Dr. Hare, Bishop of Chester, Sir Robert's brother Horatio Walpole, Matthew Concanen, and Barnham Gould, but it was only in 1731 that copies of the newspaper were ordered to be dispersed through the post office. Links may also have been established with the *Daily Journal*. In addition there were two newspapers run by "Orator" John Henley, the *Corn Cutters Journal* and the *Hyp-Doctor*. Other pro-government newspapers included papers as diverse as James Read's *Weekly Journal*, the *Plain Man*, the *Citizen*, the *Senator*, and *Pasquin*, although there is no evidence that they were in receipt of a direct government stipend. Seemingly, Walpole never attempted to set up any provincial newspapers, preferring to concentrate on centrally produced papers that could be dispersed to the regions.[23]

That these papers were primarily set up to counter any moves in the opposition press and initiate attacks when possible, is obvious from the space allotted within their pages to direct commentary on the contents of their opposition counterparts. In the penultimate issue of the *Senator* the writer "Abraham Standfast" ironically acknowledged the close bonds that existed between him and the writer of the *Craftsman*: "*Both* shall inherit the Honours of Posterity; *He* alone having been born to write, what I alone knew how to admire!" And when Lady Mary Wortley Montagu decided to set up a newspaper in defence of the government she indicated through the choice of title, *The Nonsense of Common-Sense*, that her main target was the opposition newspaper *Common-Sense*.[24]

The cost of the pro-government press verged on the prohibitive. The government bought up enormous quantities of newspapers for free distribution to all parts of the country (see below). Over a four-year period, Arnall received "*for* Free-Britons, and Writing" no less than £ 10997.6.8 from the Treasury, for instance. Even larger sums were regularly paid to John Walthoe, for printing and publishing the *Daily Courant* and the *Corn-Cutters Journal*; to him and John Peele for their part in the *Daily Gazetteer*; to William Wilkins for printing the *London Journal* and writing, and so on.[25]

It seems likely that Walpole was concerned about the expense, but perhaps he also came to feel that the propaganda network had become too unwieldy. Either reason would explain his decision in 1735 to withdraw his subsidy from the *Free Briton*, and the *Daily Courant*, and to create one main newspaper to act as semiofficial mouthpiece on political matters (although the *London Journal* and the *Corn Cutters Journal* continued to receive subsidies). The result was the *Daily Gazetteer*, to which the main writers from the other newspapers were now moved. It was this newspaper that Parson Adams in Fielding's *Joseph Andrews* declared he had not even heard of, only to be told that it was "a dirty newspaper . . . which hath been given away all over the nation for these many years."[26]

At no time in this period were newspapers that showed a consistent pro-government bias commercially successful; their popularity was well below that of their opposition brethren. In 1730 the *Craftsman* could boast of a weekly sale of 10,000–12,000 copies; whereas the *London Journal*, perhaps the most popular of the papers subsidized by Walpole, sold no more than 2,000 or 3,000 copies.[27]

It is important to realize that the government never actually owned any of the pro-government newspapers. Control was ensured through heavy subsidizing, and these newspapers remained in private hands throughout the period. According to Michael Harris, the evidence suggests that those who were financially involved formed "a quite small closed group . . . that controlled a number of important, if politically one-sided, London newspapers." He sees Samuel Richardson, John Peele, Thomas Woodward, and John Walthoe as the most important members of this group, which also included Aaron Hill, William Wilkins, and his relative Joseph Tovey (a tallow chandler who had diversified into the pro-ministerial press) and others.[28]

Little is known about the day-to-day operations of these newspapers. In a letter "supposed to be wrote to Sir R— W—," dated 1733, from James-Street, Westminster, however, an unknown writer put forward a scheme for a newspaper to supplant the other pro-government papers. He provides a sketch of what he must have considered the ideal situation for the writer of such a newspaper. This "London Gazette" should be written by a man well versed in foreign affairs and "all languages" (French, Italian, Spanish, Latin, High and Low Dutch), who should have no other employment, write all himself, never quit London, and even "have the Press in his own House, to overlook it with Care." He should be well paid so that he could frequent the Court and foreign ministers, etc. He should read all the new pamphlets and books and have direct access to "the News of a public Nature from the Ministers which the King has abroad." And on the grounds that "such Papers cannot be kept up, so as to keep other Papers down, without it has some Home-News; [t]his *London Gazette* should have all of it that can be suitable to the Dignity of the Paper."[29]

DISTRIBUTION

One of the most important elements in Walpole's propaganda network was his distribution system. It was in Walpole's interest that material favorable to his cause should be circulated as widely as possible. Consequently enormous sums were spent on buying up large numbers of every issue of the *Daily Gazetteer* and other pro-government newspapers which were then "given away" and dispersed over large parts of the country through the agency of the post office. Many pamphlets that had been accepted by the Old Corps Whig leadership were distributed in the same way—as many as 10,000 copies of each pamphlet. Proclamations, prayers, and notices followed the same routes. Other unbulky material—such as separately published poems—may well have been similarly "Spread thro: the Kingdome [sic] in hopes of being Serviceable," but this has yet to be proved.[30]

In the towns people could buy literary works and newspapers directly from the shops of booksellers and mercuries, who kept a wide range of works, the political variety included, at any given time. Political ballads and other works were cried about the streets by hawkers, who would often sing the songs for prospective customers.

Coffeehouses were very important centers for the dissemination of political propaganda. It has been estimated that in 1739 there were 551 coffeehouses (and 207 inns and 447 taverns) in London alone. Their owners complained regularly during the period of the high prices of the newspapers they were more or less forced to take in by customer demand. Each of the major establishments was paying up to £20 a year in newspapers. Some coffeehouses also provided pamphlets and separately published poems.[31] When in London, Shenstone went with his friends to George's coffeehouse where for a subscription of one shilling, they "read all pamphlets under a three-shilling dimensions [sic]; and, indeed, any larger ones would not be fit for coffee-house perusal." Since many coffeehouses were either Whig (like the St. James' coffeehouse) or Tory (like the Cocoa Tree), visitors could discuss their reading with people of a similar political persuasion, a practice which might tend to reinforce—and in some cases perhaps modify—their own interpretation of what they had read.[32]

This latter point was very important because contemporaries admitted that it was not always enough to have access to propaganda material; on occasion guidance was needed on how to interpret it correctly. Lord Hervey for some time regularly supplied his protégé

Conyers Middleton at Cambridge with pro-government publications, knowing that Middleton was "pleased with having something of this Nature the first of any Body in the Place."[33] In 1737 when the government decided to publish the letters that had passed between the king and queen and the Prince of Wales, after the long drawn out family quarrel had peaked and the prince had removed his wife—whilst actually in labor—from under the parental roof, Hervey sent copies to Middlelton. The letters had been printed verbatim, so as to allow the nation to judge unfavorably of Prince Frederick's behavior towards his parents. Middleton, however, did not know quite what to make of the documents and explained to his patron that he and "those, who wish well to ye Governmt" needed instructions about "wt we are to think & say abt it, for in all questions I shall be proud to be on Your Lordship's side, but in political ones especially always ambitious to follow you." In a subsequent letter Middleton again complained:

> I am highly obliged to Your Lordship for the corrected impression of ye Letters; & wish onely [sic] yt you had added some instructions, to enable me to comment upon them wth more advantage to ye little circles, wch I draw around me. but [sic] since Your Lordship will not point out to me ye proper places & topicks of remark . . . [34]

Lord Hervey obligingly wrote Middleton another letter in which he pointed out weaknesses in the prince's letters. This is a timely reminder that, strictly speaking, propaganda does not need to be written down to count as such. Middleton would seem to have acted informally as a local center of information and distribution of government propaganda to a small circle of Whigs. William Shenstone even claimed that "a certain person gives pensions of three pounds a-week to porters and the most illiterate stupid fellows you can imagine, to talk in his behalf at ale-houses; where they sit so long a time, and are as regularly relieved as one centry relieves another."[35]

For large-scale distribution of propaganda, however, nothing could beat the post office. In addition to being a branch of the revenue, a source of patronage, and a center of international and domestic communications, the post office functioned as a propaganda and intelligence organ. As such it was extremely useful to Walpole. Not only did the post office on occasion stop opposition propaganda from reaching the provinces, it was also the single most important agency for the distribution of propaganda. The privilege of franking newspapers and other printed material so that copies could be sent free of charge through the post was restricted—officially—to Members of the Houses of Parliament, but had been extended by custom to the clerks in the offices of the Secretaries of State and to some officials of the post office. Pro-government propaganda could thus be distributed without further cost. Opposition politicians also took advantage of this privilege. By 1730, fifty-nine Members of Parliament were regularly buying 766 copies of the *Craftsman* every week.[36]

Subsidized newspapers and pamphlets were thus sent regularly from the central post office in London to county deputies for free distribution to individuals and to inns and other places where people congregated. It was convenient in this respect that so many of the county deputies were occupied with other business, and that so many of them were innkeepers. In dispersing propaganda they were aided by other government employees such as the Customs and Excise officers.[37]

On the whole 10,000 copies would seem to have been a fairly average number of any given pamphlet to be distributed by order of the government. But some works were clearly intended for restricted audiences. That only 1,600 copies of *A Letter from a Dissenter to the Author of the Craftsman* were distributed, is logical since it was aimed primarily at the Dissenters through important members of their community. No similar explanation can be found to account for the fact that only 1,100 copies of George Henckin's *Persuasives to Impartiality & Candour in Judging of the Present Administration* were sent through the usual channels. But even in the case of pamphlets intended for a very wide audience the number of copies distributed can vary slightly.[38] There is, for instance, a difference of 200 copies between *The Conduct of the Opposition* and *A Short Argument against giving Military Officers Commissions for Life*, of which 10,200 and 10,000 copies respectively were paid for out of Treasury funds.[39]

We know, then, that propaganda was distributed to most parts of the country through a system set up by the government, but we know relatively little about what sort of a readership the Old Corps Whig leadership had in mind for this kind of material. Is it possible to discover what sort of target groups official pro-government propaganda was aimed at? Two distribution lists that have survived among Walpole's private papers at the Cambridge University Library, allow us a glimpse of how the distribution system worked. The two lists concern two pamphlets published in 1739 which are clear-cut cases of government propaganda, presenting Walpole's views on the difficult relations with Spain, which had just occasioned the debate over the Spanish Convention, *The Convention*

Vindicated from the Misrepresentations of the Enemies of our Peace and *The Grand Question, whether War, or No War, with Spain, Impartially Consider'd: In Defence of the Present Measures against Those that Delight in War*, both sold by James Roberts. The lists were drawn up by the printer or publisher of the pamphlets, to show Walpole what had been done with the copies paid for by the government.[40] Unfortunately no equally detailed distribution list is known to have survived of a pamphlet for which a fairly restricted readership was envisaged.

The two lists are almost identical, and show that 10,305 copies of each pamphlet were distributed. This must be considered a large quantity for the eighteenth century, although some pamphlets are known to have been distributed in greater numbers, especially if they catered to the public's desire for sensationalism. Sacheverell's sermon published after his impeachment, may have sold 100,000 copies, for example.[41]

For both the pamphlets on the Spanish Convention the recipients are the same, although recorded in different order. The lists are at one and the same time very detailed and tantalizingly oblique. Some people who received only one copy are mentioned by name; others—most of them either politicians or officeholders—received several copies each, and these were obviously meant for redistribution, but to whom remains a matter for speculation.

The presence on the lists of named individuals can in most cases be explained by their positions in the administration. Lord Wilmington received two copies, presumably as Lord President of the Council; Sir William Yonge three as Secretary at War, Lord Chancellor Hardwicke and Mr Speaker Onslow received six each, and so on.

The problem is, however, that these assumptions could very easily be wrong. Take the case of Horatio Walpole who received twelve copies all to himself. This could be plausibly explained by referring to his many posts in the government, his relationship with his brother Sir Robert Walpole, or the fact that he moved the address in the House of Commons on the Spanish Convention in a two-hour speech. And yet he may well have received the twelve copies quite simply because he was the author of both pamphlets.[42]

This is a problem that affects several of the people on the list since they were active within several different spheres. Did Horatio Townshend, for instance, receive twelve copies because he was a prominent merchant in the City of London, because he was a Commissioner of Excise, or because he could contribute to the Townshend-Walpole election interest in Norfolk?[43]

Some of the addressees are predictable. A substantial number of copies were sent to the various departments, with the offices of the Secretaries of State receiving the largest share.[44] One can only speculate about the final destination of these 896 copies, but it seems likely that a number of them would have gone by diplomatic bag to British representatives abroad, to keep them informed of the debate at home. Under Secretary Charles Delafaye certainly sent both pamphlets and newspapers to Stephen Pointz while he was Commissioner to the congress at Soissons.[45]

The offices of the Secretaries of State seem to have been more involved in the distribution of propaganda than the other departments, judging by the number of copies received. The Lords of the Admiralty together only got twelve copies, as did the Commissioners of Trade, for instance.

The Treasury was the most important department, but only fifty copies are marked down "To John Scrope, Esq for the Lords Commisioners and for the Clerks of the Treasury." Compared to the numbers sent to the Secretaries of State this figure seems modest, but does not take into account the enormous quantities of pamphlets sent to various employees of offices that sorted under the Treasury. Conspicuous among these were the Customs and Excise officers, whose loyalty towards the government made them constant targets for opposition attacks. The numbers tell their own story: in all, they received 4,012 copies, presumably for redistribution to important individuals, inns and coffeehouses in their local communities.[46]

All the recipients mentioned so far were clearly expected to redistribute the copies sent to them, whilst possibly keeping one for themselves. There is, however, a group of recipients who received only one copy each, presumably to keep them informed of government policy. One hundred eighty-eight copies were sent "To the Lord(s) singly by Penny-Post" and five hundred fifty-seven "To the Commons Singly by Penny Post," in other words this kind of propaganda seems to have been sent not just to Walpole's supporters in Parliament but to independents and members of the opposition as well.[47] But Members of Parliament were not the only identifiable target group for pro-government propaganda. In all seven hundred forty copies were "Sealed up and Sent to the Post-Office for the Country Clergy," and the archbishops and bishops all had copies. Key figures within the judiciary were also in receipt of copies of the pamphlets,[48] as were a few court officials. The financial interests of the City of London were represented on the lists by the Sub-Governors and the Directors of the Bank of England, and by prominent loyal City merchants.[49]

The most interesting part of the manuscript concerns those named individuals who are marked as the recipients of only one copy each. Most likely these copies were intended for them personally, an indication that Walpole thought it important to keep them informed about government politics on a regular basis. Not all the people mentioned by name can be identified with a reasonable degree of certainty,[50] but wherever identification has been possible it is easy to account for their place on the list simply by referring to the positions they held within the "Establishment." It seems natural that the Attorney General (Sir Dudley Rider), the Solicitor-General (John Strange) and Dr. George Paul (King's Advocate General) should have copies, along with Mr. Auditor Benson. The famous Whig doctors Richard Mead and Sir Edward Hulse, who attended the king and Sir Robert Walpole respectively, also feature on the list, together with a few court officials, and John Fowle of Broome, Norfolk, who was a Commissioner of Customs and second cousin of Sir Robert Walpole, for whom he acted as election manager.[51]

To sum up, it seems that pro-government propaganda of a certain kind was sent regularly and automatically to all Members of Parliament, to election managers in the districts, to important and not so important "bureaucrats" in the various departments, to key figures at Court, in the judiciary, in the church hierarchy, and in the City of London merchant community, and that an attempt was made to reach certain important members of the local communities via the Customs and Excise officers and the county deputies of the post office, notably members of the clergy.

Since copies were provided for all Members of Parliament, irrespective of political allegiance, it seems that the government made serious efforts to reach some of their opponents. There may therefore well be some substance to the accusations put forward by the *Craftsman* in November 1728, that the ministry was sending subsidized newspapers to individual subscribers to the *Craftsman*, obtaining their addresses from the copies that passed through the post office.[52]

As for the identity of individuals in the local communities who were in regular receipt of pro-government propaganda, the evidence is scant. There may, however, be a clue to the kind of people Walpole wished to reach, in a letter from one John Collier of Hastings, in which he mentions being provided with newspapers by Daniel Prevereau, Chief Clerk of Newcastle's office, who is marked down for six copies of the pamphlets on the Spanish Convention. Collier was an attorney who probably owed his place in the Customs in

Sussex to Newcastle, for whom he acted as election agent in those parts:[53]

> I have had for sometime, an Evening Post, The Daily Gazetteers & the Weekly London Journal From Mr Prevereau Of My Lord Dukes Office, From whom I receiv'd a letter last Post, that he was to Suspend Sending me any more Papers, till I made application for them to his Grace, and acquaint him what papers I desir'd. I would not presume Troubling his Grace in such an Affair, but If you please to do it, I should be glad to have The Same Papers continued.[54]

Michael Harris sees this as an example of the brisk commercial trade in newspapers carried on by government officials, and consequently draws the conclusion that Collier was paying for the newspapers himself. I believe this is false, and that here we do have an example of an individual who was receiving free papers from the government and who consequently represents the sort of person that members of the Old Corps considered it important to keep well informed about their policies. If Collier had been paying for the newspapers himself, it does not make sense that the delivery should be suspended until he had time—at somebody else's request—to reconsider whether he still wanted the same newspapers, and even less that the Secretary of State himself should stoop to take an interest in such matters. Harris's interpretation seems even less likely when it is considered that Newcastle was in debt to Collier for a considerable amount of money expended in order to keep up the government's election interest in certain boroughs.[55] On the other hand, it makes perfect sense to see Prevereau's letter to Collier as part of a ministerial drive to save money by making sure that free copies of newspapers were only delivered to people like Collier if they were really interested in receiving them.

If then, as seems likely, Collier was in fact a regular recipient of free copies of pro-government newspapers, and probably other propaganda material as well, the reason for his inclusion on Prevereau's distribution list can most convincingly be sought in his extensive election interest at Hastings. In 1734 Walpole was told that if he wanted two Whigs elected at Hastings "he must provide handsomely for Collyer [sic]," because "that town absolutely depends upon him."[56] As one of the Duke of Newcastle's most trusted election managers, it was obviously important that he should be kept up to date on Whig policies.

Politicians and others loyal to Walpole seem to have considered it part of their service to the government to distribute whatever propaganda they were sent. In 1733 Sir Thomas Robinson of Rokeby, who was part of Walpole's voting majority, wrote to his father-in-law Lord Carlisle, "I have just had a dozen of the Free Britons of last Thursday sent to me, and as many pamphlets about [the] late Excise scheme." Robinson did not specify the source for these productions but enclosed a copy of each for Lord Carlisle. Well over a year later he enclosed a copy of another work, explaining "I have had a very large parcel of them sent to me, and shall faithfully disperse them." At one point he sent "a pamphlet dispersed by the Administration, called the Grand Accuser, and have this post enclosed a poem on the glorious theme of Liberty; they are both esteemed to be well done in their different kinds."[57]

4

Pro-Government Writers: Hirelings, Volunteers, and "Bureaucrats"

When ministers, declared James Ralph, writing in 1758, "conde-scend to imploy [sic] the Pen, they either take the first that comes to hand out of the public Offices, or else have Recourse to the Col-leges: In which latter Case, the Church furnishes the Reward; and in the former the State; as Vacancies happen to fall and Pretensions can be accommodated."[1] The question of whether Ralph's words adequately reflect the situation in 1758 must be left to others; but could his remarks be used to describe the situation that obtained during the years when Walpole was in charge of the Old Corps Whig propaganda effort? Who *were* the men and women who wrote for Walpole?

At this point it is necessary to distinguish between what contem-poraries called "hirelings" and "volunteers." A hireling or hack writer wrote quite simply for money, with writing as his main occu-pation in life. A volunteer, on the other hand, had some other occu-pation or independent means, and did not rely on writing for an income. Some of them were politicians themselves. In many ways hirelings and volunteers were treated—and expected to be treated—differently. However, it is not always easy to distinguish between them. Detailed information concerning the financial and job situa-tion of some of the more obscure writers is not always available, and often the individual author's estimation of his own situation in life differs markedly from the sentence passed on him by contem-porary and later commentators. Oldmixon has often been called a hack, but Oldmixon himself steadfastly maintained that he was "early a Volunteer, and not a Hireling, in the Service," and even in opposition satire he was called "a Volunteer Tool." Warburton, however, claimed that he was "all his life a virulent Party-writer for hire, and received his reward in a small place, which he enjoyed to his death."[2]

Between these two groups there was a third, consisting of what we might call "bureaucrats," people who were already in Walpole's employ and who occasionally contributed material that could be used as propaganda. As a group they are very difficult to assess. Most of the time they behave like hirelings: their freedom to maneuver was clearly nominal. Yet, a clever "bureaucrat" was of value to Walpole—with his ingrained respect for men of business—and so there is frequently an air of self-confidence normally associated with the volunteers in their communications with the "Prime Minister." To simplify, one might say of this group that they behaved—mostly—like hacks, and were treated—mostly—like volunteers.

RECRUITMENT

In 1734 the author of *Tit for Tat* taunted Lord Hervey—"Sweet, pretty Prattler of the C[ourt]"—with the daunting task that lay ahead of him and anyone else inclined to write in support of the Government:

> But can your Arm a Weapon lift
> To battle P[ultene]y, P[op]e, or S[wi]ft?[3]

One quite sees the problem, and under the circumstances it is amazing just how many pro-government supporters remained seemingly undaunted by the prospect.

Given the high moral rectitude that opposition authors expressed on the subject of hack writers prepared to support Walpole's policies for pay, it may come as a surprise just how many of them at one point or other of their writing careers tried to come to an understanding with Walpole. Contemporaries tend to portray Walpole as recruiting actively by approaching authors who had come to his attention by publishing on the opposition side. Probably this did happen on occasion, but the evidence suggests that more often than not the initiative was taken by the writers. James Thomson, Elizabeth Boyd, Thomas D'Urfey, and Susannah Centlivre, all offered their services to Walpole and were turned down. It is said that Thomson's *Britannia*, which was written in 1727, was only published two years later, and then anonymously, because the author was "trying his luck with Walpole." In 1727 his *Poem Sacred to the Memory of Sir Isaac Newton* came out with a dedication to Walpole, describing him as Britain's "most illustrious *Patriot* . . . like Heaven dispensing Happiness to the Discontented and Ungrateful." John Gay also approached Walpole, but regarding the offer of the post of Usher to one of the young princesses as an insult, he went into "literary opposition" instead.[4] Even Nicholas Amhurst, who later became responsible for the *Craftsman* and in many ways a symbol of opposition activities, had originally offered his services to the government, and had collaborated with Sir Richard Steele and George Duckett on *Pasquin*. Arnall accused Amhurst of having "loiter'd away his Time, and spent his Fortune in haunting Lord *Cadogan's Levee*; where being disappointed, he turn'd his Rage on Sir *R. W.* whom he never spoke to in his Life."[5]

When Henry Fielding came to London in 1727 and started writing plays, many of his friends and associates were Walpole supporters, notably his cousin Lady Mary Wortley Montagu, who seems to have helped him launch his career as a dramatist. Unpublished poems by Fielding recently discovered among her papers show him praising the "Prime Minister" and attacking the opposition. For the Coronation of 1727 and the new king's birthday, he wrote two poems—now lost—but issued under the imprint of the respectable Whig publisher James Roberts. His first play was acted at the Theatre Royal at Drury Lane, which was considered the theater of the Establishment.[6]

If they had ever been employed by Walpole or angled unsuccessfully for place, authors later tended to try to gloss over this part of their lives. A tendency to leave out in collections of verse earlier poems reflecting political views inconsistent with subsequent political affiliations, is noticeable. After Thomson's attempts to come to terms with Walpole had proved unsuccessful, his fullsome dedication to Walpole in *A Poem Sacred to the Memory of Sir Isaac Newton* was promptly dropped.[7] In slurring over such matters the authors were later aided by their friends and early biographers who clearly tried to cover up something that they considered shameful.

For prospective volunteers, access to Walpole and his closest associates was easier to obtain than for prospective hacks. Their social standing was normally considerably higher, so they could approach the "Prime Minister" directly or through mutual acquaintances. The Reverend Thomas Newcomb, for instance, had been "honourd with a share of . . . regard and friendship" from the Duke of Newcastle at the time when Newcomb was living in Sussex— Pelham territory—as chaplain to another Whig grandee, the Duke of Richmond. Newcomb himself attributed the "many Honours" and "generous favours" he later received from Newcastle to the Whig bias of his poetry.[8]

On the whole, the volunteers were people whose political stance and literary exploits were well-known to contemporaries. In his first letter to Walpole the Reverend Samuel Madden—unknown to Walpole and writing from Ireland—hoped that if a newspaper was set up as a vehicle for his papers "many of y:r & our Countries friends might hereafter come in to my assistance." He mentioned specifically George Bubb Dodington (who later defected to the opposition), Dr. Edward Young, Sir William Yonge and George Lyttelton who on entering Parliament in 1735 became a prominent member of the opposition but who in the early 1730s wrote in favor of Walpole's government. Madden himself, however, wished to remain anonymous, considering political writing improper for a clergyman.[9]

It comes as no surprise that many of the volunteers were themselves politicians; of the writers mentioned by Madden only Young was never in Parliament. Lord Hervey, Soame Jenyns, and Sir Charles Hanbury Williams were likewise politicians. Others were in some way connected with the Whig aristocracy: Thomas Newcomb was chaplain to the Duke of Richmond, for instance.

The hirelings are on the whole far more anonymous, and facts about how they were recruited are few and far between. "See me then Sir whom you have made; Me who am so truly your own," William Arnall wrote to Walpole in 1734, claiming to have been taken into Walpole's "Care" in his "tender Age even as a Child." With "scarcely Three Relations living"—and those apparently in reduced circumstances—he had been denied a liberal education (fortunately Walpole's "Humanity inspired what Education had denyd"). Arnall trained as an attorney's clerk, and worked for Sir William Yonge, before he came under Walpole's "Protection" at the age of twenty. By 1734 he had been in Walpole's service for seven years.[10]

Some writers of lowly origins came to political writing through the patronage of Whig grandees. Joseph Mitchell's father, a stonemason from Ratho near Edinburgh, had worked for the Earls of Stair and Lauderdale, who later became the patrons of his son. When Joseph Mitchell moved to London they helped bring their protege to Walpole's attention.[11] Thomas Cooke was "for some time domesticated, in the family of the Earl of *Pembroke.*"[12]

Benjamin Norton Defoe gives quite a detailed history of how he became one of Walpole's hacks in a letter to Newcastle in which he complains of the treatment he had subsequently met with from the "Prime Minister:"

Sir Robert Walpole; was pleas'd to Confirm me in his Service, for a Peice [sic] I wrote after the Two Houses Address to the King, soon after

His Majesty's Accession upon their Examineing [sic] of the National Debt; tho: I had wrote Several things before, for which His Honr: was so good, as both to thank, and to reward me: But upon Sir Robert's approbation of this performance His Honr: was so kind to say to me, that he Entertain'd me, that I should look upon myself as his Man; and that I should write only for himself and ye Administration; and that His Honr: would Support and provide for me; which in innumerable instances, to the utmost of my Ability, I have done ever Since.

In this letter Benjamin Norton Defoe conveniently glossed over earlier encounters with members of the government. In August 1721 he had been arrested for writing the introduction to a "Cato's Letter" in number 107 of the *London Journal* which revealed unofficial information about the Secret Committee inquiring into the South Sea Bubble scandal. Charges were not raised against him—a fact which has been attributed to Daniel Defoe's influence with the government. It seems far more likely, however, that his release was made contingent on improved behavior in political matters. In a letter dated 1 March 1722 addressed to Charles Delafaye in Lord Townshend's office, Benjamin Norton Defoe reveals that by then he was submitting material weekly on Mondays to Delafaye's "Direction." Benjamin Norton Defoe describes his works as "Testimonys [sic] of ye sincerity of my Intentions to Perform Engagements," but reminds Delafaye that "if my Lord Townshend will not be so kind to me as he has given me reason to Expect I may have the Liberty to pursue any other measures I may think for my Advantage." Still connected with the *London Journal*, Norton Defoe was kept ignorant of the negotiations for a takeover that were going on at that time between the proprietor of the newspaper and Charles Delafaye as an agent of the government. In effect, Benjamin Norton Defoe was writing simultaneously for and against the government.[13]

Access to the "Prime Minister" was hard to obtain for obscure pretenders to his patronage. As time went by a pattern emerged of hopeful hack writers, often using pseudonyms, sending specimens of what they were capable of producing directly to Walpole. In their letters they explained this procedure by referring to their "Obscurity," and expressed suitable political opinions. Among these was a prospective writer calling himself A. B. who explained to Walpole, "If I may be so fortunate as to merit in any degree your approbation of this short Essay, I should think myself highly honoured, to have Notice of it by an Advertisement in the Courant, being not so happy as to hope otherwise of gaining Access to your Person." Sometimes the writers would stress that theirs was an "Unknown hand" but at the same time indicate that they were part of a pro-government tradition of writing. A prospective government hack calling himself Philo-Britannicus, may have chosen that pseudonym to indicate his intention of writing in the spirit of Bishop Hoadley's contributions to the *London Journal* under the pseudonym of Britannicus.[14]

Some scribblers had self-confidence enough to write directly to Walpole in their own names. Anthony Gavin, for example, who had written the bestseller *A Key to Popery*, and who was later to end up as a clergyman in the American colonies, wrote to Walpole enclosing a specimen of his "Endeavours to serve" him, with "a new way of hammering D'anvers," the fictitious writer of the *Craftsman*. If accepted, Gavin would wait on Walpole to receive his commands.[15]

Walpole was not the only prominent politician to be contacted by hopeful writers in search of government patronage. Several of them—such as Thomas Newcomb, Leonard Welsted, J. Cartwright, etc.—were attached to Walpole's interest through the Duke of Newcastle. It is noticeable that Sir William Yonge, who in 1735 became Secretary of War and who dabbled in poetry, was very active in recruiting new writers. Arnall started his career as his attorney's clerk, Concanen made his acquaintance shortly after he arrived in London from Ireland, and then became attached to Newcastle and so on. George Bubb Dodington, who "ran straight" for five years in his dealings with Walpole before defecting in 1740, was also the center of a Whig coterie of writers (Young, Aaron Hill, etc.).[16]

What ranks were the government writers recruited from? The volunteers were often politicians themselves or associated with politicians close to the centre of power. The number of clergymen among them is noticeable—Thomas Newcomb, Edward Young, Samuel Madden, Dr. Bland, Dr. Hare, etc. Other less likely professions were also represented: Ralph Courteville was an organist and Stephen Duck was a thresher. Quite a number of the authors who wrote consistently in Walpole's service were people of liberal education who for some reason could not or would not exercise their skills in their chosen professions. Matthew Concanen was bred to the law but allegedly found it "too dry for his volatile disposition." Ironically, after writing for Walpole for several years, he was awarded the place of Attorney General in Jamaica, an office he is said to have filled "with the utmost integrity and honour" for seventeen years. Joseph Mitchell's plans to become a clergyman were dashed when the Edinburgh Presbytery denied him the necessary reference because of his passion for the theater. Refusing to beg forgiveness for something he himself did not consider inconsistent with a religious vocation, he traveled to London, where he moved in literary circles and started to write plays.[17]

Most of the hack writers and even some of the volunteers are very obscure, and little is known about their lives. Only occasionally does one get a glimpse of them as private human beings: Thomas Cooke who struggled to support a wife and one daughter, who after his death became a prostitute; Thomas Gordon who was so proud of his two sons, of whom friends heard bad accounts; Joseph Mitchell complaining that John Dennis had modeled his tragedy "into stupidity of Correctness"; Raphael Courteville, who had married an heiress (£ 25,000) and for a while lived "elegantly" (country seat, coach and six) "growing a little merry over a bottle" and distributing copies of his own ballad to an unresponsive group of acquaintances. Not to mention George Verney, Lord Willoughby de Broke, a man whose poetry was "so ridiculously unlike measure," and who was besides "so mad and so poor," that Horace Walpole at one point was determined to leave him out of his *Catalogue of Royal and Noble Authors*. Lord Willoughby de Broke seems to have been an arch Tory and it is therefore strange that he received a pension from Sir Robert Walpole. He may simply have been a charity case to the "Prime Minister," and not expected to do anything in return for his pension—indeed he seems to have been so poor that he sold one of his poems in the Court of Requests himself for half a crown.[18] The only reason we know about this pension is that in 1741 he met with a robber on the road to Edinburgh ("having lost all my mony & baggage of Cloths [sic]"), and asked to have part of it paid in advance:

> I have but this six hundred a year as Sr Robert Worlpole [sic] is pleasd to Grant me to Live on.[19]

At the very lowest level we find writers so obscure that nothing remains of them but their submissive letters to Walpole offering their assistance.

EMOLUMENTS

It must not be thought that the volunteers—for all their proclaimed disinterestedness—expected fewer rewards than did the hacks. Quite the contrary: to some extent a man's social position determined how much he could ask for, and the volunteers had a much higher social standing than their hack counterparts. The words of Lady Hertford on another subject seem strangely applicable: "In this country . . . lettered aristocracy is repaid by the public, even for the slightest exertions of intellect, tenfold."[20]

The hacks and the volunteers tend to ask for slightly different things, however. The hacks nearly always ask for money pure and simple, to help them out of whatever financial trouble they happen to be in. Only the most well-established hirelings dared to raise the issue of permanent posts and sinecures with Walpole, as William Arnall did whenever suitable posts fell vacant (Clerk of the Pipe in the Court of Exchequer in Ireland, a job in Auditor Godolphin's Office, and so on). The volunteers, on the other hand, never stop asking for posts for themselves, their relatives, and their protégés.[21] Their solicitations range from the general ("some Place") to the specific. They kept a strict eye on the state of health of those who held desirable posts, and put in their bid for a place the moment the incumbent was either deceased or seemed moribund. It is very rare for a volunteer to ask the Whig leadership for money. As one pro-government pamphleteer remarked about writers on both sides of the political divide, "the great ones mean nothing more than to write themselves into Power, if they can, and the little ones into Pocket."[22] "Bureaucrats" and others who were employed by the government in various capacities, and who occasionally contributed propaganda material, expected this activity to help them gain promotion.

The hirelings and the volunteers differ in that, if a hireling receives bounty from Walpole, in most cases we can assume that as a full-time writer in Walpole's interest he owes his reward to his political writing or related activities. It is, on the other hand, much more difficult to determine whether the emoluments that fell to the share of the volunteers came as a result of their willingness to write in the Old Corps interest, because more often than not they had other political services to offer—such as their vote in Parliament or election interest in various boroughs—which have to be taken into account too. William Bryan of Bury St. Edmunds is a case in point. Assured by the Earl of Bristol that Newcastle had "exprest great Good will" towards him, Bryan informed the latter that "after having many Years endeavourd to serve the administration, without having ever been regarded by it," he would now like to "meet with some favour from it." As a voter in Cambridge and in the City of London, with freeholds in Cambridgeshire and Suffolk, Bryan approached Newcastle because he stood to lose one of his freeholds, unless help was forthcoming from the government. In typical style, Bryan discreetly presents his personal problem to Newcastle in

terms of a potential threat to the Whig election interest in certain
boroughs. What is of interest, however, is that Bryan makes it clear
that he has served the government by other means too. He encloses
not only a political poem but a sort of curriculum vitae of his literary production, the earliest poem dating back to the days of Queen
Anne.[23]

There are many indications that not only Bryan but many other
volunteers looked upon party writing as an important part of their
"service" towards the Old Corps, which consequently ought to be
rewarded. For this group the question of remuneration for services
rendered was often a complicated pattern of services performed for
the writers or for their dependents or protégés, sometimes—but not
often—combined with financial assistance.

The goal of every hack writer in Walpole's employ was to be, in
James Ralph's words, "suitably and permanently rewarded." How
suitably they were rewarded is a question on which their opinions
and Walpole's tended to differ, and this will be discussed below.
What is certain is that very few hacks were given a *permanent* reward in any shape, and were thus denied the security that they all
seem to have considered as the ultimate goal. William Arnall,
though openly admitting that "no Man had ever nobler Returns of
boundless Favours," still asked for a nonrevocable post. He reasoned that such a job would place him beyond the power of his
"most unforgiving Enemies"—the politicians whom he had "de-
fied offended and enraged" whilst in Walpole's service—should the
"Prime Minister" be ousted from power. Similarly, Lewis Theobald complained that Walpole showed him "all Kindnesses, but the
most important One . . . the settling me in some comfortable Certainty."[24]

The reason why Walpole was reluctant to grant permanent security to his writers is fairly obvious. By placing them in a position
where they would be secure for life, he placed them out of reach of
his own influence and power. A realist like Walpole was not likely
to forget this. Prudently, he kept his hacks in a totally dependent
position, feeding them with the hope that eventually they would obtain a more permanent and secure post. Benjamin Norton Defoe had
received assurances from Walpole:

> His Honr: promis'd me, and was pleas'd to repeat the promise to me of,
> a place for Life; His Honr: was so good even to add, that I might depend
> upon the very next place that then befell.

The "promise being delay'd," Benjamin Norton Defoe had continued to write "from time to time," remaining "in the Service above

twelve years."[25] Later, when he turned to writing for the *Craftsman*, the treatment he had received could be justified by pointing to his disloyalty.

Both hirelings and volunteers routinely proclaimed their "inviolable attachment" to Walpole's "Service & Interest," stressing that their loyalty would remain the same "though Favour should cease to be of Profit." Here, however, the writers had to strike a fine balance, because it was obviously not in their interest to allow Walpole to become complacent, for fear that his munificence would lessen. Writers with sufficient self-confidence therefore occasionally hint that neglect of one sort or another might lead them to defect.[26]

Even in cases where the writers' loyalty to Walpole after their preferment was never in question, however, security tended to make them less productive, as Thomas Cooke once explained to Lord Pembroke:

> It must be confessed that some poets, when possessed of affluent, or easy, circumstances, have neglected the Muses that first gave them celebrity and fortune. Welsted, who certainly had genius, does not appear to have written much after the Duke of Newcastle procured for him a place in the Ordnance Office; and we learn from Voltaire's letters to the English Nation, that, when he waited on Congreve, who was in possession of lucrative offices, the latter told him, "he did not choose to be considered as an author, but to be visited merely as a private gentleman."

This is a familiar complaint. Once Thomas Gordon was placed beyond the need to write for a living, through a regular income as Commissioner of the Wine Licenses and marriage to the wealthy widow of his erstwhile partner in writing "Cato's Letters," John Trenchard, he became indolent and spent most of his time away from London. With such examples in mind, Walpole kept his hirelings and volunteers in a state of permanent expectancy, a fact recognized by some of them. Lewis Theobald, for example, asked Warburton's advice about a promise made to him by the "Prime Minister:"

> Shall I pursue this dream of expectation, and throw away a few hours in levee-haunting? Or will it be more wise to wake myself at once from a fruitless delusion, and look on promises but as Courtiers' oratory?[27]

Nonetheless, quite a number of pro-government writers did obtain minor offices under Walpole. Ambrose Philips, for instance, was awarded employments in Ireland, Welsted a place in the Ordinance Office through Newcastle, and the journalist James Pitt a post in the Customs Office at Portsmouth, which he was rumored to have sold for £1000. He was also made Surveyor of Tobacco; as Warrant Officer in the Port of London he earned a salary of £200 a year. According to James Ralph, who also worked for Walpole for a while, James Pitt "knew how to make the most of his Master's favours, and in a few years deserted the Service." He went back to Norfolk where he had been a schoolmaster before he was recruited to write for Walpole. For pro-government writers to attain such security was, however, the exception rather than the rule. Most of them were kept waiting interminably, and this insecurity was galling to many. John Lyons, for example, criticized the way in which pro-government writers, himself included, were kept "in so tormenting & uncertain a Dependancy [sic]," suggesting as a remedy that they be given "Revocable Place[s]" as "a good Pledge for a Man's playing fair."[28]

In general opposition writers tended to portray pro-government writers as not only uneducated and incompetent but poor. Occasionally, however, it suited their purposes to create an image of writers in Walpole's employ as rolling in money. Davies claimed that "the slightest favour from the press was sure to be amply rewarded." As proof he relates a story of how after the opposition writer James Miller's *Are These Things So?* was published in 1740 "a young Gentleman of about nineteen years of age, took it into his head to write an answer to this piece . . . Sir Robert was so pleased with it, though but a flimsy performance, that he sent for Roberts, the publisher, and expressed his great satisfaction at the compliment paid him, by giving a bank note of a hundred pounds; which he desired the publisher to present with his compliments to the author."[29] This would seem to have been an extremely rare occurrence, however, and was probably calculated to encourage aspiring authors to follow in the young poet's footsteps.

On the whole Walpole was not the munificent patron of hacks that he has been portrayed as being. Oldmixon was so galled by a friend's hint that "the World generally believ'd I was handsomely rewarded for my long Labours in the Service of that Cause, which is the Basis of our present happy Constitution," and so displeased with the treatment he claimed actually to have met with, that he published his sad tale for the public to judge. Describing himself as a volunteer, he had "always thought Whiggery to be, like Virtue, its own reward." After writing actively in the Whig interest from 1710 onward, he had very little to show for it by the time he came to write his complaint in the early 1740s. His post of Collector of the Port of Bridgewater had in the end brought him financial loss, and he claims that the money he had been promised "was at first dilatorily and precariously paid . . . and at last wholly witheld." When informed in the 1730s Walpole had "seem'd astonish'd" at the scant rewards Oldmixon had met with and had doubled his income to £200 ("This is the prodigious Reward with which I have been twitted"). Even this income had led to problems because of his "depending upon it, and being almost as often disappointed." Oldmixon may be a special case because he seems to have been a bit of an embarrassment to Walpole, continuing to write as if the Whigs were still in opposition. Oldmixon was clearly too independent to be manipulated into producing the kind of propaganda Walpole wanted (see Part II), and his failure to move with the times may well have been at the root of his "Neglect and Oppression."[30]

In his doctoral thesis on the rewards for authors under Walpole, K. M. Greene concluded that Walpole was no generous patron, only handing out just enough bounty to keep them all hoping. Only if a hack writer could serve him in other ways, might he become the master of a substantial income. Ralph Courteville, for instance, claims to have earned £800 a year, despite the fact that a weekly wage for a journalist writing for one of the printer-owned papers was no more than a guinea a week. Initiated into Whig principles in 1711 "at a time our Country was in eminent Danger," Courteville claimed to have spent seventeen years in "Service to Sr Robt. Walpole . . . in which I had many singular Trusts as well at home as abroad in which I gave him such proofs of my Fidelity as Occasion'd him often to call me his Trusty Servant as well in obeying his commands in that Respect as in then writing the Gazeteer." Courteville, as his name indicates, was of French origin and seems to have had Jacobite family connections. Probably he was useful to Walpole in discovering Jacobite activities; long after Walpole's death he offered to serve the Duke of Newcastle in such a capacity for "very little encouragement" ("ever so little pecuniary Assistance").[31]

A few fortunate writers received pensions. Walpole persuaded George I to give Edward Young a pension, and George II to increase it to £200 a year. At a time when Richard Savage was still soliciting favor from prominent members of the government, he was disappointed of the laureateship—the king is said to have "publickly declared his Intention to bestow it upon him"—he wrote a poem celebrating the queen's birthday, and published it under the name of the Volunteer Laureate. The queen sent to the bookseller for a copy and gave the author £50 and a message was conveyed to Savage "that he had Permission to write annually on the same Subject; and that he should yearly receive the like Present, till something better . . . could be done for him." Several other Whigs received "bounty" so regularly that they could be said to be in receipt of revocable pensions: Leonard Welsted and the critic John Dennis both received £20 a quarter, for instance.[32]

Sometimes hacks and "bureaucrats" were given a down payment for pamphlets found acceptable for distribution. Seemingly they themselves saw the work through the printing process and were reimbursed once the pamphlets arrived at the post office for distribution. Henckins was paid £42.10.0 "for 1100 *Persuasives to Impartiality and Candour in judging of the present Administration*," whereas Monsieur Lagrelle received £150 for "a Pamphlet in Vindication of the Ministry, delivered at the Post-Office by *Joseph Crichley* [sic]."[33]

On the whole, however, pro-government writers had to exercise a great deal of patience. Joseph Mitchell complained in verse form in 1735:

> BUT you, SIR, have been sung by me
> From Seventeen Hundred Twenty Three,
> Down to this Day, in various Strain,
> At great Expense of Time and Brain.
> Yet, tho' at sundry Times befriended,
> No steps of Honour I've ascended;
> Nor find my Circumstances mended![34]

Further on in this poem, however, Mitchell admits that "taking one Year with another" he has received £500 from Walpole. His hope is for "some certain Salary | Some honest, snug, Life-lasting Place" (pp. 8, 9).

The list of writers who received bounty at one time or another is a long one, including authors as diverse as the genealogist and bookseller Arthur Collins (£100), the arch-hack Benjamin Norton Defoe (£50), Walpole's favorite journalist William Arnall (£200), John Oldmixon (£33.1.6), songwriter and solicitor to the Treasury Edward Roome (£11.9) and the playwright Benjamin Martyn (£50). In 1732 John Lyon received £100 "for Services performed," and £50 as "bounty" (repeated a year later).[35]

It should, however, be emphasized that not all sums paid to writers are necessarily specified in the treasury accounts. Certain trusted individuals associated with the propaganda effort, such as Nicholas Paxton and Samuel Buckley, often drew large sums from the Secret Service funds without specifying for what purposes the money was intended. There were also indirect ways of rewarding writers. In 1732, for instance, Joseph Mitchell solicited a post in the Stamp Office for his friend Abraham Hayes, explaining to Walpole that this would provide him (Mitchell) with "a whole Year's Provision." Obviously some agreement had been struck between Hayes and Mitchell that would benefit the latter in his "present unhappy Condition." It is also possible that some writers may feature in the Treasury records under fictitious names. In the Secret Service accounts for the last four years of the reign of Queen Anne, for instance, the name of Claude Guiot stands for Daniel Defoe.[36]

No matter how much money Walpole gave some of his writers, they never seemed to get enough. Lewis Theobald who—according to a friend—was "of a generous spirit, too generous for his circumstances," is supposed to have been the model for Hogarth's original print of "The Distressed Poet." William Arnall was another one who "squandered as fast as he received." [37] Ralph Courteville—driven "to the very last extremity"—on one occasion begged Walpole to save him "from Destruction as you have many Others" and save his person and his chattels from being seized for debt.[38] Joseph Mitchell, commonly known as "Sir Robert's Poet," was another one whose "natural dissipation of temper . . . fondness for pleasure, and eagerness in the gratification of every irregular appetite, threw him into perpetual distresses," even after his wife had inherited "several thousand pounds."[39] He wrote to Sir Robert from prison:

> By Means of your last Bounty and that of a private Friend, I was enabled to compound with my greatest Creditor and discharge some small Debts.
> For Several Months past I have had no Difficulty to struggle with, but one. It is a Debt of 28 Pounds only, for which I am at Present a Prisoner. A little more than 30 Pounds wou'd discharge me from Debt & Costs, as 50 wou'd clear me in the World at once. But, being so greatly oblig'd to your Humanity and Goodness already, I hardly dare hope for any Sum to relieve me: Tho, if you vouchsafe once more to befriend me, by Sending a Small Bill by the trusty Bearer, I promise to give you no more Trouble of this Sort again, and that I will devote my whole Time and Talents to your Service'.[40]

Nor was Mitchell the only author to write to Walpole from debtor's prison: at various times Benjamin Norton Defoe, William Arnall, and Thomas Cooke all did the same. And in 1741 Oldmixon wrote to Newcastle, "I am threaten'd with imediate [sic] Ruin & I am now drag'd to a Place I cannot mention in ye midst of all ye Infirmities of Old Age Sickness Lameness & almost Blindness & without ye means even of subsisting."[41]

Constant impecuniosity seems quite simply to have been the lot of writers for hire during the eighteenth century. Long after Walpole's death, Thomas Cooke, Ralph Courteville, and James Ralph were still soliciting favors from the Duke of Newcastle, drawing his attention to past services and promising him their undying loyalty if he would only procure for them various employments, rescue them from prison, pay their debts, give them some small "encouragement."

The main problem for the hacks was that they were on sufferance. Since Walpole preferred to pay them at irregular intervals—presumably to keep them on their toes—most authors were reduced to sending regular begging letters, their solicitations ranging from the minuscule to the astronomical. In tracking down suitable compensation, the initiative was with them: first they had to produce the goods, and if their payment then failed to materialize, it was up to them to keep reminding those in power of their obligations. But then hacks who wished to write directly to Walpole or other prominent members of the party, needed an excuse to do so, and more often than not they found it in the submission of new political works for Walpole's approval. Thus the hacks were locked in a vicious circle, and to keep them there was clearly to Walpole's advantage. Benjamin Norton Defoe, for instance, complained in 1738 to Newcastle that he had written "Several Papers" for Walpole, two of which, a letter for the *Daily Gazetteer* and a pamphlet called *A Word in Season* were "lay'd before His Honr. for approbation." For neither had he received any compensation, although the pamphlet had been published at his own expense. Ralph Courteville made a habit of sending issues of the *Daily Gazetteer* to Walpole, pointing out which productions were his.[42]

Things had clearly not changed much since 1715 when Sir Richard Steele complained to Newcastle:

> I will never hereafter do more than my part without knowing the terms I act upon, and I think what I have said deserves a good establishment for life . . . In one word, My Lord, the purpose of this letter is to lay my dissatisfactions before You, and to declare on what foundation I will enter into the lists. I cannot turn so much time that Way and be supported by assistants equall [sic] to the Work for lesse [sic] than a 1000 l, a Year. And before I enter upon the Argument I hope to receive 500 l. or be excused from so painfull [sic], so anxious, and so Unacceptable a Service.

Less than two months later he wrote:

> It was upon Your Lordship's intimation to Me that I should be supported
> in it, that I have lately appeared in Publick as a Writer; But I find that
> care of me is not to be taken, except I passe [sic] through sollicitations
> [sic], which will take up more of my time, and quiet of mind than it is
> Worth. I have Therefore desired My Lord Townshend to excuse my
> going on in the affair which I have undertaken, since the part off [sic]
> the ministry is not performed to Me.[43]

The payment or nonpayment of writers was only one aspect of
the general eighteenth-century problem of a society living on
credit. Writers who produced political propaganda were in much
the same situation as wigmakers, tailors, and others who produced
items of necessity or luxury for the upper classes: they received
payment as and when it suited their patrons to recompense them.

The slowness and inadequacy of government accounting is also
extremely noticeable, and helps throw further light on the hacks'
problematical existence, although individuals higher up in the social scale were also adversely affected. This is illustrated by what
happened in 1744 to Joseph Bell, Controller of the Inland Office of
his Majesty's Post Office, a staunch political supporter of Walpole
and a key figure in the dispersal of propaganda. When Walpole's
factotum Nicholas Paxton died, Bell asked Newcastle to,

> speake [sic] to his Majesty to give me some assistance, all the money I
> had of my own in the world was four Hundred pounds, which is all lost
> in Paris, and the £72: owing me by Mr Paxton for the Country news
> papers paid for out of my pocket, for the Government's Service, I take
> now for Granted is all lost, as he is dead, I could here name the many
> Services performed by me for the late King, and his present Majesty.[44]

Indeed Bell could have mentioned some services: he and Paxton
had saved Walpole from impeachment by refusing to give evidence
to the committee established by Parliament to investigate the last
ten years of his administration (when Paxton after his release
waited on Walpole, Lord Fitzwilliam "in the height of zeal, took
him about the neck and kissed him").[45] It is truly significant that a
man who had been so central to Walpole's propaganda effort as Joseph Bell was left vulnerable to strokes of chance. This, however,
is typical of eighteenth-century bureaucracy: officeholders were expected to forward money of their own to cover their expenses until
their accounts could be passed by the Treasury, a process which in
extreme cases could take years.

During the eighteenth century dedications were, of course, rewarded with cash payments. James Thomson dedicated one of his poems to Sir Spencer Compton (the Speaker) and George Bubb Dodington (Lord of the Treasury) and received twenty guineas from the former and fifty pounds from the latter.[46] A request for permission to dedicate was widely recognized as an indirect petition for money. By the 1730s twenty guineas had become customary, and the practice ridiculous, since authors often dedicated their works to people with whom they were not personally acquainted. This was certainly the case with many pro-government hacks who wrote for permission to dedicate their works to members of the Old Corps Whig hierarchy.[47]

An author might receive a substantial financial reward if prominent politicians decided to sponsor a subscription of their literary productions. For this to happen both the writer and his work had to be sufficiently respectable. Thomas Gordon's translation of the works of Tacitus was published in this manner "and being patronized by Sir Robert Walpole, formed a very lucrative speculation." It was also important that the work in question should be (relatively speaking) nonpolitical. When Samuel Buckley, for instance, published his *Thuanus* in 1735, he explained to Walpole that one of the leaders of the opposition, Lord Carteret, was "a great Promoter" of his undertaking and had "engaged his Friends in both Houses in my favour (it being no Party-Question)." Just how lucrative such a subscription could be, can be documented in the case of Lord Hervey's promotion of Dr. Conyers Middleton's history of Cicero. Middleton is said to have pleased the Royal family by toning down the authoritarianism of the Emperor Augustus, since contemporary writers often drew a parallel between George II and Augustus. Throughout the process Hervey read the work and suggested changes, a practice which allowed him to discreetly oversee the political contents.[48]

Before declaring himself willing to undertake the subscription—a thing he had never done before—Lord Hervey discussed the possibility of a subscription with other politicians, among others the Speaker and Sir Thomas Winnington. He was in favor of publishing the work in two volumes at a price of two guineas, as it would render the work not only "handsome" but lucrative ("of all the People I shall ask to subscribe, it will be just as easy to get two Guineas as one"). Middleton objected that "ye generality of my Subscribers must be men of Professions, wth whom ye difference of a guinea would be of great weight," and suggested that they "add half a guinea onely [sic] for the larger paper, to take in all ye richer sort."[49]

Middleton roped in some of his friends to help disperse proposals among their acquaintance. Hervey provided franks.[50] As the subscription got under way, Hervey seems to have entered into the spirit of the game. He was determined to make "this Subscription the most universal one that was ever known in England." To start with he clearly made it every good government Whig's duty to subscribe personally and to force his friends to subscribe and distribute proposals. He read parts of the work to Princess Amelia. He also employed "Emmissarys," Old Corps Whigs like General Churchill and Henry Bromley,[51] and wrote to Dr. Clarke at Winchester, and to an acquaintance at Oxford "to pick . . . up all the subscribers they can lay hold of." He wrote in the same manner to the opposition Whig politician Lord Chesterfield who happened to be at Bath, an indication that he considered the work acceptable to people of all political persuasions and that he did not wish to make a party issue of the subscription:

> for my acquaintance in town, those I see I sieze [sic], & my message by my Emmisarys to those I do not see is, that I shall never think any body that can or does read that will not subscribe to such a subject treated by such an Author . . . & have declared I am indifferent whose List any body is in, but those that are in none I will give no quarter to for I look upon it as my affair as much as yours [Middleton's].[52]

The result of this hustle and bustle was a subscription list that included six members of the Royal family, and on which Old Corps Whigs featured prominently. Lord Hervey himself had more than five hundred subscribers on his own list, and had himself put down personally for twenty-five copies. The subscription was so phenomenally successful that it enabled Middleton to purchase a farm at Hildersham. Stephen Duck was another writer whose literary productions earned him considerable financial success, largely due to the queen's interest in him. Not only did she award him a pension but she patronized subscriptions of his works "with uncommon Ardour, and incited a Competition among those who attended the Court, who should most promote his Interest, and who should first offer a Subscription." For one of the playwright John Mottley's benefit nights the queen on the prince's birthday "did the author the singular honour of disposing of a great number of his tickets, with her own hand, in the drawing-room, most of which were paid for in gold, into the hands of Colonel Schultz, His Royal Highness's privy-purse, from whom Mr. Mottley received it, with the addition of a very liberal present from the Prince, himself."[53]

Swift claimed that the Whigs after their dismissal from office in 1710 employed "a set of writers by subscription," and it seems that this practice of clubbing together to raise money for authors persisted, even after return to power ensured that they had other monetary sources on which to draw. Stephen Duck certainly benefited from such money raising activities: the Rev. Alured Clarke had "collected between twenty and thirty guineas for him at Winchester" to be added to "the money that has been gathered for him."[54] In one of Joseph Mitchell's begging letters in verse, *A Sick-Bed Soliloquy to an Empty Purse* printed in 1735—this time addressed to Lord Stair—the author describes how he wakes with a hangover after a Bacchanalian night on the town to find that his purse is now "poor indeed, a Poet's Purse." His plan is for the purse itself to intercede with Stair for relief:

> . . . Go, empty as thou art,
> Trembling and plaintive to my Patron STAIR,
> Who knows but, from his well-known generous Hand,
> Some golden Medals of our *Cæsar*'s Stamp,
> Of *Charles* or *James*, of *William, Ann* [sic], or *George*,
> (For all alike are Guineas good to me,
> Who make no Party Matter of the Gold)
> May happily be dropt? Or, shou'd he rather chuse
> (O that he wou'd!) to put thee in his Fob,
> And at a lucky Season pull thee out,
> Wretch as thou art, among his Noble Friends,
> Bless'd both with Pow'r and Will to help a Bard,
> How chang'd, how charmful, wouldst thou then return![55]

One extraordinary phenomenon is the publication of appeals for redress from members of the public for alleged ill-treatment by political patrons. Arthur Collins, as a last resort, exhorts patrons to step forward, if "some are yet remaining, who have Spirit and compassion, to intercede for some Provision that may be a recompense for him." Oldmixon did exactly the same. In publishing his case he claimed that "instead of Prejudices taken against me in an Opinion of large Favours and Emoluments received, I rather merit Pity for having found nothing but Neglect and Oppression." The public, he points out, have it in their power to recompence him for "labouring Day and Night in the Service of *Liberty* and the *Reform'd Religion*" by buying his *History of Christianity*.[56]

Robert Whatley went one step further when he wrote a pamphlet about his case of alleged neglect in an obvious attempt to blackmail Walpole into dispensing patronage. Whatley presented the pamphlet to Walpole in manuscript, and left it up to him whether it was to be published or suppressed. This depended entirely on what Walpole chose to do about the man and his ambitions: "It is *yet* an *absolute Secret*; my desire is it may ever continue so." Here Whatley obviously misjudged the "Prime Minister" who was not one to submit quietly to blackmail and whose case could not be harmed by a pamphlet which proved by its very existence that he was not in the habit of showering appointments on any Tom, Dick, or Harry who simply took it into his head to be one of his supporters "both in speaking and writing."[57]

DEMANDS AND OBLIGATIONS

After the Hanoverian Succession, a great writer like Congreve was patronized by the Whigs seemingly without any view to what he might or might not include in his writings. His plays were politically neutral, yet for the Whigs it was a matter of prestige and interest to provide him with an income of over £1,200 a year. Without writing party material, Congreve had high political value, simply because he was a professed Whig and had the personal influence exercised by all distinguished writers at that time.[58] A general hardening of attitudes had, however, long been under way, and by Walpole's time writers patronized by the government had become, as it were, politically accountable.

Unless they were both rich and independent, writers had very little freedom in relation to their political patrons. In 1733 Richard Venn was offered "his own terms if he would write for the government, but he was told he must at the same time go thorough stitch and do as directed, which he with scorn refused." When word reached the Tory Lord Oxford that William Oldys was trying to make "interest with Sir Robert Walpole, through the means of Commissioner Hill," he declared to Oldys that "though he could not do as grand things as Sir Robert, he would do that which might be as agreeable" if Oldys could disengage himself "from all other persons and pursuits." Oldys consequently resigned a £20 annuity from "a nobleman, who might have served me in the government . . . that I might be wholly independent, and absolutely at my Lord Oxford's command."[59]

In an age of patronage, ingratitude was considered one of the major sins. How seriously many contemporaries took their obligations to their patrons is clear from an episode that took place precisely in the Earl of Oxford's own family. Conyers Middleton, who at the time when Lord Hervey sponsored the subscription of his *Life of Cicero* had become "a very zealous Whig," had started his career as "a strong Tory" under the patronage of the Earl of Oxford.[60] The two men fell out when Middleton was accused of expressing unorthodox religious views in a work which Oxford had read and approved before publication. When Middleton failed to obtain the expected support from his patron on this occasion, he took refuge with the Old Corps Whig side. He explained his decision in a letter to Oxford, resigning all the emoluments he had received from his old patron. He clearly considered this the only honorable way of extricating himself from a relationship that no longer worked either for patron or protégé. Another dependent of Lord Oxford's, Minschul, published an anonymous defence of Middleton, and was promptly dismissed when the authorship was discovered. Minschul appealed to Middleton whose advice plainly shows that basically he accepted a patron's right to expect loyalty from his protégés:

> . . . as his Lordship might have good reason to be disgusted, at your taking such a step, whilst in his service, & without his permission; so I advise you to throw yourself at his Lordship's feet, & ask his pardon in the best manner you are able; with promise of writing nothing for the future, but what he shall order & allow.[61]

In most cases a patron could exert subtle or not so subtle pressure on writers he supported. The Rev. Alured Clarke was anxious to shield Stephen Duck—the favorite charity case in Court circles—from the worst excesses of patronage. He asked that "the Thresher poet"

> should not be obliged to make verses upon any particular subject without her Majesty's order . . . it would be a great advantage to him to have some time for storing his mind with as much proper knowledge as he can before he engages in a new work, it is a pity he should be diverted from it by every one that has any curiosity to gratify in setting him upon some employment of their own.[62]

A satirist or a panegyrist with a patron had better get the politics right. They clearly had to accommodate themselves as best they could to their benefactors. In 1732 Richard Savage published a panegyric on Sir Robert Walpole, for which he received twenty guineas. In his *Life of Savage* Dr. Johnson commented:

As he was very far from approving the Conduct of Sir *Robert Walpole*, and in Conversation mentioned him sometimes with Acrimony, and generally with Contempt, as he was one of those who were always zealous in their Assertions of the Justice of the late Opposition, jealous of the Rights of the People, and alarmed by the long continued Triumph of the Court; it was natural to ask him what could induce him to employ his Poetry in Praise of that Man, who was, in his Opinion, an Enemy to Liberty, and an Oppressor of his Country? He alleged, that he was then dependent upon the Lord *Tyrconnel*, who was an implicit Follower of the Ministry, and that being enjoined by him, not without Menaces, to write in Praise of his Leader, he had not Resolution sufficient to sacrifice the Pleasure of Affluence to that of Integrity.[63]

Similarly, at the height of the Excise crisis, before Thomas Cooke's defection to the opposition, a dissident Whig friend engaged in "the *cause of liberty*" wrote: "I am convinced no person would act more in that way, than yourself had you the necessary fortune to support your sentiments." Few were prepared to be as honest about this as Joseph Mitchell:

As I have defil'd much fair *Paper*, so 'tis no less true, that much foul *Paper* have I *burn'd* . . . I have even sacrific'd some *favourite Pieces* to the Flames, for Fear of offending the *Good*, the *Great*, or the *Weak* ones of the Earth. I have almost *circumcised others to Death*, to gratify *Persons I was oblig'd to*, in Spite of my own *Judgment and Taste*. I wish I cou'd say, I have not also publish'd *not a few*, which I dislike, out of mere *Ceremony* and *Compliment*: But, both by what I have *printed*, *mangled*, and *destroyed*, the *Revenue* has gain'd considerably. In this Respect my *private Vices* have turned to *public Benefits*.[64]

As these examples indicate, sincerity cannot be expected from Walpole's writers. It was rumored that when James Sterling and Matthew Concanen came to London from Ireland in the 1720s they determined on the basis of a flip of a coin that Concanen would write in defence of the ministry and his friend offer his services to the opposition. This anecdote may well have been based on no more than ill-natured hearsay, yet it illustrates the predicament faced by all would-be scribblers at the time. A choice of political allegiance had to be made, and consequently speculations about their sincerity or lack thereof are likely to be most uncertain. Self-interest was after all recognized as a natural and totally acceptable force at the time.[65]

Many Whig writers were of course quite beyond Walpole's control. These were private gentlemen who published occasionally, pseudonymously, and at their own expense, without the knowledge of the government, and who were consequently restrained only by their own conception of what might at any one time be politically expedient. Probably most of these productions did not differ markedly from works sanctioned by Old Corps Whig politicians; self-appointed defenders of the ministry had only to consult the pro-government newspapers to find out precisely what was official policy at any given time. But there were always the eccentrics. Sir Alexander Brand of Brandfield in Scotland, for example, regularly wrote birthday poems to the king, the Prince and the Princess of Wales, attending at Court in person while his circumstances permitted. In 1727 he printed a collection of these poems, which conform in every way to standard poems on the subject issued through the pro-government press, except that he refers repeatedly to his own private affairs: his "Years Infirmities and Disasters," his knowledge of languages, his fifty years of happily married life, his previous business activities (Director of the Fishery with interests in Danzig and Thorn; manufacturer in Scotland of "Gilt Leather, Cheaper by 50 per Cent" than the foreign variety), his literary production (poems to the Royal family, the Duke of Argyle, and Sir Robert Walpole), and his plans to build "*a Canal to be cut at his own Expense, from Leith to the Palace of Holyred-house [sic], and to set up the King's Statue on Horse-back, and Prince* William's *there to convince the World of his great Loyalty, and that he is no Bankrupt,*" together with detailed complaints of his son's behavior (fatherly forgiveness obtainable subject to specifications). If redress is obtained through the good offices of the queen, Sir Alexander is ready to rear another statue (of Prince Frederick this time), but he threatens to "*buy Land either in England or Hanover, being determin'd not to live among Scotch Justices of the Peace, &c. who have insulted him in Coffee-houses, and in the King's Garden, concerning which a Process now depends before the Lords of Session.*"[66]

Clearly Sir Alexander Brand consulted no one but himself before publishing. A surprising number of volunteers were, however, willing to work closely with key members of the Old Corps Whig establishment in an effort to produce works with the maximum propaganda effect, thereby exposing themselves to the same kind of political pressure that was part of a hack writer's very existence. Walpole and other leading Old Corps Whigs obviously could not treat these volunteers like hacks and simply tell them what to write and when. The pressure exerted on them was much more subtle, but not different in essence to that exerted on the hirelings. What Walpole demanded from his hacks can be summed up in William Arnall's description of his own contribution: "faithful Zeal and constant Application."[67] Whereas "faithful Zeal" was also expected of the volunteers, Walpole was in no position to demand their "constant Application."

Any writer who wanted to come to the notice of Walpole had to express the correct political sentiments right from the start, as the prospective hack A. B. did in his first letter to Walpole. He announced his wish to "employ the small share of Talents Nature has allotted me, against these Ennemies [sic] of their Country who under the cloak of Patriotism, are designing the subversion of all Government." "Who Can lamely Submit to see ye Best and Greatest villifyd?" were the words of Philo-Britannicus to Walpole, on submitting a character sketch vindicating the "Prime Minister" to the world. Mitchell described his friend Stuart to Walpole in a poetic letter of introduction as "one of Us, and has a World of Zeal."[68]

Once a hack was in Walpole's employ, or a volunteer had come to his attention, their loyalty had to be unwavering. The letters that these writers directed to Walpole abound in protestations of the most disinterested and unchanging loyalty towards his interests. Walpole was therefore unlikely to be impressed with Eustace Budgell's assurances that he had "never yet wrote So much as one Single Craftsman," as long as he added "I do not affirm, Sr:, that I have no manner of acquaintance with the author or authors of those Papers, or that I may have never Said Something over a glass of Wine, which may have been looked upon and caught up as a lucky hint." As will be shown (in Part III), one of the positive moral elements of the Old Corps Whig ethos was that of political constancy and consistency, used as a stick to beat opposition members who had defected from Walpole's camp. For writers financially dependent on the government, therefore, the only solution to disenchantment with government policies was retirement. According to Joseph Turner, this is what his friend Edward Young did ("See *Young* retires, with one fair Branch of Bays, | Resolv'd to keep, whate'er he won of Praise"). By 1730 Young was complaining to close friends that after more than seven years of service he had still not received any preferment. Young continued to enjoy his yearly pension of £200, a fact which perhaps prevented him from writing *against* the government, although his conscience (or the influence of friends such as Dodington) may no longer have allowed him to write actively *for* the government.[69]

For the volunteers it seems to have been very important to distance themselves from the hacks, as the Irish clergyman Samuel Madden did in a letter to Walpole:

> I beseech you Sr. not to impute any little labour I have taken (or shall
> be able to take) this way to self Conceit or impertinence or a low merce-
> nary zeal, but to such noble & honest motives as animate your self &
> every true Patriot when all our great Interests are at Stake.

Naturally the volunteers drew the line between themselves and the
hacks on the basis of independence of opinions.[70]

Seemingly the hacks were equally anxious to divorce themselves
from the prevailing *image* of the hack, and thereby distance themselves from fellow hirelings. Occasionally they even go so far as to
try to impress on Walpole that their zeal, as reflected in various
works written for his service, was sincere and had nothing to do
with mercenary considerations. William Arnall, for example, who
in 1733 was under a cloud for financial malpractice, wrote thus to
his patron,

> Have you so often forgiven the base, the ungrateful, the false and the
> faithless will you then crush me with Severity whose Heart is Irre-
> proachable whose Hand was never prostituted to do you Wrong who
> have neither sought nor made Friends amongst your Enemies but all
> your enemies mine? Have I been the Man that ever wished to become
> Independent of you or that after having asked and accepted your Favour
> allowd myself to oppose and insult you? Have I been the Man who after
> having listed Myself to asperse and injure you enterd into your service
> when the Cause of abusing you would no longer support me? Have I
> been the Man who ever shewd myself wary of appearing in your Vindi-
> cation and whilst I incessantly solicited your Favour meanly endeavourd
> to make your Enemies imagine that I had no Hand in your Service?[71]

Is there evidence to support Arnall's contention that his own loyalty was maintained against a background of political opportunism
and disloyalty among the pro-government writers? Walpole's late-
eighteenth-century biographer William Coxe claimed that some
hacks "not unfrequently [sic] propagated in private conversation,
and even in public clubs, disadvantageous reports of the minister,
and declared that high rewards induced them to write against their
real sentiments."[72] And it is certainly true that in some cases hack
writers defected from the opposition to the government and vice
versa. That they were vulnerable to economic offers is understandable, since few of them earned as much as Arnall. Consequently
defection was as much the rule as the exception among the hirelings. Thomas Cooke and Benjamin Norton Defoe both ratted on
Walpole. Ralph Courteville wrote for the opposition before being
recruited to write on the pro-government side, and was at one point

suspected of Jacobitism. According to Warburton, James Ralph, who had come to London from the American colonies together with Benjamin Franklin in 1724, was "detected in writing on both sides on one and the same day."[73]

The most spectacular case of disloyalty among the pro-government writers, however, concerns Benjamin Norton Defoe, who had worked for the opposition before he was recruited to write for Walpole. In 1739 Defoe was taken up by a warrant from the Duke of Newcastle because of his involvement with the *Craftsman*. Having thus been caught with his finger actually in the opposition pie, Daniel Defoe's son had no option but to admit that he had taken "refuge in ye Craftsman," excusing himself by referring to the extreme poverty to which he and his family had been reduced ("not till my Innocent Motherless Children were reduced to the last bitt [sic] of Bread"). There is little reason to doubt that Benjamin Norton Defoe was in dire financial straits. For years he had been describing himself as "in the greatest Extremity of Distress." In petition after petition he recounted his sob story: a most numerous family (seventeen children in less than seventeen years of whom he had buried fourteen), his wife's death of a miscarriage, the remaining three motherless children, and so on. Probably his distress was very real. His father, however, saw things differently. Daniel Defoe, himself untrustworthy in money matters, complained on his deathbed of "ye Injustice Unkindness and I must say Inhuman Dealing of my Own Son wch: has both ruind my family and in a word broken my heart." Defoe père claimed that he had trusted his "Two unprovided Childn:" to his son, only to find that he suffered "them and their poor Dying Mother to Beg their Bread at his door, and to crave as if it were an Alms, what he is bound under Hand and Seal Beside the most Sacred promises to supply them with, himself at ye Same time living in a Profusion of Plenty." It seems quite characteristic of Benjamin Norton Defoe, that having been caught flagrante delicto working for the enemy he immediately offered to double-cross them by making the situation "turn to the Service of the Government." Indeed there seems to be little reason to doubt his assertion that, given suitable compensation, he "would be willing to Sacrifice every Interest" of his own to Newcastle's "Command."[74]

Some writers were not cut out by temperament to be protégés for long, and the least suitable of them all was Richard Savage. Extravagant and permanently impecunious, with an ego that rendered him servile and self-assertive by turns, he always, according to Dr. Johnson, "asked Favours of this Kind without the least Submission or apparent Consciousness of Dependence, and that he did not seem to look upon a Compliance with his Request as an Obligation that deserved any extraordinary Acknowledgements." He also had a tendency to criticize over his bottles people that he adulated in verse. For a while he was patronized by Steele, who gave him an allowance, offered his natural daughter in marriage with a dowry of £1000, or alternatively help to obtain a post in the government. When Steele heard that Savage—not famous for his patience—had ridiculed him in company, he withdrew his support. For a while Lord Tyrconnel "received him into his Family" and allowed him a pension of £200 a year. When this arrangement came to an acrimonious end, Savage actually blotted the name of his ex-patron out of his own copy of *The Wanderer*, and Tyrconnel was so incensed that he came with "a Number of Attendants" to beat Savage at a coffee-house. Savage actually published a panegyric on Sir Robert Walpole who rewarded him with twenty guineas and at some point gave through a friend of Savage's "a Promise of the next Place that should become vacant, not exceeding two hundred Pounds a year." It is easy to understand why Walpole failed to keep his promise. Even Savage himself "did not indeed deny that he had given the Minister some Reason to believe that he should not strengthen his own Interest by advancing him, for he had taken Care to distinguish himself in Coffee-Houses as an Advocate for the Ministry of the last Years of Queen *Anne*, and was always ready to justify the Conduct, and exalt the Character of Lord *Bolingbroke*, whom he mentions with great Regard in an Epistle upon Authors, which he wrote about that Time, but was too wise to publish." In the end Savage confronted Walpole at his levee. This must have clinched matters.[75] Walpole preferred his writers to be like Joseph Mitchell who was noted for his strong sense of gratitude.[76]

MIDDLEMEN

In his book on the newspaper press during the Walpole era Michael Harris has stressed that the relationships that existed between the journalists working in the London press and their political backers "probably involved some very variable forms of personal contact," but that these are remarkably difficult to pin down. One reason for this is, quite simply, that communications of this nature are easier and, above all, safer to conduct through conversations than through letters. Occasionally, people explain to Walpole that they are only communicating by letter because they have been, as one of them complained "too much cramp'd at your Levee to speak my Tho'ts [sic]," or that they are prevented by illness from waiting on him ("Nor should I have troubled you with Epistles but that my Fever hangs about me . . . which makes it Advisable for me not yet to stir").[77]

Some historians have claimed that "there is scant evidence of direct personal intervention by Walpole" and that he "usually chose to rely on intermediaries." The research carried out for this book, however, indicates that Walpole was far more active in propaganda matters than has generally been thought. In his *Walpoliana* Lord Hardwicke remarked:

> Sir Robert seeing what an ill-use was made of the press against him, spared no expense to defend his conduct in the same way. The writers he employed were by no means of the first-rate; but when he and his brother took the trouble to direct or overlook their performances, the case was very different.[78]

Walpole seems to have had direct relations with a number of writers, giving advice on how to handle specific issues, and remonstrating with them when he disapproved of the line they had taken. In 1722 Sir Richard Steele wrote,

> It is a mortification to me to be, in any way, interrupted in what I do under your observation and patronage, for I am as much raised in the pleasure of Life by your conversation, as I am exalted in any hopes I may form, with regard to my fortune, from your favour.[79]

Similarly, Leonard Welsted sent an "unfinishd draught" of "another treatise" directly to Walpole. He expressed confidence that Walpole would understand the "Scheme & intention" and hoped that the "Prime Minister" would agree with him that such a piece would be "seasonable & of service att this time." Welsted acknowledged having received "Testimonies of regard & favour" from Walpole and assured the "Prime Minister,"

> I shall at all times exert myself to produce what may be worthy of your care & protection, & lay out my whole industry & zeal in your cause, which, I know, will allways [sic] be the cause of the public.[80]

Both Steele and Welsted had such a high standing not only in literary circles, but in society in general, that Walpole could not offend them by turning them over to middlemen. However, not only certain volunteers but some of the hirelings too seem to have had ready access to the "Prime Minister." In this respect, at least, Walpole was no snob. William Arnall, for instance, seems for most of his career to have enjoyed his confidence. All the evidence indicates that Arnall had frequent meetings with Walpole and that he often took orders directly from "the Great Man" himself. In April 1733 Arnall wrote to explain why he had not attended Walpole *the last fortnight*: in the middle of the Excise Crisis he "saw no Room . . . to be Heard."[81] Occasionally they communicated through Thomas Gordon or Nicholas Paxton, the éminence grise of pro-government propaganda.

Apparently the hacks—and even some volunteers—considered it necessary to obtain Walpole's permission to write and publish on certain issues. Arnall, for instance, asked for permission to defend the Excise scheme after its defeat, announcing his intention of coming to see Walpole to obtain his "Hearing,"

> What you Sr have said for it would put to Shame all those who have appeared against it. But this hath been confined within the Walls of one Assembly And none are equal to the Task of supplying the Want of those Arguments without Doors unless They have your Instructions. It is this that I humbly apply for and If Sir this be Vouchsafed to me my Industry in Improving it to the best Uses will be equal to my Gratitude for having been distinguished by so desired a Favour.[82]

Problems arose chiefly when a hack misjudged the situation and was considered to have exceeded his instructions. This is what happened when Benjamin Norton Defoe wrote and published a freelance pamphlet, defending Walpole against aspersions cast on him by Eustace Budgell. Once the piece was published, Norton Defoe had been assured by Edward Walpole, Sir Robert's son, that "it was a very clever peice [sic] Exceeding well done; and that to his knowledge His Father liked it very well; and look'd upon it as the properest Reply that could be made." Thus encouraged, Norton Defoe "in hopes it might be agreeable and Serviceable" to Walpole, had decided to ensure a wide circulation for the pamphlet by giving away "above two hundred of a twelve penny pamphlet; more than were Sold." Apparently Defoe was never recompensed either for writing or for dispersing free copies of his work. Clearly, Walpole considered that Defoe should have asked for permission to print:

> . . . such is the fate of an unhappy necessitous Man; when I attended your Honr: all I got, was seemingly your Hon.r's displeasure; Your Hon:r reprimanded me for presumeing [sic] to Enter your Hon:r as you

was pleas'd to Express it, in the Lists, with Such a wretch as Budgel [sic]; who you dispised [sic] as much as the Dirt under your Shoes.[83]

Obviously, Walpole could only deal personally and regularly with some of his more trusted writers, and then only if the matters in hand were considered important by the writers themselves or Walpole. A number of middlemen start to appear as intermediaries between leading politicians and writers or journalists.[84] That the hacks—and even some of the volunteers—did not expect Walpole to handle their cases personally is clear from their letters. As early as 1721 a writer calling himself J. C. wrote to Walpole to give him the chance to peruse a pamphlet before it went to the press, and announced his willingness to wait on him "or any person whom you shall please to appoint, in order to explain any part which may not be clearly enough exprest." One Thomas Digges showed a similar awareness that "the Multiplicity of Affairs" might prevent Walpole from examining his material personally, suggesting to Walpole that he "referr [sic] it to any Person You think proper, and . . . under Your Encouragement proceed to the perfecting of it."[85]

Satirical prints hostile to Walpole often feature characters that lead hack writers literally by a string through their noses. In one such print Dr. Conyers Middleton leads Court Evil (the opposition sobriquet for Ralph Courteville), but there is also a figure riding postilion for Walpole's State Coach, and the engraved verses explain:

> 'Tis he de Coachman [Walpole] does confide in,
> Of all de Hackneys to have the guiding.[86]

This character has been variously identified, and there has always been a tendency to believe that Walpole must have consigned the care of pro-government propaganda to one single individual. The evidence, however, indicates that there was never one middleman, but several middlemen.

In their search for one individual responsible for Walpole's propaganda effort, historians have suggested several likely candidates, in particular Nicholas Paxton and Thomas Gordon. Although they were both actively involved in Walpole's propaganda effort, they seem to have had very different roles to play.

Nicholas Paxton had a rather sinister reputation. Probably the one referred to as "yon fell Harpy hov'ring o'er the Press" in Paul Whitehead's *Manners*,[87] he was, as already mentioned, paid a regular salary to inspect newspapers and pamphlets published all over

the country for any treasonable or libelous material. His legal train-
ing enabled him to give advice on when to initiate prosecutions. As
Solicitor to the Treasury, Paxton was also entrusted with enormous
sums of money. Over a period of ten years close to £95,000 passed
through his hands, but little is know about how this money was
spent, since much of it was Secret Service money, and Paxton refused point blank to answer any questions put to him by the committee appointed to enquire into the last ten years of Walpole's term
in office. In their report the committee complained about "the great
Difficulty they labour under, from this obstinate and contemptuous
Behaviour of Mr. *Paxton*, who appears to have been directly or indirectly concerned in most of the Transactions, into which they
have hitherto enquired; and when they consider the very large
Sums, which have been issued to him, during the Time of his being
Sollicitor [sic] to the Treasury, and that no effectual Methods were
ever taken to oblige him to account for any Part thereof." Paxton
meddled more actively than most in elections, so it is likely that
large sums went into keeping up the government election interest in
various boroughs. He also seems to have been the paymaster for
hacks and informers, one of the latter complaining that he had applied, unsuccessfully, for recompense from Paxton "as directed."
Paxton's role in Walpole's propaganda effort was seemingly two-
fold. As overseer of the press he advised on legal matters and was
very much involved with attempts to suppress or restrict the circulation of opposition material. As paymaster in general he came into
close contact with writers for hire, and directions from Walpole to
various journalists and writers were often transmitted through him.
However, he seems to have been much more involved with the practical side of opposition propaganda than with directing the actual
contents of pro-government propaganda.[88]

Thomas Gordon seems to have been more directly involved with
the pro-government writers, especially perhaps the hacks. He set
Benjamin Norton Defoe to write for the *London Journal*, presum-
ably before it and they became part of Walpole's propaganda effort.
Later Gordon acted as overseer for Arnall in his work for the *Free
Briton*, a fact which Arnall is said to have resented. Gordon was
also associated with the journalist James Pitt who wrote for the
Daily Gazetteer, and with the printer John Peele,[89] admitting to an
Old Corps Whig friend who had been shabbily treated by the gov-
ernment:

> Nor am I half so sanguine a man as Jno Peele takes me to be—I have
> often felt bitterness of heart, when I have appeared all Joyful to him
> about our public matters & Men.[90]

A man of good family, with a liberal education, with considerable experience in political writing, a reputation as a translator and writer, Gordon would seem a much more likely character to direct the pro-government writers in their efforts to defend Walpole's administration, than the more obscure Paxton. For how long Gordon remained actively involved in Walpole's propaganda effort, is, however, matter for speculation. In a letter written to a friend and dated 1 July 1740 Thomas Gordon reveals meticulous knowledge of current events and mentions seeing Walpole from time to time, but states: "I spend all my time at the Hill, except my short Intervals of Business."[91] These are not the words of a man responsible for Walpole's propaganda effort on a day-to-day basis.

A few poets prepared to write in support of Walpole's government had the kind of independence that comes with great wealth and high social standing. Charles Hanbury Williams was a Monmouthshire landowner, a Member of Parliament, a personal friend of Sir Thomas Winnington and Henry Fox and other prominent politicians, Paymaster of the Marines, and later, after Walpole had retired as Lord Orford, to become Lord Lieutenant and Custos Rotulorum of Herefordshire and a Knight of the Bath. Hanbury Williams was clearly both too rich and too independent to be manipulated. Any attempts to direct his works would have been deeply resented. He was, however, quite willing to listen to his friends, and often changed his works so as to fit in with their ideas about what was politically expedient at any given time. All his works, from love poems for his various mistresses to bitter satires on opposition politicians, passed through the hands of Henry Fox, who encouraged, criticised, suggested topics, changes, and additions. In this way Fox acted informally as both literary and political adviser to his friend.[92]

Most pro-government writers, however, were financially dependent on some patron or other, and thus part of the basic structure of patronage on which contemporary society was based. Prominent Whig politicians who had protégés among the writers were in a position to influence them politically. Among the more active politicians in this respect were the Duke of Newcastle, Lord Pembroke, George Bubb Dodington (who later joined the opposition), and Sir William Yonge.[93] Yonge, for instance, had served both as Lord of the Treasury and Lord of the Admiralty before becoming Secretary at War in 1735. He belonged to the powerful group of Old Corps Whig friends, which surrounded Sir Thomas Winnington and Henry Fox and included prominent politicians like Lord Hervey and the not so prominent politician but gifted satirist Sir Charles

Hanbury Williams. Sir William Yonge was himself an author, collaborating with his protégés Concanen and Roome on a ballad opera based on Richard Brome's *The Jovial Crew*, and writing jointly with Winnington and Hanbury Williams "one or two political ballads before Lord Orford went out." Yonge's personal interest in literature, together with his high rank, politically and socially, may have qualified him for the delicate task of maintaining close relations with a number of pro-government writers, and acting as an intermediary between them and Walpole. Lewis Theobald once explained to a friend that Walpole had turned him over to Sir William Yonge "as a Remembrancer & Intercessor for me to his Favour." As an active recruiter of pro-government writers, it was only natural that Yonge should continue to lend them support and encouragement. James Ruffhead, for instance, put a poem called "Seasonable Admonitions" at Walpole's disposal, "by the Comendations [sic] of Sir William Yonge."[94] In a poem published in 1733 Yonge is urged as Walpole's friend to "watch o'er the *Letter'd State*," and "WALPOLE's Pow'r engage | To free from blind *Stupidity* the Age" in which it pays to write for the opposition. In other words Yonge is encouraged to act as patron on a large scale. Commentators have been unable to account for the fact that Yonge, according to Lord Hervey, "without having done anything . . . particularly profligate—anything out of the common track of a ductile courtier and a parliamentary tool—his name was proverbially used to express everything pitiful, corrupt, and contemptible."[95] Perhaps Yonge's involvement with government propaganda explains some of this unpopularity, although an ugly divorce may also have contributed.

The more actively involved politicians like Sir William Yonge were in recruiting, the more writers they would have to control or influence—and support. To be cynical, in many cases these writers became assets—along with local election influence, family connections, etc.—that Whig politicians had to offer in return for a place at the center of political power.

The strength of such a system is that it allowed for close contacts between patron and protégé during which subtle pressure could be brought to bear on the latter, who might well learn to internalize his patron's values if his own were different at the outset. The weakness of the system resides in its dependence on the political consistency of the patron. Sir Robert Walpole's last few years in power were clouded by internal dissent within the ministry itself, and it would seem that some writers were hedging their bets. A knowledge of the tension that existed between Walpole and the Duke of

Newcastle may well have informed a letter which Leonard Welsted addressed to the latter in 1738. Reminding Newcastle of his "intended kindness" to him, Welsted explained:

> if I have the happiness of being countenancd by your Grace, I shall be less in danger of being injurd from any quarter, & in a much better way of being befriended.

Perhaps this was Welsted's way of ensuring continued favor in the event of a ministerial reshuffle.[96]

It would also seem that some business was contracted at regular meetings where several writers attended. Joseph Maubey relates that when his friend Thomas Cooke, who was "all his life a strenuous assertor of Revolution principles," came to London in the early 1720s at the age of about twenty, he soon struck up an acquaintance with Thomas Tickell, Ambrose Philips, Leonard Welsted, Sir Richard Steele, John Dennis, and "others, whose political opinions agreed with his own." Cooke became a member of a club which included Joseph Maubey's maternal uncle Joseph Pratt and "several literary characters" who met weekly at the Spring Gardens, afterwards at the Vine and Royal Oak Inn. It was presumably to this club that Lewis Theobald later introduced William Warburton. Known as the Concanen Club, it was presided over by Matthew Concanen, and included members such as the critic John Dennis, the young poet George Moore Smythe, and Thomas Cooke and Edward Roome. At these meetings new projects were initiated, and sometimes became the object of collaborative work. It was at such meetings that the campaign against Pope, in which the young Warburton participated, was orchestrated. They were all joint authors, for instance, of a letter attacking Pope (signed W. A.) which they had inserted in Mist's *Journal* for 8 June 1729.[97]

Perhaps it is also worth pointing out that certain government offices were dominated by people who were closely concerned with propaganda, and although this is pure speculation, it seems likely that pro-government campaigns were hatched in such places as the Wine Licence Office. By 1740 all five Commissioners had been promoted during the Walpole period, and three of them had been actively involved with pro-government propaganda, but in different capacities. Thomas Gordon, who was or had been one of the most important middlemen on whom had devolved the task of overseeing a large section of pro-government propaganda; the arch-Whig Henry Harris, a close friend of Winnington, Fox, Hanbury Williams, and other important Whigs, who described himself as a former hack writer ("I once Lived my self, I own, by my Wits, as it is called—but Damned Unpleasant it was!") and Anthony Corbiere who had served the Secretaries of State as translator, private secretary, Under Secretary and decipherer.[98]

Working Relations Between Writers and Politicians

Writers who submitted their work to Walpole very often proclaimed their willingness to change the material to suit Walpole's purposes, or even to suppress the work altogether. John Ker, for instance, who had made himself "an Advocate for the Cause of Liberty in a Poem addressed to the British Senate," sent a copy to Walpole with the following message:

> I am conscious of having written it with a hearty Zeal for Freedom and your Admiration. If you, Sir, think fit to disapprove of it, I assure you it shall for ever dye, the Impression being at my own Charge and in my own Hands.[99]

And from Ireland Samuel Madden sent material "to be publisht when & how you please, with whatever corrections those you entrust them with think best," explaining,

> I am sensible both my want of abillity [sic] & skill for such a Work & my distance from the scene of business, & being depriv'd of all proper instruction & information, must make them very defective; but if you think they are worth my own attendance or the care of others to alter or improve them, they & I are absolutely at your service, if such trivial things can be worth your service.[100]

Several other writers express diffidence. E. J., for example, claimed that he only submitted his treatise in manuscript because "I am uncertain, as this is my first attempt of ye sort, whether I have put some things on the right foot or no; whether this treatise is a defence, as intended, or a real invective: for I look upon an awkward defence as ye worst sort of invective."[101]

It is quite clear that submitting a manuscript and offering to make required changes was not a mere matter of form. The writers often refer to alterations which they hope will remove "all objections" to their schemes. In 1732 one of Walpole's press spies advised strongly against prosecuting opposition writers since in his view party scribblers were mere slaves controlled by stronger members of the bookselling trade. If this was true of the opposition writers, it seems to have been no less true of their pro-government counterparts. In Michael Harris's words "the author was obliged to pay for increased financial security by giving up some degree of independence." He claims that compared to the opposition writers the journalists that wrote for the government were under a much more "formal and consistent oversight." None of them seem to have had any financial stake in the papers for which they wrote and were therefore in a financially dependent position.[102]

It would, however, be wrong to think that the volunteers who submitted their works to Walpole were not subjected to the same sort of political pressure as the hacks. Just like the hirelings they were often kept waiting for permission from Walpole to publish their works. Just like the hacks they had access to the government printing and distribution network, and could be subject to some form of supervision. When, for instance, Oldmixon, who thought of himself as a volunteer, in 1723 issued a *Critical History* intended as a counterblast to Lord Clarendon's history and to Eckart's *History of England* (which had "treated the glorious Struggle by the Parliament in *Forty-two*, as a flagrant *Rebellion*," a view which had consequences for how one looked upon the Glorious Revolution), "Two honourable Persons near the Ministry, who had the printed Sheets as they were work'd off at the Press . . . express'd very great Satisfaction in reading it." Of the published work "Thousands were dispers'd in a short Time." And when William Somerville submitted his poem *The Chase* to the queen through Charlotte Clayton (later Lady Sundon), explaining that he wished to dedicate the work to the Prince of Wales, Dr. Freind of Westminster School and Stephen Poyntz were asked to read it and propose emendations. At their suggestion Somerville changed a simile at the end of the section devoted to the Hare Chase. It was feared that the original simile might be "misapplied." In substituting the image of Orpheus set on by the Bacchanals, the author explained to Mrs. Clayton: "Thus, Madam, I am equally unmerciful to poets as ministers, when they will suit my purpose or embellish my poem. I beg you will believe that I am and ever will be firm and inflexible in those honest principles upon which the Revolution was founded."[103]

It was clearly safest to submit works for consideration, even if they were not intended as political propaganda, but merely touched on high politics or prominent politicians. This is what the Dean of Christ Church John Conybeare did, when he found himself under the necessity of referring to the Duke of Newcastle's actions in a

certain affair. He simply submitted the relevant passages, expressing the hope that they would not be found to be "disagreeable Either with Truth, or . . . profound Respect."[104]

Frequently, having once offered to let Walpole or one of his
trusted agents have a look at their unpublished material, the writers
were caught in a trap. Often these works remained—and no doubt
at times designedly so—among Walpole's papers, and the authors
were then forced to write to remind the "Prime Minister" of their
existence, or risk his displeasure by publishing without the consent
that had after all been solicited. In 1733 Thomas Cooke informed
Walpole that his "Collection of State Poems" had "now been
printed three Weeks; six of which I have, at different Times, submitted to you: and as they remain in the Printer's Hands till I have
the Honour of your Commands, I hope I shall be no longer without
them." It also takes very little imagination to guess at what was
behind the following letter to Walpole,

> Tho my Intention was well meant, in submiting [sic] the Pamphlet in
> Manuscript, to your Honors Judgment, yet I now fear it was Imprudent,
> considering how precious every moment is, to one incessantly busied,
> in concerns of the utmost weight & Importance. I therefore humbly beg
> pardon, for that, & this presumption. But as I have since made several
> additions thereto, in defence of the Ministry, & other alterations; & that
> some Friends think it will be of use to the admtion [sic], was it soon
> printed; I propose so to do, unless your Honors [sic] pleasure should be
> signified to the contrary.[105]

It would seem that occasionally hints were sent by people who
did not themselves wish to write the material. The proprietor of the
Gentleman's Magazine Edward Cave, for instance, after spending
some time in the visitors' gallery in the House of Commons during
a debate, and hearing an opposition politician make a digression
about the weekly writers which was later "applauded as unanswerable," wrote "a Sketch for a Reply" and sent it to Walpole as "a
Mean [sic] to furnish a Hint to any of your Friends." This could of
course be modesty on Cave's part, but perhaps he simply meant
what he was saying.[106]

Some of the political works seem to have been commissioned, in
that certain authors were encouraged to write on specific topics in
specific ways. More often than not, however, the initiative seems to
have come from the writers, who sometimes presented their
schemes or their finished documents to Walpole or his deputies for
approval. If permission to publish was forthcoming, the writers had

access to the pro-government publishing network. Of course, writers did not need to go via the Whig leadership with their manuscripts. Printers, booksellers, and publishers could be contacted directly, and the political polarization ensured that authors were likely to contact those who were known to be working for the government. It is significant that when in 1741 one Thomas Dicey who claimed to have "been permitted to Write for upwards of Three Years in the Gazetteer without any Obstruction," had one of his works refused, it was to Walpole that he wrote to complain, enclosing a copy of this 'Letter design'd for the Gazetteer sent many Days since, and not incerted [sic]."[107]

Unfortunately, the best documented example of how writers and politicians cooperated on creating propaganda concerns a political pamphlet, and not what we normally think of as fiction. However, since it helps to illustrate the process it has been included here.

In 1735 the so-called Bank Contract episode occurred. The opposition accused Walpole of having been present at a meeting held in 1720 between the directors of the South Sea Company and the Bank, at which, it was alleged, certain financial malpractice had been covered up. Several Whig writers were actively at work on this difficult case. One John Adlam was busy trying to recover material that might be of service in "this Controversy, if continued," for Walpole's benefit enclosing and commenting on pamphlets issued from opposition quarters. He also offered advice on how to deal with the crisis, proclaiming himself "ready to assist in explaining this Affair in any Capacity or Method that may be thought proper."[108]

Thus William Arnall was but one of several to work on this case. He had already "embarked in this Controversy and . . . appeared in it not without Some Reputation and Success," when he obtained a sneak preview—a measure of his influence in press circles—of "the Craftsman now in the Press on the Bank Contract." He immediately wrote to Walpole to ask his permission to pursue the matter further, if the *Craftsman* should publish more on the subject, thereby providing "sufficient Scope for an Answer." His requests to Walpole in that connection are revealing:

But that I may be in the right Method of Enquiring & Thinking concerning this Affair I will beg Your Permission to be heard a very few Minutes on Tuesday Morning; and will with all the Application which I am Master of endeavour to make your Adversaries as despicable as they are false malicious & unjust. Desiring only in my own Behalf that . . . you will allow me to aquit [sic] myself in the Course of it as is expected from me And that you will indulge me from Time to Time with such short Hearings as may not be troublesome or inconvenient for You.

Before he had time to send this letter off to Walpole, Nicholas Paxton turned up with a printed copy of the *Craftsman* in question and Arnall consequently enclosed it for Walpole's perusal.[109]

Arnall was granted a meeting on the following Tuesday, and Paxton wrote to assure Walpole that nothing would be published before then. Informed by Paxton of this decision, Arnall wrote to Walpole that, "nothing was intended till I could obtain the necessary Light in a Matter of so much Importance." He also provided Walpole with transcripts of two documents relating to the case, one seemingly an opposition pamphlet. And when the two men met, according to Arnall, Walpole laid down certain "Rules" for how Arnall was to present the case.[110]

Originally Walpole had intended that Arnall should write on the subject as early as September 1731. For this purpose Arnall had been provided with "the Case between the Bank and South Sea Company" which he assumed had been drawn up by "Mr. Townshend." The "Case" had remained unreturned among Arnall's papers. On looking it over, he doubted whether a certain passage from a speech quoted in the "Case" would be "fit to be mentioned," since he foresaw that the opposition might use it in a certain way in their campaign. He therefore gave it as his "humble Opinion" that "it will be the most prudent Method of stating this Case to proceed according to the Rules you laid down last Tuesday."[111]

A month later, Arnall wrote to Walpole, who was in Norfolk, to assure him that he thought it his "Duty to consider the Business of the Bank Contract with all possible Application" so that whenever Walpole thought fit to give him "further Commands" he would be able to render him "more effectual Service."[112] This was perhaps intended as a reminder to Walpole that Arnall needed his permission to go on with his work. Arnall sent Walpole word that he had managed to ascertain that a minute book of the South Sea Company did exist—as alleged in an opposition pamphlet—and that Walpole was mentioned as having been present at the meeting in question. The inference was that henceforth this fact could no longer be denied with impunity, although in Arnall's opinion "The Author of the Consideration on the Publick Funds [Walpole himself] is never the less to be justifyd in the same Manner as if such a Book did not exist He knowing nothing of its Existence till this Moment."[113]

ANONYMITY OF AUTHORSHIP

As Arnall insinuated in a letter to Walpole (quoted earlier), it is a fact that many hacks—and a few volunteers who considered their social position inconsistent with party scribbling[114]—tried to keep their association with Walpole and his administration a secret. Some of them may have done so out of pure timidity, or aristocratic disdain for publicity, but quite often the desire for anonymity was motivated by a wish to avoid an anticipated hostile reaction from their surroundings, should their political commitment become generally known. Malachi Postlethwayt claimed that he had lost several friends by engaging in the Excise controversy "which tho' conceald as much as possible, has unluckily come to light."[115] The political polarization at the time was certainly strong enough to break up friendships. Sir Charles Wyndham complained that when he and his friend Sir Charles Hanbury Williams became Members of the House of Commons their "different ways of acting in Parliament . . . reduced great intimacy within the cold & narrow bounds of bare civility."[116] A perennial complaint among hacks was that their loyalty towards Walpole had earned them not only unpopularity but enmity in opposition quarters. This some of them tried to use as a lever in their dealings with Walpole, since only a permanent nonrevocable post could shield them from the wrath of their political enemies, should Walpole be forced out of office. Arnall, for example, put in for a permanent post on the following grounds:

To ask Employments of an uncertain Tenure would not I think be proper for one in my Condition Since in such a Case I must continually remain exposed to the Power and Vengeance of your most embitterd Enemies . . . faithful Zeal and constant Application to deserve your Care have thus exposed me to such bitter such immortal Hatred.[117]

During the eighteenth century it was of course quite normal for writers to publish their works anonymously or pseudonymously. To identify the author of individual contributions to the newspapers is most of the time well-nigh impossible, and for good reasons. Thomas Cooke once told Sir Hans Sloane in confidence that he wrote for the *British Journal,* insisting that this must go no further, since "Secrecy in that Point is one of the Articles betwixt the Proprietors of the Paper & Myself."[118] Although the title pages of poems addressed to the Royal family or to Sir Robert Walpole frequently reveal the identity of their authors, writers were on the whole anxious to remain anonymous, especially if they had high social standing. Often this anonymity was no more than nominal: Soame Jenyns's collected poems were published with the author's arms instead of his name emblazoned on the title page. And Sir Charles Hanbury Williams's response to a friend's suggestion that one of his panegyrics should be published with his name, is suggestive: "I think your Saying to everybody that tis mine is Sufficient, & better to print it without a Name."[119]

A gentlemanly reluctance to seem to wish to see one's name in print cannot often explain the anonymity of the kind of material that has been examined for this book. But there were other reasons why authors of politically sensitive material sought to remain anonymous during the Walpole era. Unlike their opposition counterparts, pro-government writers did not risk prosecution initiated by the government. Private suits for libel could be brought, however, although few contemporaries seem to have resorted to this expedient.

In the early eighteenth century there was still a tendency to settle such matters privately. If they were discovered to have reflected too severely on their peers, aristocratic satirists risked being ostracized from polite society for a while, or—more seriously—they might be challenged to a duel. William Pulteney and Lord Hervey fought each other over the authorship to a hard-hitting political pamphlet, with Walpole's enemies claiming that the "Prime Minister . . . stirred up the Lord *Harvey* to challenge Mr. *Pulteney*; hoping that the point of the young Gentleman's Sword would dispatch his Rival."[120]

At the other end of the social scale, people involved in propaganda were vulnerable to other types of attack. In 1733 Lord Walpole happened to be in the audience when comments on his father and on the Excise scheme were inserted into a pantomime, and promptly went behind the scenes and "corrected the Comedian with his own Hands very severely." A similar thing happened to William Wilkins, who was considered "the favourite printer of the Whig party" (although his disloyal behavior during the Excise crisis may have changed that). Having inserted in his newspapers certain mock advertisements which satirized William Pulteney and alluded to his wife's relationship with Lord Bolingbroke before her marriage, Wilkins was assaulted at the Crown Tavern in Smithfield by a posse of thugs and beaten within an inch of his life. Seemingly the aggressors were led by Mrs Pulteney's brother Captain Samuel Gumley, a military gentleman of irascible temper and Jacobite sympathies.[121] The attack on the Whig publisher James Roberts by ruffians in 1721 may have been politically motivated.[122] Hawkers were subject to the same occupational hazards. In 1740 a hawker singing a ballad which reflected on the Duke of Argyll, who had recently been metamorphosed into an opposition politician, was set on by a Scotsman who,

> coming by, and not liking the music, began to cane the offender very handsomely; who, pulling out a long, sharp-pointed knife, and being assisted by two more (imagined to be the authors of the song) attacked the gentleman in his turn, who drew his hanger, planted himself against the church wall, and, with the assistance of the mob (who were equally disobliged at the impudence of the ballad) made so good a defence, that he put the enemy to flight, and remained master of the field of battle.[123]

Once the identity of the author of a satirical work was discovered, the risk of repercussions was a very real one and could only be avoided by the kind of resolute behavior shown by Lord Hervey, when a bookseller obtained a copy of a satire in which he had reflected on one of his own friends. The poem was not meant to have a wider readership than the Richmond family, but now it was published. Lord Hervey set to work immediately to turn his satire into an attack on another friend, who was conveniently dead, and presenting this manuscript as the original, blamed the discrepancies between his manuscript and the printed version on the malicious intentions of the publisher. With a little help from the Richmond family, Hervey persuaded his friend that he was innocent.[124]

Anonymity was clearly a necessary precaution for most writers. Henry Fox, who acted as literary and political adviser to his friend Sir Charles Hanbury Williams, warned him not to show his poems to anyone but him, since this represented the only way to get them printed.[125] In some cases, however, anonymity of authorship may have been dictated by the wish to heighten the propaganda effect of certain works. Suppressing the name of the author was one way to avoid giving potential readers any clues to the political bias a given work was likely to have. Combined with a deliberately misleading title page, anonymity of authorship could be a very effective method of insinuating a pro-government poem into opposition hands.

II

How to "Set the Nation's Happiness to View"

HAPPY BRITANNIA, coud'st thou know thy State,
Conducted by a *Minister* so great;
Who! spite of Faction, burns with honest Zeal,
And toils unwearied for the Common-weal;
Plots, Menaces, and Madness dares defy,
Thy Int'rest ever chiefly in his Eye;
And, conscious of Integrity serene,
Shuns no fair Trial, and desires no Screen.
No more thy Care to watch o'er *Europe's* Fate,
And hold in Balance ev'ry jarring State!
No firmer Heav'n on ATLAS' Shoulder stands,
Than safe thy Treasure in a WALPOLE's Hands.
                              (Joseph Mitchell, *Congratulatory Verses*)

5
Propaganda—Eighteenth-Century Style

As shown in the preceding sections, the organization of a pro-government propaganda apparatus to deal with an increasingly vociferous opposition, was part of Walpole's efforts to defend his government and consolidate his own position as "Prime Minister." Newspapers were sponsored, writers employed, printers, booksellers, and publishers engaged to ensure that a positive image of government policies and personalities was conveyed to the public. A sizeable amount of propaganda might therefore be confidently expected.

In view of Walpole's reputation as a philistine who held men of letters in contempt, it is not surprising that the part played by literary works in his propaganda campaign should always have been considered as very minor. A cursory look at the pro-government newspapers tends to confirm this view: poems, for instance, would seem to have been introduced only when other copy was lacking, and although they can often be attributed to pro-government poets, they were not always political in tone.

However, newspapers represented only one outlet for political works, and there is plenty of material to testify to the importance that contemporaries attached to political writing. Even for a period when every gentleman was expected to be able to produce verse effortlessly, the sheer amount of poems and other literary works published separately and exhibiting a clear pro-government bias is remarkable. Politics also extended to the theater, and many plays are whiggish and pro-government in tone.

In many cases it is possible to prove that specific works received varying degrees of encouragement from Walpole and his associates, who clearly looked upon literary works as an integral part of their propaganda effort. In fact, the extent to which they seem to have made little or no distinction between literary material and straightforward political pamphlets is striking. Also many political pamphlets make use of quite "literary" techniques, often starting off

101

with political theorizing and ending up with allegories, dreams, fictional conversations, etc.

However, one major problem facing anyone inclined to study political literature of the eighteenth century—be it pro-government or opposition in slant—is the fact that so much of the relevant material is either anonymous or pseudonymous. Where the identity of the author is not known, it becomes almost impossible to trace the publishing history of individual works through scattered references in private letters or official documents. This raises the question of what kind of material should be considered as propaganda.

It is well documented that certain authors wrote consciously in "Walpole's service" and that some of them regularly submitted material for inspection by "the Great Man" himself or one of his trusted colleagues. However, both writers and politicians are habitually vague about the identity of specific works when referring in their letters to such transactions, which in many cases must have been conducted at private meetings rather than through correspondence. Only exceptionally is it possible to trace a work from its first conception in the mind of the author, through modifications suggested by friends, politicians, editors, or political overseers, to the finished product, published in a form intended to have a felicitous effect on an imagined readership.

A narrow definition of propaganda as "polemical literature aimed at manipulating its readers' political perceptions," presupposes the existence of a propagandist with a notion of the target reader, a polemical objective, and a polemical strategy,[1] since the task of the propagandist (who is not necessarily identical with the author) is to try to persuade others to adopt his own (real or feigned) opinions on certain political subjects or to reinforce such views in people who already think along similar lines.

It would be tempting to say quite simply that any work that serves to reinforce a certain political stance, irrespective of whether the author's political intentions are known, and irrespective of whether the work has been approved by a specific political group, is automatically to be considered as propaganda. From this perspective any anonymous work with contents consistent with pro-government policies would fall into the category of pro-government propaganda. Since, however, there is plenty of evidence to suggest that all political groups tried to disperse disinformation by publishing works in political disguise which conformed in most respects to the expectations of a rival group's readers, but were intended to put across some particular subversive point or other (see below), it is hazardous to attach a "Tory," "Whig," or "Opposition Whig" label to individual works solely on the basis of their political contents.

Moreover, even where the name of the author of a specific work is known to be a government supporter—even a parliamentary supporter—such a work cannot automatically be classed as pro-government propaganda. It would seem that Parliament had its share of backbenchers who were not always too well informed about government strategies and who were therefore likely to publish confidently what politicians closer to the center of power would have considered ill-advised or downright stupid. Pro-government pamphleteers frequently complain that Walpole is made "answerable for all the indiscreet Things that may be publish'd in his Favour; Things which it is not to be supposed he could have Leisure enough to write, or Inclination enough to read."[2] Such works are, of course, interesting in themselves as constituting perhaps a more genuine expression of party feeling than the more censured works that only reached the public after prominent politicians had vouched for them.

If we see the existence of a propagandist as a prerequisite for considering any given work as propaganda, it follows that all literary productions that appeared in newspapers supported by Walpole, can automatically be regarded as propaganda, since this is precisely what the *Daily Gazetteer* and other newspapers were set up to produce.

The same goes for separately published works for which a political genesis can be constructed. Thomas Cooke's *Poems on Affairs of State*, for instance, clearly received Walpole's stamp of approval, since it can be proved that the author "at different Times" before publication submitted six of the nine poems to Walpole for inspection, and that the printed copies of the book remained in the printer's hands for at least three weeks awaiting "the Great Man's" pleasure.[3]

However, it is simply not feasible to establish a direct link between author and politician for each and every work, and it would therefore be impossible to write a history of literature used as pro-government propaganda based only on works for which such a direct link has been established. It has therefore been necessary to adopt a fairly pragmatic approach:

Anonymous or pseudonymous works with a clear pro-government bias have been accepted as propaganda when published by booksellers or publishers known to have worked for Walpole. As a strategy this is far from foolproof since it necessarily includes people like Thomas Cooper who published on both sides of any political question. However, other publishers employed by the Government, seem to have been very circumspect about the political bias of anything they published "without authority," as was only natural if they wished to retain the custom of the Old Corps. Printers and booksellers like John Peele, Samuel Buckley, and James Roberts would therefore be unlikely to handle material likely to offend those in power. For instance, those works studied for this book which were published by James Roberts—known as "the favourite publisher of the Whigs"—conform in terms of contents so consistently to government policy at any given time that it is tempting to see Roberts's name in the imprint as conferring on the works in question a semiofficial standing.

For the purpose of this book, works by Old Corps politicians have been considered as propaganda, unless there is a special reason to suspect that their authors were too far removed from the center of power to know what was considered politically expedient by the party leadership. In such cases, a distinction between propaganda and nonpropaganda has been drawn on the basis of whether the works were published through the usual pro-government channels—interpreted as official approval—and works for which other outlets had been found.

It should perhaps be emphasized that propaganda does not necessarily have to be published to count as such. Circulating poems in manuscript seems to have been far more prevalent during the eighteenth century than is currently realized. Works in manuscript, however, have only been counted as propaganda when it can be proved that efforts were made to circulate them, in however restricted circles.

I have also accepted as political propaganda all works written by authors known in a general way to have been writing for Walpole or one of his adjutants, and also writers dependent on aristocratic patrons sympathetic to the Old Corps, a group which included grandees like the Duke of Newcastle, the Duke of Richmond, and so on. Special attention has been paid to the authors who ratted on Walpole, and care has been taken to identify the precise moment of their apostasy, although this is often made abundantly clear, not merely by a complete change in political vocabulary, but also by a change to a different publishing network.

If this strategy seems to allow little or no room for a consideration of the opinions and idiosyncrasies of individual writers, it is precisely because in very many cases their dependent position rendered them vulnerable to pressure from their patrons and their political allies.

Seen from Walpole's point of view a total lack of sincerity may not have been a problem, so long as the writers in question continued to churn out the kind of material he wanted. In fact it may well have been an advantage in some cases, because the writer, if he were privately of another political opinion, would know better what sort of arguments and what manner of putting them forward would be likely to impress the target group of readers. It has to be remembered that several prominent Whig supporters, like Thomas Winnington and Henry Fox, had converted from Toryism, and their presence on the periphery of the propaganda scene may indicate that Walpole found their knowledge of Tory ways of thinking useful.[4] It also seems likely that Walpole's own experience as leader of a joint Tory/dissident Whig opposition during the Whig Schism may have given him some valuable insights into the potential vulnerability of an opposition of a similar composition.

It may in some cases have been much trickier for Walpole to deal with freelance material written by well-meaning supporters, since for such productions he was inevitably held personally responsible. Certain Whig authors continued to write as if they were still in opposition, never quite adjusting to the idea that if they wished to remain on good terms with the Whig leadership their job was now, not to spout high-flying Whig theory, but pragmatically to defend Walpole by justifying his policies and measures. Used to writing in opposition, they were unwilling or unable to adapt. This is clearly what is at the root of Oldmixon's complaints:

> I could not learn in the Country, that there had been a strange and unhappy Revolution in the State of *Whiggery*, that *Things* were dropt, and Persons put in their Places, and that there were Writers, who pretending to be *Whigs*, had little Regard for old *English* Principles, and employ'd all their Time and Talents in varnishing over temporary Expedients, which perhaps were not the Effect of Choice, but Necessity, more for the Sake of Particulars than of the Publick . . . This Prostitution of Whig Principles by certain *Letter-Writers* in Journals, Courants, and other Daily Papers, I knew could not be laid at my Charge; for I had never written a Word in Vindication of any particular Person or Persons, nor of any Measures, but what I thought tended to promote the publick Interest, Security, and Peace.[5]

That Whig ideology changed gradually, once political power had been concentrated in Whig hands, has been well documented by H. T. Dickinson, and is a constant complaint among some members of the older generation of Old Corps Whig supporters. Writing to

Lord Chancellor Hardwicke, Lord Somerset promised grudging support over election matters, but complained:

> My principles hath their ffoundations [sic] Established on the ffundamentall Principles of the true old whiggs in fformer times when the Libertys & the Propertys of the People were their cheifest [sic] care & considerations much more in those dayes, then it seemeth now to bee by the present whiggs in this Generation for most of the modern actions are not consistent with those old Principles.[6]

6

The Rationale Behind Walpole's Propaganda Effort

The amount of money that Walpole was prepared to spend on propaganda indicates how much value he attached to this activity, but raises the question of what he actually hoped to achieve by this massive spending. Given the amount of corruption the "Prime Minister" was prepared to exercise at election times in order to retain a majority in the House of Commons, where was the need to keep a whole thriving business going in order to put his own views across to the electorate? And which groups was he trying to reach—his own followers, his opponents, or waverers?

It seems reasonable to infer that the administration stepped up its propaganda effort largely because their attempts to suppress opposition material were no more than moderately successful. In the long run the government could not base its defence on a strategy of suppressing or buying off criticism, or restricting the distribution of opposition material; consequently Walpole recognized and acted on the need for an expanded propaganda organization. Starting off as a purely defensive campaign, over the years it came to include far more aggressive tactics.

Both in their letters and in their literary output Walpole's supporters show a sophisticated approach to propaganda, in which modes and times of production were subservient to considerations of the way in which a particular work could have the maximum effect on an imagined readership.

AN ANTIDOTE TO POISON

The government professed to welcome opposition criticism through the press. John Lyons, the author of *The Danverian History*, expressed the official view as follows:

107

Whomsoever would form for himself a just History of his own Times, need never be at a loss for the *Truth* of the Current Transactions of National Affairs, nor seldom for the *Reasons* and Motives of them, our *Party contentions* contributing very much towards this, provided, a Man can restrain his own Passions, and not indulge himself in such Sympathies and Antipathies as may obstruct an equal observance. For, the Writers of Opposite Interests and Principles are constantly watching for, and laying open each others Failings, from whence a great *Good* is produc'd by them, tho' they seldom or never design any such thing, too often the contrary is their Aim, even Imposition and Deceit: but a prudent Man, when he sees any Proceedings arise from Prejudice, and pursu'd with Passion, is ever suspicious of Injustice, and guards against it.

Although John Lyons clearly sees, or professes to see, opposition scrutiny of the government as a good thing in itself, he sounds a note of caution:

A Narrative of a fictitious Fact *is a* real Fact *to the Person perfectly deceiv'd, and produces the same Passions, Emotions, and other Effects.*[1]

Clearly then, there was a risk that ill-intentioned or ignorant people might be misled by one-sided information, especially if this was deliberately misleading. It followed that in order to redress the balance opposition propaganda must be countered by pro-government propaganda. Opposition sympathizers like Lady Marlborough naturally took the opposite view. In her opinion it was the papers sponsored by the government that "impose on very ignorant people, a great many of which are in the country."[2]

It is difficult to determine what effect propaganda, whether of the government or the opposition kind, actually had on contemporary popular opinion, but clearly politicians from both sides must have agreed with Oldmixon that a good effect was "a necessary Consequence of the Dispersing." From the provinces election managers routinely reported to the Old Corps Whig leadership that opposition propaganda was credited in the local community and would have a pernicious effect unless "the Edg [sic] of it be taken off by something handsomely written on the Other Side."[3]

Government supporters put their faith in the theory of "the antidote," based on the idea of the body politic as an organism subject to illnesses and imbalances analogous to those that afflict the human body.[4] Regarding opposition propaganda as so much poison introduced into the body politic—Bolingbroke's "persuasive *Poison*,"[5] for instance—they considered that in order to restore it to health the government must show "as much Diligence in the distributing the Antidote" as their adversaries use in the spreading of the poison: "the Antidote ought to keep pace with the Poyson." However, the self-evident practical problems involved in the exercise were not lost on contemporaries. Making the antidote available to people potentially infected by the poison, involved reaching the same readership as the opposition, and as one pamphleteer remarked sardonically, even if you succeeded in handing the antidote to the sick nobody could actually force them to swallow it.[6]

Despite its shortcomings, the theory of the antidote partly explains why pro-government writers and officials felt so strongly that attacks from the opposition should not be allowed to go unanswered. Propaganda was seen largely in terms of a shouting match, with the two sides scoring points off each other. If a political group failed to respond to allegations or representations put forward against them, their opponents were considered to have won, and they to have lost, a point. Not to counterattack would be tantamount to admitting that the allegations made by their opponents were true. There were, after all, times when both sides admitted defeat, when the facts were so strongly against them that they saw no way of defending their position. When in 1743 an opposition print called "The Confectioner" attacked George II for showing a preference for his Hanoverian over his British troops at the Battle of Dettingen, Sir Charles Hanbury Williams wrote to Henry Fox,

> What may we not expect to hear When Malice has Reason for its foundation to build upon . . . the Banquet is over & the reckoning coming— How is it to be paid? By a Fine speech of Ld C[artere]t's to prove the good the Hanoverian artillery did at Dettingen. Suppose in answer to that, that Ld Talbot should rise with the Print you sent me in His Hand and cry out Confectioner by way of Answer—If the fact is true It wont admit of a reply. and I scarce know a Man in the house of Lords Except Ld DeLawarr that would attempt one.[7]

The highest praise was showered on pamphlets that allowed for no response from the other side. Oldmixon boasted of having written a pamphlet which "Mr *Harley*'s Advocates could take no Hold of it, no Answer to it ever attempted; it bore several Impressions, and was twice pirated," just as Arnall was proud to have written an answer to an opposition production that was considered "unanswerable." In fact there was a tendency among contemporaries, if they were not too prickly, to show respect for good blows from their opponents. When Sir Thomas Winnington defected from the Tories to the Old Corps Whigs in 1729, he declared that he had been "sufficiently bated" by all his "old friends" in the opposition and especially "handsomely and cleverly abused" by William Pulteney, whose satire he had taken care to return "in pretty strong terms."[8]

In this way each side kept a close watch on whatever was published by the other. Walpole supporters involved in the propaganda process were avid readers of the *Craftsman* and opposition productions in general, in the same way that opposition writers regularly scanned the pages of the *Daily Gazetteer*. At his own request, the *Craftsman* was sent regularly to the government supporter Stephen Poyntz, while he was acting as a diplomat on the Continent, for instance. In fact, it was often felt that the newspaper writers had lost sight of a wider audience: "As to the Craftsman and Gazetteer, their Disputes rather concern themselves than their Readers."[9]

Since the same attitude prevailed on both sides of the political divide, an atmosphere was created in which any attack, whether initiated by the government or the opposition, would be bound to unleash a paper war, and new works could be expected to appear on both sides in a quarrel that would either peter out into increasingly feeble productions or be pushed aside by the introduction of new issues and other arguments. Thus the separately published opposition poem *Are these Things So?* was answered by an opposition and a pro-government poem entitled respectively—and predictably— *Yes They Are* and *No They are Not*. These works were followed by, among others, *What of That?* and *Have at you All*—the political bias of each being fairly easy to determine from the titles. This literary debate was summed up in the pro-government poem *Pro and Con*:

> PRO met with *Con*: . . . Says *Con* to *Pro*,
> Tell me, old Friend, *Are these things so*?
> For once the honest Truth declare,
> And boldly answer, *Yes, they are*.
> *What Things*, says *Pro*? Sir, *They are not*;
> Or if they are then, *What of that*?
> Will you a *Weather-mender* prove,
> And teach the God of Day to move?
> Equally modest your Design,
> T'instruct our Planet how to shine.
>   Don't beg the Question, *Con* replied,
> But let the Truth by Truth be tried.
> I say they are, will dip in Gall,
> And prove it too, *Have at you all*.[10]

In this particular case some answers in prose also turned up, but on the whole there seems to have been an unstated convention that an attack should be answered in the same form, an ode for an ode, a ballad for a ballad. Often, indeed, a poem based on—say—a particular satire by Horace, would be answered by an imitation of the same poem.

The need to retaliate had an unfortunate effect on much run-of-the-mill political literature, since often writers quite clearly did not envisage a readership with a politically eclectic taste. Their works—whether in prose or poetry—contain an inordinate amount of preliminary résumé—predictably slanted—before they eventually get to the point of putting their own case across. Only in the more sophisticated works has the discussion become internalized.

THE UNBIASED MUSE

One of the most regular complaints to appear in pro-government productions was that the opposition writers in their tendency to see everything in extremes and corresponding inability to see the finer points of any argument, were showing a bias that was irresponsible and unacceptable. They and their promoters were routinely depicted as irrational fanatics who must never be trusted with real power.

In his doctoral thesis Simon Targett has shown that Walpole's newspapers—with the exception of Orator Henley's *Hyp-Doctor* and the *Corn-Cutter's Journal* which also received encouragement—tried to establish a tone of almost extreme moderation, seeking to present the government, its supporters in general, and more specifically its writers, as men of reason and moderation, who remained unruffled by the excesses committed by the opposition.[11] By appealing ostentatiously to reason and not passion, they indirectly defined their readers as men and women of moderation and intelligence who would remain impervious to opposition attempts to influence them.

This approach was dictated partly, one suspects, by considerations of the dignity expected of writers associated with the government, but also reflected the basic Old Corps Whig ethos. Sir Lewis Namier is supposed to have said that being a Conservative involves accepting man's limitations, and the Old Corps Whigs, once in office, developed similar attitudes. The limitations inherent in man's nature meant that imperfections in the political system had to be expected and accepted. This is the gist of a pamphlet published in 1733 by James Roberts called *A Persuasive to Impartiality and*

Candour in Judging of the Present Administration, for which the author George Henckins received £42 and 10 shillings for 1,100 copies delivered at the post office for distribution around the country, and which consequently can be assumed to express the official position down to the last comma:

> A State of perfect Happiness is not to be obtain'd here: If we are of all others the nearest to it, let us rejoyce, though our Good be mingled with some Evil.[12]

The insistence on moderation was also based on considerations of what was most likely to have an effect on the kind of readership they were trying to influence. In a letter dated 1733 *"supposed to be wrote to Sir* R—— W——*,"* the writer puts forward the scheme, referred to earlier in this study, for a new pro-government newspaper to supplant those already in existence. In his view, these are rendered ineffectual by betraying too strong a party spirit, since the readers of a newspaper "when a strong party Spleen appears in it . . . throw it away, and often with a Curse." The projector is of the opinion that "when all Abuses are left out of such Papers, and when small Turns, almost imperceptible, are constantly given to what is related without any Anger, the wisest of Men, and the most artful on the other Side, scarce know how to contradict it, and are caught in a Net." The writer of the projected newspaper should therefore be "very careful to give a small and slight Turn to all the News in Favour of the Administration, but so as to keep up the Character of an impartial Writer."[13] William Arnall indirectly expresses a similar attitude in an attack on the opposition's way of writing:

> A cunning Calumniator will allow some good Qualities in the Object he abuses, on Purpose to be believed, when he charges him with bad Qualities. But to condemn in the Lump, to make Men hideous and wicked without Allay, will ever and justly pass for *Reviling*; and a Reviler, when he is known to be such, forgoes the Success of his Trade.[14]

Quite a number of pro-government writers seem to have adopted this theory of how best to persuade readers of authorial sincerity and honesty. By allowing individual opposition figures some good traits—all within reason—they were left free to attack their opponents more forcefully. The typical pro-government writer tried to present himself as rational and moderate and only too willing to do justice to the individuals he was in fact satirizing:

> Each Human Creature view'd through Passions Glass,
> May either seem an Angel, or an Ass.
> Most Workman-like nice Characters he draws,
> Who artfully adheres to Optic Laws;
> Provides a Medium ting'd; but tinges fuller,
> When he inclines to strike a stronger Colour.
> Takes in those Rays precisely which he needs;
> Rejects and scatters all the rest, like Weeds:
> With Ease a clear Complexion turns to yellow,
> Or Man of Honour to a worthless Fellow.
>
> But if delusive Tinctures thrown aside,
> The *Prism of Truth* be faithfully apply'd;
> Mens blended Qualities we disunite,
> Each viewing in its own peculiar Light.
> By such Transmission unconfus'd they play
> Before our naked Eyes, in just Array:
> Perfections, Vices, all distinct appear,
> Ingredients of a mingled Character.[15]

In conformity with the idea that in order to obtain the trust of the reader the writer must be prepared to allow his targets some small degree of merit, the poem acknowledges Pope as a great poet, but attacks him for putting his great talents to such poor political use. Likewise Bolingbroke is credited with,

> Imagination, Intellect, both strong;
> Inflexibly he leans to what is wrong.[16]

The procedure is extremely simple: a minor point is conceded, something praiseworthy is found, but only the better to lend force to the main attack.

This is probably one explanation for the popularity of "the dialogue." By its very nature it made it possible to allow the representative of your opponents a few hits, indirectly or directly admit to certain failures, and yet so orchestrate the conversation that it builds up to a grand finale in which the character that represents your own view is allowed to get the better of his opponent. Such a poem is *The Three Politicians: or, The Dialogue in Verse between a Patriot, a Courtier, and their Friend. Concluding with an Exhortation to Admiral Vernon.* This poem was printed for T. Cooper in 1741, some time after the war with Spain had broken out. The "Patriot"—in immoderate language—attacks the "Courtier" ("The Man is paid, and pension'd for his Praise") and the government for being too timorous in their dealings with Spain. The "Courtier," on the defensive, explains that governmental dithering had been motivated by a wish for peace and admits that this approach has proved unsuccessful. However, now that war has been declared, he shows himself as confident that the British will win, whereas the "Patriot" betrays the very timorousness in the face of war that he has just accused the pro-government spokesman of harboring.

Of course pro-government writers payed no more than lip service to the ideal of reasonable moderation, and far from all pro-government propaganda conformed to this kind of pattern. In view of the prevalent ideas about the need—indeed the obligation—to answer false (or even inconveniently true) allegations, and in the face of mounting opposition hostility, the government found itself under the necessity of defending itself with any means at its disposal. "When Dirt is to be thrown, He is the ablest Man that hurls the most," remarked "Elkanah Pikestaff" sardonically, in the pro-government newspaper the *Senator*.[17] If the opposition descended to gutter level, then the government felt justified in defending itself in kind. Pro-government writers were not at all averse to a bit of mudslinging. In a letter to Walpole, offering his services in a literary capacity, the Rev. Samuel Madden admitted that the *Craftsman* had a "greater Reputation for Wit, & Talents for dispute" and that it was "a superior Master of the arts to catch the Crowd." His recommendation, hardly consonant with the spirit of Christian forbearance, was to,

> begin an attack against them in a method & manner entirely new & that there was no way so effectual to defeat them, as to turn their own Cannon against them & ridicule them; for besides that this is no reasoning age nor our People so fond of strong arguments as biting Jests, I was persuaded if once the laugh could be turn'd against them the mob would desert them & they must be undone.[18]

Increasingly, pro-government writers showed that they were willing to return an eye for an eye. In fact some of them were more than willing to strike the first blow. Although some of the pro-government journalists—such as James Pitt—remained "almost entirely defensive," there were others, such as William Arnall, of whom it has been said that the opposition writers "could not dismiss him with a sneer of contempt. He was too adept at drawing them out into combat and engaging their energies in squabbles over personalities rather than issues." It has been suggested that Walpole valued him especially for his willingness to "trade insult for insult."[19]

In conformity with the theory behind all mudslinging pro-government writers concentrated their attacks on individuals rather than on their principles. There was, however, clearly a differentiation to be observed here. A certain moderation is noticeable in the main-stream pro-government newspapers, more hard-hitting but basically respectable works were issued under the imprints of various members of the book trade. The prominent Whig wholesale publisher James Roberts, for instance, was obviously very careful about the political bias of what he published. But for less respectable and downright insalubrious productions alternative channels had to be found, since the government had no wish to be directly associated with such works. In an effort to cover their tracks the government could arrange for disreputable works to be published by little known booksellers. For instance, the scurrilous attack on the Lord Mayor *The Barber Turn'd Packer* (London, 1730), probably written by Lord Hervey, was printed for A. Moore, which David Foxon believes to be a fictitious name.[20] This may have been the practice also in cases where it was seen as expedient that potential buyers and readers should not be able to guess at the political slant of the work by simply looking at the imprint. After all, any informed contemporary reader would have known that the pamphlet or poem he held in his hand was certain to be a pro-government production if it bore the imprint of James Roberts, just as John Nutt's imprint would have alerted him to the likelihood that he was about to read an opposition production.

A QUESTION OF TIMING

Pro-government writers were acutely aware of the ephemeral nature of much of what they wrote. As one hireling explained to Walpole, two pamphlets "were begun the Day after the Short view was Publish'd but the Author was taken Sick about ten days after & Continud [sic] so for above two months. & then the Town was enterd on other Disputes. so much that he did not carry them on farther as thinking it after the time."[21] In a letter torn at the edges, Hervey gave the following explanation for why he was not going to publish one of his works:

the World is at present so busy'd on other Mat[ters the] Subject of this Pamphlet so little now the subject of Thoughts or Conversation; that few would read it & th[ose who] did, would only have their attention engaged without an[ger] raised or any Concern for its Effect.[22]

The right moment had to be sought, and consequently the letters of pro-government writers are full of references to works that either "cannot appear at this time" or works that the author considered "Seasonable."

But just as the time might pass, the time might suddenly become right for a specific poem or other work. Madden wrote to Walpole that he wanted to print his poem "Bermuda," since Walpole "is often mention'd in it with honour & that the War with Spain makes a number of Passages very Seasonable for these Times."[23]

The theater occasionally revived plays that could be given a new actuality by altered circumstances. At the height of the Jacobite invasion of 1745, John Ford's *Perkin Warbeck* was played to enthusiastic and patriotic audiences (for years "Perkin Warbeck" had been a sobriquet for the Pretender in pro-government works). When Addison's *Cato* was revived in 1737, the Prince of Wales cheered with the opposition, who read into it an attack on Walpole.[24]

A curious episode took place over Samuel Madden's *Memoirs of the 20th Century*, which was printed "with such very great dispatch, that three printers were employed on it," namely Roberts, Woodfall, and Bowyer. Only the last mentioned printer actually knew the identity of the author. Together they printed an edition of 1,000 copies. According to one report, "the book was finished at the press, March 24, 1732–3; and 100 copies were that day delivered to the Author. On the 28th a number of them were delivered to the several Booksellers mentioned in the title-page; and in four days after, all that were unsold were recalled, and 800 of them given up to Dr. Madden to be destroyed." Other reports claim that "900 of the copies were delivered to Dr. Madden, and probably destroyed" and that "the edition was suppressed on the day of publication." Why this satire, which is superior to most pro-government satires should have been suppressed remains matter for speculation. Perhaps Madden's cover was blown, and his authorship revealed. As a clergyman he considered party writing inconsistent with his vocation and was most anxious to remain anonymous. Perhaps it had something to do with his dedication to the Prince of Wales. John Nichols refers to this dedication as ironical, but this must be incorrect. Samuel Madden had already dedicated his play *Temistocles* to the Prince of Wales to whom he acted as chaplain, and who at that time was not yet officially part of the opposition to his father's government. Perhaps something happened to make that dedication inappropriate. In any case, for some reason it was decided that it would not be a good idea to publish the work at that point in time or perhaps at all.[25]

It was not totally unheard of for works to be suppressed in this way after they had been printed. Walpole seems to have actively intervened to stop one of Odell's "Poems in favour of the Ministry, and against Mr. Pope" from being published. According to William Oldys, the poem in question was "printed by the late Sir Robert Walpole's encouragement, who gave him ten guineas for writing, and as much for the expense of printing it; but through his advice it was never published, because it might hurt his interest with Lord Chesterfield and some other noblemen who favoured Mr. Pope for his fine genius." Something vaguely similar happened in 1737 when Lord Hervey sent to Conyers Middleton the printed version of the letters, already referred to, that had passed between the Prince of Wales and his parents "this Moment come from the Press . . . scarce dry." Hervey explained in a postscript: "since I wrote to you this morning, I have recieved [sic] Instructions, not to give out any Copys of [the] Paper I enclosed to you, till some alterations are made in it; & therefore Beg you will not show it till you hear farther from me." Middleton later received permission to show the imperfect copy, as long as he did not part with it and promised to burn it as soon as the revised copy arrived in the post. The changes were "minute, tho many," with the exception of an omitted date which was "material."[26]

CATERING TO DIFFERENT AUDIENCES

T. N. Corns, W. A. Speck, and J. A. Downie's identification of the target readers for both pro-government and opposition propaganda as "the uncommitted sections of the political nation," does not do justice to the sophisticated thinking that underlies the attempts of political groups to reach different audiences for various productions. Writers and politicians had their minds firmly on a potential readership for any given work, taking into consideration such matters as whether the time to publish was exactly right and whether the average reader's attention span was likely to be overstretched ("I dare say the performance is well executed; but my fear is least it should lose part of its use by being so very long. Could it not be shortned [sic]?").[27]

That an attempt was made to reach specific audiences for specific works, of this there can be no doubt. When Ralph Courteville wanted to insert a letter in the *Daily Advertizer* commenting on matters relating to the City officials, he explained to Walpole: "In my humble Opinion this would not be a wrong Scheme; But I shall not attempt it without you approve it—nor should I do it in any other Manner than as one of their own Body." Similarly, in 1732 Arnall prepared for Walpole's inspection some papers "on the subject of petitions for the repeal of the Tests," for which he suggested the following mode of publication:

> . . . if it may be proper to publish them only as the sentiments of a private Dissenter, offered to his misguided brethren, they shall then be sent to a dissenting bookseller, in an unknown hand, and by a fit person, to be published as an accidental pamphlet arising in the controversy among the Dissenters themselves.[28]

Underlying Courteville's and Arnall's suggestions is the assumption that people would be more likely to pay attention to the opinions of a member of a group to which they could be defined as belonging, especially on matters touching themselves as part of that group. This was followed up by an attempt to circulate works to members of the groups at which they were aimed. On 19 December 1733, for instance, 1,600 free copies of *A Letter from a Dissenter to the Author of the Craftsman* were dispersed "by Order of the Right Honourable Sir Robert Walpole" and "sent to the Dissenters in Town & Country." At six pence a copy this transaction cost the government the relatively modest sum of £40, since only a moderate number of newspapers were given away.[29]

The question of audiences is a difficult one and subject to much speculation. Politically speaking, there were three possible target groups: government supporters, opposition adherents, and the uncommitted. Attempts were made to make government propaganda available to members of all three groups. It was of prime importance to reach loyal government adherents, who would need periodical reassurance that their political views were sound and beneficial to the country. Surrounded by opposition neighbors, they needed to be regularly supplied with the right information about government policies and a positive interpretation of recent political events. Ignorance would leave them vulnerable to attack. The *Senator*, for instance, was set up to appear regularly for the duration of one parliamentary session, and to counter any moves made by the opposition press. A regular reader of this newspaper would be well equipped with arguments against the maneuverings of the opposition. The *Senator* happens to be both well-written and amusing, but for pro-government readers periodicity was strictly speaking more important than the literary quality of the propaganda they were supplied with.

The politically uncommitted part of the nation might well be influenced by the same kind of material as those who were already Walpole supporters, although in their case the quality of the propaganda was likely to be far more important. It was, however, crucial that pro-government propaganda should also be made available to opposition supporters, as evidence that the government was capable of answering the charges brought against it, although the opposition adherents were unlikely to be swayed by the same kind of propaganda. If the government writers were to have any hopes of influencing them, alternative methods had to be employed. The first consideration was to ensure a sympathetic reading. This could only be done by camouflaging works to look like opposition productions and infiltrating them into the publishing networks of the opposition. Such works written in political disguise were designed to look like opposition productions in every way but to put across some subversive point or other. Nor was this practice confined to pro-government circles. In 1717, for instance, Daniel Defoe complained that "there had been a Letter publish'd in print, sign'd R. W. and said to be written to the Earl of *Sunderland*" which was attributed to Walpole and was in fact a forgery.[30] Similarly, in 1740 Sir Charles Wager was informed that,

> The Inclosed is what is calld here the Short Writting [sic] letter Sent to the Coffee houses here from the Dublin post office: as comeing [sic] from the Secretaries office In London, it is so Impudent a piece: I thought it my Duty to acquaint you with it & have the original by me; these scandallus [sic] peices [sic] hath Corrupted the peoples Minds here beyond Expression.[31]

Social considerations also entered into the question of readerships. There can be no question, for instance, that the *Daily Gazetteer* and Orator Henley's *Corn-Cutter's Journal* and the *Hyp-Doctor* were likely to appeal to very different people. Socially and intellectually, Henley's newspapers were aimed at a readership less sophisticated, less likely to be influenced by rational arguments, than that envisaged for the *Daily Gazetteer*. In view of this fact, it is significant that after the reshuffle of 1735 when the *Daily Gazetteer* was started and Walpole withdrew his subsidies from two pro-government newspapers, he continued to pay a subsidy to Orator Henley, even though Henley was considered disreputable by many contemporaries, Whigs included. Conyers Middleton reported from Cambridge that Henley was unlikely to draw much of an audience to his projected public lectures since "ye young ones will be prohibited from going to ye Orator, & ye old will be ashamed to go."[32]

Considerations of the social stratification of readerships obviously entered into the choice of literary forms for political messages. When authors decided to use the ballad form, for instance, they had in mind a wider and considerably less educated readership than the one they must have envisaged when employing certain other poetic forms. The *Grub-Street Journal* put it concisely when it claimed that "the streets are alive with ballads; the Court resounds with odes." In an ironic dedication to "The Author of a Poem, Intitled An Ode to Mankind" (i.e., Robert Nugent), the pseudonymous author (Tim Scribble, i.e., Ashley Cowper) wrote:

> Your Scheme of Government is founded on Principles so just, so clear, and I may add, so *new*, that I thought every Method should be taken to propagate it; nor knew I any so effectual for this Purpose, as a *Ballad*—An Epitome of it under that chearful [sic] Form, will naturally make deeper and more lasting Impressions, than the noblest Precepts deliver'd with the solemn Brow of an *Ode* — Besides, Sir, Works of that sublime *Cast* seldom reach the *Many*, for whom *Yours* are confessedly *calculated*; nor, indeed, have they *Parts* to understand, or *Taste* to relish them— But a *Song* lies level to all Capacities, is readily retain'd in the Memory, and therefore always at hand for *Use* as well as *Delight*—By this means, too, we shall co-operate in the Great Work, and by our joint Labours for the Good of the Common Cause, we shall imitate *Nature*, who rolls stately *Tides* to enrich and adorn proud *Cities*, but pours humble *Streams* for the Refreshment of smaller *Towns* and *Villages*.[33]

Contemporaries were clearly not blind to the way in which a political message might be enhanced and become more effective, if conveyed through verse:

> For any Accusation, in smooth Verse, will always sound well, though it is not tied down to have a Tittle of Truth in it; when the strongest Defence in poor humble Prose, not having the harmonious Advantage, takes no body by the Ear.[34]

Verse is of course easier to memorize than prose, especially if there is a tune to go with it. Some of the poetry was set to traditional tunes and was intended to be used in connection with gatherings of the faithful to keep up the party spirit between and during elections. The title page of the poem *The True English-Boys Song* specified that it was "to be sung round the bonfires of London and Westminster." Other songs and ballads of all political descriptions were presented as "proper to be sung at elections,"[35] as envisaged by the opposition writer James Bramston:

> Some certain Tunes to Politicks belong,
> On both Sides Drunkards love a Party-Song.[36]

Some Tunes were Tory, just as others were Whig. An example of a ballad song with Whig associations was "Lilibullero," which was held to have contributed considerably towards creating popular anti-monarchical resentment during the Exclusion crisis, and was thus said to have "sung James II off his throne." Contemporaries were therefore convinced of the efficacy of the ballad as a political weapon. As William Bryan explained to the Duke of Newcastle: "the Ballad of Lillebullero [sic] had a surprizing effect . . . and as Pieces of this kind will be more read among the People in general than what is serious and argumentative, they will be more likely to be influenc'd by 'em at the time of Elections." Consequently, political writers were prepared to write political ballads for mass consumption. As John McAleer has pointed out, "what both Jacobite and Hanoverian ballad makers sought was not a place in literature but success for the cause they served."[37]

Too much must not be made of the question of different audiences for printed works, however, since there is plenty of evidence to suggest that contemporaries kept a close watch on what emanated from all sides. Before Fox and Winnington became Whigs, for instance, the latter sent the former "all the pamphlets of any credit that are yet come out," and this included poems by pro-government writers as well as opposition pamphlets.[38]

Nowadays it is often taken for granted that the aim of the propagandist is to reach as comprehensive a readership as possible. This was not always a safe assumption during the Walpole period, however. If poems and other works in manuscript were widely circulated they would sooner or later fall into the hands of a printer or publisher, and in such cases it is all too easy to assume that this was the author's intention in the first place. Such was not always the case, however, and if the identity of the author were known, an unauthorized edition might cause untold embarrassment. Sometimes the decision to circulate a poem in manuscript was motivated quite simply by a wish on the author's part to choose his own audience. In this way the readership could be restricted to a small circle of friends, who shared the basic views and assumptions of the author, thus helping to reinforce group feeling among them. Any country house gathering between the parliamentary sessions could function as the perfect restricted audience for certain political poems, for instance. To such gatherings at the houses of his friends, Sir Charles Hanbury Williams would bring his "whole Escritoire." While his friends—Whigs to a man—went shooting, Hanbury Williams, who was a disastrous shot, would write satire. At friendly gatherings like these he would show even poems that reflected badly on members of the Old Corps Whig leadership, poems which he would not wish a larger audience to see. Probably certain poems were thus used in the internal power struggle within the party. Hanbury Williams participated at several of the annual meetings at Walpole's country seat Houghton (three weeks for the select in the spring and the more comprehensive "congress" that lasted for six to eight weeks in the autumn), and probably he behaved in much the same way there.[39] There is at least evidence of poetic activity of a nonpolitical kind at Houghton, involving Lord Hervey, Thomas Winnington, Henry Fox, Sir William Yonge, and Sir Charles Hanbury Williams, and it seems unlikely that other more political works would have been excluded.[40]

To circulate a manuscript to a restricted circle could be most effective. So long as the work in question did not proliferate, this method not only allowed the author to choose his own audience, but to ostentatiously exclude others from this audience. Pope, for instance, wrote some verses against Hervey and showed the poem to people in manuscript. Rumors of the existence of this poem soon reached the other side, causing as much unpleasantness in the anticipation of a possible printed edition as the reading of the poem would have done.[41] When Hervey defected to the opposition in 1743 his erstwhile friend and political ally Sir Charles Hanbury Williams promised Henry Fox that he would do his best to finish a satire on Lord Hervey in time for their next meeting in Parliament. This may of course be pure coincidence, but if not, it is not difficult to imagine the discomfort to Hervey if a manuscript were being passed around among a laughing group of former friends together with glances in his direction.[42]

Even when printed, works need not be published. This again allowed the author to choose his own readership, as the Jacobite William King did when he had his poem *The Toast* printed in a limited edition and gave away copies to friends, extracting a promise from each that they would not show it to anybody else without asking his permission.[43]

Attempts were also made to instill proper Whig principles in the young. Shakespeare's *Julius Caesar* was acted "*by some young gentlemen at a private school near* London, *just after the* Spittlefield *riot*." Thomas Newcomb who was attached to the school, provided both a Prologue and an Epilogue. In the latter, spoken by the young actor who played Mark Anthony, the political moral to be drawn from the play was pointed out in no uncertain terms:

> You see of what odd stuff a mob is made
> And in five hours what antick tricks they play'd;
> Who seldom in one point two days agree;
> Ranting for *Brutus* now, and now for me;
> As the whim takes, and as their leaders guide,
> For you, for me, for this, or any side:
> Who'er they like, on whomsoe'er they fall,
> 'Tis neither right nor wrong — but blunder all:
> By the first paper lying in their way
> Still biassed — and the Journal of the day:
> Duty and peace, if *Osborn* [James Pitt of the *Daily Gazetteer*] they meet;
> Faction and flame, if *Caleb*'s mobbing sheet,
> Left on each compter weekly to supply
> The evening falshood, and the morning lye.

In the same poem Newcomb endows the word "Patriot" with a sinister meaning, in keeping with pro-government contempt for the way in which the so-called "Patriots" had appropriated that word, but quite startling in view of the age of the actors and presumably the audience:

> War pleases now, peace will delight him soon;
> And leagues he lik'd in *May*, disgust in *June*.
> So like to ours in all their works and ways,
> Sure patriots first appear'd in *Cæsar*'s days.[44]

THE MAIN TASKS OF A POLITICAL WRITER

Milton Percival has described the pro-government writer's "daily pother" as to "deny, minimize, ratiocinate, and reassure."[45]

Faced with unpleasant facts pro-government writers could choose to simply deny their existence. When Gay's *Beggar's Opera* was first staged, for instance, "Abraham Standfast, Esq." of the *Senator* pretended that the play was not at all antigovernment in tone, and claimed that the opposition was wilfully misinterpreting the work. To prove his point "Standfast" described a conversation with his barber, who claimed to have detected a political dimension in Miss Violante's famous rope dancing act:

Ah, Sir, those same Plays mean a great deal more than every body knows; Did you ever see Violante's *Rope-Dancing? Why d'ye ask, Mr. Razor?—Because, Sir, asking your Pardon, are you sure you knew [sic] the Meaning of it?* The Meaning of a Rope-dancing, Mr. *Razor!—Ay, Sir, Why there it is. You Country Gentlemen, asking your Pardon, are ignorant of these Things.* Violante, *Sir, means one of the greatest men in England.—*The Deuce she does.—*'Tis even so, Sir: what d'ye think she wears those white Pumps and Stockings to the Top of her Thighs for? only to look like a Knight of the—you understand me.—*That's strange—*But true, Sir: Her high Leaps plainly mean her Ambition; and the Danger of her Trade shows she will do any Thing to get Money. Why, Sir—*You'll please to wash your self, good Sir.—*What d'ye think she holds that long Pole in her Hands for?* Why to Poize herself with it—*Nothing like it, I assure you, Sir; that long Pole, Sir, means nothing more nor less than a White Staff, and now the Secret is out, ha, ha, ha, ha.*[46]

To deny unpalatable truths was not always advisable, however, if it involved advancing a direct lie. Citing advertising as a case in point, one commentator sees disinformation as "not so much a matter of blatant lies as of concealing or twisting the truth," sometimes involving no more than a change of emphasis.[47] Pro-government writers often chose this approach and deliberately misinterpreted events. One extreme example of this occurred when Walpole withdrew the Excise scheme in 1733. That night London was alive with the ringing of bells, people illuminated their houses and made bonfires, and Walpole was burnt in effigy at Temple-bar, in King Street, Bishopsgate-street, and other places. The *Daily Courant* dealt with this massive expression of popular support for the opposition over this issue by ascribing all the hullabaloo to the anniversary of the coronation of King William and Queen Mary, which it happened to be.[48]

In the first number of the *Daily Gazetteer* in 1735 Arnall explained in some detail the task set before him and other writers on the government side:

The Cause which we have undertaken is, to vindicate Publick Authority from the rude Insults of base and abusive Pens; to refute the Calumnies, and the injurious Clamours, of factious dishonest Men; to expose the Insincerity of Mock Patriots the little Arts and mean Practices of which they are notoriously guilty, in seducing Mankind, and misleading the People from their Duty to their Destruction: To set the Proceedings of the Administration in a true and faithful Light; to inculcate the most affectionate Zeal for the *Sacred Person* of the KING: the just Regard which every *Englishman* ought to have for all the Branches of his illustrious Royal Family; and the most vigorous Resolution to transmit the Crown in the *Protestant Line* to the latest Posterity, as the only Security which we can have, under GOD, for our Religion and Liberty.[49]

Although this description covers the basic duty of presenting the government's version of events, it comes nowhere near defining the main job of the pro-government writer. His was the task of providing alternative myths to counter those propagated by the opposition writers, and thereby substitute positive images of the Royal family and the Whig leadership for the prevailing negative ones. Nor does Arnall's definition give any indication of the fierce battle which was fought over the meaning of certain important words and concepts.

Both sides tried very hard to appropriate the symbols of the other. The Jacobites, had, for instance, made oak leaves a symbol of Jacobite hopes for the future. Ordinary people made political statements by wearing oak leaves on anniversaries associated with the House of Stuart. The Old English Oak Tree was too good a symbol of national identity for the Whigs to allow it thus to be appropriated for narrow Jacobite use. In a *Dialogue between an Oak and an Orange-tree* printed for James Roberts in 1716, the two trees chat amicably about their status as political symbols, setting each other straight with regard to popular misconceptions. The Orange-tree is pleased to symbolize the restoration of liberty and the overthrow of Popish tyranny through the intervention of the House of Orange, but reassures the Oak that rumors of Whig designs on the Established Church are "the silly Fears of poor deluded People, which have been raised by the Industry of artful and designing Men." The Oak admits to being deeply disturbed by the symbolic use that the Jacobites are making of its leaves. Personally in favor of "the present happy Government, and that Best of Princes, who is at the head of it," it vows:

> I'll never more consent thus to be made a tool of. If they will force me to appear on the Return of that Day, I'll discover every Design they form, and tell the most secret Expressions.[50]

In a propaganda situation even nonpolitical works could seemingly be used to deflect attention from more important and potentially controversial moves on the government's part. It was said of a play by "the other Samuel Johnson," for instance, that "Sir Robert Walpole promoted the success of this piece as far as lay in his power, making it serve to engage the attention of the public from some state designs of his own, which were at that time ready to be put in execution."[51]

III

"The Spirit of a Faithful British Subject Running Thro' Em All": Important Themes in Pro-Government Works

7

A Nation Truly Fortunate

The more successful the opposition was in its efforts to portray Walpole as a bungling and corrupt statesman at the head of an incompetent cabinet totally unworthy of the trust reposed in them, the more self-evident became the need to present the general public with an alternative image of the people in power and especially of Sir Robert Walpole himself.

It has been suggested that both the government and the opposition simply adopted certain themes and stock images from earlier campaigns in their paper wars. That they did so is hardly surprising, considering how whole works were occasionally altered for re-use in different contexts. Thomas Cooke's poem "To Alphenus" would not seem to have been aimed at any one in particular, but was later used, in modified form, as a satire on William Pulteney.[1] A tract written by the poet John Hughes, who was "firm to the revolution and the protestant establishment," on the 1715 Jacobite uprising but not published, was first printed, with a preface, by his nephew during the rising of 1745.[2] One of the most extraordinary productions in this connection was published without an imprint in 1731 under the title *The Lord Bishop of London's Caveat against Aspersing Princes and their Administration. Applied to William Pulteney Esq; And the Lord Viscount Bolingbroke, Occasioned by their Present Political Debates.* An outspoken condemnation of opposition based on selfish motives (envy, pride, ambition, interest) as "contrary to *Reason, Religion,* and the avowed Doctrine of the *Church of England,*" neither politician mentioned in the title is directly alluded to, for reasons that become clear in the postscript which identifies the pamphlet as "a Substance of a most excellent *Assize* SERMON, preached by the Right Reverend Father in God, Dr. *Edmund Gibson,* Lord Bishop of *Lincoln* (now our worthy Diocesan) in the Year 1705" (pp. 4, 10, 26). There is also evidence to show that even political prints were sometimes used over again when circumstances allowed, much in the same way that old plays could be made to comment indirectly on political events taking place a hundred years or more after the death of their authors.[3]

Certainly basic themes of political corruption were ready to hand for any writer to appropriate and modify to suit his or her own political purposes. However, writers on both the opposition and the government sides developed over the years—and the longevity of Walpole's reign must here be taken into account—themes and symbols so much their own that authors had no difficulty faking the air and manner of the opposite side so as to produce works in political disguise.

A number of the themes adopted by the opposition had originally been part of a tradition of Whig satire developed during the party's years in opposition (the corrupt nature of politics, incapable politicians promoted to high office through interest, the all-pervading influence of money, etc.). In adopting such themes, the opposition writers cleverly narrowed the focus of this satire to Walpole until he, through their joint efforts, emerged in print as a monster of iniquity, a corrupt and corrupting politician whose private and public lives were equally despicable. As the opposition proceeded to monopolize these old Whig themes, and as the political climate hardened, pro-government writers had to all but discard them. Just as the Tories after the Glorious Revolution had to moderate—at least officially—their views on passive resistance and hereditary right, the Whigs, once in power, put less and less emphasis on the doctrine of how power corrupts.

It follows that some themes that were relatively innocent in the early and mid-1720s were no longer considered in the same light by the 1730s, a fact that few critics seem to take into account when discussing the political contents of contemporary works. Some literary productions have been labeled "opposition" although the themes they contain were at the time of their composition still considered innocuous and were not uncommon in pro-government works. Edward Young, for instance, who was a Walpole supporter, adopted many such themes in his *Universal Passion*, published 1725–26.[4]

As one might expect, pro-government authors paint a picture of Britain that is diametrically opposed to the opposition image of a nation in which corruption is sapping the foundations of public and private morality, in which the new financial institutions are shifting wealth and influence away from the landed gentry into the greedy hands of a new class of moneyed men devoid of any feeling of responsibility towards less fortunate groups in society, in which men have become so morally bankrupt that they prefer wealth to political integrity, private to public interest, a dishonourable peace to war with honor.

According to pro-government writers Britain under the two first Hanoverian Kings was a nation blessed by Providence and fortunate in every way:

> Our neighbours share not half the blessings,—giv'n
> To us, thro' Bounty of *all-gracious* Heav'n!
> (What of That?, p. 6)

> While I survey the blessing of our isle,
> Her arts triumphant in the royal smile,
> Her public wounds bound up, her credit high,
> Her commerce spreading sails in ev'ry sky.
> (Edward Young, Universal Passion)[5]

In such poems Britain was often contrasted with less fortunate countries in terms of the natural advantages providentially given to her but denied to others:

> How does his [Heaven's] Justice distant Lands afflict,
> Here Earthquakes terrify, there spreading Plagues infect.
> The frighted Towns, thro' dark Destruction mourn'd,
> Their Palaces to stately Ruins turn'd.
> The falling Turrets in Destruction Great,
> Bury whole Cities in the Grave of State.
>   While here . . . [6]

Britain was a country in which "*Freedom* and *Property*, Twin-sisters, kiss":

> While *Peace*, and *Plenty* bountiful of Hand,
> Pour forth their mix'd Abundance on the Land,
> Commerce improv'd, thy Fleets securely ride,
> And foreign Riches flow from ev'ry Tide.[7]

This is rather typical of the kind of panegyric verse written at the time. When writers employed by Walpole extol their country they all tend to focus on trade, peace, plenty, liberty, stability, the rule of law, and protection of property, as interdependent elements that together form a society which is truly blessed by fortune:

> Beneath thy Care [Walpole's], bless'd with the Sweets of Peace,
> The Muse shall flourish, and each Art increase;
> Faction shall droop, Disloyalty lie dead,

And Commerce once again uprear her Head;
Nations unite in Friendship's sacred Chain,
The Sailor's surest Passport on the Main:
The wealthy Merchant shall complain no more;
His be the Treasure of each distant Shore.[8]

Liberty ("Goddess ador'd by *Britain*'s isle") is normally the *sine qua non*:

From her kind bosom let her show'r
   On her lov'd earth, and fav'rite land,
Superior bliss, and envy'd pow'r,
   And smiling peace, and wide command.

. . . .

That ravag'd by no wasteful war,
   That her [Britian's] glad fields with harvests shine,
Th'effect of thy indulgent care,
   O prince belov'd! and *Walpole* thine!

While industry, with all her arts,
   Crowds, with full sheaves, the golden plains;
Seen by the joy, which fills all hearts,
   That *plenty* lives, where *freedom* reigns.[9]

In her recent book on the gradual forging of a British national identity in the century or so following the union with Scotland in 1707, Linda Colley has shown that Protestantism—under threat from hostile Catholic countries and a Catholic rival dynasty—was instrumental in shaping a specifically British identity. Britain was the most powerful country in Europe to uphold the Protestant faith, and this allowed Britons to see themselves as part of a nation with a distinctive role to play, and even to interpret their material prosperity as a sign of God's favor to a chosen people. All through the seventeenth and eighteenth centuries it was commonplace for clergymen and writers to compare Britain's beleaguered state as champion of the true faith to Israel's struggles with neighboring peoples. Colley also notes how Handel in his oratorios regularly compared Britain to Israel in terms of the deliverance of the Israelites from danger through the agency of leaders inspired by God.[10] This was a theme that pro-government writers found it particularly easy to adopt. In *The Statesman* George Spiltimber compares Walpole to Moses both in terms of what he has done for the country and the ingratitude that the people show him in return. He also implicitly equates the Stuarts with Pharaoh:

Scarce greater Blessings sprung from Touch divine
Of him, who led a chosen Nation forth
From cruel *Pharaoh*'s arbitrary Sway,
To Liberty, and *Canaan*'s fertile Land;
When yielding Rocks gush'd forth in copious Streams,
To quench a People's Thirst; who joyous quaff'd
The cool Refreshment; yet, their Wants supply'd,
Unthankful, to their Murmurings return'd.[11]

As Linda Colley has shown, to eighteenth-century Britons Catholic France was—in modern jargon—the great "Other." This was the case in both opposition and government propaganda. But whereas the opposition claimed that Walpole's policies were changing the fine balance between king, lords, and commons as a prelude to the introduction of political tyranny on the French model—chains and wooden shoes in contemporary iconography—pro-government writers tended to use France as a contrast to offset and enhance their own positive image of contemporary Britain. In panegyrics of this kind Britain was frequently juxtaposed to France and other neighboring countries with regard to political liberty. This seems to have been the case throughout the Walpole period, despite the fact that for much of it France and England were diplomatically linked. French totalitarianism was too good a contrast to the conditions that obtained in England to be passed over. Ashley Cowper's poem "*On the Bustos of Sir* ISAAC NEWTON, *Mr. LOCKE*, &c. *set up by her late Majesty Queen* CAROLINE *in the* Hermitage *at* Richmond. Anno 1732" was addressed to those not fortunate enough to be born in Britain:

Behold, O *Stranger!* new from foreign *Lands*,
Where *Slaves* obey what lawless *Will* commands;
Where *Statues* to the proud *Oppressor* rise,
And hood-wink'd *Faith* has put out *Reason's* Eyes;
Behold! the Honours CAROLINE ordains
To these *Great Souls*, who *wrote* to break your *Chains*!
Unerring *Nature's* equal *Laws* to shew,
Prescrib'd to all *above*, and all *below*.
Example rare! O *Britain blest!* to see
Thy *Queen* declare for *Truth* and *Liberty*.[12]

In pro-government works the praise of Britain as a trading nation is particularly noticeable. In one of his early poems Thomas Cooke refers to commerce as "the Great Support, the Goddess, of our Land." And his "London, an Ode," first printed in the *British Jour-*

nal, is a veritable hymn to London and her commerce as the most important element in Britain's expansionist policies:

> *London*, of the fairest Isle,
> The ornament and Honour stands;
>   Lo! her Streets with Plenty smile,
> Diffusing Blessings thro her Lands!
>   See, her floating Castles ride,
> Bringing Wealth with ev'ry Tide:
>   On the *Tagus*, and the *Rhine*,
> Fruitful bleeds for her the Vine:
>   For her the Sons of *India* toil
> Beneath the burning Eye of Day;
>   They strip the aromatic Soil,
> And send to her their Sweets away.
>   The distant Sun for *London* shines;
> For *London* teem the golden Mines.

Cooke also employs what by then had already become something of a literary cliché, the metaphor of London as the heart that pumps life-giving blood into the body of the world and receives it back.[13]

In pro-government works trade is seen as totally dependent on peace. As the opposition in the 1730s became increasingly vociferous on the topic of alleged Spanish depredations against British sailors, the government forces tried to stem the tide of popular bellicosity by appealing to reason and the interests of the merchant community. In a letter, Newcastle's Under Secretary Charles Delafaye expressed the opinion that Britain "as a Nation of Merchants ought not to be over fond of War & Heroism," and in pro-government pamphlets the needs of a country dependent on trade are stressed again and again. The poets followed suit, and produced a number of poems that expressed antiwar feelings. In *Patriotic Love*, printed in 1737 when the war fever was considerable, Hildebrand Jacob praised Walpole for his pacific disposition. Similarly, Joseph Mitchell in "Poltis King of Trace" had in 1726 tried to stem the tide of emotional prowar feeling by asking whether the goal was really worth the effort.[14] And William Parrat made little of the anti-Spain propaganda in the opposition press ("Why, for a slight Offence, a War proclaim"). At the same time an effort was often made to present the king as firmly in charge of world politics ("While Distant Empires stand in aw [sic], | And, sheath the Sword, least he should Draw").[15]

In several pro-government pamphlets it is alleged that the opposition's warmongering was dictated less by outrage at Spanish depredations than by party political tactics. The "Patriots" only wished for a war so that they might later criticize the way in which it was conducted:

> Alike pernicious, either weak Design,
> To keep *Gibraltar* still—or to resign.
> To have the Treaty sign'd, they loudly call;
> 'Tis sign'd—and now it has undone us all.
> By *Fleury* manag'd, or by *Philip* made,
> They guess, by Instinct, it has spoil'd our Trade;
> And prophecy, by strange discerning Skill,
> Before the Terms are known, they must be ill.[16]

That the opposition had found a topic on which the ministry was divided, and which was therefore likely to fuel internal dissension, was predictably passed over in silence.

Once war with Spain had been declared in 1739, the government writers naturally had to change tactics. From then on, they maintained that the government had been right to try to avoid a ruinous war, but since all peaceful attempts to reach an agreement with Spain had proved unsuccessful, Britain must seek a just revenge.

Although pro-government writers tried in this way to defend government policies in general by projecting a positive image of the nation in which the grumbling of a dissatisfied faction is insignificant when seen against the happiness and contentment of the nation as a whole, they tended to concentrate their efforts on building a positive image of the most important political leaders. As we shall see, the Royal family naturally came in for their fair share of adulation, but it is noteworthy how much space was allotted in pro-government works to the "Prime Minister."

8

"O Fav'rite Son of Heav'n":
An Alternative Image of Walpole

Shou'd we have a Land Flood, or a Summer too dry,
Or a Ship lost at Sea, or a House that should fall,
O swear the great Man was the Cause of them all.

This extract from the anonymous poem *Dawley, Danvers, and Fog's Triumph* neatly encapsulates the exasperation felt by many Old Corps Whig supporters in the face of the massive campaign waged against Walpole.[1] In opposition eyes Walpole could do no right. He was blamed for every setback, failure, or negative occurrence, irrespective of whether he had the power to avoid or remedy them. One supporter noted ironically,

> (For all our Woes, from Earth and Heaven, of late
> Have sprung from dire Corruption in the State;
> Our Fevers, Agues, Winds, and heavy Rain,
> All the sad Fruits of thy unrighteous Gain).[2]

There was an element of truth in such complaints. Paul Langford has pointed out, for instance, that the victory of William Pulteney's friend Admiral Vernon at Portobello was "quickly registered as an opposition rather than a national triumph," whereas for his defeat at Cartagena, "Walpole was held personally responsible."[3] That Walpole could not be expected to control atmospheric conditions, became an especially noticeable theme in pro-government works after war was declared with Spain and opposition writers criticized the inactivity of the fleet:

> Go thou vain Mortal, charge the subject Sea,
> And bid the rising Waves thy Nod obey;
> Tell the dependant Winds how long to blow,
> And all thy dreadful Might and Greatness show;
> Perhaps they'll follow thy supreme Command
> Nor tempt the Fury of thy pow'rful Hand.
>
> *(Come on Then*, p. 5)

Bertrand Goldgar and other critics have demonstrated how writers more or less loosely associated with the opposition over the years succeeded in creating an extremely negative image of Sir Robert Walpole. In opposition works he was presented as the unscrupulous commoner who had arrogated to himself all power, who, through the corrupt use of public funds, had made his position at the helm unassailable by reducing Parliament to a state of bribed somnolence, whose ever-increasing private fortune testified to his own lack of scruples in money matters. In a sense this massive campaign was a measure of his success; as one critic has remarked on quite a different subject: "No one inveighs very long against failures."[4]

If ever there was a politician in need of having his image smartened up it was Sir Robert Walpole. The prevailingly negative image of him created by the opposition had become so standardized that authors could allude to it very effectively simply by using certain adjectives which had become contaminated by their frequent use in connection with Walpole as a character. In response to the opposition's successful portrayal of Walpole as incompetent and corrupt, it was necessary to present the public with an alternative view of him. Clearly, one of the main tasks of the pro-government writers was to try to take the ironic twist out of the expression "the Great Man," as it were.

Joseph Mitchell may well have been right when he claimed that this effort was long in getting off the ground:

> For Years had WALPOLE, good and great,
> Upheld and grac'd the *British* State,
> Ere any *Bard* of Skill and Spirit
> Attempted to record his Merit!

Mitchell claims to have been the first such poet to attempt ("with *Caledonian* Bravery") to fill this vacuum, and to have been followed by Eusden, Beckingham, Young, Dodington, "*et cetera.*" This accords well with Milton Percival's observation that the opposition only started to single Walpole out for specific attention in the mid 1720s.[5] With the launching of *The Craftsman* in 1726, however, the opposition became so formidable that Walpole definitely needed to have writers at hand to present his version of things to the public.

Occasionally they comment directly on specific policies, like John Mottley:

> Him, by whose Schemes, her Land *Britannia* sees
> Unburthen'd of her *Debts*, by *Wise Degrees*;

> Him, to whose Praise th'enlarg'd *Insolvent* rears
> His grateful Hands, and gives Adieu to Tears.[6]

More often, however, they refer to his policies in very general terms ("O! Born to make thy *native happy Isle* | Rejoice in *Plenty*; and in *Freedom* smile"), or concentrate on presenting a positive view of Walpole's character. In their panegyrics on the "Prime Minister" they simply deny the reality of the opposition image of Walpole. So far from being a "bungler," as his enemies claimed, he was a clever politician: in control of events, able to shoulder the enormous responsibilities laid on him. (But even Lady Marlborough admitted as much: "The chief must have great talents, or he could not have compassed what he has").[7] His public life was one of constant attention to business, sacrificing time and effort to the common good. They continually stress the consistency of his political life ("how early did he appear in the glorious Cause of Liberty and his Country, and with what immoveable Firmness and Constancy hath he on all Occasions maintained its true Interests!").[8] In private life he emerges as affable and sociable, with a great capacity for friendship. Not surprisingly, he is described as "insensible to Satire's Stroke":

> WALPOLE is easy, when, to please the Mob,
> You call him *Knave*, his *Honour*, or plain *Bob*.[9]

In such exercises pro-government writers were predictably guilty of gross exaggeration. Frequently their encomiums become involuntarily funny. George Spiltimber, a gentleman of Gray's Inn, echoed Horace when he dedicated his poem *The Statesman* to Edward Walpole rather than to his father since to draw Sir Robert's attention—if only for a moment—to read a dedication to himself would be "to interrupt the Happiness of my Country." In the same way Mr. Withers worried that "The Land may suffer, by my guilty Song."[10]

It would be tempting to say quite simply that in general the pro-government writers attributed to Walpole whatever traits they happened to think of as positive. To them he was, "WALPOLE the Great, the Wise, the Good, the Just," a statesman "try'd in all Things, and in all Things great." He was the patriot "to whom no Merit e'er apply'd in vain. | Of whom the worthless can alone complain | Who ne'er deceiv'd his Friend, nor broke his Vow."[11]

However, a familiar pattern can often be detected in panegyrics of this kind. Walpole is nearly always praised for his leadership qualities, which ensured that his term in office became noted for stability despite the opposition both within Parliament and "out of doors." In stressing the basic stability of government under Walpole, they emphasized particularly "how *long* thou didst endure the *Weight*, how *well*." This insistence on stability is often reflected in the choice of metaphors that tend to indicate solidity, permanence, dependability. He was the strong, reliable statesman who "like a *steady Guide*, dost *boldly* steer, | Tho' *treach'rous Rocks*, and *Monsters fell* are near." In combination with the standard pro-government image of the opposition, branded individually and collectively as unstable, unpredictable, inconsistent, ruled by emotions, blind to reason (see below), Walpole was habitually portrayed as the fixed center in the midst of swirling uncertainty:

> Through *Billows*, *Storms*, and *Insurrection*, too,
> Thou steerst the *freighted Bark*; and sav'st the *noisy Crew*.[12]

Henry Fielding, for instance, used the same familiar cliché in a begging letter in verse, addressed to Walpole in manuscript in the early 1730s but only published in 1738:

> While at helm of state you ride,
> The nation's envy, and its pride;
> While foreign courts with wonder gaze,
> And justly all your counsels praise,
> Which in contempt of *faction*'s force,
> Steer, tho' oppos'd, a steady course.[13]

There is nothing here to distinguish Fielding's choice of metaphors in describing Walpole and the opposition from similar works by pro-government writers:

> What, tho' a grumbling, disappointed Crowd,
> Like Sea-surrounding Billows, rage aloud!
> Fixd, as the *Isle* amid the foaming Deep,
> Your envied Place, and easy Temper keep.
> Long, amid Storms and Hurricanes of State,
> You've stood our Pilot, and maintain'd your Seat.[14]

One rather suspects that in the last example Walpole was only saved by his sex from a complete identification with Britannia herself.

As will be shown, when writing satire pro-government writers do not often risk setting up Walpole and the Old Corps Whigs as a positive ideal against which opposition supporters could be judged, but when they do, it is precisely Walpole's strength, ability, and authority they tend to emphasize. In *An Epistle from a Nobleman to a Doctor of Divinity* published by James Roberts in 1733, Lord Hervey derides a would-be statesman of the opposition ilk who,

> Thinks he's so wise no *Solomon* knows more:
> That the weak Texture of his flimsey [sic] Brain,
> Is fit the Weight on W—'s to sustain;
> In *Senates* to preside to mould *the State*,
> And Fix in *England's* Service, *Europe's* Fate.[15]

The sheer weight of business that Walpole had taken on his shoulders is a recurring theme in panegyrics written in his honor and expressed in varying imagery. To try to take over from Walpole would be like presuming to wear Achilles's armor ("its very weight would pull you down"). Joseph Mitchell referred to Walpole several times as "the Atlas of the State,"[16] and speculated on what would happen if he were to die:

> How soon, *Britannia*, wou'd thy Beauty fade?
> What equal Hand wou'd hasten to thy Aid?
> Long, very long, Ye Pow'rs, suspend his Fate;
> On Him depends the Safety of the State.
> While He, our *Atlas*, its vast Burden bears,
> What need to fear the Falling of the Spheres.[17]

The theme of Walpole's overwhelming responsibilities is often combined with accusations—well-founded in some cases—of people's ingratitude towards him. In *The Statesman's Mirrour* Walpole is advised to resign, because his honors and riches are no compensation for the heavy burden laid on him by his office. At the beginning of the poem we almost suspect irony:

> While lab'ring you, the pond'rous State support,
> And Poise, alone, the Country and the Court;
> With Laws defend us, and with Morals grace,
> And wake all Night that we may sleep in Peace:
> Must you, with Cares oppress'd, for ever groan,
> And be the only Wretch in *Britain* known.

As we read on, however, it becomes clear that the poet is indeed "a friend" as he has claimed to be. The people are satirized for their ingratitude:

> What? tho' thy Toils have thus enrich'd the Land,
> They know thee not, nor bless the Giver's Hand!
> With bitter Spight, thy Kindness, they return,
> And mad, at once, with Wealth and Envy burn!

After a long catalogue of the wonderful things Walpole has done for Britain ("What's left to ground a wish upon?") his reward is ingratitude:

> Crown'd with Success, the shining Course is run!
> Now count thy Gains, thou pack-horse of the State,
> Whom Men, mistaken, call the Wise and Great;
> And is't for this, thou'st given the Whole of Life
> To factious Discord, and the noisy strife?
> Robb'd home of Peace, and sold the genial Hour,
> For painted Trifles, and for gilded Pow'r?[18]

In their effort to give Walpole what in American political campaigning is known as "an image overhaul," pro-government writers were largely responding to opposition attacks. Whilst often pretending that Walpole was in no need of defence,

> Honour, that solid shield on which you trust,
> Takes from each foe the pleasure of a thrust;
> Strong to defy, and steady to endure,
> Her orb resistless, and protection sure;
> Faction's weak shafts all glancing from the steel,
> Which from their point does no impression feel;
> Each passage stopt, and bounding back from you,
> Pierce the dire Fury from whose arm they flew,[19]

it is clear that—explicitly or implicitly—they addressed a number of criticisms leveled at the "Prime Minister" from the opposition quarter. The more prevalent of these will therefore be discussed below under separate headings.

Walpole and Corruption

Many contemporaries were persuaded that under Walpole the corrupt use of public funds was on the increase. The opposition press hammered home the message that by distributing posts, pensions, sinecures, and more straightforward bribes, Walpole was able to influence the voting pattern of individual politicians and consolidate a parliamentary majority. Thanks partly to the influence of Lord Bolingbroke, allegations concerning corruption were omnipresent in opposition propaganda, not only because this was an effective way of attacking the government, but also because many contemporaries accepted the theory that if corruption were allowed to spread unchecked in a society, the liberties of its citizens would gradually be eroded, and tyranny would inevitably ensue. This was the accepted explanation for the downfall of the Roman Republic, and many opposition writers feared that a similar fate might befall Britain.[20]

Since the idea that the independence and liberty of a country relied entirely on the civic virtue of its citizens was central to traditional Whiggery, Lord Bolingbroke had found an extremely effective basis on which to embarrass the government. By claiming that Walpole and his supporters were deviating from traditional Whig values he made it very difficult for the pro-government writers to retaliate. This approach also allowed Bolingbroke to lend respectability to the opposition. Recognizing that many contemporaries considered a formed opposition in Parliament as prima facie seditious, Bolingbroke redefined the activities of the opposition in terms of a patriotic duty to oppose forces that would ultimately destroy British liberties. In doing so, as Quentin Skinner has shown, Bolingbroke cleverly reduced the old Whig ideas on patriotism to a question of denouncing corruption in the form of placemen and pensions.[21]

Opposition propaganda often gave the impression that Walpole had invented corruption single-handedly (which, decidedly, he had not), but more often claimed that corruption under him had reached unprecedented heights (which it, arguably, had). So successful was the opposition in tarnishing Walpole's image in this respect, that he has come down to us as a man so cynical that he found the exercise of large-scale corruption entirely congenial. This is so much part of our conception of him that elements that do not conform to it are ignored. Sir Robert once said to a poor man to whom he had given an insignificant post in the Revenue, "Never do a *little* Thing, and never Wink at a *great* one," but it is for claiming to know the price of almost every member of the House of Parliament, that he is remembered, although he may have been misquoted.[22]

For pro-government writers corruption was naturally an extremely sensitive subject. Potentially there were three ways of handling this issue. Government supporters could try to dismiss the opposition's persistent allegations as simply unfounded. Or they could acknowledge that corruption was part of the political system but deny that a political elite had to be virtuous in any sense of the word to govern well. Or, as Shelley Burtt has pointed out, whilst accepting the existence of political corruption, they could redefine civic virtue in terms of a more privately oriented virtue, "a quality that disposes to behavior beneficial to the public but not for publicly oriented reasons." Burtt claims that pro-government writers opted overwhelmingly for the third solution. It was certainly rare for government supporters to maintain that contemporary political life was completely devoid of corruption. Similarly few Old Corps Whigs went as far as to embrace wholeheartedly Mandeville's theory that human beings are by nature corrupt, but that their individual selfish acts turn into public benefits, although Burtt does not rule out the possibility that Mandeville's Whig patrons originally may have thought of his theory in terms of a potential justification for the use of corruption.[23]

In electing to acknowledge the existence of corruption, whilst redefining civic virtue, pro-government politicians and writers built on and modified the views expressed in the "Cato" letters printed in the *Daily Journal* in the early 1720s and written by John Trenchard and Thomas Gordon. The two authors were both Whigs, but of the old-fashioned idealistic type (at least in their writings), and their criticism of the government over the South Sea Company scandal together with their constant charge that Whig principles were being abandoned, proved embarrassing to the ministry. Consequently Walpole arranged to have the *Daily Journal* bought up ("Cato's Letters" moved to another newspaper), and after Trenchard's death, persuaded Thomas Gordon to join his camp.[24]

While the opposition located the threat to political liberty in the vulnerability of individual politicians to corruption, "Cato" asserted quite simply that corruption "has its Root in human Nature." Therefore even the best regulated political system can only hope to reduce its scope, not obliterate it completely: "Men will be Rogues where they dare." This point of view pervades the following extract from a friendly letter written nine months after Walpole's resignation by the journalist James Pitt, who had retired but remained loyal to Walpole, to Thomas Cooke, who had done neither:

You are always railing at men in power, prithee be a little more philosophical, wisdom and experience teach us, that men in like circumstances are generally the same. Men in power are not worse than men out of power, nor do persons in public life deserve harder words than persons in private life: they both carry their designs and particular views, by the proprest methods they can think of, without any great regard to the rectitude or morality of the means. There are as great R[ogues] at the Exchange as at the Court end of the Town, and I beleive [sic] *greater*; for in proportion as men advance in funds they advance in virtue too, or at least, will save appearances better.[25]

For "Cato" civic virtue, although rooted in self-interest, consisted in the honest discharge of duty and maintaining "a vigilant attitude towards the inevitable corruption." Pro-government writers naturally tended to put nearly all the emphasis on the first of these imperatives. That they should have adopted and developed "Cato"s' ideas about corruption is quite logical. Although Burtt does not explicitly make the connection, it is significant that one of the men behind the "Cato" letters went on to act as probably the most important middleman between Walpole and writers associated with him, Thomas Gordon.

Although in general they accepted corruption as an inevitable part of life, pro-government writers often denied the existence of political and financial corruption in specific cases or with regard to specific individuals. An attempt was made to portray Walpole himself as above suspicion, for instance. In *Pro and Con* he was described as,

> Not one, who anxious to be Great,
> Bears for himself the Toils of State;
> And minding nought but private Good,
> Drops like a Leech when full of Blood.

(p. 10)

But in defending Walpole personally from corruption, pro-government writers were very much on the defensive. It is not hard to detect a certain bravado in some of their lines ("Here W—LE lives to check *Corruption's Swing*"). It is, for instance, rather amusing to find Joseph Mitchell describing Walpole as a fierce latter-day Ladon curled protectively around the Treasury. This was so much at odds with the general image of Walpole that Mitchell, who often wrote directly for the "Prime Minister" and an inner circle of Whig supporters, probably intended it to be received as an amusing exaggeration:

> Safe in his Hands a Nation's Treasure lies,
> Who knows its Wants, and best can raise Supplies;
> And, undesiring, guards the charming Prize.
> So, round the tree, that bore *Hesperian* Gold,
> The sacred Watch lay curl'd in many a Fold:

His Eyes uprearing to th' untasted Prey,
The sleepless Guardian wasted Life away.[26]

The standard way in which to address the issue of corruption in general was to follow "Cato"s line. Instead of denying the existence of corruption *tout court* they accepted—with varying degrees of resignation—corruption as an inevitable part of any political system. "Age after age *incorrigible* sins" wrote James Ruffhead in *Seasonable Admonitions*, published in 1740.[27]

It is easy to see the attraction to pro-government writers of a view based solidly on the Christian dogma of man's fall into a state of sin. If post-lapsus man was by nature corrupt then it was not possible to claim—as opposition spokesmen did regularly—that they alone had the moral stamina to rule Britain without the use of corruption. Their "holier than thou" attitude could be exposed as hypocrisy, since nobody can claim to be untainted by the general human condition. This basic Old Corps Whig tenet was used to justify a pragmatic attitude to the use of morally doubtful means to ensure a state of stability. Pensions and places could be justified on the grounds that they could contribute towards the stability of the state apparatus at a time when many forces were at work to undermine that stability.

It is this pragmatic attitude that lends such a worldly air to much Old Corps Whig writing. At times this can be quite startling. Joseph Mitchell, in his poem "To a Right Honourable Grumbletonian," applies a tale from Aesop about a fox who turns down an offer by the hedgehog to rid him of a swarm of flies. The fox reasons that this lot will soon have drunk their fill of his blood, and if chased away, will only be replaced by another swarm who have as yet received nothing and are consequently likely to be more ferocious. Aesop had "sav'd the mighty W——E of those Days" by applying this story to human conduct,

> But the instructed *Britons*, cautious grown,
> Will trust no craving Candidates unknown.
> Our present Flies will soon have suckt [sic] their Fill,
> They *Gratis* serve, and keep their Places still.[28]

The opposition frequently referred to a "Golden Age" in which honesty had prevailed and corruption was unheard of. It was not always clear how far back you had to go in history to find this ante-lapsus state, but it was obviously before Walpole's time. Pro-government writers, for obvious reasons, rejected the idea of a "Golden

Age." They tend to take the view that man's nature has always been the same:

> Not wondering at the World's new wicked Ways,
> For Virtue now is neither more or less,
> And Vice is only varied in the Dress;
> Believe it, Men have ever been the same,
> And all the Golden Age, is but a Dream.[29]

In pro-government works the point is made again and again that corruption is simply part of the human condition. An extreme example of the pro-government post-lapsus view of man is present in Mitchell's "The Patriot":

> WHEN publick *Debts* make publick *Taxes* rise,
> And threaten'd *War* demands enlarg'd Supplies,
> Wilt Thou, O *W[alpole]* for one Year, assign,
> To *sinking Funds* those *Perquisites* of thine?
> *N[ewcastle]*, *T[ownshend]*, to be *truly Great*,
> Say, Will ye serve, *unhir'd*, the *British* State?
>
> . . . .
>
> Or, wou'd ye, *Ch[esterfield]* and *P[ulteney]*, boast
> *More generous Conduct*, did *ye rule the Roast*?

The poem also refers to the *earlier* conduct of certain "Patriots" whilst still members of the Government ("Wou'd they not *be* what they've already *been*").[30]

Although this is an extreme case, Mitchell adopts a typical pro-government strategy. Very seldom is an attempt made in satirical attacks on the opposition to present the government as an absolute ideal against which its opponents are judged and found wanting. A down-to-earth, pragmatic government like Walpole's did not lend itself easily to this kind of treatment. Instead pro-government writers try consistently to drag everybody else down to the same level by drawing attention to corruption in other places, for instance, in the City (which they viewed with jaundiced eyes due to the links between the opposition and certain City authorities). In 1737 there were thus several attacks on the future Lord Mayor Sir John Barnard, linking him with alleged corruption in the City. When the opposition, in 1731, was glorying in the fact that the printer of the *Craftsman* Henry Haines had been found innocent of sedition by what in their circles was known as "the Honest Jury," a very scurrilous pamphlet portrayed "the new Dozen at Westminster" as "One

Half . . . Knaves, and the other Half Fools" ("Besides they had touch'd what came out of the *Mint*").[31]

Of all aspects of corruption, the issue of placemen and pensioners was the most worrying to the opposition. Bills to prohibit placemen from sitting in Parliament became, in Professor Plumb's word, "perennial." Just how important the issue of placemen (and the pressures they could be exposed to), was to an opposition sympathizer, is revealed in a letter written by the formidable Duchess of Marlborough—known as "Mount Ætna" in certain pro-government circles:

> I have made a settlement of a very great estate that is in my own power, upon my grandson, John Spencer, and his sons: But they are all to forfeit it if any of them shall ever accept any employment, military or civil, or any pension from any King or Queen of this realm, and the estate is to go to others in the entail. This I think ought to please every body.[32]

Although opposition spokesmen tried to give the impression that the conferring of pensions and places on politicians on the basis of their political loyalty rather than on their abilities was a new development under Walpole, this was hardly the case. Although there are grounds for believing that corruption was on the increase under Walpole, who was an excellent organizer in this field as in any other, it was already well entrenched in society long before Walpole's rise to power. There can hardly have been a member of the House of Commons—of whatever political description—who had not had to sully his hands good and proper in giving bribes to obtain the requisite number of votes. Hypocrisy was the order of the day. Given to much rhetoric on the subject of the government's use of patronage, and to grand gestures of the kind indicated in the passage quoted above, Lady Marlborough elsewhere talks glibly of places she has obtained for her own family members.[33] There was clearly a case of double standards here, as one pro-government writer pointed out:

> A Patriot's Place is a Reward,
> A Courtier's is a Bribe:[34]

WALPOLE THE COMMONER

In 1725 the Rev. Robert Wodrow from Scotland remarked in his diary on how "all things run very smooth in England as to publick matters in Parliament. Thus, though he have no relations, no family, and scarce any freinds [sic] among the great familys [sic] and nobility in England, yet, by his interest in the House of Commons, and the necessary dependance upon him every body must have, and his exquisite managment [sic], he [Walpole] stands his ground."[35] A certain section of society resented the fact that Walpole as a commoner had arrogated to himself the power that had traditionally been held by a member of the aristocracy. At least, Walpole's lack of aristocratic credentials is often pointed out in works hostile to him and his government, in which he is often portrayed as an ambitious upstart. It is not possible to say what effect these works had on contemporaries, but they seem to have influenced one or two modern historians who have attributed to Walpole a downright underprivileged start in life.[36]

Walpole came of solid country gentry stock, and a place in Parliament was therefore more or less his birthright. However, his rise to political preeminence was spectacular and disapproved of by many. His elevation to the knighthood in 1725 was bad enough, but a year later when he added—as the first commoner since 1660—the blue ribbon of the Garter to the red ribbon of the order of the Bath, aggressive squibs like the following started to circulate freely:

> Sir Robert, his Interest and Merit to shew,
> Laid down the Red Ribbon and put on the Blue;
> To Two Strings already this Knight is preferr'd,
> Odd Numbers are lucky, we wait for a Third.[37]

Charges of Walpole's overwhelming ambition were on this occasion countered by Charles Beckingham, and others, by a presentation of Walpole as the reluctant recipient of the honors conferred on him by the king, since he himself "Good alone for Good pursues":

> The noblest Natures must comply
> To wear the Wreaths their actions raise:
> His Looks a graceful Resignation tell:
> He takes the Glories he has earn'd so well.[38]

In order to emphasize the legitimacy of Walpole's position as a commoner at the head of the government, writers sympathetic to his cause tend to stress the fact that he owes his position to the king himself ("Well does the Nation's universal Voice | Greet with a Peal of Joy the Sovereign's Choice").[39] The pro-government line was that whoever criticized Walpole as unsuitable for high office, was indirectly attacking the king's judgment, since the monarch indisputably had a constitutional right to choose his own servants. "Thee, the Monarch chose" George Spiltimber wrote in *The Statesman* (p. 8). This, it is implied, ought to be unanswerable.

His lack of illustrious ancestors may well have been a sore point with Walpole himself, however, since his writers frequently address this question of pedigree, and in a bewildering number of ways. Some of them chose to portray Walpole as a man of great lineage, as Spiltimber did:

> From the Great NORMAN, down to NASSAU's Reign:
> Where some with Titles, all with Virtue, shone
> Illustrious, Ennobled, and Rever'd.
>
> *(The Statesman, p. 6)*

Other writers emphasized that Walpole was "descended of a Family, the Antiquity of which needed not Titles to make it Honourable." The genealogist Arthur Collins provided proof of Walpole's "Family being in England before the Conquest," and felt that his efforts entitled him to some place under the government. "Walpole, who com'st of ancient Race" wrote Francis Manning, without going into details.[40]

Most pro-government writers chose in this way to elevate Walpole in terms of traditional marks of social superiority: ancient lineage, obscure titled ancestors, paternal acres. Few of them elected, like Joseph Mitchell, who came of humble stock, to glory in Walpole's status of commoner and his meritocratic rise to prominence:

> So, while great GEORGE the Sceptre wields;
> And ev'ry Land to BRITAIN yields;
> A *Commoner* supports the Crown,
> And gives the Nation its renown!
> What Marks of Royal Favour are too great
> For this distinguish'd ATLAS of our State?

Mitchell even went on to suggest that Walpole deserved to be made a duke, and in another poem, written when Walpole moved into Downing Street number ten, insisted that Walpole was "noble" in a different sense:

> First noble Master of this honour'd Dome!
>
> . . . .
>
> Long live its worthy Owner, Lord, and Guest,
> Of ev'ry needful Quality possest,
> Greatest in Pow'r, in doing Good the Best.[41]

In Mitchell's verse Walpole's status as a commoner is seen as an asset rather than a disadvantage since it makes him easier of access to "Men of all Degrees, | From Peer to Peasant":

> To such a Patriot-Minister may press
> All sorts of Subjects, certain of Access.
> No Lordly Pride, Austerity, Grimace,
> Or studied State appears upon his Face;
> Open, yet serious; tho' majestick, plain;
> Reserv'd with Ease, and pleasant without Pain
> Whom do his Words invite in vain to come,
> Or from his Levee send despairing home.[42]

WALPOLE AS PATRON

One of the chief charges against Walpole was his alleged contempt for men of letters. He was seen as a minister with a strictly utilitarian approach to the question of offering patronage to authors. In opposition works Walpole emerged as a philistine with no taste for or knowledge of literature, whose active dislike for men of letters led to a refusal on his part to take on the expected role of patron to the best writers of the day. As a commoner, they claimed, he probably did not even recognize such inherently aristocratic obligations. To some extent Walpole was a victim of the king's lack of generosity in matters of patronage. While in office, Walpole is said to have confided to a friend that his two major problems were: Hanover and the king's disinclination to part with money.[43]

Walpole himself wrote what Professor Plumb has called "dull, solemn, heavily argued common sense," and the assumption is that these were precisely the qualities he valued in his writers. Horace Walpole admitted that his father "happened never to have any good writers amongst the numbers he paid."[44] However, Walpole senior was hardly the country bumpkin in such matters that he has been represented as being. He would seem to have been a reasonable scholar in his younger days. According to William King—Oxford academic, Jacobite, and no friend of his—"SIR ROBERT WALPOLE, who by his oratory raised himself from a small estate to the height of power . . . had not any great stock of learning. He was indeed not unskilled in the classics; some knowledge of those authors he could not but retain, as he had been formerly a fellow of a college in Cambridge." An admirer commented, after his death, that "he understood the best Authors well, but he seldom quoted them, and was abundantly more attentive to what they said, than to their Manner of saying it."[45] Walpole referred to himself as "no scholar, and no reader," and in retirement at Houghton complained that he derived "no pleasure from such pursuits." This is often quoted as proof that he actively disliked literature. However, he is also said to have burst into tears when it dawned on him that a hectic life in politics had rendered him unfit for a quiet life of reading. Walpole's cultural interests lay more in the direction of paintings than literature. His interest in paintings seems to have amounted to a passion; Dudley Ryder noted in his diary, "He owns it himself that he cannot see a fine picture and be easy till he has it."[46] Walpole's private collection of paintings was sold after his death by his grandson to Catherine the Great of Russia and is now in the Hermitage.[47]

Pro-government authors tend simply to deny the opposition thesis that Walpole despised authors and was no patron of literature. They refer—without a trace of irony—to Walpole's "Love of Letters" as a given fact. Philip Frowde, who had been to Eton with Walpole, claimed that Walpole had early acquired "a Taste the most just and Distinguish'd," and concluded that he had brought "the *Learning* and *Arts* of *Greece* and *Rome* into the *Cabinet*."[48] And Joseph Mitchell praised Walpole ("Mine and the Muses' Patron") and the queen,

> In Numbers, such as you, your self, would use,
> Did *Europe* give but Leisure to your Muse.[49]

Writers who had never met Walpole but were striving to come to his attention, addressed him in similar fashion. They simply followed an older custom of praising political leaders for their patronage of literature. One hopeful schoolmaster from Newcastle addressed the "Prime Minister" to his face as "an Excellent Patron of true Literature."[50] This sentence was clearly meant to be taken seriously, but if it had been found in a work by Pope, Swift, or other writers loosely associated with the opposition, it would obviously have been interpreted as an ironic remark.

In fact it was quite usual for panegyrists during the 1720s to speak of Walpole as a learned man. "Still Learning's Cause (Thyself how learn'd!) defend | And be to drooping Sciences a Friend!," wrote poet laureate Laurence Eusden. And John Withers described Walpole as "The Man, distinguish'd by peculiar Parts, | Refin'd by Studies; exercis'd by Arts."[51]

In *The Monument* Joseph Mitchell tries to present Walpole to himself and others as a great patron: "WALPOLE, who lives but to support and save" is urged to set up a monument in memory of Sir Richard Steele, who will then be able to boast in the Shades that it was raised by "th' ablest Judge and truest Friend of Men":

> Well, to the dead, may WALPOLE stretch his Care,
> Whose great Protection all the living share.[52]

It has been suggested that Leonard Welsted, Sir Richard Steele, and Ambrose Philips "were aware that Walpole did not conform to their ideal of the patron, and at the same time they were unwilling to accept their own awareness. They refused to surrender the idealized image for to do so would be to abandon their fondest hopes." This is probably quite true, but in addition to plain wishful thinking there also seems to have been an attempt on foot to mold Walpole into a munificent patron of literature. Some writers seem to be actually *willing* Walpole to become the patron, if not of literary merit in general, at least of their particular attempts. Joseph Mitchell, for instance, in one of his many poetical requests for a post, asserts that the "Prime Minister" "for All, can do whate'er he will."[53]

The critic John Dennis, who was in yearly receipt of £20 "bounty" from government funds, admitted that all was not perfect, but made the case that good poets had always been neglected by the English. Quoting him, the editor of *The Twickenham Hotch Potch* claimed that great sums were now "squandered away upon four objects (an impertinent *Scotch*-Quack, a Profligate *Irish*-Dean, the Lacquey of a Superanuated [sic] Dutchess, and a little virulent Papist)" (i.e., Arbuthnot, Swift, Gay, and Pope, here marginalized geographically, morally, socially, and in terms of religion).[54]

In confronting the issue of patronage, pro-government writers could not avoid commenting directly or indirectly on their own situation. William Arnall, who had benefitted considerably in a financial sense from his association with Walpole, defended himself against aspersions cast on him by the *Craftsman*, by proclaiming:

> . . . however *scandalous* He may think it, or would have it thought, I shall never be *asham'd* to own *any* Obligations to Sir *R. W.* whatever they may be; which Acknowledgment is so far from being a Reflection upon my *Integrity*, that to do otherwise might justly redound to my *Infamy*.

Arnall reminds his readers that "this *Great Man* was once the *Idol* even of *one Mr. A[m]h[urs]t*; and that others have as much Right to *defend his Administration*, as that *Time-serving* Writer had to *flatter his Person*." Quoting Nicholas Amhurst's own admission that he had once been "a *Garret-Pensioner* to a *Little Britain Printer*," Arnall concludes that he himself might "with *equal* Reputation receive the Pay of a *Gentleman*." This is typical of their strategy of hitting back by dragging everybody down to the same level.[55]

On the whole pro-government writers seem to have been acutely aware that their productions were viewed with critical eyes by a section of the literary community. This is especially true of the journalists. James Pitt explained to the readers of the *London Journal*:

> The prejudice we have to encounter at present is, that writers for a court are slavish venal prostitutes; and writers against a court, men of generous sentiments and probity.[56]

But other writers show a similar awareness. Joseph Mitchell presented himself as shrugging off criticism in a nonchalant manner: as long as he pleased Walpole's taste he remained indifferent to the verdict of the critics ("Dogs bark, Swine grunt, and Asses bray").[57]

This awareness would not seem to have sapped their self-confidence, however. Joseph Mitchell's family in Scotland—neither rich nor cultured—actually thought that he had been Poet Laureate. "He was, I have heard, somewhat elated with his learning & parts, but this elevation of mind is I believe pretty common to the greatest part of the Literati," wrote John Graham who came to Ratho— Mitchell's place of birth—as schoolmaster almost twenty years subsequent to his death. In his verse epistles to Walpole Mitchell wrote humorously of himself as "Immortal MITCHELL, WALPOLE's Poet!," playing Horace to Walpole's Maecenas.[58]

THE PRIVATE MAN

Pope's description of Walpole in his private hours, conforms in many respect to the image of Walpole's private self that his minions tried to create:

> Seen him I have, but in his happier hour
> Of Social Pleasure, ill-exchang'd for Pow'r;
> Seen him, uncumber'd [sic] with the Venal tribe,
> Smile without Art, and win without a Bribe.
> Would he oblige me? let me only find,

> He does not think me what he thinks mankind.
> Come, come, at all I laugh He laughs, no doubt,
> The only diff'rence is, I dare laugh out.
> *(Epilogue to the Satires, Dialogue I*, ll. 29–36)

The same aspect is stressed, for instance, in Joseph Mitchell's poem "The Shoe-heel," written in 1727:

> How amiable WALPOLE with his Friends,
> His old, well-try'd and honest Friends, retir'd
> From publick State and Care! Whether a Pot
> of sober *Porter*, healthful English Drink,
> Or Punch more potent, he vouchsafe to taste,
> Social, good-humour'd; or a Hunting rides,
> Easy and free, as rural *Squire*, unvers'd
> In Policy and Government Sublime.[59]

It would seem that this image of rural bonhomie was close to the image Sir Robert Walpole personally wished to project of himself. He is said to have—probably ostentatiously—opened his game-keeper's letters before reading state dispatches, and he also liked to sit for his portrait wearing sporting dress.[60]

Walpole's private life frequently came under opposition scrutiny. Here again he was declared to be morally corrupt. He and his wife lived quite separate lives, putting up with mutual infidelities. Double standards ensured that his leniency towards Lady Walpole in this respect was often criticized more severely than his own liaison with Molly Skerrett, whom he married after the death of his first wife, and by whom he had an illegitimate daughter.[61]

However, nasty attacks were also leveled at Molly Skerrett, and even her daughter, after Walpole on his resignation obtained for the latter a patent of precedence as an earl's daughter. In a poem posing as a reaction by the women to her elevation ("Yet know, Vain Maid! The Noble British Fair | Still keep their Virtue, and their Honour clear"), it is—surprisingly—not her illegitimacy or her mother's lack of virtue, that is the issue:

> We pity you the harmless Cause of Wrong!
> On *him* your Vengeance wreak, ye Female Throng!
> Within thy Vein her richer Blood doth roll;
> One Drop of his *contaminates the Whole*.[62]

Although pro-government writers took every opportunity to paint Walpole as a fond father (for instance, on the death of his daughter

Lady Malpas),[63] they naturally observed silence on the subject of his relationship with his first wife, his mistress, and his illegitimate daughter. This is particularly noticeable in the poems written in 1738 to celebrate the nuptials between Walpole and Molly Skerrett, in which the parents of a strapping young daughter were addressed as if consummation had just taken place. In a simply dreadful poem "Printed for the Author" called *The Greatest Statesman and the Happiest Fair, A Pastoral, Humbly Inscribed to the Right Honourable the Lady WALPOLE* the Rev. George Lumley of Merton College describes their meeting, makes them utter the most frightful platitudes (Walpole: "All things more beauteous than before appear, | And strive new Graces, now my CHARMER's here," p. 6), and (by passing over in silence ten years of extra-marital cohabiting) draws a direct line from the first awakening of Walpole's amorous passion to the tying of the matrimonial knot:

Thus each consenting, they in *Marriage Bands*,
Did jointly pledge their *willing Hearts* and *Hands*;
The KING, the NOBLES, COMMONS, All approve.
Their HAPPY NUPTIALS, and their HEAV'N-BORN LOVE.

(p. 8)

9

"The Best of Princes": The Royal Family in Pro-Government Works

In 1736 the ship carrying King George II back to England from that year's "Hanoverreise" was delayed by westerly storms. Asked how the wind was for the king, one of his subjects answered "Like the nation—against him." This joke, related by Lord Hervey, serves to illustrate with what marked lack of enthusiasm many of his British subjects regarded the monarch.[1]

The Jacobites were, of course, in favor of a Stuart restoration. While historians argue about the extent to which Tories were committed to the Pretender's cause, everybody agrees that all Whigs— with one or two eccentric exceptions—were in favor of the Hanoverian Succession.[2] This, however, did not imply that they were automatically enthusiastic about individual members of the Royal family. Both George I and George II were personally unpopular with many Britons who supported their title to the throne on principle.[3]

As the opposition attacks on the administration became increasingly daring, the Royal family also came in for a considerable amount of personal satire. In the days when Thomas Cooke was still writing for Walpole, he accused Caleb D'Anvers, the fictitious writer of the *Craftsman*, of conducting a campaign against the Royal family itself:

> After he had endeavoured long in vain to render the Minister odious in the Eyes of his Prince, he toiled with the same Ardour to make the Prince odious in the Eyes of his People; nor could the Majesty, nor the Sex, of the Queen protect her from the impudent Malice of his Pen.[4]

This was an often repeated complaint. And pro-government writers often attributed this campaign to a wish on the part of the opposition to topple the Hanoverian Royal family:

Whilst *the Opponents* had any Hopes of removing the Minister by approaching the King, it is very true that all their Shot was level'd at that single Mark; but when they despaired of gaining their Point that Way, and thought removing the King was the only Way to remove the Minister; the Tables were turn'd, and instead of collaterally hurting the Interest of the King, by imputing all his Measures to the Folly and Wickedness of an *ignorant, corrupt* Minister; they threw away the Mask and the Scabbard, turn'd the Point of their Weapons directly to the King's own Breast, and endeavour'd to cast the same *Odium* and Ridicule on the Person and Character of the *Master*, that they had formerly done on those of the *Servant*.[5]

The opposition often took care to emphasize that they had no wish to attack the king; their aim was simply to berate the evil minister who had—it was claimed—acquired an unconstitutional influence over the monarch. Both in the theater and in separately published poems the "majesty misled" theme was prevalent. However, to claim that the king was either fooled or dominated by his "Prime Minister" and that a rescue operation was consequently called for, was in itself insulting to the monarch in an age when ministers were still regarded as his personal servants. This was of course regularly pointed out by pro-government writers:

The Opposition 'through the *Sides* of the *Minister*, strike at the *sacred Person* of the King: for tho' they couch their Meanings in *ambiguous Terms*, 'tis intelligible enough: None but *His Majesty* has the Power of *choosing* and *changing* the *Ministry* ; and they might, with *equal Modesty*, say, that the *King* was at the Head of a *Conspiracy* to introduce *Slavery*; as to say, that *he* appoints *Instruments* to accomplish it.[6]

When pro-government writers, in trying to justify Walpole's position as "Prime Minister," stressed that he owed his elevation directly to the king, and that attacks on him were in reality attacks on the monarch ("They censure thee—but mean, by thee, their King"), opposition writers countered by accusing Walpole of skulking behind the throne.[7]

THE HANOVERIAN SUCCESSION

The Hanoverian Succession underpinned the Whig domination of contemporary political life. Because of the Jacobite threat, it was of course very important for pro-government writers to present the public with a positive image of the monarchy and justify the right of the Hanoverians to the British throne.

Important days of commemmoration were made the occasion for much public celebration in honor of the House of Hanover. In Bath on the anniversary of the king's birthday in 1734, for instance, the pro-government side marked the day with big dinners and provided "a Bonfire & Drink for ye Mob." Charles Delafaye reported to Newcastle that "there was universal Mirth & Duty & Respect for the King & ye Royal Family: whoever were otherwise minded (if any there were) lurked in Holes & Corners." Even Mother Lindsey, presumably the proprietor of a brothel—"who is, & ever was, *Whig a bruler*"—gave an Entertainment.[8]

Politically one could actually be guilty by default: local gentry who failed to ring bells and provide entertainment on important days of celebration were taken note of. Even to absent oneself on such days was considered suspect.

As H. T. Dickinson has shown, the Whigs, once they had consolidated their dominant position in contemporary politics, tended to tone down the importance of Locke's theory of the social contract, which had been so useful to them in justifying the Glorious Revolution. That the relationship between ruler and ruled was determined by an original contract which could be dissolved by the people if the king failed to comply with the original terms, was a theory far too dangerous in a situation where an unpopular Royal family of German extraction was threatened by the reality of an alternative dynasty, admittedly with little enough to recommend it, but distinctly more British in its antecedents. Consequently, the social contract theory was modified to agree with the new circumstances. However, the Old Corps Whigs naturally remained hostile to the theory of the divine right of kings and would have agreed wholeheartedly with the Prince of Wales's protégé Robert Nugent's lines about how monarchs "Can claim no nearer Kindred to the Skies: | *Earth* is their *Parent*, thither *Kings* should bend; | From her they rise, and not from Heav'n descend."[9]

References to theories of kingship crop up repeatedly in pro-government writing. Soame Jenyns mocked the basic Tory attitude of nonresistance to unsuitable kings in "An Essay on Virtue":

> No servile tenets wou'd admittance find,
> Destructive of the rights of human kind;
> Of power divine, hereditary right,
> And non-resistance to a tyrant's might:
> For sure that all shou'd thus for one be curs'd,
> Is but great nature's edict just revers'd.[10]

And in an ode published in 1738 Francis Manning includes the following stanzas about the assassination of Charles I, in which the author tries to blend outrage at the beheading of the king with an indictment of the Stuart transgressions that caused it:

> For Royal Blood, by Subjects shed,
>> What Invocations can atone?
> What Law or Force, by Justice led,
>> Enough revenge th'invaded Throne?
>
> What Hand is there so rash to try
>> From deep Remembrance to erase
> A Crime of such a purple Dye,
>> Which Story will to Ages trace?
>
> Flagitious Deed! abhorr'd by all
>> But those who did the Sentence sign,
> *Yet Faults, that caus'd the Father's Fall,*
>> *Were they avoided by his Line?* (my italics)

The answer to this rhetorical question is an emphatic negative, and the poem goes on to assert the basic right of subjects to take action against an unworthy king, by praising the results of the Glorious Revolution: William III, the Hanoverian Succession, King George II, and other members of the Royal family.[11]

In contemporary plays the events leading up to the Glorious Revolution are dramatized again and again, but in disguised form. One case in point is Benjamin Martyn's *Timoleon* (1731) which Christine Garrard sees as "one of the first Patriot dramas." This play would seem to have been a pro-government production, however. In his dedication to the king Martyn claimed that George II had "condescended to patronize a Performance, written with an Ambition to render Your People easy under your Government." The author praises "the Happiness of Your MAJESTY's Government" and claims to have used George II as a model for "the Virtues of a King, who is a Blessing to his People." In *Timoleon* the main character returns from the wars to find that his brother Timophanes is abusing the power lodged in him by the state. One of the upholders of liberty prays:

> O thou Almighty! awful, and supreme!
> Redress, revenge an injur'd nation's Wrongs;
> With Pity view her violated Laws,
> Her trampled Rites, her butcher'd Patriots:

> Hear suff'ring Virtue groan beneath Oppression,
> Hear, and relieve it! *Jove* eternal, hear!

The play revolves around the necessity of deposing a king who has failed to respect the laws of the land. In the fifth act, Timoleon and the patriots try—ad nauseam—to make Timophanes repent before they finally slay him, thereby emphasizing that a king can only be legitimately overthrown if he breaks the laws and if all other means have been tried.[12]

Pro-government writers tend to emphasize that George I and George II actually *deserve* to be kings:

> Hail, mighty Monarch! whose Desert alone
> Would, without Birth-right, raise Thee to a Throne![13]

In his poem *Ratho* Joseph Mitchell gives a truly Whig view of monarchy; "the guardian *Genii* of the Good and Great" aid those monarchs who "merit first, before they mount a Throne." This tendency is perhaps what worried an Old Corps Whig supporter and writer of occasional verse like J. Wainwright, a Baron of the Exchequer in Ireland, who on producing two prologues in 1731 explained:

> I own the two last lines of the first, which are new, are owing to some doctrines which I have lately seen advanced by the State writers, which seem to me to take away all regard to the King's birthright.[14]

As far as the pro-government Whigs were concerned, the title of George I and George II to the British throne was not in dispute. Consequently they do not often argue about it in print: in their works the Hanoverian Succession is very much taken for granted. Explicitly or implicitly, however, the message was driven home that the only true king of England came from the House of Hanover: hence the constant harping on the impeccable Protestant antecedents of the Royal family.

Indirectly, attention is also drawn to the Hanoverian family's right to the British throne by the way in which the Royal family is constantly connected with the past. In view of the many references to William III, one would have been forgiven for thinking that the Hanoverians were directly descended from the prime beneficiary of the Glorious Revolution. Stephen Duck, for instance, wrote:

> Immortal WILLIAM! by whose prudent Cares,
> We yet enjoy the Fruits of all our Wars;

Our Laws, Religion, Liberty, and Peace,
And ev'n the Blessings of the BRUNSWICK Race.[15]

When Princess Anne in 1734 married the Prince of Orange this connection was stressed repeatedly. In *The Gods in Debate: or, No Bribe like Beauty* the East wind—known as the Protestant wind—is eager to waft a new Prince of Orange over to England to join his Royal bride, and Jove himself declares:

> "From this Pair shall succeed
> "(So the Fates have decreed)
> "A Scourge to keep Tyrants in Awe;
> "And while *Liberty*'s Care
> "Shall fall to my Share
> "The World ne'er shall want a *Nassau*.[16]

Another obvious way to remind people of the Hanoverian Royal family's right to the British throne, was to keep alive the Jacobite threat. In many pro-government works the end of Queen Anne's reign is seen as a time of great danger, when the Tory government came close to restoring the Stuart line. This allowed them to present George I as the great deliverer:

> But lo! pale *Albion*, ripe for Ruin made,
> Menac'd by Foes, and by false Sons betray'd,
> To Thee, as to a Guardian-Angel, flies,
> And home-bred Frauds and *Popish* Chains defies!
> Just in a timely Hour, 'ere yet too late,
> Just in th' important Crisis of our Fate,
> Thee Providence gave to the *British* Throne,
> By Laws, by Birth-Right, and Desert Thy own.[17]

Some historians argue that Walpole exaggerated the Jacobite menace for political reasons. His campaign was intended to discredit not only those Tories who were accused of being Jacobites, but also the moderate Tories and dissident Whigs willing to cooperate with them in the opposition. The threat of Jacobitism was calculated to make the Old Corps Whigs join ranks, and to induce moderate opposition Whigs and Tories to question, among other things, the policy of attacking Royalty in the press. Compared to the Stuart alternative, the Hanoverian Royal family seemed a good thing to practically all Whigs, and perhaps even to a large proportion of the Tories. As will be shown in a subsequent chapter, however, the attitude towards Jacobitism in pro-government propaganda was ambiguous. On the whole, the Stuarts were presented as part of a Catholic and authoritarian tradition, and Jacobites as a potential fifth column. However, in their efforts to discredit the descendants of the House of Stuart, and their Jacobite supporters, Walpole's writers were hampered by the need to portray the Jacobite threat as an insignificant or spent force doomed to failure ("Since GEORGE serene looks down on Faction's Blast").[18]

The numerous offspring of George II and Queen Caroline were a godsend to pro-government writers. By their very existence the young princes and princesses promised future dynastic stability, a fact which was stressed repeatedly in pro-government writing, as for instance in Leonard Welsted's *A Poem to Her Royal Highness the Princess of Wales. Occasioned by Her Late Happy Delivery, and the Birth of a Princess*:

> . . . . *Britons*, This is She,
> Who shall your Tow'r, and Bulwark be!
> With CAROLINE, who wipes the Stains,
> And Griefs away, of former Reigns:
> Nor *England's* Angel now bemoans
> Her childless Queens, and barren Thrones.[19]

Linda Colley has remarked on the difference between Jacobite and pro-government propaganda in that, whereas "Jacobites dealt essentially in personalities and romance," there was no equivalent personality cult of the Hanoverians who were "vindicated in terms of what they did and what they abstained from doing."[20] This is everywhere apparent in pro-government writing. Cibber even went as far as to suggest about George II:

> *If private Views could more prevail,*
> *Than Ardour, for the Publick Weal,*
> *Then had his Native Martial Heat,*
> *In Arms seduc'd him, to be Great.*[21]

And Joseph Mitchell, in the last of the following lines from *Ratho*, not only praises the king for his constitutional actions but implicitly compares George II favorably to the Stuarts who were suspected of harboring notions of arbitrary rule:

> O! crown his Reign, as he preserves the Land,
> Persists the Pattern of Imperial Sway,
> Makes righteous Laws, *Himself* the first t' obey.[22]

Elsewhere Joseph Mitchell praised the unauthoritarian leanings of the Royal family since the Revolution, and marvelled at the Queen's choice of statues for her Hermitage at Kew:

> What Sov'reign e'er immortaliz'd the Foes
> Of arbitrary Sway, who durst oppose
> Encroachments on the Int'rests of Mankind,
>
> . . . .
> Princes th' uncommon Virtue rarely shew,
> To honour Men, who publick Weal pursue;
> Teach that their Pow'r is but the People's Will,
> And, for their Welfare, to be practis'd still!
> But CAROLINE, unforc'd, and by free Choice,
> In this peculiar, first, Distinction Joys,
> From common Fate to rescue ev'n the Dust
> Of Patriots pious, learned, wise and just.

In Mitchell's view the statues of Locke, Newton, Clarke, and Woolaston proved that the British people were secure in their liberties ("Judge, from the Choice, how safe your Interests are").[23]

INDIVIDUAL MEMBERS OF THE ROYAL FAMILY

Linda Colley sees the Royal family itself as largely to blame for the bad press they received. She points to the fact that the first two Hanoverian kings never tried to be kings for all their subjects. By promoting only Whigs to high office, they were correctly perceived as Whig kings, and as such could not expect to command the respect of every section of society. In view of the fact that they never visited Wales, Scotland, the North of England, or the Midlands, their frequent visits to Hanover served as so many reminders of their foreign origins. Also George I and George II seem to have remained indifferent to the task of building up a suitable public image that might ensure wide popularity. Linda Colley relates how George I entered London for the first time, "driving along in pitch darkness as if deliberately to outrage the crowds of Londoners who had waited long hours to see him." Neither he nor his son tried to fully satisfy the public's enthusiasm for pomp and circumstance as an outward expression of stability and continuity. The Georges were too private, too frugal, perhaps even too insecure in their new setting to indulge in the kind of ceremonies that, better than the spoken word, could act as propaganda for their right to the British throne. George I lived a retired life, except during the years 1717–

1720 when he tried to outvie the Prince of Wales who was at the head of the opposition.[24]

Although panegyrics on the first two Georges tended to concentrate on their constitutional role as protectors of the Protestant faith and the life and liberties of their subjects, propagandists also had to find ways of praising individual members of the Royal family for their personal character traits. Given the unpromising material would-be panegyrists had to work with, they often found themselves in the position of having to invent suitable characteristics without basis in fact, and this lent an extra air of sycophancy to their panegyrics. Contemporaries naturally took it for granted that such works were written with ulterior motives. Among the elegies written when Queen Caroline died there was, according to the sarcastic Lady Marlborough, "one very remarkable from a Dr. Clarke, in order to have the first Bishoprick that falls," which stood out from the "nauseous panegyrics . . . that make one sick, so full of nonsense and lies, that almost every body knows to be so."[25]

Pro-government writers did their best to project positive images of individual members of the Royal family, although it has to be admitted that they did not make a very good job of it. On the whole, the verse written in praise of the House of Hanover is uninspired stuff. Frequently these poems become involuntarily funny, as when Joseph Mitchell urged the Northern bards to write panegyrics on the king: "O sing great GEORGE, and save yourselves from Dust." And in 1734 the young William Dunkin—soon to acquire a reputation as a political turncoat—wrote *An Ode to be Performed at the Castle of Dublin, On the 1st of March, being the Birth-Day of Her Most Excellent and Sacred Majesty Queen Caroline.* In this truly wretched production the return to his wife of George II—at that time merely Elector of Hanover—from the battlefields of the War of the Spanish Succession was described in the following manner:

> What Shouts of publick Joy salute her Ears!
> See! see! the Reward of her Virtue appears.
> From *Audenard*'s Plain
> Heap'd with Mountains of Slain,
> The Dread of *Gallic* Insolence,
> Grac'd with Spoils,
> Reap'd by Toils
> In Godlike Liberty's Defence,
> The *Hanoverian* Victor comes,
> Black with Dust, and rough in Arms,
> From the Noise of Fifes and Drums

He comes, he comes, he comes
To gentler Love's Alarms.[26]

It has been claimed that after the Glorious Revolution there was a relationship between political ideology and poetic style in the sense that "the extravagant rhetoric of Gallic and late Stuart panegyric evoked absolutist views of kingship incompatible with the moderate principles of Whig and Tory loyalists." Instead of flamboyant hagiography, tact and restraint were called for in the case of "constitutional" monarchs. One wonders whether this theory can really explain the marked lack of warmth in even the most obvious pro-government productions. After all, even many arch-Whigs found it difficult to muster enthusiasm for individual members of the Hanoverian Royal family. Commentators have remarked, for instance, on the anti-German attitude that prevailed in England during the Walpole period, and especially on the lack of any positive German associations in popular works.[27]

To be fair, the two first Hanoverian monarchs can hardly be said to have had the personal qualities that inspire successful panegyrics. Clearly there was a limit to what one could do with a Royal family of German extraction at whose head one unremarkable monarch with a slightly sinister reputation was succeeded by another just as lacking in regal bearing, neither of them exactly noted for their sense of humor or for linguistic prowess. Both George I and George II had irascible tempers, and were not allowed to forget it (in opposition prints George II can easily be identified as the figure kicking his hat). Even so, initially George II seems to have been popular, if only because he compared favorably with his father. One modern historian has described him as "a monarch of considerable shrewdness and political skill," but many of his subjects considered him gross and uncharismatic, and he was certainly not interested in literature. Although the number of Command Performances during his reign was actually higher than under Queen Anne, for instance, many were merely pantomimes; and to his Vice-Chamberlain he said, "My Lord Hervey, you ought not to write verses; it is beneath your rank: leave such work to little Mr. Pope."[28]

However unpromising individual members of the Royal family were as material, however, it was expected that a certain amount of panegyric should be produced for special occasions. In Ireland in 1730 government supporters provided a premium of £100 "for Exercises in the College on His Majesty's Birth Day". In 1727 poems in honor of the new king and queen were read publicly all over the country. At Westminster School, for instance, the students performed in front of a distinguished audience "from the Cabinet, from the Senate, from the Church, from the Bench, from the Bar, from the Court, from the Camp."[29] Such poems tended to emphasize the dynastic stability that allowed for a peaceful transfer of power from father to son, and often included praise for Walpole, Townshend and other important officers of the state.[30] Clusters of poems appeared regularly in connection with Royal birthdays, the Royal nuptials of 1733/4 and so on. The death of Queen Caroline in 1737 also occasioned much elegiac verse. The poets laureate did their bit as best they could, and were met with a storm of opposition laughter for their pains. Variations on the "return and celebration motifs" characteristic of Restoration panegyrics were carried on from Stuart times, addressing the king on his safe return from a voyage. Since the love the two first Georges bore for their German electorate resulted in frequent visits to the Continent, contemporaries had recurrent opportunities for exercising their talent—or lack of it—for this kind of writing.[31] Such verses were published by private individuals on their own initiative but also by public bodies such as the universities and major schools. On the occasion of the marriage of the Princess Royal to the Prince of Orange "The Vice-chancelour [sic], masters, & Scholars" of the University of Cambridge each—as an "Act of their Duty and Loyalty"—wrote verses for a manuscript book to be presented to the king.[32]

Only a direct threat to the existence of the House of Hanover could inspire panegyric flights out of term. Whenever political events suggested that the Hanoverian Succession under certain circumstances might be vulnerable, pro-government writers responded with an increased output of poems written in honor of the Royal family. According to Milton Percival, the ballad writers always "in the employ of the Whig ministry rather than the crown, found it expedient to praise the king only when Succession itself seemed threatened, or Walpole's government, endeavoring to manipulate public opinion, raised the cry of a threat." The discovery of the Atterbury plot in the early 1720s and the Jacobite Rising in 1745 thus occasioned reams of patriotic verse in honor of the Royal family, whereas during the 1730s, a time of relative Jacobite inaction, only a relatively modest number of loyal ballads were published.[33]

Poems written in honor of the first two Hanoverian kings tend to emphasize their military exploits. Neither George I nor his son could be accused of lacking courage, since both men had personally taken part in the wars on the Continent in the days before George I became king of England. This was eagerly seized on by pro-government writers, not always with felicitous results ("Heav'ns! how the Heroe fought at *Audenarde!*"). References to their well-established bravery often served as a contrast to unfounded allegations that the Pretender and his son were cowards. An opposition was easily established between the king ("While GEORGE defends, fear thou [Britain] no *Romish* Gloom") and the Pretender ("Who twice for long-expected Empire drew, | Twice saw the distant Foe . . . and seeing flew?"). In pro-government works the Pretender and his son prepare for battle by bowing to their saints and counting their beads.[34]

Both George I and his son were regularly compared to the Emperor Augustus—an Augustus ribbed of authoritarian tendencies:

The second *Caesar* mildly sway'd his *Rome,*
Sooth'd all the *Nine,* and taught all Arts to bloom;
Thence sprung the Glories of the *Roman* Name,
That roul [sic] for ever in a Tide of Fame:
Britain! un-envious view th' *Italian* Plains!
See *Rome'*s blest Times restor'd!———Thy own AUGUSTUS reigns![35]

When they remembered—and the Opposition was unlikely to let them forget—that Augustus's rule had been notable not just for the eminence of contemporary poets but for political excesses, the king was described as a superior Augustus:

With Vices unstain'd, of more unblemish'd Fame,
(A Praise that ne'er cou'd reach the *First Augustus*
Name).
He once was Vitious [sic], Cruel, False, Unjust:
Tho' LORD of Nature styl'd, *The Slave of Lust.*
All we can say t'excuse, is, Heav'n did join
Him to a LIVIA, not a CAROLINE.[36]

With regard to Queen Caroline pro-government writers had more material to work on. Lively, interested in religious and philosophical debate, quite accomplished as a singer, she could plausibly be portrayed as interested in the arts ("*Superior* to the *Pomp* of Britain's *Throne,* | In *Arts* she reign'd *unrival'd,* and *alone*"). She was also seen as learned to the point of being an intellectual ("While Rival *Sages* her *Decision* wait, | To solve some subtle *Point* of high *Debate*"). Since the king could not by the wildest stretch of the imagination be portrayed as a true patron of literature, it was very important that the queen should be presented as filling this role, as "the universal patroness of learned men."[37]

Queen Caroline had another asset: in her youth she had refused an offer of marriage from the future Emperor Charles since it would have entailed changing her religion, and so she could be portrayed as especially devout and devoted to the Protestant faith.[38] The poems written in her honor also tend to emphasize her matchless qualities not only in her official capacity as queen—regent during her husband's sojourns in Hanover, patron of the worthy, protector of the unfortunate—but in the private sphere as dutiful wife and mother. In verses addressed to the queen on her birthday in 1728, Philip Frowde rhapsodized:

> She shines our Model of domestic Life,
> The tender Parent, and endearing Wife;
> The gracious Mistress, who from Pomp descends
> To meet her Servants in the rank of Friends;
> Swift to redress the Injuries of Fate,
> And raise the Wretched from his abject State;
> Curious to learn where modest Merit grieves,
> She finds the Haunt; and found, its Care relieves.
> Nor languish now the Few, who dare explore
> Nature's Recess, and dig the secret Ore;
> By Sympathy of Soul, unurg'd, she moves,
> To patronize the nobler Arts, she loves.[39]

Queen Caroline's death in 1737 was a great personal loss to the king. On one occasion Princess Amelia actually removed all the queens from the pack of cards, so that her father would not be constantly reminded of the deceased.[40] In Jacobite circles, on the other hand, it was gleefully reported that "A Bell Man in the City of London has extremely diverted the people, his Rhyme on the Occasion of M[adam] Caroline's Death was,

> O Cruel Death! why hast thou been so unkind
> To take Our Queen & leave Our King behind."

Others showed their disrespect in indirect ways. It was reported of Lord Chesterfield, who by then had defected to the opposition, that he neither went into mourning nor presented his condolences at Court, and that the Duchess of Bridgewater and another lady were turned out of the Chapel of St. James's for wearing white gloves.[41]

Pro-government writers, on the other hand, described the nation as united in mourning. Stephen Duck, the thresher poet who had personally benefitted from the queen's bounty, wrote a poem describing a vision in which before the queen's death he saw Britannia herself beg the Almighty to spare "One sacred *Life*, so precious

to my Isle." Britannia is joined by all Britons from the king himself
down to the widows and orphans who had experienced the queen's
charity ("Three Kingdoms beg Thee to avert her Death"). God,
however, explains that since the queen has reached perfection—in
terms of piety, learning and virtue—a few more years of life would
change nothing, and so the death sentence is told for "The Noblest
Queen that ever grac'd a Throne."[42]

In other poems mourning the death of the queen, however, pro-
government writers actually admitted that she had been far from
omni-popular with her subjects. In these poems, the theme of ingratitude predominates. In *The Dream* the deceased is lauded to the
skies for her loyalty to God, king and country, while her subjects
are accused of treating her badly:

> SAY, what Returns to Heav'n, and Her you made,
> Who daily felt the Good for which she pray'd?
> Was it in Zeal, and Holiness of Life,
> In Love, and Hatred of domestick Strife?
> Was it in Duty and Obedience seen,
> And did you bless the Pow'r that bless'd the Queen?
> To you I speak, ye *Britons* but in Name,
> Who, void of Duty, Reason, Manners, Shame,
> Did, by blaspheming her, at length provoke
> Her God, in Ire, to strike the avenging Stroke.
> Were you not mutinous, perverse, ingrate?
> Self-conscious, self-confessed, you answer That.

The poem contains a dream in which the late queen herself is made
to say of her British subjects:

> As soon as you were mine, to me you were
> As dear as Children, and as much my Care;
> But I, as fondling Mothers often prove,
> More froward made you by Excess of Love.

She ends by exhorting them to make the king's task easier by showing him respect and by ceasing their discord.[43] The queen's death
was made the occasion for countless such appeals for unity, not always in language suitable to achieve such an object:

> Henceforth let Party-Fury cease,
> The Worm that prays upon your Peace.
> Trust not a giddy, factious Fry,
> That dare both King and Laws defy,
> That prostitutes the Patriot's Name,

> To set your Houses in a Flame,
> And rather than not glut their Hate,
> Would risk the Welfare of the State.[44]

The House of Hanover was not exactly famous for happy father/ son relationships, and this obviously presented panegyrists with a problem. When George II succeeded his father in 1727 Charles Beckingham in his poem to celebrate the occasion, simply chose to ignore the strained relations between the deceased and his son even though these had been so pronounced that for a time the Prince of Wales had headed the opposition to his father's administration. Instead Beckingham emphasized the continuity of the royal line (George I's "Virtues . . . remount the Throne"), and even made "the Royal *Shade*" himself praise his son and heir.[45]

The same basic situation was repeated in the next generation. Prince Fredrick's sympathy for the opposition had been noticed as early as 1729, although for many years his position remained ambiguous. In 1733, for instance, the prince turned down an offer granting his requests for marriage and a separate establishment, because it had been made contingent on his public recognition of Walpole as the king's minister and friend. However, that same year he refused to endorse the opposition position on the Excise scheme, even though he was under pressure to do so. Only in 1737 did the Prince of Wales officially become the figurehead of the opposition, thus lending respectability to their activities. After this it became very much more difficult to claim that they were acting in an unconstitutional way. This gave a much needed boost to the opposition which had withered slightly since Lord Bolingbroke's withdrawal to France in 1735, disillusioned with William Pulteney, Lord Carteret, and their parliamentary supporters, in whom he recognized a strong opportunistic streak akin to his own.[46] The Prince of Wales's residence became the focus for much opposition activity, and Prince Frederick sought to make his own court as much of a contrast to that of his father's as possible. Possibly the prince's chosen role of patron of literature should be seen in this light. James Thomson, David Mallet, Henry Brooke, and Richard Glover were among the writers whom he patronized.[47]

Pro-government writers tended to ignore the bad relations between father and son. The king was proclaimed to be unenvious of "Merit equal to his Own."[48] The prince was on no better terms with his mother. On her death in 1737, one or two pro-government writers chose to address themselves directly to Princess Amelia rather than to the Prince of Wales, only referring in general to how the queen's blood and example would in her children "speak the precious Nurture of their Root."[49] Most pro-government writers simply observed silence on the subject of the family quarrel. In *The Statesman*, for instance, Spiltimber praises the king and his younger son the Duke of Cumberland, but remains conspicuously silent on the topic of the heir to the throne. You do not have to be a deconstructionist to detect a "silence in the text" when one pro-government writer starts by praising the king and goes on to speak in flattering terms of the late queen, the Princess Amelia, and the Duke of Cumberland, in other words almost every adult member of the Royal family with the exception of Frederick Prince of Wales, as in Francis Manning's "The Second Ode to Augustus Cæsar Imitated."[50] Moreover, the extensive use of the theme of ingratitude in connection with the Royal family would have served as a subtle reminder to contemporary readers of the ungrateful behavior of one subject in particular.

10

The Attack on the Opposition

As time went by, forces in the government came to realize that attack is often the best defence. Although pro-government writers still devoted much time to projecting a positive image of Walpole and his administration, it was altogether more efficacious to bring the war into the enemy camp, by attacking the opposition, collectively and individually. It is no exaggeration to say that pro-government writers were far more successful in their attacks on the opposition than in their attempts to eulogize the government. According to G. A. Cranfield, provincial newspapers favorably disposed to the government—there were but few, and none of them in receipt of a subsidy—hardly ever included material in open praise of Sir Robert Walpole and defence of his policies. Instead they "might reprint the more vicious attacks of the ministerial organs in London upon the Opposition newspapers."[1]

How ineffectual panegyrics on Walpole could be is exemplified by the following extract from an ode to Walpole carried on the front page of the *Daily Gazetteer* for 24 April 1738:

> This is the Sovereign Man, Compleat;
> Hero; Patriot; glorious; free;
> Rich, and wise; and fair, and great;
> Generous WALPOLE, Thou are He.

Given that "almost identical verses appeared frequently in the opposition papers, which relied heavily on sarcasm as a political weapon," Cranfield is surely right to assume that such a production would have been "greeted with shrieks of mirth by all Walpole's opponents."[2] The effectiveness of such verse must have been limited, the reader's response entirely dependent on his political convictions: whereas a government supporter might have had his view of the "Prime Minister" confirmed, an opposition adherent would almost certainly have considered the poem an example of the sycophantic adulation to which government writers were supposedly prone.

Instead of publishing works which would please friends to the government but which would almost certainly prove counter-productive in confrontation with politically hostile readers, it was clearly preferable to adopt an alternative approach. Direct attacks on the opposition would not only please friends but—hopefully—embarrass enemies. In a letter to Walpole written some time after 1727 Samuel Madden pinpointed the main problem confronting government propagandists:

> You know well Sr. how vain it is to reason with anyone, who will never be convinc'd or silenc'd, but will still have the last word.

According to Madden an aggressive campaign against "the Craftsmen" would be more effective than the defensive tactics mostly employed to try to justify Walpole's policies. He proposed "to begin an attack against them in a method & manner entirely new & . . . turn their own Cannon against them & ridicule them; for besides that this is no reasoning age nor our People so fond of strong arguments as biting Jests, I was persuaded if once the laugh could be turn'd against them the mob would desert them & they must be undone."[3]

Gradually pro-government writing became markedly more aggressive. This is noticeable, not only in the field of literature, but also to some degree in other areas, such as political engravings. In the late 1720s and in the 1730s the opposition was allowed to dominate the production of prints which consequently remained almost exclusively hostile to Walpole. In the early 1740s, however, the pro-government side suddenly proved capable of taking the lead in such matters, by inaugurating an attack on the opposition which clearly drew blood. Starting with "The Motion," which was most unusual in selling at 3d (half the usual rate), the campaign involved several prints on the government side.[4]

"THE HAUGHTY, THE AMBITIOUS, AND THE REVENGEFUL"

> YE guilty Sons of busy Faction, tell
> What real Evils justify your Tongues,
> Which slander him, by whose unerring Hand
> Religion, Law, and Freedom, stand secur'd?
>   (Spiltimber, *The Statesman*, p. 8)[5]

The campaign against Walpole's government had planted opposition politicians and writers firmly on the moral high ground. By attacking "the Great Man" and his allies as corrupt they presented themselves—explicitly or implicitly—as a morally superior alternative to the status quo. As they became increasingly successful in creating an image of Walpole as responsible for a new wave of corruption spreading like an insidious disease throughout contemporary society, it became imperative for pro-government forces to hit back. They did so by presenting to the public an alternative version of the political views and tactics of the opposition, and by launching a full-scale attack on the morality of individual politicians. On the whole, the methods employed by various writers associated with the government are so remarkably consistent as to deserve the name of a campaign.

Old Corps Whig adherents seem to have had few illusions about the possibility of prolonged periods of political consensus. In the words of one pro-government pamphleteer "it is usual for all Malecontents [sic] to rail at the Times, and at Ministers, as the Authors of such Times." Historians have claimed that the government denounced all opposition as de facto unconstitutional. This is a simplification: although some pro-government writers took this line ("None thine [Walpole's], but who, at once, are *Britain*'s Foes"), many government supporters did not profess to see oppositions as necessarily undesirable, but as an inevitable consequence of the existence of parties. According to Under Secretary of State Edward Weston "Partyes there must be, there will, & for the Safety of this Countrey [sic] there always ought to be."[6] Similarly, Arnall wrote in the *Free Briton*:

> Opposition, however it is practis'd or complain'd of, is neither unnatural or new. It ever was in the World, and ever must . . . for Opposition is the Test of Truth, the Touchstone of pure Virtue; and conscious Worth will have Courage enough to bear that Test, as guilty Fear will shun it: But if that Touchstone is taken away, Mankind have no Security against Deceit, which must pass undetected, because unexamined . . . Whoever assumes more Authority than any Man ought to be trusted with, cannot atone for the Crime by discharging it well.[7]

Not only publicly but privately, government supporters expressed approval of oppositions so long as they were temporary and restricted to specific issues. In 1733, after the massive opposition campaign against the Excise scheme had resulted in its withdrawal, Charles Delafaye, who as Under Secretary of State was involved with the organisation of pro-government propaganda, wrote informally to a colleague and friend that he was "apt to think that such little shocks, now & then, settle a Constitution ye firmer upon its true bottom."[8]

Using as their starting point a basic acceptance of the inevitability and even necessity of oppositions as a phenomenon in political life, pro-government writers launched a severe attack on the specific opposition that confronted Walpole. What the "Prime Minister" and his allies objected to was a permanent opposition, one that was regarded as automatically hostile to all government policies, what contemporaries called a "General Opposition." "There is as little Sincerity in finding fault with *every thing*, as in objecting to *nothing*," wrote one ministerial supporter.

> DEFECTS, tho' e'er so small, in troubled States,
> Sow great Complaints which *Faction* cultivates;
> *Sedition* springs, as ill Weeds grow, apace,
> And some rob *Janus* of his double Face:
> These worthy Zealots sure have plainly shewn,
> By *Publick Good* they only meant their *own*.[9]

In their works pro-government writers routinely expressed the view that the opposition to Walpole was based not on principles but on opportunism, and that its members were united only in a wish to discredit the administration at any cost. A typical example can be found in *Lord B[olingbro]ke's Speech upon the Convention*, clearly a response to the opposition production *Sir xxx [Robert Walpole's] Speech upon the Peace* in which Walpole was presented as demanding unconditional loyalty from his supporters in the parliamentary division over the Convention with Spain. In the pro-government version Lord Bolingbroke—debarred by his Jacobite past from sitting in the House of Lords—explains to an extra-parliamentary assembly of opposition politicians exactly what is expected of them in the same division. The suggestion made by "orderly S[andys]" that the Convention be read, does not meet with approval:

> And what would you read it for BOL[INGBRO]KE crys,
> Would the Gentleman trust to his Senses or Eyes,
> My Maxim (no bad one) Sir, always has been
> To blame Things unheard, and condemn them unseen.
> *Derry down*, &c.
>
> This Consideration alone must be had,
> Whatever our Enemies do *must* be bad;

Let your Judgments for ever be rul'd by your *Hate*,
Sir ROBERT's a Fool, *Harry Fox* can't debate.
                              Derry down, &c.

Allow not a Foe to have any Pretence
To Honour or Honesty, Courage or Sense;
To our Friends be *these Virtues* and Qualities granted,
'Tis but just to bestow 'em where most they are wanted.
                              Derry down, &c.

. . . .
And this desperate Step was agreed to by all,
Let ENGLAND be *ruin'd* but WALPOLE *must fall*.
                              Derry down, &c.[10]

As time went by the government campaign gathered force and
the paper war settled into a familiar pattern. In their attacks on their
opponents, pro-government writers played blatantly on the fear of
the unknown. They portrayed the opposition as so unreliable and
unpredictable that a political change in their favor would bring the
very stability of the state into jeopardy. Joseph Mitchell, for instance, expressed the opinion that,

> . . . oft the worst Abuse
> Changes of Hands in Government produce.
> The ticklish Seat ascend new Charioteers,
> And quite o'erturn it by their loose Careers.
> From PHEBUS self, the World no hazard ran;
> But cou'd not bear one Day his vent'rous Son:
> He thro' new Ways the flaming Chariot drove,
> And all was Fear below, and all was Fire above.[11]

In pro-government works the opposition is seen as a stark contrast to Walpole. Whereas the "Prime Minister" is described, as already mentioned, by the use of metaphors suggesting strength,
permanence and stability, opposition politicians are seen as unsta-
ble, swayed by emotions which they are unable or unwilling to ana-
lyze. They are the "Sea-surrounding Billows" to Walpole's "Isle,"
the "foaming Deep" to his "Pilot." In fact nature imagery is often
used to emphasize the unpredictable and volatile character of the
opposition, precisely because nature is fundamentally beyond
human control. Thus to try to mollify the opposition is to try "to
court the wind"; by extension their actions are likened to those of
weathercocks; individually and collectively their supporters behave
like "angry curs," and so on.[12]

Mostly, the opposition is portrayed as totally opportunistic,

> the Foes of such a Minister, who in mere Opposition to his Schemes, promoted domestic Confusion, a foreign War, and a total Interruption of Trade, that they might have the Pleasure of complaining of it; that such Men as these should be honoured with the Name of Patriots, even by the Dregs of the People, will strike succeeding Ages with Wonder.[13]

The tendency in the opposition press to insinuate that Walpole and other statesmen were guilty of corruption but without offering any proof was particularly resented. In Philip Frowde's *The Fall of Saguntum*, one of the true patriots says to the rebels who have been the victims of disinformation:

> . . . Is to asperse, to prove?
> Sad then should be the State of Innocence.
> Shall bare assertion have the force of truth,
> And weigh the Tenor of our Actions down?
> No, 'tis from them, when other Proof is wanting,
> That Men should form their apt and surer Judgments.[14]

Allied to this theme is the regular accusation that the opposition was behaving in an ungentlemanly manner. When Paul Whitehead criticized the government in his *Manners*, he was told that he might have been a tolerable poet "Hadst thou but been a little better bred."[15]

The opposition was accused—more or less openly—of conspiring with Britain's enemies. In a panegyric on Walpole John Mottley, publishing under his own name, voiced delight that despite the fact that she was "by base Minds at *Home* assisted, *Spain* | Submits, recedes, prevaricates in vain."[16]

Paradoxically, however, the opposition is often described as acting contrary to logic, simply because individual members instead of using their reason allow themselves to be swayed by emotion. Led astray by their own enthusiasm, resentment, etc., they are presented as a dangerous alternative to Walpole's government. Typically in Lord Hervey's poem *The False Patriot's Confession; or, B[olingbro]ke's Address to Ambition*, Lord Bolingbroke decides to retire from the world of politics, only to find:

> This Course *my* Reason bids *me* steer,
> But if by cursed Chance I hear
>   *Of W[alpo]le's* hated Name,
> Again Ambition swells *my* Breast,

Envy and Rancour break *my* Rest,
And REASON I DISCLAIM.[17]

Not only were opposition writers and politicians accused of being swayed by emotion themselves. Again and again pro-government writers accused them of addressing themselves to their readers in ways not calculated to engage their reasoning faculties but to appeal to their emotions—not to mention inflame their passions—thereby evoking that greatest of eighteenth-century fears. In *The Grand Accuser the Greatest of all Criminals*—a pamphlet published by James Roberts in 1735 of which 9797 copies were distributed free of charge[18]—the anonymous author says of Bolingbroke:

> . . . he has certainly very great abilities, and though he could entertain Men of Virtue and of true Taste perfectly well, if he proposed to write to such, yet, sacrificing his Conscience to his Politicks, he looks round him, computes what Sort of Readers are most numerous, most disposed to receive his Lectures with Applause, and to believe (or pretend to believe) and propagate his Assertions: And then he charges boldly those Ministers whose Destruction he seeks, with enormous Crimes against their Country, in the most outrageous and violent Terms, adapted to the Taste of the Vulgar, the more to incite their Passions (pp. 14–15).

The opposition was seen as particularly dangerous because it was willing not only to exploit popular expressions of discontent but to take the initiative in fomenting extra-parliamentary activity. This was coupled with the larger issue of the threat of Jacobitism ("the Craftsmen, those disturbers of the publick Peace; who if not prevented may in time shake our happy settlement, to exalt themselves").[19]

In regular attacks on the opposition's close links with "Fellows of no Name, no Authority, Figure or Interest in their Country," pro-government writers played on the fear of the mob, which was naturally all-pervasive in a society vulnerable to street violence through an almost complete lack of law-enforcement officers. The claim made in a poem by the dissident Whig James Miller that "the *Will of Heaven* is the *publick Voice*," would certainly not have been endorsed by Walpole and his allies. In fact, one suspects that most contemporaries—irrespective of their political convictions—would have agreed with Joseph Mitchell's assertion that "a *Mob* is ever on the blundering Side."[20]

The most frightening thing about the mob was of course its unpredictability. A standard complaint among Walpole's supporters is "the confused Clamour of the Peoples [sic] capricious Voices."[21]

The common people are assumed to "praise without Cause, and without Cause dislike":

> To lead Mobs by Reason's an idle Pretence,
> Mobs cease to be Mobs when govern'd by Sense.[22]

The tenuous connection that existed between the opposition and the lower sections of society was exploited for all it was worth by writers associated with Walpole. In an age when to be "low-born" was automatically equated with ignorance, insularity, dependence, volatility, and so on, it was fairly standard to accuse one's opponents of being low-born, irrespective of the party allegiance of either accuser or victim; but it was a point that pro-government writers returned to again and again, especially in connection with the support that the opposition received from the City. In one poem Lord Bolingbroke is made to say of the Lord Mayor of London:

> He'll summon the wise C[ommo]n C[ounci]l together,
> From the *Maker of Scales* to the *Seller of Leather*:
> We'll call 'em all *Merchants*, and sure they'll agree
> To what's offer'd by B[A]RB[E]R, and written by ME.

Bolingbroke goes on to recommend that "every Man that is Liberty's Friend" should mix with the populace in order to incite violent and seditious acts ("And do you thro' those Numbers remember to tell | How *dy'd the De Witts*, and how *Buckingham fell*."[23]

Nor was the opposition's attempt to appeal to non-parliamentary groups attributed to political considerations alone. The motivation was often seen as personal, such as an undignified wish for praise:

> You scorn a Bribe, you say—tho' meanly proud
> Of that vile Bribe,—the Praises of the Crowd.[24]

More important, however, than their attacks on the relative obscurity of many opposition sympathizers was the pro-government writers' systematic attempt to wrestle opposition politicians away from their position of moral preeminence. This was done by consistently reducing their political actions and sentiments to the level of private frustrations, ambitions and desires. "If the Possession of Place influences Men, does not want of Place influence them as much?," asked one pamphleteer, typically refusing to construct an ideal pro-government standard against which the opposition could be judged.[25]

A pretence of moral superiority was certainly a very strong element in contemporary opposition propaganda. While denouncing placemen and other government supporters as corrupt and self-seeking, they themselves professed to be activated by nothing but the most high-minded and sincere patriotism. Pro-government writers tried to turn the tables on them by attributing their choice of political loyalty to private ambitions. Walpole himself said in a speech:

> My great and principal crime is my long continuance in office; or, in other words, the long exclusion of those who now complain against me . . . The Jacobites distress the government they would subvert; the Tories contend for party prevalence and power. The Patriots, from discontent and disappointment, would change the ministry, that themselves may exclusively succeed . . . They clamour for change of measures, but mean only change of ministers.[26]

Variations on this basic theme, are everywhere apparent in the works of writers associated with Walpole. As one might expect, digs at the opposition were inserted when Sir William Yonge collaborated with Concanen and Roome in turning Richard Brome's *The Jovial Crew* into a ballad opera. Performed at Drury Lane in 1731, and later revived at Covent Garden for "a very successful run for several nights," it includes songs like the following:

> *Here comes a Courtier polite, Sir,*
> *Who flatter'd my Lord to his Face;*
> *Now Railing is all his Delight, Sir,*
> *Because he miss'd getting a Place.*
>
> *The Courtier, he begs for a Pension, a Place,*
> *A Ribbon, a Title, a Smile from his Grace,*
> *'Tis due to his Merit, is writ in his Face.*
>
> *But if by mishap, he shou'd chance to get none,*
> *He begs you'd believe that the Nation's undone.*
> *There's but one honest Man—And himself is that One.*[27]

The pro-government print "The Acquittal" (See detail on the jacket) shows Walpole standing unharmed amidst impotent arrows marked "Ambition," "Want of Place," "Disappointment," "Self Interest," "Sham Patriotism," "Affected Zeal," "Resentment," "Malice," "Prejudice," "Revenge," "Disaffection," "Want of Pension," "Pique."[27] Similarly, pro-government writers invariably portray opposition politicians as activated by a self-interested desire for power, places, pensions and money. Typically, Walpole was warned that,

> The Crowds that court thee, court with Friendship's Face;
> The Face speaks Friendship, but the Heart, a Place.
> Deny them that, and tho' so oft they swore,
> They PATRIOTS turn . . . and vote with you no more,
>
> . . . .
> The *Faction's* self for thee no Malice knows,
> They are thy *Places*, not thy *Person*'s, Foes.
> By them, the *Statesman*, not the *Man*, is fear'd;
> Thy *Pow'r* is hated, but thy *Truth* rever'd;[29]

And in his *Manners of the Age*, Thomas Newcomb wrote sarcastically:

> In every age, what numbers have we seen
> Made Patriots, by resentment and the spleen;
> By pious wants, whose morals strangely mend,
> In place their own, when out, the nation's friend?
> A kind repulse, a lucky discontent,
> Has to the soul its virtues often lent;
> Fill'd it with parts, and probity all o'er,
> Dark'ned with guilt, or dullness curst before;
> *Bessus* grew upright, righteous, just and wise,
> Soon as the post he lost, had clear'd his eyes;
> Found, the first day he did from court depart,
> Fresh virtues budding in his holy heart;
>
> . . . .
> How great a patriot then had *Britain* lost,
> Had *George* still smil'd, and *Bessus* held his post!
> Lov'd by his prince, and trusted with a place,
> He might have wanted still, both parts and grace.[30]

In work after work the message was hammered home that the Tories and the dissident Whigs were nothing but hypocrites who only payed lip service to the patriotism and personal sacrifice advocated by "Country" ideology. That their actions in opposition were motivated by personal rather than self-effacing motives is in the poem *The False Patriot's Confession; or, B[olingbro]k's Address to Ambition*, written by Lord Hervey, indicated by the frequency with which the persona uses the words "I" and "my," and for fear that this fact should go unnoticed, the first person pronouns are all printed in italics. The list of base motives for opposition activity is a long one. One pamphlet charged the opposition with spending more than ten thousand pounds "to turn the Election; I mean the Town of B____d." In "The Muse's Commission to Sir R. Walpole" Joseph Mitchell mentions all the objects of beauty at Houghton, "Things which, however *Fog* amd *D'Anvers* rave; | *St John* and *Poultney* [sic] wou'd be glad to have," as though Lord Bolingbroke and Pulteney were paupers. In similar fashion, the City's opposition to the Excise scheme is attributed to the high incomes that certain merchants derived from illegal trade, a practice which this scheme was designed to suppress.[31] In *The Grumbletonians, or The Dogs Without-Doors*, written by Henry Carey, and, judging by the poor quality of the paper and print, aimed at a mass market, two mastiffs are so jealous of their master's favorite hound, that they are turned out of the house. Here they succeed in disrupting their master's business ("These ugly Currs kept such a Rout, | That no one durst stir in or out"), but being let back into the house, they behave in the most submissive manner:

> These currs who were so fierce before
> Now crouch and wriggle on the Floor:
> Fawn at the very Servants Feet,
> And tremble least they should be beat.
>   Next they traverse the Kitchen round,
> To see what Prog is to be found;
> Where, having fed to hearts desire,
> They stretch'd themselves before the Fire.

The poem ends with an exhortation to the reader to discover the moral of the tale.[32]

The theme of the potential danger to the state represented by faction, is a recurring one in plays written by Walpole supporters. Philip Frowde's tragedy *The Fall of Saguntum*, performed in 1727, is a case in point. An embittered faction (of two) plot the downfall of Saguntum. One of them is Murrus—a Pulteney-like character—who is "bold, vindictive, and impetuous," jealous of all rivals, given to exaggerated speech (he is warned not to "think opprobrious language makes a Patriot"). Moved by ambition and resentment, willing to sacrifice the public good to their own private interest, the conspirators are even prepared to betray Saguntum to the besieging army led by Hannibal. In order to further their seditious ends, they exploit Murrus's popularity with the common people. By feeding the easily led masses incorrect information designed to work on their prejudices, the traitors foment a rebellion ("what is to Reason just, | Will not of Force convince an inflam'd

People"). A few heroic characters confront the internal and external enemy. In his introduction to the printed play, Frowde compared their bravery to that of Walpole, who when the Hanoverian Succession was in the balance, "dared . . . to display the utmost *Force* of *Eloquence* at a *Crisis*, when to endeavour only to teach us the Ingloriousness of such a Desertion, *preposterously* became little less than *capital*." A contemporary audience was, however, likely to see a far more immediate application in a play that denounced faction and emphasized the need for unity. Lewis Theobald's prologue reminded the spectators that internal dissension had paved the way for Nero's rise to power. And the play ends with the governor praising his people for being fundamentally virtuous (although occasionally misguided). Saguntum can take pride in the fact that "(the Partner of his Crime, tho' late, repenting) | One single Traitor did these Walls contain." He appeals for unity, especially when faced with an external enemy.[33]

Although, opposition politicians were—collectively and individually—portrayed as self-seeking and opportunistic, and their much publicized opinions as based on private considerations rather than on genuine political principles:

> Each picqu'd, dissapointed, Ambitious, & proud,
> With heads very hot, & tongues very loud,
> No Coolness, no Judgment, their passions to curb;
> & Just as much Knowledge as Serves to disturb,[34]

it is clear that in their campaign, pro-government writers differentiated sharply between the different groups that were co-operating together in the opposition.

"THE JACOBITES, THE EASILY LED, AND THE OPPORTUNISTS": DIVIDING THE OPPOSITION

Christine Gerrard has described the opposition as "individuals or alliances of individuals motivated by a variety of factors" and "nothing like a political party." Writers and politicians hostile to Walpole, however, tried to portray the opposition as united in terms of political ideology and goals. By describing Whig/Tory labels as obsolete, and insisting on the reality of a Court/Country dichotomy they could preserve some kind of unity between the various groups within the opposition and at the same time present a united front to the outside world. The measure of their success can be gauged by

the fact that occasionally modern historians have taken this propaganda at face value. When one historian, for instance, in order to
prove the meaninglessness of Whig/Tory labels, quotes an opposition pamphlet rebuking Lord Perceval (former opposition advocate
turned government supporter upon the fall of Walpole) for using the
obsolete terms Tory and Whig instead of the more valid labels
Court and Country, he is overlooking the fact that it was in the *interest* of the opposition to maintain that the old party divisions were
extinct.[35]

Old Corps supporters refused to accept this image of the opposition as unitedly devoted to a Country ideology. In the late 1730s
Walpole himself distinguished between three groups in the Opposition: "the Boys [Lord Cobham and his allies], the riper Patriots [the
associates of William Pulteney and Lord Carteret], and the Tories."[36] Not surprisingly, in pro-government works the Whig/Tory
distinctions clearly exist. Implicitly or explicitly men are seen as
belonging to the Whig or Tory camps. Whereas good Whigs remain
loyal to Walpole, bad Whigs defect. Consequently the opposition,
consisting of Tories and dissident Whigs (which could be further
subdivided on demand), could be presented as consisting of mutually incompatible political groups with but one thing in common:
their inveterate hatred of Walpole. It would of course be tempting
to see in pro-government works proof of the non-existence in the
Walpole era of a "Country" party, but it would be naive to overlook
the very obvious fact that just as it was clearly an opposition policy
to use the nomenclature Court/Country, pro-government writers
were equally interested in keeping up the belief that the old party
distinctions were still valid, that Tories were Tories and Whigs were
Whigs, no matter what some of the latter group had managed to
fool the Tories into believing.

In pro-government works the opposition was presented over and
over again as consisting of mutually irreconcilable groups united
only in their wish to supplant Walpole and his allies in office
("Lions may couple now with lambs, | When Whigs embrace with
Tories"). Whereas in one fairly respectable pro-government pamphlet the opposition was defined as "this *Scylla* and *Charibdis* [sic],
this Jacobite and Republican-party," in another far more scurrilous
production it was described as comprising "an *invenom'd Set* of
Men," who "like *Beasts*, of *different sorts*, shut up together, *forget*
their *natural Enmity* to *satiate* their *common Lusts*, and *care not*
what kind of *Monsters* are produced betwixt them, so their *brutal
Appetites* are but *gratified*."[37]

If the opposition could be presented as a conglomerate of separate parts with different interests, forever threatened by internal dissention, then clearly they would emerge as a poor alternative to Walpole's stabile rule. In his poem *The Faction, A Tale* Ashley Cowper tells a story about "some far distant *Latin* State" in which the anger of a violent opposition is diffused by "a Man of subtile Parts" who has succeeded in gaining their confidence. Granting their first premise "that Times were ne'er so bad as now," he advises against condemning those in power en bloc; the innocent should be allowed to retain their posts. He therefore proposes to parade the senators before the crowd one by one so that those found guilty can be discarded and "others nam'd to fill their Place." The outcome is predictable:

> So many Men, so many Minds;
> And 'twas more easily agreed
> Who shou'd go *out*——than who *succeed*
> Each stiffly did his Friend propose,
> And each the other did oppose,
> So that at length it came to Blows.

To drive home the message—which hardly needed driving home—the poem was "Humbly Inscrib'd to Messrs. Craftsman and Compy [sic]."[38]

The Opposition Whigs

The worst pro-government malice was reserved for the Whig members of the opposition. At this point a distinction has to be made between the older and the younger generation of opposition Whigs, for it is noticeble that most pro-government ire was aimed at the older generation of former Whig allies who had deserted the Old Corps Whig cause, while the younger generation who were "untainted" by a former alliance, were given far less attention. It is natural that special treatment was reserved for prominent "Patriots" such as William Pulteney, the Duke of Argyll, and George Bubb Dodington who had ratted on Walpole. The slow trickle of deserters had to be taken seriously, as a threat to Walpole's power base. On the whole, however, pro-government writers tend to try to play down the importance of this trend. In *The Oak and the Dunghill; A Fable*, for instance, these defectors are seen as so many falling oak leaves. Although they contribute to the growth of the dunghill, the oak pretends to be undismayed by this fact:

But be they thine————New Seasons spread
New Honours, o'er my rising Head.[39]

This seeming indifference to the defections is given the lie by the
fact that every spectacular desertion from Walpole's camp was
hailed by a barrage of personal satire, branding the deserter as a
traitor. These works were clearly intended to embarrass the culprit,
by isolating him from his erstwhile allies and rendering his transi-
tion to the opposition camp as difficult as possible. They were also,
one suspects, calculated to increase group feeling among the loyal
and act as a deterrent for any individuals hovering on the brink of
defection. All these works made the same very obvious point: loyalty towards any political group whatsoever could not be expected
from people, who through their political apostasy had proved themselves to be basically unreliable.

Whatever reasons the older dissident Whigs may have had for
withdrawing their support from Walpole, their motives for transfer-
ring their loyalties were rendered uniformly suspect in works with
a pro-government slant. In *A Hue and Cry*, for instance, they are
portrayed as a pack of hounds which has broken out of the kennel
in Westminster "for want of *proper Care being taken of 'em*" (p. 1).
In *A Coalition of Patriots Delineated* they are "disturb'd with a
Lustre superior to their own." To make room for them in the cabinet would therefore be "to cut down the *Oaks* that the *Shrubs* might
flourish" (pp. 20, 24). And a humorous evocation of the flimsy pretext on which a government supporter might desert to the opposition is implicit in Thomas Gray's remarks in a letter to Horace
Walpole dated 1736:

> I think this is the first time I have had any occasion to find fault with Sir
> Robert's mal-administration, and if he should keep you in town another
> week, I don't know whether I shan't change my side, and write a
> *Craftsman*.[40]

Sir Charles Hanbury Williams, who was himself part of Walpole's silent voting majority in the House of Commons, was well
placed to observe and—when necessary—distort their motives. In
his poems, for instance, George Bubb Dodington's change of sides
was attributed variously to his failure to obtain a much-solicited
knighthood or peerage ("He's on this grown a patriot," "A Grub
upon Bub"), and to his alleged dismissal from office ("Argyle's
Decampment"). Similarly, Lord Hervey who had once been a personal friend, was after his defection described as "the court wretch,
who now depriv'd | Of Post . . . | From that one cause opposes."[41]

In Hanbury Williams's scheme of things, people did not simply leave the Old Corps of their own accord, they were thrown out.

The older generation of dissident Whigs were extremely vulnerable to satire since they could be portrayed as deserters from the right cause. A slightly unusual method would seem to have been taken with George Bubb Dodington. In his pro-government days he had written a panegyric on Walpole, which went through four editions in the year 1726. Shortly after Dodington's defection in 1741, a new edition was brought out. No more effective way could perhaps have been devised to discredit a one-time adherent who had fled to the enemy. A contemporary reader could be trusted to apply to Dodington himself his attack on Walpole supporters who joined the opposition because of frustrated ambitions. In the poem Dodington contrasted such behavior with that of "an honest Man"—Dodington himself, thinly disguised—who would remain "In Power, a Servant; out of Power, a Friend."[42]

Forced—in Hanbury Williams's words—to "Unvote his votes of twenty years" ("Argyle's Decampment"), a dissident Whig like Argyle laid himself open to attacks based on the discrepancy between his actions and professed principles before and after the defection to the Opposition. Among the books in a mock library catalogue written by Thomas Newcomb there was "A Collection of learned and curious speeches against Pensions, Excises, and Standing Armies; written by a noble Ducal author, who voted eighteen years for Pensions, Excises, and Standing Armies."[43] In "Earle and Dodington: A Dialogue," to take another example, Sir Charles Hanbury Williams used as personae to confront each other the new opposition convert George Bubb Dodington, laboring to master the new rhetoric, and Giles Earle, Lord of the Treasury, who according to Lord Hervey had professed himself "always ready, without examining what it was, to do anything a minister bid him."[44] When the latter makes the highly questionable claim that "Walpole now has got the nation's voice, | The People's Idol, and their monarch's choice," the following exchange of opinion ensues:

Dodington: When the Excise scheme shall no more be blam'd,
When the Convention shall no more be nam'd,
Then shall your minister, and not till then,
Be popular, with unbrib'd Englishmen.

Earle: The Excise and the Convention! D[am]n your b[loo]d
You voted for them both, and thought them good;
Or did not like the triumph of disgrace,
And gave up your opinion, not your place.

Cornered in this way, Dodington admits to having spent "years in ignominy" as a placeman under Walpole, and claims—not very convincingly—that his current opinions are sincere.[45]

The idea behind this writing is not to promote Old Corps standards as morally superior to opposition practice, but simply to cut the latter down to size. The basic similarities between the two are stressed: their careers having crossed each other, they have in common their willingness to desert one master for another for purely self-interested reasons, as well as their disloyal criticism of former leaders and sycophantic adulation of present ones. The only difference between them is that what Dodington attempts to conceal behind high-sounding verbiage, Earle admits openly.[46]

The message is again a very worldly one: those who claim to be morally superior are shown to be no better than the people they condemn. A common ploy in pro-government productions is to show the opposition politicians as performing the kind of actions which they criticized in others. In Sir Charles Hanbury Williams's "Argyle's Decampment," for example, Dodington, who as a defector to the opposition ranks would be expected to denounce corrupt elections in no uncertain terms, is caught handing out pocket boroughs to his dependents:

> "Oh, Damer, Tucker, Raymond, Steward!
> "To Eastbury all welcome;
> "Two of you shall for Weymouth serve,
> "And two shall serve for Melcomb."[47]

The fact that several members of the opposition, dedicated to the denunciation of parliamentary corruption in the form of pensions and places, were pensioners in the Prince of Wales's household, could be exploited in pro-government propaganda, once the prince had officially joined the opposition. In "A Political Eclogue" Sir Charles Hanbury Williams puts the following attack on the dissident Whig George Lyttelton into the mouth of the Tory Edmund Lechmere:

> But does not one thing stare you in the face?
> All the whole country knows you have a place;
> And, I assure you, think it the same thing,
> Whether you have it from the Prince or King.[48]

After the general election of 1741, when the influence of the Prince of Wales and the Duke of Argyll, in the Cornish and Scottish boroughs respectively, had ensured that most of these seats were filled with opposition members, Hanbury Williams wrote "Unhappy England, still in forty-one," which neatly illustrates this tendency to portray the opposition as acting contrary to its own professed ethical norms. In this poem Cornwall and Scotland, representing the opposition, are likened to "two common strumpets," and we are invited to laugh at them as they,

> Go forth and preach up virtue through the land;
> Start at corruption, at a bribe turn pale,
> Shudder at pensions, and at placemen rail.[49]

As every contemporary reader knew full well, and as the use of the image of prostitution implied, Cornwall and Scotland could not have been won without quite as much electoral corruption being exercised on the opposition side as on the government side.

The political cynicism that informs this and other pro-government poems will perhaps strike many readers as chilling, but seen against the prevailing "holier than thou" attitude of much opposition writing, may well have struck some contemporaries as positively refreshing. This poem exemplifies the extreme antihypocrisy of much pro-government writing. In straightforward panegyric attention is naturally drawn to the excellence of the status quo. In satire, this is, however, relatively rare. In their refusal to construct a conventional positive standard against which the opposition could be judged, pro-government satirists project an image of Walpole's supporters as superior to their opposition counterparts only in the sense that they are not hypocrites, and in that their political actions and opinions are seen as consistent and of one piece.

Pro-government writers laid great stress on political consistency and the virtue of remaining faithful towards one set of ideas, and consequently towards the same party. They tended to build their own ethos around this concept. Two years after the fall of Walpole, Hanbury Williams characterized himself as "Stedfast in principle, and stiff in party, | To Pulteney adverse still, to Walpole hearty," and Joseph Mitchell was giving the highest praise to his patron Lord Stair, when he said of him that he was "Whether with honest *Place* and *Pension* crown'd | Or unrewarded, ever faithful found!"[50] A change of opinion, especially if attended by a corresponding change in political allegiance, was regarded as highly suspect, raising serious questions about a man's integrity.

It was, of course, possible for a government supporter to disagree with Walpole on separate issues without automatically becoming the object of a smear campaign. This was, for instance, proved by

Lord Lonsdale who in 1735 resigned the Privy Seal because of a
general dislike of the management of public affairs. The important
thing, however, was that Lord Lonsdale did not joint the opposition.
In Hanbury Williams's "An Ode to Viscount Lonsdale," written in
1743, Lonsdale's independent attitude is the standard by which the
more recent deserter from the ranks of the Old Corps, Lord Hervey,
falls short:

> How different from this wretch is he
> Whose only view is to be free,
>   Careless of all beside;
> Nor in his most unguarded hour,
> Courts popularity or power,
>   Thro' vanity or pride.
>
> Such is the man, so just, so brave,
> Neither the king's nor people's slave,
>   But to his conscience true.[51]

The Tories

On the whole, pro-government propaganda devoted less attention
to the Tories than to their dissident Whig allies. This is logical
since, in general, people who hold radically different views, whilst
disagreeing wholeheartedly, may well feel a respect for each other
that they naturally withhold from defectors from their own point
of view. Walpole himself expressed respect for "honest Shippen,"
despite the fact that he was notorious for his Jacobite sympathies.
According to Horace Walpole his father always said, "I will not say
. . . who is corrupt, but I will say, who is not, and that is Shippen."
And Shippen reciprocated: "Robin and I are two honest men; he is
for King George and I for King James; but those men in long cra-
vats only desire places, either under King George or King James."[52]
It is also true that Walpole had a general policy of not upsetting
the Tories needlessly.[53] In pro-government works, when the Tories
are not equated with Jacobites, and thus seen as potentially dangerous, they tend to be treated good-humoredly as country bumpkins:
ignorant, insular, with extremely limited vision, yet basically loyal
to their misguided principles. A typical example of such relatively
good-natured satire is to be found in Soame Jenyns's "Epistle,
Written in the Country, to the Rt. Hon. the Lord Lovelace then in
Town":

> The cloth remov'd, the toasts go round,
> Bawdy and politics abound;

> And as the knight more tipsy waxes,
> We damn all ministers and taxes.[54]

And in "A Political Eclogue" Sir Charles Hanbury Williams presents Edmund Lechmere (Member of Parliament for Worcestershire) as a Squire Western type of Tory: blunt, ignorant, more concerned about his private cares than about public issues, and able to sum up his politics in one line ("My principles to you I'll freely state, | I love the church, and Whiggism I hate"). Despite these negative attributes, Lechmere's outspokenness is contrasted favorably with the hypocritical and declamatory speeches of the dissident Whig George Lyttelton, which it helps to expose.[55]

Modern historians disagree about whether the Tory party consisted predominantly of Jacobites, or whether most of them were loyal subjects under the two first Hanoverian kings. Many government supporters followed Walpole's lead and saw a potential Jacobite in almost every Tory. Sir Charles Hanbury Williams wrote to a friend: "It is usually said take away the Torys that joyn them & the Jacobites would make a very slender appearance, I am just of the contrary opinion Take away the Jacobites & where will you find a Tory?" This is probably an exaggeration, but Jacobitism was certainly still a potent force in certain parts of the country, with the staunch government supporter the Rev. Meadowcourt reporting from Oxford: "the same measure of leaven is still fermenting in this learned lump."[56] Nobody doubts, however, that the possible connection between Jacobitism and Toryism could be exploited by Walpole and his writers whenever they wanted to discredit not merely the Tories themselves but the dissident Whigs who were prepared to co-operate with them.

It was at one and the same time necessary and useful for the government to keep alive a constant reminder of the threat that Jacobitism posed to the stability of the state. In the words of Sir William Yonge, at that time Lord of the Treasury, "the Spirit of *Jacobitism* seems to lie dormant in private Corners, till a more proper Season offers to exert itself."[57]

The Jacobite slur was used regularly to discredit individual Tories, whose links with the dissident Whigs are normally emphasized. In *The Barber Turn'd Packer. A New Ballad*, for instance, the Lord Mayor John Barber is singled out and accused—rightly, as it happens—of being in favor of James III, and his involvement with the *Craftsman* and one of its patrons, William Pulteney, is made explicit.[58]

Since it was impossible for them to express their opinions openly,

Jacobites were, by the nature of things, hypocrites. They could therefore plausibly be portrayed as a dangerous set of men willing to tell any lies, and thus untrustworthy in all situations ("So tho' I drink with Mr. *Mist* | The Tory-rory Journalist, | To take Suspicion off at home | I drink as well with Mr. *Roome*"[59]).

In anti-Jacobite works a connection is naturally established between Jacobitism and the Catholic faith. In *The Humble Petition of his Grace P[hili]p D[uke] of W[harto]n* the persona grovels at Walpole's feet. Exiled on the Continent, the duke wants permission to return to England and attempts to smooth over his Jacobite associations. Warton's blatant hypocrisy is humorously made evident through his inability to divest himself of his Catholic terminology:

> 'Tis true I told a Priest with Gravity
> I loath'd Heretical Depravity
> But my true Reason, by the Mass,
> Was Zeal for the Illustrious Race,
> Yes, by our Lady, Sir, I swear
> Stark Love to th' House of Ha[nove]r!
>
> . . . .
>
> If timely Succour You will bring,
> And reconcile me to the King,
> Eternal Duty will I swear
> By ev'ry Saint i' th' Calendar.

There was a long tradition of anti-Catholic literature in England. David Wagner has documented the existence of a groundswell of anti-Catholic erotica, emphasizing the hypocrisy and covertness of individual members of the Catholic church, especially Jesuit priests. Antonio D. Gavin, who later offered his services to Walpole, wrote *A Masterkey to Popery* (Dublin, 1724), a bitter attack on the Catholic Church to which the author had once belonged. Charles Beckingham, Nicholas Rowe, Ambrose Philips, George Sewell, and many others wrote anti-Catholic plays, portraying Catholicism as inconsistent with British liberty, thereby connecting the House of Stuart with absolutism.[60]

However, in their campaign to discredit the opposition by stressing their Jacobite associations, the government was handicapped by a wish to avoid giving status to the cause itself. This sentiment— with regard to the whole opposition—is voiced by John Mottley in a panegyric on Walpole:

> To name thy baffled, disingenuous *Foes*,
> *Who* would thy Toils for *Britain*'s Weal oppose,

> Is drawing *Thee*, dishonest Task! too weak,
> And giving Them that Honour which they seek.

Pro-government writers could not attack all Tories as secretly in favor of a Stuart restoration without giving the impression that Jacobitism was a major force. For this reason the attitude towards Jacobitism in pro-government works is ambivalent. Although individual Tories were regularly accused of being Jacobites, Jacobitism is just as regularly portrayed as a lost cause with but few adherents, a strategy sometimes extended to the entire opposition.[61] In a poem published just after the Hanoverian Succession it is claimed that with the exception of a few wretches who will be trusted no more:

> We find on Tryall,
> The Nation is Loyall.[62]

The description of Jacobitism as a spent force is most forcefully conveyed in Samuel Madden's *Memoirs of the 20th Century*, which was withdrawn from circulation only days after publication (see Part II above). This satire consists of the private letters of the descendant of a disgruntled opposition politician in the days of Walpole. This descendant is Prime Minister under "George VI." Among the dispatches he receives from ambassadors abroad, there is one from the envoy to the Vatican in which the then Lord Hertford describes a meeting with "an old Gentleman who is actually the lineal Descendant of one of our ancient Kings, who abdicated his Throne thro' a violent Aversion to the Northern Heresy, and his zeal to this See . . . He is certainly Great Great Grandson, to the Person who is once or twice mention'd in the Histories of the glorious Reigns of *George* II. and *Frederick* I. under the Name of the Pretender." Considered as "a Piece of Antiquity," the Vatican allows him "2000 l. a Year, and a beneficial Place, of first *Valet de Chambre* to his Holiness." The whole description of this octogenarian suggests a lost cause. Attended only by "a few Highland gentlemen," he has followed his father's example and never taken the title of king. Nor does he have an heir, for his five children—all in occupations relating to the Catholic faith—are illegitimate. Extremely devout and with "a saturnine melancholy Severity of Manners," his links with Britain are severed to the point where his ignorance of the English language makes it necessary for him and Lord Hertford to converse in Italian.[63]

No matter how ambivalent the official campaign against the Tories often was, amongst themselves the Old Corps Whigs kept up a reminder of the wounds inflicted on some of their number by Queen Anne's Tory government. Horace Walpole relates how his mother used to sing "On the Jewel in the Tower," a ballad recounting Walpole's steadfastness and incorruptibility under persecuting Tory hands, and that she liked to dwell particularly on the last verse in which her husband's rise to preeminence was prophesied.[64]

DIVIDE AND RULE

Any political occurrence that pointed to a divergence between the two main groups that formed the opposition, either in terms of ideology or interest, was seized on by pro-government writers to emphasize the basic incompatibility of Tories and their Whig allies. One such episode occurred when Tory members of the House of Commons marched out of Parliament rather than support Samuel Sandys's motion to remove Walpole from the king's "presence and counsels" forever. The Tories reasoned that to attempt to dictate to the monarch in such matters was unconstitutional. This breach between Tories and Whigs in the opposition was made much of in pro-government writing:

> Great *W[a]lp[o]le*'s Downfall was our Drift,
>   That we might gain our *Ends*;
> But by this last malicious Step,
>   We have made his *Foes* his *Friends*.[65]

At the 1741 general election two dissident Whigs and two Tories, all of them violently antigovernment, opposed each other at the Worcester election. Once again writers close to Walpole had a field day. Here was irrefutable proof that the opposition was united in name only. This episode was exploited by Sir Charles Hanbury Williams in "A Political Eclogue," which reads as an effort to portray Tories and dissident Whigs as so different in terms of personality, aims and principles as to render their cooperation in the opposition ludicrous ("One sighs at Walpole's everlasting sway, | While t' other mourns th' excessive price of hay"). The poem is a rendering of a fictitious conversation between two of the contenders, Edmund Lechmere (Tory) and George Lyttelton (dissident Whig), in which the latter attempts to persuade the former to withdraw from the contest by urging familiar "Patriot" arguments: the obsolete nature of Whig and Tory labels, the need to avoid all schisms in "the party" opposing Walpole. The mockery results from the juxtaposition between "the Patriot" Lyttelton, with his moral bombast, and "the Grazier" Lechmere, with his ignorant but honest outspokenness. Lyttelton's high-sounding rhetoric is reduced to a cloak which barely covers the selfish ambition that it is intended to disguise, since he is clearly determined that Lechmere should be the one to sacrifice his personal wishes to the Country "party" so as to allow Lyttelton himself to continue in "full pursuit of glory." Asked why he intends to oppose Lyttelton at the polls, Lechmere's response is simple:

> Because, Sir, you're a Whig, and I'm a Tory.
> Howe'er with us you the same schemes pursue,
> You follow those who ne'er will follow you
>
> . . . .
> And tho', with you, Sir Robert I abhor,
> His Whiggish heart is what I hate him for;
> And if a Whig the minister must be,
> Pult'ney and Walpole are alike to me.[66]

It was not always a question of the Whigs following "those who ne'er will follow you," however. The beauty of the situation, from the point of view of a pro-government writer, was that either group could be portrayed as the dupe of the other, all depending on which group he wished to attack at any given time. So sometimes the Whigs are seen as "governed and led by the worst and most inveterate of the *Tories*."[67] Occasionally the Jacobites are named specifically as the sinister eminences grises manipulating other members of the opposition ("*many* do not see the *Consequences* of what they are *put upon*").[68] More often than not, however, the Tories were portrayed as the victims of dissident Whig deceit.

This was all part of an ill-disguised attempt to sow dissention between the groups, mostly along Whig and Tory lines, by playing on their respective fears and prejudices. In *The Citizen's Procession*, for example, the anonymous author claimed that as far as their joint efforts to squash the Excise scheme were concerned, the landed gentry (largely Tory) was being hoodwinked by the City interest (largely dissident Whig): the merchants' real reason for fearing a scheme designed to "cure Frauds, and protect the fair Trade," was to safeguard their lucrative smuggling activities, which would eventually enable them to buy up all the land, and so supplant those "who in *Liberty's Cause bore the Heat of the Day*" (i.e., the Tories). And in *The Countryman's Answer to the Ballad, called, Britannia Excisa*, the "Chorus" reads:

> Lords of Manors and yeomen,
> Freeholders and gem'men [sic],
> Drink a health to King George, your friend:
> 'Tis his gracious intent,
> With his good Parliament,
> To bring the Land-tax to an end.[69]

It is logical that pro-government writers sought to divide the opposition by concentrating on themes that were likely to upset one group more than the other. This may well explain why there is such an emphasis in much pro-government propaganda on the opposition's willingness to flirt with the common people, since it is well-known that Tories "feared anarchy far more than absolutism," and therefore had a deep-seated fear of the mob.[70] By stressing the rabble-rousing activities of certain dissident Whig politicians, pro-government writers hoped that the Tories—more than their opposition Whig brethren—would be upset, and that this would serve to create divisions between them.

By insisting on a basic Whig/Tory polarity within the opposition, pro-government writers had clearly found a weak spot. Not only Walpole's allies but many of his opponents were suspicious of the group headed by William Pulteney and Lord Carteret, who were suspected of merely using other opposition Whig groups and the Tories as "scaffolding" in order to obtain places for themselves whenever Walpole would be forced to resign.[71] This had of course been a major theme in the government press for well over a decade, but in the late 1730s several members of the opposition started to voice similar sentiments. Bolingbroke's comments on the subject in a private letter written in 1740, for example, could with only small adjustments have been inserted in one of the newspapers subsidized by Walpole:

> Is it not manifest, that two or three men have been laboring some years to turn a virtuous defence of the constitution, and a virtuous opposition to maladministration into a dirty intrigue of low ambition? that they are preparing to continue Walpole's scheme of government in other hands, and that the sole object of their pretended patriotism is to deliver over the government of their country from faction to faction.[72]

This is, of course, exactly what happened when Walpole was forced to resign in February 1742.

In trying to divide the opposition, pro-government writers also operated on a personal level, exploiting any private animosities between individual leaders. Such divisions could be maintained or widened by pouring salt into already existing wounds. This was clearly the intention behind the mock advertisements that caused the printer William Wilkins to be physically assaulted. They alluded in no uncertain terms to the affair that Mrs. Pulteney had had with Lord Bolingbroke before her marriage. In the course of their relationship Bolingbroke had once written a dispatch whilst in bed with the then Miss Gumley, and using her naked posterior as a writing desk, had signed it "from the most beautiful bum in Christendom." The letter in question surfaced at a meeting of the committee assembled to inquire into Harley's administration. Seeing the letter, Walpole attempted to extract it—his enemies claimed that he did so in an ostentatiously discreet manner calculated to draw Pulteney's attention to what was happening. Whether or not this was Walpole's intention, Pulteney intervened, protesting that there must be no suppressing of evidence, and insisting that the letter be read to the entire committee. After this its contents became common knowledge. Here was a point that might be exploited. It would not only brand Pulteney as a kind of cuckold, it would also serve to keep alive already existing ill-will between two leaders of the opposition:

> In a few Days will be reviv'd, By the same Company that acted last Winter, At the Great House near *Piccadilly*, next Door to the *Dispensatory*, An Entertainment in Grotesque Characters called the CABAL: Or HARLEQUIN a Patriot. The Part of HARLEQUIN by Mr. SQUAB. To which will be added, the *Metamorphosis*; Or the LADY a WRITING-DESK. In which HARRY GAMBOL has promised to play his Original Part of SECRETARY, and the LADY will not fail to perform her's with her usual spirit.[73]

PRETENDED PATRIOTS: DEBUNKING OPPOSITION RHETORIC

> Then were they taught *Sedition*'s Catechism;
> CORRUPTION, LIBERTY, AND PATRIOTISM![74]

Whilst still a writer in Walpole's employ, Thomas Cooke once likened the opposition to Ericthonius "the upper Parts of his Body . . . lovely and graceful, those from his Thighs downwards . . . the resemblance of Serpents . . . all beautyful above, and a Monster below":

> When we read the Writings of a certain Author, we see the Words *Liberty*, *Virtue*, my *Country*! and all the specious Terms of Patriotism; but

at the Bottom we discover *Malice, Ambition,* and all the other tyrant Passions of the Soul.[75]

One pro-government pamphlet warned: "when we see *Men* seiz'd with an *unsual* [sic] *Fit of Kindness* for their Country, and appear to act contrary to their former avow'd *Principles* and *Practice,* 'tis time to suspect a *Fraud.*"[76] Thomas Newcomb's mock library catalogue included "An Enquiry into the nature and origin of modern Patriotism; shewing, that the loss of Power is the source and parent of Honesty; the great incentive to Virtue and Integrity; and the chief promoter of a man's Love to his Country." The government position was quite simply that, "Place is the aim—when freedom is the cry."[77]

Pro-government writers concentrated much of their effort on puncturing opposition rhetoric. There is no doubt that members of the Opposition were prone to use a lot of high-flown metaphors and that they referred very freely to abstract notions, such as "freedom," "patriotism," "love for one's country," and so on. In pro-government writing this rhetoric is presented in a uniformly negative way. At best, opposition language is described as a standard formula with no basis in reality; at worst, it is seen as a cloak to hide unacceptable private ambitions. Again Thomas Newcomb's mock library catalogue is instructive:

A new Set of sounding Words, and terrifying Phrases; carefully collected into one volume, for the use and advantage of young patriots and statesmen at clubs, fairs, coffee-houses, and bear-gardens; which being artfully disposed, and methodically digested into easy and flowing periods and sentences, without the least truth, sense, or meaning naturally form themselves into satires, sonnets, and lampoons against the government.

N.B. The ingenious author of this collection begs leave to inform the publick, that if any Worthy gentleman is desirous to abuse his Majesty, the Ministry, or Parliament, in the handsomest manner, he may have it done at very reasonable rates, by the said Collector; who, since his late exclusion from court, has made this sort of writing his usual diversion and employment.[78]

Over the years the opposition, or at least part of it, had, for instance, managed to arrogate to itself the name of "Patriots." This was a constant irritant to pro-government writers:

> O, Wretched Name! how thou'rt abus'd of late!
> A Step-stone vile, to mount the troubl'd State;

A Mask deceitful, to conceal from Sight,
Fraud, Envy, Avarice, and burning Spight [sic]!
(The Statesman's Mirrour, p. 10)

The word "patriot" became so contaminated for Walpole's supporters that when Sir Charles Hanbury Williams in 1746 was in the
process of writing a panegyric on the Duke of Cumberland he was
"almost ashamd [sic] to put in the Epithet *Patriot* in the eighth
Stanza. becausc Ld Bath [Pulteney] &c have so vilify'd that Sacred
Word, but it is the True One, & Ld Bath can no longer decieve
[sic]." In 1741 "Philo-Georgius" presented himself to the Duke of
Newcastle as "at the greatest Distance from the Temper of . . . Modern Patriots, who take a pleasure in complaining & Trouble the waters on purpose to find their acct In fishing In them."[79]
   In one of his poems Hanbury Williams described a Patriot as one
who "of Virtue will prate like a saint on a tub."[80] And in several of
his political works dissident Whig personae are allowed to "prate
of Virtue" in such a way as to expose their rhetoric as consisting
only of hollow phrases. This is noticeable, for instance, in "The
Chairman's Speech to the Secret Committee," which was published
soon after Walpole's fall from power and which ridicules the in-
quiry into the last ten years of Walpole's premiership as a parody
of justice. The Chairman, Lord Limerick, is made to lament that
Dodington had not been chosen to sit on the committee since "the
intimacy he once had with the Earl of Orford [Walpole], and the
entire affection he now bears his country, must have been of the
greatest service." Here the phrase "the entire affection he now
bears his country" is simply opposition jargon for "now that he has
joined the opposition against Walpole." Similarly in the poem mentioned earlier entitled "A Political Eclogue," in the confrontation
between Edmund Lechmere's Tory down-to-earth honesty and
George Lyttelton's dissident Whig high-sounding rhetoric, the former is seen as vastly preferable to the latter. Lechmere's outspoken
approach helps expose the fact that Lyttelton uses language to cover
his own selfish plans for the future. And the final words are given
to Lechmere, who more than implies that Lyttelton's words and
thoughts are at odds:

> "What tho' my words are not, like your's, refin'd,
> "Rough tho' they are, they always speak my mind.
> "Freeholders with such language well dispense,
> "And before all the flow'rs of eloquence,
> "Prefer an honest heart, and common sense.[81]

A normal ploy for pro-government writers was to appear to be allowing the readers a look behind the fictional scenes. In *The Three Politicians* Will [Pulteney] says in an aside to Harry [Boling-broke], as they are preparing to impose on the independent Whig Sir Joseph [Jekyll]: "Now let's have much *Wit*, with some appear-ance of *Vertue*. You know 'tis necessary." Forewarned in this way, the reader has no difficulty in recognizing the opposition rhetoric for what it is: cant devoid of all real meaning. The conversation between the three men is overheard by the young drawer at a tavern "who was himself a great *Dabbler* in *Politicks*, read *Fog* and the *Craftsman*, hated *Ministers* and *Excises*, and had a Warm liking for the *Chevalier*." After hearing the conversation, however, "he be-gins to think there are some *Honest* Men in *Place*, and not a few K[na]ves out of *Power*."[82]

Specific Butts for Satire

At least on the surface pro-government satire was far more con-cerned with individual politicians than with general political issues. This practice conforms with the overriding principle behind all mudslinging: in assailing an opponent it is normally easier and more effective to discredit his character than to try to bring his ideas into disrepute. Attacks on individuals rather than on policies were of course very much the norm in the first half of the eighteenth century. Horace Walpole claimed that parliamentary debates, "where no personalities broke out, engaged too little attention."[83] At the same time, it is clear that pro-government writers through the use of personal satire wished to make a political point by insinu-ating that opposition Whigs and Tories, notwithstanding their ag-gressive statements to the contrary, represented no real alternative to government policies, and that their opposition to Walpole was based merely on a wish to supersede him and his allies in office. By focusing on individual politicians and reducing their choice of political allegiance to the level of private ambitions and frustra-tions, pro-government writers sought to undermine the opposition claim that their opposition to Walpole was based on a wish to intro-duce "New Measures" and not "New Men."

Only a few opposition politicians can be said to have been sin-gled out by pro-government writers for regular satirical attention, as representatives of the political groups to which they belonged. It has been calculated that there were 132 dissident Whigs in Parlia-ment after the general election of 1741, but only a handful of these are satirized with any regularity in pro-government works. The same is true of the Tories.

The choice of these victims to represent the whole constellation of politicians that pro-government writers set out to discredit, was largely determined by their places of trust at the head of the opposition, but not only by that. It is noticeable that writers associated with Walpole tend to avoid commenting too freely on the Prince of Wales, who from 1737 onwards was at least nominally at the head of the opposition. This immunity to attack seems to some extent to have spilled over onto his closest associates, who were not satirized as regularly or as virulently as the representatives of the dissident Whigs who looked to Lord Carteret and William Pulteney for leadership. This preference probably reflects an awareness on the part of pro-government writers of where the *real* power in the opposition was located. It is also possible that considerations of respect and even reversionary prudence were instrumental in shielding the heir to the throne from the worst excesses of pro-government satire.

It is also noticeable, that of the two leaders of the "Patriot" Whigs, William Pulteney and Lord Carteret, the former was far more consistently and aggressively satirized than the latter. This curious fact gives rise to speculation. It may be that the unequal load of obloquy cast on these two politicians reflects the fact that already in the eighteenth century the House of Lords was considered less important politically than the House of Commons (on Walpole's fall he persuaded Pulteney to accept a peerage, and joyfully remarked that he had "turned the key of the closet upon him").[84] It could even be that the relative dearth of attacks on Lord Carteret reflected a hope on the government side that Carteret might be persuaded to return to the fold (Carteret seems to have been well liked in certain pro-government circles for his refusal to pander to the masses). If such were the case, it would not do to alienate him further by frequent and vicious attacks. It is also possible that Carteret was spared simply because he did not participate much in the propaganda effort against Walpole; unlike Pulteney, he did not publish pamphlets or write in the *Craftsman*.[85]

Then again, perhaps Carteret was allowed preferential treatment simply because his personality did not lend itself to satiric treatment in the same way that Pulteney's did. Whereas Carteret by all accounts was aristocratically indifferent to other people's opinions ("He will but promise if you praise, | And laugh if you abuse him"),[86] William Pulteney seems to have been acutely sensitive to criticism. Touchy and irascible, he would appear to have been constitutionally incapable of hiding his irritation whenever a satiric attack hit home. This, of course, added to the pleasure felt by those pro-Walpole politicians who could observe him and his allies in the House of Commons. He had proved by the episode that led to his duel with Hervey, whom he took to be the author of a pamphlet actually written by Sir William Yonge, that he could be baited.[87]

As a butt for pro-government satire, William Pulteney also had other elements to recommend him. As one of the leaders of the opposition he was sufficiently eminent to warrant constant satirical attention. He had been one of Walpole's most loyal adherents before he resigned and joined the opposition in 1726. He thus fell into the category of deserters, which received special treatment by pro-government writers. Vulnerable to attack on the basis of his former political record, pointed references could be made on occasion to his activities in connection with the Atterbury case, his voting record, parliamentary speeches on specific issues, etc.[88]

In addition William Pulteney had one ruling weakness that could be exploited effectively in satirical attacks on him: he was notorious for his avarice. Heir to the Pulteney estate which yielded £10,000 a year, he had acquired a fortune through marriage to Anna Maria Gumley, the daughter of a wealthy glass manufacturer, had left himself open to charges of legacy hunting by twice inheriting fortunes from people to whom he was unrelated, was thought to have employed some questionable methods in acquiring wealth, and was found on his death in 1764 to have been worth £400,000 in money and £30,000 a year in land. What he had acquired of wealth, Pulteney would not easily part with. He was famous for making undignified economies, his daughter complaining to a friend about "bad paper, bad ink, & wretched pens." Even his friends did not deny that he had "rather too great a love of money; but . . . not near so great as it was commonly reported and reputed to be," and while they claimed that he devoted a tenth part of his yearly income to charity, they conceded that he was "very strict and exact in all his accounts and payments." It was, therefore, probably quite typical of Lord Bath that although he contributed towards the education of his nephew, the future playwright George Colman the elder, he exacted interest on a loan to the young man, who on presenting his uncle with a gift, received advice to the effect that "there are few friends worth valuing so much as to make oneself a farthing the poorer for."[89] After the fall of Walpole, Pulteney was accused of stinginess towards the writer of the *Craftsman* Nicholas Amhurst who "died, it is supposed of a broken heart; and was buried at the charge of his honest printer."[90]

Even his strong points were turned against him. Pulteney seems to have had considerable talent as an orator: "When he spoke, he had the art to persuade all who heard him, that he felt every sentiment which he uttered. He was pointed, gay, facetious, pathetic, or diffuse, as the argument required; whatever rhetorical weapon he chose to brandish, he was sure to come off victorious, for he was master of them all." In pro-government works, however, he was described as a man whose "frothy Eloquence" was calculated to deceive people and excite the mob to actions detrimental to the stability of the state.[91] Pope was building on a long tradition on the pro-government side when he later in the unfinished "One Thousand Seven Hundred and Forty," satirized Pulteney more memorably than any of the pro-government writers had ever done:

> Thro' Clouds of Passion P[ulteney]'s views are clear,
> He foams a Patriot to subside a Peer;
> Impatient sees his country bought and sold,
> And damns the market where he takes no gold.[92]

A writer who wished to satirize Pulteney had, in short, plenty of material at his disposal. In *A Poetical Essay on Vulgar Praise and Hate*, a typical attack on Pulteney, the anonymous author concentrates on all the elements outlined above, one after the other. He accuses Pulteney of avarice ("He ventur'd Life—nay, more his Money too!"), attributes his political apostasy to private ambition ("He thought his Merit *vast*, his *Rise* but *small*"), and concentrates on the discrepancy between his voting pattern as a one-time Walpole supporter ("Did any thing which might deserve a Smile, | Was Warm in ev'ry Part they could allot, | For Armies spoke, and sanctified a Plot") and as a leading member of the opposition ("With wonted vehemence He harangues the H[ouse], | Against the Things He did Himself espouse"). A long description of Pulteney's alleged shortcomings, and his willingness to co-operate with anybody in opposition to Walpole in order to further his own ends ("Caball'd with Men o'ercharg'd with Public Hate, | And even with branded Traytors to the STATE"), leads up to the question:

> Could one believe that such a *Character*,
> Should even among the Populace seem Fair?
> Yet so it is————and Numbers on *Him* gaze,
> As one whose Merit even Transcends our Praise,
> Yet from those Acts, if we the HERO scan,
> Shew us a meaner Creature————if you can?

> Or dare to say that Reputation's Right,
> Which Leans on Pride, Disloyalty, and Spite.

Pro-government writers extended their attack on Pulteney to include his wife, with whom he is said to have "lived in the vinegar bottle."[93]

Next to Pulteney, the man who received most direct attention in pro-government satire is clearly Henry St. John, Lord Bolingbroke. Although Bolingbroke had been at the head of the Tory government right at the end of Queen Anne's reign, his association with the Jacobite court at Saint-Germain before and after the Hanoverian Succession effectively debarred him from participating in parliamentary debate. He did, however, take an active part in opposition politics, operating as a mentor for both Tories and dissident Whigs, and helping to shape the various groups into what he called "the Country party" which by presenting a united front would emerge as a viable alternative to Walpole's Old Corps Whig. He was thus one of the founders of the *Craftsman*, contributed essays to the newspaper, and thus participated actively in political debate. Naturally Walpole supporters like Henry Harris distrusted him:

> More Mischief was sown in this Country by that Man, under false pretences to Virtue, than ever could have happen'd by the Influence of the most profligate Examples in the World.[94]

In their attacks on him writers associated with Walpole tend to concentrate on two aspects. For one thing, they routinely remind the public of Bolingbroke's known Jacobite connections, claiming that his allegiance to the Pretender was not a thing of the past but still a prime mover behind Bolingbroke's policies. In *A Hue and Cry*, for instance, some of the dogs that have escaped from their parliamentary kennel are marked J. R. (James Rex) and others G. R. (George Rex) but as the mark "of the first is burnt in, and the latter only clipt, so the G. R. is almost (if not quite) worn out in some." All the dogs, irrespective of markings, have been caught by "a *certain Vagabond*, notorious . . . for enticing of Hounds, and carrying them beyond Sea for the Service of a *foreign Prince*."[95]

Secondly, pro-government writers very often highlight Bolingbroke's devious position as a man who actively interfered with contemporary politics despite the fact that his treasonable past debarred him from taking a seat in the House of Lords. To them he was "the *Grand Incendiary*," whose "fine Italian hand" stirred up trouble in the best Machiavellian tradition, and who through more or less secret negotiations was able to manipulate opposition politicians, and through them inflame the unthinking mob.[96]

His ultimate aim—they alleged—was to reduce Britain to utter chaos as a necessary preliminary for bringing over the Pretender. This is clear, for instance, from "The Confession, Impenitence, and Despair of Hal. Gambol [Bolingbroke]," to the tune of "The Dame of Honour," in which Bolingbroke as a persona says:

> I preach that *Peace* will ruin *Trade*,
>   A *War* enrich the *Nation*;
> That *Harmony*'s a Tune ill play'd,
>   And *Order* is *Desolation*:
> That *Laws* will eat up *Liberty*,
>   And *Freedom* quite *enslave* us;
> And that a popish *Tyranny*,
>   The only thing is can *save* us.[97]

Uniformly identified as a Jacobite, Bolingbroke was automatically seen as a person whose word could not be trusted. In 1732 a physician at Guilford named Swithin Adee published *The Craftsman's Apology. Being a Vindication of his Conduct and Writings: In Several Letters to the King*. The persona is Lord Bolingbroke, who in four letters tries to convince the king that he is innocent of treasonable connections with the Pretender's court. True, he did leave hurriedly for France after the death of Queen Anne, but "A Notion so weak can your Council advance, | That all must be wicked who travel to France?" By the second letter Bolingbroke almost admits to his treasonable activities but makes light of them:

> I pretend not indeed to be free from all Crimes,
> Which a Friend would impute to the Fault of the Times;
> But Offences and Errors all human————and such
> As a Man might commit—without sinning too much.

Bolingbroke counters any suspicions that he is politically active behind the scenes by describing himself as leading a pastoral existence in the country ("When my Capons are cram'd, and my Pullets are fed | With what inward Content do I waddle to Bed?"). Besides he is old and decrepit ("My Friends all before, I come puffing behind"), and leads a life divorced from politics:

> The *Post Boy* and *Craftsman* perusing by Fits;
> And scarce know the Time when your Parliament sits;
> At Pooll [sic] at *Picquet*, or a Game at *Quadrille*,

> With my Spouse and *Dick Francklin*—the Top of my Skill;
> Or perhaps in an Eve, when I've little to do,
> I may venture a Shilling with *P[ultene]y* at *Looe*;
> A pamphlet perus'd, or a News-Paper read,
> And creep, when my Prayers are finish'd, to Bed.
> This is all my Employment; just after I dine,
> A Sermon at Three, and my Bible at Nine;
> (A Game now and then at *Black Gammon* I play)
> And a Prayer for your Majesty closes the Day.

In his place he recommends Pulteney to the king as a good Secretary of State ("Himself, the weak Projects of *Spain* to have spoil'd; | Would have got the good Duchess of *Parma* with Child").[98]

Pro-government writers also latched onto the fact that Bolingbroke's wife had perjured herself to obtain some property, solemnly swearing in a court of law that she was not married to Lord Bolingbroke at a time when they were in fact secretly married. Here was another wife that could be used in mock advertisements.[99]

In pro-government writing Bolingbroke is uniformly described as a person for whom the end justifies the means, and who is consequently ready to perjure himself upon the smallest occasion. In *Lord B[olingbro]ke's Speech Upon the Convention*, for instance, he is made to say to his followers,

> For *once* I'll speak Truth, since all here are Friends,
> This cursed Convention won't answer our Ends:
> But 'tis easy its Meaning to construe away,
> And I'll make it speak what it ne'er meant to say.

In fact, in this poem Bolingbroke as a persona behaves very much in the way that opposition writers pictured Walpole as acting as leader, and not merely in his lighthearted lack of respect for the truth. Bolingbroke has absolute control over his supporters, who react to his speech with thundering applause; he brooks no opposition (promptly turning down a motion by Sandys), explains that the truth as such is irrelevant and must always be made subservient to immediate political objectives, and spells out the opposition priorities ("either our Party, or *England*'s undone"). He also reveals that he is not without corrupt election interest ("I'm sure of the M[ayo]r"), and lets drop that he has interest enough in boroughs and City institutions to initiate many local petitions against the government ("Let *Petitions* be drawn—Let L[ON]D[O]N begin, | Each *Port* in the Nation will follow, but *Lynne* [Walpole's borough] | What the *City* shall say I *myself* will prepare . . .").[100]

The royal pardon which allowed Bolingbroke to return to England after years in exile had been obtained while Walpole was in power. The normal theme of ingratitude towards the king and his "Prime Minister" could thus be applied to Bolingbroke with a vengeance, although the truth is that Walpole had been opposed to his restitution. A variation on the theme of ingratitude is found in *A Letter From Walpole to the Lord Bolingbroke* in which the anonymous author attributed the opposition's anti-French stance to Bolingbroke and charged him ironically with ingratitude towards the country which "so kindly received and entertained you when your Guilt made you fly your own Country."[101]

In conformity with the opposition practice of lumbering Walpole with nicknames (Sir Bluestring, Sir Blue, etc.), pro-government writers did their best to provide nicknames for prominent opposition politicians. Among the names that stuck were Harry Gambol for Lord Bolingbroke and Squire Squab and William Wildfire for William Pulteney. The sobriquet Harry Gambol goes back to Queen Anne's reign.[102]

THE *CRAFTSMAN* AND OTHER OPPOSITION NEWSPAPERS

One may suspect that one of the reasons why William Pulteney and Lord Bolingbroke were at the receiving end of more antigovernment satire than any other opposition politicians was their involvement with the *Craftsman*. As founders of, and active contributors to, the main opposition organ, they were representatives—indeed the embodiments—of a phenomenon that pro-government writers must have found extremely frustrating. Right from the start the *Craftsman* had acquired a high reputation for writing. According to the Jacobite Member of Parliament William Shippen, pro-government authors were—at least on one occasion—"entirely outwrote by the other side." Even such a dedicated Walpole supporter as Samuel Madden admitted in a private letter to the "Prime Minister" that the *Craftsman* had "a greater Reputation for Wit, & Talents for dispute, than those who every Week write against him" and that the newspaper had shown itself "a superior Master of the arts to catch the Crowd." The press informer "John Smith" felt that the writers associated with the *Craftsman* were worthy of government notice, whereas "the rest of the crowd of Political Railers carp for Bread & throw out impudent Scandals to avoid Starving."[103]

Frequently pro-government writers tried to treat the *Craftsman* as so much below contempt as to be scarcely worth taking notice of, with Thomas Newcomb suggesting that Walpole was less envied for his "sovereign's smile, | And *Britain*'s love, than *Danvers*' hate."[104] That this was no more than a pose is suggested by all the attention lavished on the newspaper in pro-government productions. It is true to say that from its first inception in 1726 the *Craftsman* was like the proverbial thorn in Walpole's side. Despite James Bramston's assertion in *The Art of Politicks* that "who puts Caleb's Country-Craftsman out, | Is still a secret, and the World's in doubt," it was of course generally known that Nicholas Amhurst, under the pseudonym of Caleb D'Anvers, was responsible for the day-to-day activities of the newspaper, but that Pulteney and Bolingbroke were occasional contributors. Opposition Members of Parliament were called informally "the danverians" by government supporters. At the same time pretended ignorance on this subject could occasionally be part of a strategy to annoy those involved, as when one pro-government pamphleteer remarked on "the *Craftsman* and *Fog's Journal*, those infamous Retailers of Lies, Scandals, sedition, and Treason: At once the Demonstration and the Reproach of that unlimited Freedom we enjoy, and the Lenity and Goodness of that King and that Government which the Authors are hired to defame. If any of the worthy Authors may be offended at my supposing they are paid for their Labours, let this plead my Excuse, that I imagine it impossible for any Man who affects the Name of a Gentleman, to suffer such Obloquy and *Billingsgate* to drop from his Pen."[105] Both William Pulteney and Lord Bolingbroke were sometimes attacked under the name of Caleb D'Anvers, but normally such attacks were directed at Nicholas Amhurst, "Truth and Reason's Foe," whose pen could, with verisimilitude be presented as venal ("For he fights, like a Switzer, alone for his pay").[106]

In 1729 John Mottley wrote an amusing attack on the opposition in *The Craftsman; or the Weekly Journalist, A Farce*, in which a political dimension is added to the traditional theme of lovers who can only be united in matrimony by fooling stubborn old fathers. In this farce Sir Whimsical Watchit, "*an old Country Knight, a great Admirer of the Author of the* Craftsman," of "*Grumble Hall* in the County of Warwick" has a lovely daughter, Melissa. She is in love with Caleb D'Anvers's cousin. As part of the young people's plan, the hero, although of a different political persuasion, has prevailed on his cousin to let him use his lodgings and write two or three issues of the *Craftsman*, although he readily admits that he has "not naturally the Spleen and Rancour, nor all the abusive Talents of the real Author of the *Country Journal*." In fact the young man leaves most of the business of writing the papers to his man Trap, who complains that "one Fort-night more qualifies me for a Mad-House":

> What a Heap of Inconsistencies Have I every Day jumbled in my Head! Murders and Marriages, Balls and Burials, Sonnets and Slander, Epigrams, Riddles, History, Houses o' Fire, Law, Love, Mathematicks, the Plague, the Pox, with the whole Family of P's. Some Things indeed we fling into the Fire, but then we are forc'd, you know, to transcribe all the Nonsense that comes from the *Squirts*, the *Squibbs*, and the *Squats*, altho' they oblige us to contradict this Week, what they made us affirm the last; not to mention our Articles of Foreign News, and the Difficulty of picking such Things out of them as may serve the Turn of your Cousin's Patrons.

When asked what material has come in, Trap replies that "*Sham-Title* the Bookseller" has sent over another article about the Knez Menzikoff and various insalubrious stories, and that "Mr. *Pestle* the Apothecary in *Abchurch-lane*" has requested that his advertisement should be repeated "only let the long Worm be transferr'd from the Farriers Wife at *Westchester*, to any Body you think fit in the *North* (Cousin D'Anvers: "That Worm has been voided by at least fifteen People already").[107]

This often genuinely funny farce expresses familiar pro-government complaints about the *Craftsman*, summed up in Sir Whimsical's praise of the man he takes to be Caleb D'Anvers:

> You have deserv'd well of every honest *Englishman*; Odd you have maul'd the other Side; and tho' you can't with Truth or Safety, come to Particulars, yet you have pay'd them off with *Inuendo's*. O how I admire your excellent Invectives! 'Tis no Difficulty to abuse a Person that we know is an ill Man; but the Art is to make a *Woolsey* or a *Menzikoff*, of one we are convinc'd is honest and deserving, when we are resolv'd to hate him. This is what we all love you for.

The reason Sir Whimsical approves of all this is that he foresees that both he and Caleb D'Anvers will be able to obtain places once Walpole is disposed of, a consideration that weighs heavily with him when he decides to dispose of his daughter in marriage to the impostor.[108]

Pro-government writers ridiculed the opposition press—and especially the *Craftsman*—on several counts, particularly on the way in which the newspaper constantly sailed close to sedition, while taking care through the liberal use of parallels, italics, historical allusions, etc. to escape prosecution. In a pamphlet published in

1731, Caleb D'Anvers was proclaimed dead ("In vain we cry'd out, in vain we held our Tongues; | for oh! he was *dead! dead! dead!*"). Buried with him in a coffin inscribed "*Caleb D'Anvers, Esq; Patriot-General of Great Britain,*" and lined with the title pages of several of his pamphlets, is a complete set of his "*Weekly Lucubrations,* neatly bound in *Spanish* Leather, on the Back of which, are letter'd—*Dirt to Dirt, Mire to Mire, Dung to Dung.*" The wailing and lamentations occasioned by the death of "the Patriot-General" emphasize the ephemeral nature of the writing contained in the newspaper:

> Where [are] the shrewd *Remarks* thou hast written on History, and where the History thou hast *forg'd* for the sake of those Remarks? Where are now thy harmless *unmeaning Parallels,* thy *innocent well-grounded Innuendo's,* thy well-loved *Capitals,* and witty *Italicks?*[109]

That the opposition was distorting history in order to provide what Howard Weinbrot has called "legal camouflage" was a constant complaint:

> The *Craftsman* finding that the Character of *Sejanus, Wolsey,* or any other of the wickedest Ministers that have been delivered down to us by Historians, would, upon the least Wink of his to his usual Readers, be applied by them to a Minister now in Being, has been very industrious in exhibiting all the bad Ministers he could muster up, in the blackest Colours: In this he indulges himself the more freely, because he thinks it the safest, and knows 'tis the most mischevous [sic] Way of defaming . . . The *Craftsman* was hugely delighted with the Fall of the *Knez Menzikoff* in 1727, because it furnished him with such a Picture of that Minister as he thought the Generality of his Readers would easily fancy had the Resemblance of another. It was with peculiar Pleasure therefore that in one of his Papers he inserted two of the Articles charged upon *Menzicoff,* distinguishing the applicable Words by Italicks . . . But least any of the dullest of his Admirers should have simply imagined that the Charge against *Menzikoff* was against *Menzikoff,* he resumed the same Subject in another Paper, and directly explained his Meaning, by pretending to Explain the *Knez's* Title of *Toxteth* . . . "*Taxtaker: Whether . . . This may be translated a* Lord of the Treasury (*who amongst us, hath the Care and Superintendency of all the publick Taxes*) *I can't say.*"[110]

Many pro-government works set out to ridicule this ploy used so regularly by the writers for the opposition, and of which they and their readers never seemed to tire. In the dialogue of *The Oak and the Dunghill,* the Dunghill (the opposition) hurls the following invectives at the Oak (Walpole):

Thou Plunderer! grown rich by Crimes:
Thou *Woolsey* of the modern Times!
Thou curst *Sejanus* of the Plain!
Thou Slave, of a *Tiberian* Reign!
Empson and *Dudley*!————————Star and Garter!————
A *Knez*!————a *Menzicoff*!————a *Tartar*! (p. 4)

Some pro-government pamphleteers pointed out "how easy such Historical Masks and Daggers are to be found."[111]

Unfortunately, many pro-government writers followed the *Craftsman*'s lead and searched history for examples of unscrupulous politicians who for opportunistic reasons had raised oppositions against lawful authority and exemplary administrations, and sinister and evil factions that had brought destruction and chaos to happy and well-regulated communities. Thomas Cooke settled on the traitor Edric as a parallel to Lord Bolingbroke. In a print entitled "The Funeral of Faction" Faction is carried to "*the Family Vault*," which is inscribed "*to the Memory of Wat Tyler Jack Straw Kitt the Tanner Jack Cade*."[112] In these exercises they did not scruple to follow the example of their opposition counterparts and bend history to suit their own purposes. In answer to the opposition's list of ministerial villains, on which the names of Wolsey and Pierce Gaveston featured prominently, pro-government writers produced that of excellent statesmen (Morton, Audley, Sir Edward Poynings, Burleigh, Clarendon, Somers, Godolphin, etc.).[113] When opposition writers lauded to the skies monarchs who had been "patrons of the spirit of liberty" and ruled without "first ministers" (Queen Elizabeth, Edward III, Henry V) pro-government writers produced touching portraits of monarchs who had had the wisdom to choose excellent ministers in whom they reposed complete trust (again Queen Elizabeth, Edward III, Henry V).[114] Tickell complimented the queen *On Her Majesty's Re-Building the Lodgings of the Black Prince, and Henry V, At Queen's-College Oxford* in 1733. In praising these two princes, Tickell expressed the hope that Prince William would wish to "grace | His Mother's walls":

How would that Genius, whose propitious wings
Have here Twice hover'd o'er the Sons of Kings,
Descend triumphant to his ancient seat,
And take in charge a Third PLANTAGENET.[115]

Both sides had their favorite historical figures, and criticized those of their opponents. Veritable battles were fought over the interpretation of specific episodes in English or general history. As

Christine Gerrard has shown, this was especially true of the reign of Queen Elizabeth, with both sides scouring her reign for indications that the great queen would have favored their particular policies. With regard to more recent history the argument often focused on the great Whig hero the Duke of Marlborough and the Tory peace treaty of Utrecht:

> When two vile Statesmen [Harley and Bolingbroke] in dire
> Compact join'd,
> Fully in all Things, but in Honour, skill'd,
> Employ'd their Arts one Woman to betray;
> And fond of Greatness at their Country's Cost,
> Sunk in an Hour, ten Years successful War.
> > (George Spiltimber, *The Statesman*, p. 7)

> Ungrateful Country! [France, this time] to forget so soon,
> All that great ANNA for thy Sake has done:
> When sworn the kind Defender of thy Cause,
> Spite of her dear Religion, spite of Laws;
> For thee she sheath'd the Terrors of her Sword,
> For thee she broke her General————and her Word:
> For thee her Mind in doubtful Terms she told,
> And learn'd to speak like Oracles of old.
> For thee, for thee alone, what could she more?
> She lost the Honour she had gain'd before;
> Lost all the Trophies, which her Arms had won,
> (Such, CESAR [sic] never knew, nor PHILIP's Son)
> Resign'd the Glories of a ten Year's Reign,
> And such as none but MARLBOROUGH's Arm could gain.
> For thee, in Annals, she's content to shine
> Like other Monarchs of her ancient Line.[116]

The quarrel over historical personages extended to earlier times as well, however. In 1732 Lord Bolingbroke's attack in the *Craftsman* on the corruption of Athens under Pericles, was followed promptly a week later by a defence of Pericles in two of the newspapers sponsored by Walpole.[117] The fact that both political groups were in competition for the appropriation of historical figures, is recognized in the following lines, with a note attached, of a poem written by the opposition sympathizer Paul Whitehead:

> Down, down, ye hungry Gazetteers, descend,
> Call * *W---e Burleigh*, call him *Britain*'s Friend;

* See these two Characters compar'd in the *Gazetteers*; but lest none of those Papers should have escap'd their common Fate, see the two Characters distinguish'd in the *Craftsman*.[118]

One government supporter predicted that with time the Walpole era would become the subject of debate for rival political groups intent on appropriating the past:

> As we now struggle, future Times
> Shall struggle, with Imputed Crimes.
> When we shall rest, false Patriots still
> Shall call their own, the Public Weal,
> Bent some great Statesman to o'erthrow,
> Shall on our Age their Praise bestow;
> In WALPOLE's Times it was not so.
> He then shall swell the Trump of Fame,
> And faction skulk behind his Name;
> Mouth'd by each Patriot proud and surly,
> They'll play him off as you do *Burleigh*
>
> (*Pro and Con*, p. 4)

Nobody seems to have expected history writing to be a politically neutral activity in Walpole's days, although few went as far as Mrs Catherine Macaulay allegedly did later in the century: she was accused of systematically destroying any manuscripts containing unflattering information about the Stuarts that she came across in public libraries. The emphasis on "the exemplary significance of historical study" had become part of the Whig tradition by the 1690s. Following this tradition, Bolingbroke saw history as "philosophy teaching by examples."[119] Naturally, such an attitude towards history encouraged deliberate distortion. In the words of William Oldys, under certain circumstances "History descends as corrupted to posterity through the willful partiality of the knowing, as through all the involuntary imperfections of ignorance." It is therefore small wonder that Walpole himself once stopped his son Horace from reading aloud to him from a history book with the words, "O do not read history, for that I know must be false."[120]

Pro-government writers routinely accused opposition newspapers of jeopardizing the very stability of the state. Often the Jacobite specter was raised. In the *Senator* we are told of *Mist's Daily Journal* and the *Craftsman* that "both their Schemes are Jacobitism," but whereas the first is "bold & generous" the other is "cautious and subtle."[121] After Mist was prosecuted in 1728 he changed the title of his newspaper to *Fog's,* and it was generally accepted that the paper had become emaciated as the owner was forced to tone down its political contents. Not so in some pro-government eyes. As far as they were concerned the owner was still a Jacobite, and consequently his newspaper remained the same. In *A Coalition of*

Patriots Delineated we find the following characterization of the two main opposition newspapers, which contradicts everything that has most recently been said on the subject of *Fog's*:

> The CRAFTSMAN is *something* the more *cautious* of the *Two*; he guards his *Treason* best; and plays an *under Part*; and appears to have a little of the *Fear* of the *Gallows* before his Eyes; whilst his *worthy Brother*, and *Fellow-Labourer* FOGG [sic], seems to have thrown off *all Restraint*: The *Craftsman* is *underhand*, doing the JACOBITE's *Druggery*, their *dirty Work* for them; but the OTHER *audaciously*, and with *Impudence* not to be match'd, *speaks out*; he *scorns* to *disguise* the Matter, as almost *every Paper* he writes will *witness*; He not only *provokes* [sic]; but even *defies* the Justices of *his Country*. (p. 27)

Despite its contemporary reputation, it has to be admitted that the *Craftsman* was repetitive, to say the least. Erasmus Philips, whose *Country Gentleman* folded in 1726 after a run of less than a year, complained that neither Walpole's "vices nor his blunders could furnish materials to fill up two essays a week."[122] When this newspaper changed hands and its name to the *Craftsman*, its patrons, however, remained undeterred, and faithfully filled the pages of the (first twice-weekly, later weekly) newspaper with variations on the same basic theme: Walpole's unconstitutional, corrupt, and incapable use of power. New events and policies gave them the possibility of presenting their material from new angles, but basically their strategy remained unchanged. They focused on financial and moral corruption, the unconstitutional subversion of the liberties of British subjects, and mismanagement in general. When pro-government writers claimed that the language employed in opposition propaganda had over the years became standardized to the point of being practically meaningless, they naturally targeted an opponent considered as formidable as the *Craftsman*. A ballad entitled "Journalists Displayed," first printed in two rival newspapers, is a case in point:

> DEAR Friend, have you heard the fantastical Chimes,
>   *Ribbledum, Scribbledum, Fribbledum, Flash,*
> As sung by the *Journalists*, all of our Times?
>   *Satyrum, Traytorum, Treasondom* [sic], *Trash.*
> Popery, Slavery, Bribery, Knavery,
> Irruptions, Corruptions, and Some-body's Fall,
>   Pensions and Places, Removes and Disgraces,
>   And something and nothing, the Devil and all.

These Sparks they eternally harp on a String:
    Ribbledum, Scribbledum, Fribbledum, Flash,
And this is the Song they on *Saturdays* sing,
    Satyrum, Traytorum, Treasondum, Trash;
Popery, Slavery, Bribery, Knavery,
Irruptions, Corruptions, and Some-body's Fall,
    Pensions and Places, Removes and Disgraces,
    And something and nothing, the Devil and all.

In poreing you need not your Spirits to pall,
    Ribbledum, Scribbledum, Fribbledum, Flash
For when you've read One of them, then you've read All,
    Satyrum, Traytorum, Treasondum, Trash;
Popery, Slavery, Bribery, Knavery,
Irruptions, Corruptions, and Some-body's Fall,
    Pensions and Places, Removes and Disgraces,
    And something and nothing, the Devil and all.

To frighten the Mob, all Inventions they try,
    Ribbledum, Scribbledum, Fribbledum, Flash
But Money's their Aim, tho' their Country's the Cry,
    Satyrum, Traytorum, Treasondum, Trash;
Popery, Slavery, Bribery, Knavery,
Irruptions, Corruptions, and Some-body's Fall,
    Pensions and Places, Removes and Disgraces,
    And something and nothing, the Devil and all.

That the Joke is a stale one, we very well know,
    Ribbledum, Scribbledum, Fribbledum, Flash,
'Twas just the same, Ages and Ages ago,
    Satyrum, Traytorum, Treasondum, Trash;
Popery, Slavery, Bribery, Knavery,
Irruptions, Corruptions, and Some-body's Fall,
    Pensions and Places, Removes and Disgraces,
    And something and nothing, the Devil and all.

I'll tell you the Way, these Complainants to quell,
    Ribbledum, Scribbledum, Fribbledum, Flash,
Give all of them Places, and all will be well,
    Satyrdum, Traytorum, Treasondum, Trash;
'Twill be no more Slavery, Bribery, Knavery,
Irruptions, Corruptions, and Some-body's Fall,
    But stand up for Royalty! punish Disloyalty!
    Stock it and Pocket the Devil and all.[123]

11

"When Wit with Malice is in League Combin'd": Pope Unmasked

The story goes that some time after Alexander Pope's death in 1744, Hanbury Williams, on being rowed up the Thames past the poet's house at Twickenham, insisted on keeping to the opposite bank, and holding his hat under his arm, quoted Falstaff's line "I am afraid of that *Gunpowder*, *Percy*, though he be dead." Clearly Sir Charles counted himself lucky to have been one of the few pro-government writers to have escaped Pope's ire, although there may be a reference to him in the unfinished poem "One Thousand Seven Hundred and Forty," lumped together with "Hervey and Hervey's school, F[ox] H[anbury] H[inton]."[1]

His reputation as a satirist made Pope a dreaded man in pro-government circles. Commenting on Lord Hervey's literary attacks on Pope, Hanbury Williams wrote to his friend Henry Fox:

> Would a prudent man choose to engage Mr. Pope? His English may not be grammar but 'tis intelligible, and his abuse may not be true, but 'tis very lasting.[2]

When a pro-government author published a work under his own name, a feeling of unease at the prospect of possible reactions from Pope and his friends can sometimes be discerned. Writing to thank Thomas Cooke for including kind references to himself in his latest work, Lewis Theobald hoped that this would not draw upon him "some sneer from Mr. *Pope*'s immediate partisans." Similarly, when the young Warburton provided some criticisms of Pope to be included in a work by Theobald the latter insisted that as "a very reasonable caution . . . what is gleaned from them should come out anonymous; for I should be loth to have a valued friend subjected, on my account, to the outrages of Pope, virulent though impotent." Asking advice from Warburton, Theobald explained, "my diffidence of my own strength, and my conviction of yours, makes me

216

very desirous to be safe before I venture to launch out too far."
When Stephen Duck moved to the vicinity of Pope's neighborhood
at Twickenham, Dr. Alured Clarke was worried: "the friendship
and assistance of Mr. Pope would be very serviceable to him, or, at
least, it would be prudent not to expose him to the malice of the
Dunciad Club, which perhaps might be the case if some little court
be not paid." Under the circumstances, it is less cause for wonder
that many pro-government writers treated Pope with tact than that
so many of them actually did take part in a literary campaign
against him and his allies. Cibber was far from the only one of their
number who tried to "have the last Word" with Pope.[3]

Of opposition writers, Pope certainly got his lion's share of pro-
government attention, far more than Fielding, Gay, and even Swift,
although the last mentioned was sometimes linked with Pope under
various appellations ("the *Marmozette* [sic] and *dingy Dean*," for
instance).[4]

It is hardly surprising how many of the writers ranged against
Pope were of the pro-government side, even though for many years
the attacks on him concentrated on literary matters: on his translations of the *Iliad* and the *Odyssey*, and his edition of Shakespeare.
Both as a translator and as an editor, Pope was vulnerable to criticism. Although he had translated Homer with great spirit, his limitations as a Greek scholar were exposed in confrontation with more
knowledgeable opponents. Thomas Cooke, Matthew Concanen,
and Lewis Theobald, among others, pointed to passages in Pope's
translations where he had clearly misunderstood Homer's words.
Pope retaliated by accusing them of pedantry in *The Dunciad* and
in *Peri Bathous*. Joseph Mitchell is said to have persuaded Pope,
with whom he had become acquainted on his first arrival in London
in the early 1720s, to leave him out of *The Dunciad*. But most authors on the Walpole side were, of course, satirized in this work and
a number of them responded to the challenge. Thomas Cooke, for
instance, attacked the work in his *Battle of the Poets. In Two Cantos*, and in the *Letters of Atticus*. The literary quarrel that ensued
was so violent that although Pope—according to his sister, Mrs
Racket—continued his evening walks "he would take Bounce with
him; and for some time carried pistols in his pocket."[5]

For a long time subsequently critics tended almost automatically
to take Pope's side in this literary quarrel. A more balanced view is
now being put forward, however, which exonerates Theobald and
his friends from the worst charges of dullness in this respect. In
criticizing Pope as translator and editor they were basically correct.[6]

The interesting thing is that even these early attacks on Pope, ostensibly nonpolitical in their concern with his literary abilities and general knowledge, may in fact have been at least partly politically motivated. In a short biography of his friend Thomas Cooke, published serially in the *Gentleman's Magazine*, Joseph Maubey declared that: "The spirit of party ran high in the time of *George* the First; and, as Cooke was considered as an excellent Greek scholar, perhaps party first induced him to enter the lists against Pope" (of course the use of the word "party" here does not automatically suggest "political" party). There is also a suspicious ring to Theobald's assertion that he had originally intended only to write emendations and remarks on Shakespeare, but the subscribers requested an edition (which became a competitor to Pope's edition) "and some Noble persons then, whom I have no privilege to name, were pleased to interest themselves so far in the affair, as to propose to Mr. Tonson his undertaking an impression of Shakespeare with my corrections."[7] There would not seem to have been a concerted pro-government campaign against Pope at that time, however. A prominent Walpole supporter like Joseph Mitchell wrote flatteringly of Pope and Swift and their group as late as 1729, and they on their side subscribed to his *Poems on Several Occasions*, published by Pope's protégé Lawton Gilliver in that same year.

At what precise moment Pope came to be considered as associated with the opposition, is not clear. There had, of course, been tension between him and certain Whig writers as early as 1713 over Addison's *Cato*. A year later Sir Thomas Burnet (Whig) inserted a satirical compliment to Pope in his friend George Duckett's *Homerides*, on the grounds that "friends in Town" insisted that "the Compliment to him seemed proper, because that Addison & the rest of the Rhiming Gang have dropt their Resentment against the *Lordlike Man*." Despite attempts by Garth to make the two men friends, Burnet considered Pope "an illnatured little false Dog" and expressed dislike for Addison's "caressing Pope, whom at the same Time he hates worse than Belzebub & by whom he has been more than once lampooned." Burnet was, however, prepared to concede that Pope "did not want for a great deal of very diverting Satyrical Wit."[8]

For most of his career Pope tried to present himself as politically nonpartisan, his ethos that of a reasonable man, independent in his political comments ("In Moderation placing all my Glory, | While Tories call me Whig, and Whigs a Tory"). This was, however, not a view of Pope shared by pro-government writers. In response to Pope's assertion in the notes to the *Odyssey* that he was no party man, Concanen later claimed that this was "no way reconcilable to several Passages in the *Dunciad*," instancing two examples of "*Royal-Slander*." And about the *Miscellanies*, Concanen wrote: "If I mistake not, the greatest part of them are political inflammatory Pamphlets."[9] Simon Varey has suggested that the Scriblerians may "after all" have been connected with the main opposition newspaper and that Pope was "close to the *Craftsman*" while Arbuthnot, Gay, and Swift "had something to do with the paper."[10] In 1731 Orator Henley certainly accused Pope of writing for the opposition:

> We are told that Mr. P[op]e wrote the Poem call'd *The Dawley Farm* and the *Norfolk Steward*, besides several Letters in *Fog* and *Craftsman*; if so, he is very ungrateful to some of his Subscribers and Benefactors. But is Gratitude to a Protestant a tye on a Papist . . . ?[11]

Howard Erskine-Hill believes that Pope was not generally held to be writing opposition satire before the year 1734,[12] and it is certainly true that as late as 1733 we find, for instance, Paul Whitehead in his anti-government poem *The State-Dunces* urging Pope to write for the opposition in defence of William Pulteney ("Can *Pope* be silent, and not grateful lend, | One Strain to sing the *Patriot*, and the *Friend*; | Who nobly anxious in his Country's Cause, | Maintains her Honours, and defends her Laws"). However, many pro-government writers and supporters in general regarded Pope as a political enemy long before 1734. Ambrose Philips's "constant cry was, that Mr. P. was an *Enemy to the Government*."[13] And the critic John Dennis is recorded as saying:

> I regard him . . . as an *Enemy*, not so much to me, as to my King, to my Country, to my Religion, and to that Liberty which has been the sole felicity of my life . . . Reputation (as Hobbes says) is *Power*, and *that has made him dangerous*. Therefore I look on it as my duty to *King George*, whose faithful subject I am; to my *Country*, of which I have appeared a constant lover; to the *Laws*, under whose protection I have so long lived; and to the *Liberty* of my *Country*, more dear to me than life, of which I have now for forty years been a constant assertor . . . to pull the lion's skin from this little Ass, which popular error has thrown round him; and to shew that this Author, who has been lately so much in vogue, has neither Sense in his thoughts, nor English in his Expressions.[14]

In certain pro-government quarters, Pope, as a Catholic, was almost automatically suspected of harboring sympathies for the House of Stuart. It has to be remembered, after all, that Pope grew up in a pro-Jacobite environment: at the age of twelve he started to write an epic on the subject of Alcander, driven from his throne, a work which he burnt "by the advice of the Bishop of Rochester, a little before he went abroad," exiled for life by Parliament for his participation in the Jacobite plot named after him.[15] Pope's behavior to the queen was considered highly suspect:

> The late Queen Caroline declared her intention of honoring Mr. Pope with a visit at Twickenham. His mother was then alive; and, lest the visit should give her pain, on account of the danger his religious principles might incur by an intimacy with the Court, his piety made him, with great duty and humility, beg that he might decline this honour. Some years after, his mother being dead, the Prince of Wales condescended to do him the honour of a visit. [The prince humorously asked how Pope reconciled his "love to a Prince" with his "professed indisposition to Kings"][16]

Others claimed that Pope's action had nothing at all to do with his mother but was done "to gratify the ridiculous pride and passions of Swift." Whatever the reason, his actions rendered him suspect to pro-government writers. Alured Clarke wrote to Mrs Clayton: "I am not fond of paying compliments to Mr. Pope; I think he deserves them not from anybody that has a true love for the Royal Family."[17]

The relationship between Pope and Walpole himself is extremely hard to pin down. Pope was by his own admission "civilly treated by Walpole." At some point before his death in 1721, Pope's friend Secretary of State James Craggs offered Pope a government pension of £300, explaining that "as he had the management of the secret-service money in his hands, he could pay . . . such a pension yearly without any one's knowing" ("I declined even this").[18] In 1725 Pope received £200 from the Treasury as encouragement to translate the *Odyssey*,[19] with the "Prime Minister" and the Secretary of State Lord Townshend later subscribing for ten sets each of the work. Pope and Walpole had several mutual friends, staunch Old Corps Whigs like Samuel Buckley and William Fortescue. The latter seems to have worked "to keep the two men on polite terms" in the late 1720s. Walpole visited the poet at Twickenham in 1725, and as late as June 1730 Pope dined with Walpole at his house in Chelsea.[20]

Even in the late 1730s Pope continued to treat Walpole with what one critic has called "guarded respect." In 1739 he wrote to Swift: "The Ministerial Writers rail at me, yet I have no quarrel with their Masters, nor think it of weight enough to complain of them."[21] Walpole's strange immunity from attack is acknowledged by Pope himself in the *Epilogues to the Satires*:

> Sure, if I spare the Minister, no rules
> Of Honour bind me, not to maul his Tools.

These lines raise the question of what "rules of Honour" bound Pope to spare the minister. Howard Erskine-Hill accepts the possibility that Walpole may have had some kind of unspecified hold on Pope, at least between 1724 and 1728. E. P. Thompson has speculated on the possibility that Walpole may have had evidence linking a member of Pope's family to Jacobite activities and that he was holding the threat of exposure over Pope's head.[22] I think this unlikely since Pope uses the words "rules of Honour," which would hardly cover a case of blackmail. Besides, the references to Walpole in Pope's published poems seem warmer than could have been expected in such a case. William Warburton was later to link Pope's reticence on the subject of Sir Robert Walpole to gratitude in connection with preferment obtained for his friend Edward Southcote, a priest in the Catholic Church:

> Poor Mr. Pope received just such a favour from Southcote, and he never was easy till he got him a rich Abbey in Flanders, which he did by the interest of Sir Robert Walpole and his brother Horace, with the Court of France; on which account it was, he always spared those two in his Satires, and highly complimented the elder.[23]

Warburton's testimony deserves attention, since few of his contemporaries can have been more in the know. Although he eventually became so friendly with Pope as to be appointed his literary executor, Warburton was for many years associated with pro-government writers such as Matthew Concanen and Lewis Theobald, participating actively in their campaign against Pope. Warburton's story is confirmed by Joseph Spence who added the information that when the Abbey became vacant Pope wrote a letter "the next morning, to Sir Robert Walpole, (with whom he had then some degree of friendship) and begged him to write a letter to Cardinal Fleury to get the Abbey for Southcote."[24]

As time went by, it became more and more difficult for Pope to pretend to be politically neutral. Inspired by his friend Lord Bolingbroke, his verse became increasingly suspect to Old Corps Whig readers. Paul Whitehead was not the only opposition writer to suggest that the government was afraid to touch Pope:

> Pope writes unhurt—but know, 'tis different quite
> To beard the Lion, and to crush the Mite.
> Safe may he dash the Statesman in each Line,
> Those dread his Satire, who dare punish mine.
>
> *(Manners*, p. 14)

Perhaps Walpole felt about Pope as President De Gaulle is said to have felt about Jean-Paul Sartre and his acts of civil disobedience: "On n'emprisonne pas Voltaire." However, the following lines of Pope's poem "To Augustus," first published in 1737, appear to have been discussed in the King's Council:

> Let Ireland tell, how Wit upheld her cause,
> Her Trade supported, and supplied her Laws;
> And leave on SWIFT this grateful verse ingrav'd,
> The Rights a Court attack'd, a Poet sav'd.

But a proposal to have Pope arrested was rejected. Since the allusion was to the last reign it "was decided to avoid a confrontation, and the government press would appear to have been held back."[25] This decision was probably based on more than a reluctance to imprison the most distinguished poet of the age and invite bad publicity. A successful legal prosecution was no foregone conclusion even at the best of times, but when the government had to contend with an opponent of Pope's obvious intelligence, the outcome would have been uncertain, to say the least. Pope's political allusions are at the same time so obvious and so discreet that to have brought him to court would have been hazardous. His assertion in "Windsor Forest," for instance, that conditions in Britain under Queen Anne were such that "peace and plenty tell, a STUART reigns," could not but sound a Jacobite note, given that the poem was published at a time when the queen's health was failing and not everyone was willing to accept the future Hanoverian Succession. To prove in a court of law, however, that this had been Pope's intention would obviously have presented government lawyers with a major problem.[26]

It has been suggested that Walpole for many years hoped that he could persuade Pope to write for him, or at least remain neutral in the polemical warfare between opposition and government writers. This was not only because he feared Pope's abilities as a satirist. As already mentioned, Walpole intervened to suppress one of Odell's poems satirizing Pope. Significantly, this was not done to shield the poet, but because Walpole feared that the attack "might hurt his interest with Lord Chesterfield and some other noblemen who favoured Mr. Pope for his fine genius." We can only speculate on the identity of the "other noblemen," but Lord Chesterfield went into opposition over the Excise scheme in 1733. As several other doubtful government supporters defected to the opposition at about the same time (notably Lord Cobham), Walpole could presumably afford to pay less attention to Pope's popularity with some of his own supporters. It would seem that the pro-government writers were then free to attack Pope on political grounds, for soon Concanen and others were using Pope's translation of the Thersites sections against him ("But chief he glory'd with licentious Stile, | To lash the Great, and Monarchs to revile"). Newcomb accused Pope of being willing to countenance politicians who "Inspire sedition, faction raise;| Insult thy king————thy country sell."[27]

Even before the attacks on Pope became explicitly political, writers associated with Walpole saw themselves as forming a team in a war between themselves and Pope and his allies. Thus Lewis Theobald could describe Leonard Welsted as "a Gentleman of our Faction." Clearly outsiders recognized the basic two-partite structure of the contemporary literary scene. In subscribing for a set of Theobald's edition of *Shakespeare Restored*, Lord Tyrconnel made it clear that as a friend of Pope's his name was not to appear on the list of subscribers. The editor, anxious to include Tyrconnel's name, urged that "Shakespeare I apprehend to be of no Party: & that I shall have the Names of many Persons of Quality very intimately attach'd to Mr. Pope, & Advocates for all his Merit," but to no avail. He had to be content with "his Money *tacito nomine*."[28] Similarly, when Pope's "Epistle to Burlington" was published, and the poet was accused—rightly or wrongly—of having modeled his Timon on the Duke of Chandos to whom he owed favors, Theobald wrote to Warburton,

> Pope, as you'll find, has lent me an accidental lift by his
> Poem on Taste: for the Duke of Chandos, whom I never
> knew or approach'd, has subscrib'd for 4 Setts of my
> Shakespeare on Royal Paper.[29]

The polarity was such that people's reactions to new works were in some measure determined by whether or not they belonged to the same group as the author. In 1733 Anthony Henley wrote to Thomas Cooke,

> You surprise me at the Slight you put upon the Essays which Mr. *Pope*
> now owns, since I was influenced by you to read them, whether from

the Worth of the Thing, or your Recommendation, I cannot say, but I will endeavour to think ill of them, since you disapprove them.[30]

Similarly, contemporaries often felt that attacks on them were not only undeserved and unfair, but motivated solely by their allegiance to one group or the other. Conyers Middleton complained to Lord Hervey:

> I was surprized to find my name at it's [sic] full length in Pope's last piece, for I had always receiv'd civilities from him; but he does me ye greatest honour, when he treats me as Your Lordship's friend . . . I cannot guess ye reason of his joining me wth *Bland*; one, who receives not a penny either from Church or State, wth ye best beneficed Clergyman in ye Kingdom; & it is a little discouraging, My Lord, to stand exposed to envy & Satire wthout so much as a trench or breast work to defend me.[31]

POPE AT THE RECEIVING END

The stupid way to deal with Pope—fortunately not adopted too often—was simply to deny that he was a great author. In one pamphlet he was described as a "simple *Sonnateer*" who has been flattered into thrusting himself "into the Rank of *mock Patriots* and *Statesmen*,"[32] And Lord Hervey—unadvisedly—chose the same approach:

> But had he not, to his eternal Shame,
> By trying to deserve a Sat'rist's Name,
> Prov'd he can n'er invent but to defame:
>
> . . . .
> In Glory then he might have liv'd and dy'd;
> And ever been, tho' not with Genius fir'd,
> By School-boys quoted, and by *Girls* admir'd.
> So much for *Pope*—And were I not afraid. . . .[33]

It was far more common, however, for pro-government writers to acknowledge Pope's undoubted qualities as a writer ("Both when you Stroak [sic], and when you Strike, you Charm"), and then attack him for putting his great talents to such poor use ("But, say, this Justice done the Poet's Fame,| Are *Poetry* and *Probity* the same?").[34] Pope's poetical virtuosity made him doubly dangerous. In pro-government eyes he was a "Syren-Charmer, with a Dæmon's Heart!"[35] whose vision was completely distorted:

> Those who deserv'd the axe and rods,
>   In thy own lov'd *Octavius'* days,
> Make pious hero's, saints, and gods,
>   In *British* verse, and *Tw*[ickenh]*am* lays.
>
> . . . .
>
> Go plot, be false, in fraud excel;
>   Inspire sedition, faction raise;
> Insult thy king———thy country sell;
>   If thou canst sin, good [Pope] can praise.[36]

The explanation for this distorted vision is to be found either in Pope's bad nature ("born to blacken every virtuous Name"), or—more commonly—in his politics ("To *Spleen* he prostitutes his noble Art, | Alike a Bigot in his *Verse* and *Heart*: | With Him the Best of *Patriots* are but *Tools*, | *All*, but his Party, if not worse, are *Fools*").[37] In most pro-government works Pope's bias is attributed to his involvement with the opposition and particular emphasis is placed on his friendship with Lord Bolingbroke. In *The False Patriot* Pope's ruling passion is found in his "Devotion to a Friend," and Pope is urged to:

> Recall your Muse, lur'd into Faction's Cause,
> And sing, great Bard, of Heav'ns and Nature's Laws:
> But sing unsquinting; keep a guiltless Eye;
> Nor dart Contagion at the Standers-by.
> Beware how prostitute your noble Theme
> To Party-Views, and Politician's Dream:
> Nor taint immortal Lines with mortal Rage;
> Posterity will mourn the spotted Page.[38]

Privately and publicly government supporters expressed regret that Pope had turned away from other literary pursuits. "It is a thousand pities that the author of Windsor Forest and the Essay on Criticism should have soiled his genius so much as he has done of late years with Swift, &c.," Alured Clarke wrote in a private letter.[39] And after Paul Whitehead had published his poem *Manners*, for which the printer was summoned to the House of Lords, several poems claimed that it was precisely manners that both Whitehead and Pope lacked:

> Till these appear, ——— *Pope*'s but a specious Knave;
> A Tool to Envy, and Ambition's Slave;
> Link'd with Division, Prejudice and Hate,
> In Anarchy would fain involve the State.[40]

Through his political associations, Pope came in for much the same treatment as individual opposition politicians. Standard themes were modified and applied to him. Typically, his political commitment was attributed not to a disinterested concern for public matters but to private considerations. He was accused of writing antigovernment poetry for money, and miscellaneous financial malpractices were laid at his door ("his continued *Impositions* on the over-fond Publick in the exorbitant Price of his *Works*, and the mean *Arts* he has been known to use in *palming* them on the *Unwary* in *various Shapes*").[41]

The theme of inconsistency is also prevalent. Thomas Newcomb, for instance, charged Pope with applying different standards to Whigs in office and to former officeholders—like Lord Cobham—who had gone into opposition:

> But since hemm'd in with *villains* all around,
> Not one lean virtue near a court is found:
> Why heap'd on *Cobham* such rare gifts, and grace?
> [Pope:] . . . What? ask a reason? when he lost a place!
>
> Whoever quits his golden key or staff,
> I reverence, I adore . . .
> . . . .
> We pour the patriot chrism, and in a trice,
> You view him clear, and purg'd of every vice.[42]

Since Pope never renounced his Catholic faith, he was left vulnerable to accusations of Jacobitism, especially in connection with his poetical comments on the Royal family. In *The Statesman* George Spiltimber described Pope as "an Idol Worshipper" (with regard to both Bolingbroke and the Pope), a man to whom "Merit's a Crime, and Title a Reproach; | Yet wantons Praise on those who least deserve, | On perjur'd Prelates [Atterbury], and attainted Peers [Bolingbroke]; | And, studious of an ill-acquir'd Applause, | Superbly stiles himself fair Virtue's Friend. | This abject Slave to superstitious *Rome*, | Insults that Liberty he still enjoys" (p. 15).

The point was often made that one of Pope's faith ought to feel gratitude towards the government for the religious freedom that obtained in Britain. One scurrilous pamphlet convicted him of ingratitude since he had "personal Obligations to many of those against whom he levels his *Satyrs*, and their *Lenity* to those of his *Persuasion*." In the same pamphlet the question is asked: "can he trace no Footsteps of Vice but in *those* who, as Friends to *general Freedom*, humanly tolerate those of his religious *Profession*?"[43] Implicitly or explicitly, Pope was reminded that his Tory allies were less tolerant in religious matters.

The theme of ingratitude became habitual in connection with Pope. To denounce him for showing ingratitude to Walpole and his allies for abstract benefits was nowhere near as effective as to accuse him of ingratitude towards his own friends. A partial list of subscribers to his works was, for instance, published, with annotations indicating which "particular Friends, familiar Acquaintance, or bountiful Subscribers" Pope was supposed to have satirized.[44]

The best known case of alleged ingratitude on Pope's part involved, of course, the Duke of Chandos, who was thought by many to have been the model for Timon in "An Epistle to Burlington." The identification was taken for granted in pro-government works, which consequently stress Chandos's generosity to Pope. According to Hawkinson "a certain animal of diminutive size" had asked "a nobleman of the first rank" to subscribe a guinea for one of his works. After dinner ("one of several") the nobleman handed him a bank note for £500 "and desired he might have but one book."[45] In *Of Good Nature* Pope is likened to "an Adder, swoln [sic] with cherishing," and Chandos himself is treated with predictable respect:

> Enlight'ned now the World is undeceiv'd,
> Who censures You—can never be believ'd.[46]

All of a sudden the Duke of Chandos became the object of much pro-government adulation. Welsted, for instance, in a poem "Occasion'd by the Character of Lord Timon. In Mr. Pope's Epistle to the Earl of Burlington" lauded Chandos to the skies.[47] In an anonymous poem printed for J. Wilford, Chandos was described as "A Pattern to the Great, to all a Friend | Who all Men love, and All, but You, commend."[48] The more deserving of praise Chandos could be portrayed to be, the worse Pope's alleged attack on him would seem.

Modern critics have long discussed whether Pope had Chandos in mind when he created Timon, or whether his failure to identify specific targets clearly enough rendering him "vulnerable to the accusation that he had attacked his benefactor, the duke of Chandos, rather than Walpole."[49] His detractors may even have misinterpreted the poem on purpose. I have no new evidence to offer in this particular case, but it was certainly not unknown for authors of works which invited political strictures to be—wilfully or not—misinterpreted. In 1730, for instance, Welsted wrote to George

Bubb Dodington to protest his innocence of any acts of literary disloyalty towards him. Admitting that he had included "a slight raillery" of Dodington's friend Edward Young in a recent production, he assured Dodington:

> . . . as for the first Ode of Horace, which I had the honour to address to you, I hope it is not in the heart of men to conceive, that I *foresaw* and *wilfully designed the ridicule*, which I found with *grief* followed upon it; or that I could be guilty of such low and wretched disingenuity and impertinence.[50]

The theme of ingratitude, used ad nauseam in connection with Pope, would seem to have drawn blood. Only an attempt to escape criticism on this head, can explain some of Pope's actions. Pope allegedly planted a false sheet of the 1743 version of *The Dunciad* on Cibber "in order to elicit a real attack . . . so that Pope could then respond by putting Cibber . . . into the 1743 version."[51]

Another element in the pro-government campaign that Pope is likely to have found hurtful was the constant harping on what Lady Mary Wortley Montagu called his "wretched little Carcass." References to Pope's physical handicap are legion in attacks on him ("Nature her self shrunk back when thou wert born, | And cry'd the Work's not mine"):

> Let *P—pe*, no more, what *Ch—nd—s* builds, deride,
> Because he takes not *Nature*—for his *Guide*;
> Since wond'rous *Critic!* in thy *Form* we see;
> That *Nature*'s self may *err*—as well as *He*.[52]

The "Deformity of his *Mind*" was said to answer to "that of his *Body*." "It was the Equity of righteous Heav'n, | That such a Soul to such a Form was giv'n," wrote Lady Mary who also described Pope's handicap as "the Emblem of thy crooked Mind, | Mark'd on thy Back, like Cain, by God's own Hand."[53]

Once a correspondence was established between Pope's "Pigmy size" physically and mentally, his setting himself up as a judge of true taste could be presented as ludicrous:

> As well thy *Stature* might the *Standard* be,
> And Six *Foot high* be rank *Deformity*.

Pope had a tendency, it was claimed, to aggrandize himself and what belonged to him:

His House, a Box, a Fairy Ring, his Lawn,
A *Lilliputian* Grot, his cool Retreat,

. . . .

His Fountains, Puddles, which, Straw Pipes might fill,
Or Baby Cupids, pissing thro' a Quill:
His Witches [sic], Cracks, fill'd with squab Deities,
A tiny *Jove*, and Infant *Hercules*.
His Library, of Books no ample Store,
His own Works neatly bound, and little more.

This, it is implied, is at the root of his charges against Chandos's grand scheme for his country seat.[54]

Pope's crooked shape and the abbreviation of his name in print (A. P—E) led to the inevitable comparison in much satire between the poet and a mischievous monkey: "they give you the same Idea of an *Ape*, that his Face, and his Shape, and his Stature do, and his Nature ludicrously mischievous."[55] In one print Pope is portrayed with an ape's body as an effigy of Martin Scriblerus to which the following inscription is suggested:

Artist, no longer let thy Skill be shown,
In forming Monsters from the *Parian* Stone;
Chuse for this Work a Stump of crooked Thorn,
Or Log of Poison Tree, from *India* born:
There carve a *Pert*, but yet a *Rueful* Face,
Half man, half Monkey, own'd by neither Race.
Be his Crown Picked, to One Side reclin'd,
Be to his Neck his Buttocks closely join'd;
With Breast protuberant, and Belly thin,
Bones all distorted, and a shrivell'd Skin.
    This his Misshapen Form: But say, what Art
Can frame the monst'rous Image of his Heart.
Compos'd of *Malice, Envy, Discontent*,
Like his Limbs crooked, like them impotent.
But, Sculptor, since by thee this can't be done,
Nor will these Passions live in Wood or Stone;
Thine be the Task to carve his Carcass whole,
The *Dunciad* only can describe his Soul.[56]

Occasionally, the satirists went even further and compared Pope to the devil himself. This is one thing he had in common with Sir Robert Walpole.[57]

More important was the place accorded to Pope in the pro-government attack on satire as a genre. The frustration of pro-government writers is easy to detect and understand. A fine satirist like Pope was a threat, and in order to attack him and other opposition writers the pro-government side presented satire—especially personal satire—as inherently immoral and only to be handled by writers with the highest moral integrity, into which category Pope—as far as they were concerned—did not fall.[58] "Nor Dignity nor Innocence is spar'd, | Nor Age, nor Sex, nor Thrones, nor Graves rever'd" wrote Lady Mary Wortley Montagu, who in the same attack on Pope gave a definition of satire that she —for one—never tried to live up to:

> *Satire* shou'd, like a polish'd Razor keen,
> Wound with a Touch, that's scarcely felt or seen,
> Thine is an Oyster-Knife, that hacks and hews;
> The Rage, but not the Talent to Abuse;
> And is in *Hate*, what *Love* is in the Stews.
> 'Tis the gross *Lust* of Hate, that still annoys,
> Without Distinction, as gross Love enjoys:
> Neither to Folly, nor to Vice confin'd;
> The Object of thy Spleen is Human Kind:
> It preys on all, who yield or who resist;
> To Thee 'tis Provocation to exist.[59]

Conclusion

During the eighteenth century there was no escaping politics. The basic division of society along pro-government/opposition lines can be reconstructed from almost any surviving correspondence. In 1734 Charles Delafaye reported to the Duke of Newcastle from Bath, that although high society met together in the assembly rooms "without Distinction of Partys," he could give "a long List of Nobility & Gentry of both sides of ye Question."[1] A meeting of the leaders of the opposition was scheduled and when they started arriving another correspondent wrote: "We don't converse quite so much as We did, they now grow very strong, Windham [sic] is not yet come, Bathurst is here. Her R[oyal] H[ighness] behaves to admiration tis impossible to describe Her Zeal upon every thing where the Ministry an [sic] Publick are concernd . . . you need not fear any thing from the West whilst she is at the head of our Troops here, tho the Enemy are superior in Number."[2] Once Bolingbroke and the other leaders had left, there seemed to be "nothing stirring amongst them but Gaming."[3]

People flaunted their political opinions in public. Political prints were designed for fan mounts so that women could display them in drawingrooms. In honor of the House of Stuart the society of the Independent Electors of London—Jacobites to a man—had themselves painted wearing plaid waistcoats, and some people were observed to wear plaid at the Lichfield races as late as 1747.[4]

Even the illiterate part of the population would be confronted with a great deal of propaganda. Political ballads were often sung by hawkers in the streets, and political demonstrations of various kinds were not uncommon. In 1721, for instance, several "gay gentlemen hired a hearse and two or three mourning coaches and all the best music in the opera . . . and in this way serenaded the town . . . the conceit was the burying of the South Sea."[5] In Ireland in 1737, when the value of the gold coin was altered, a black flag was hung out from the top of St Patrick's in Dublin and the bells tolled as if for a funeral.[6] And when during the Excise crisis the pro-government *Daily Courant* was publicly burnt by the hangman at Tem-

231

ple bar for containing "false and scandalous reflections on the merchants and traders of this city, for their opposition to the Excise," this ceremony may well have had an effect on many who had not read that particular newspaper, and indeed on many who could not have read that or any other newspaper.[7]

The lower classes were certainly far more likely to be influenced by nonverbal political propaganda of the kind mentioned above, than by the printed propaganda produced by either the opposition or the government side. The Duchess of Richmond—renowned for her beauty—could conceivably have made more of an impression than any number of election ballads, when she contributed to party warfare in the Sussex general elections of 1734 by "dropping Orange cockades" from an upstairs window.[8] Since people in general were impressed by public spectacle, it was essential that days of Hanoverian commemmoration should be celebrated in style: thus every year the day of the king's coronation, for example, was "concluded with Bonfires, Illuminations, Ringing of Bells, and all other Demonstrations of general Joy."[9]

This is a timely reminder that the audience for the printed works used as propaganda both on the opposition and on the government side naturally was limited to the fairly well-educated section of society, and that literary works were only one part—albeit an important one—of contemporary propaganda. In terms of target groups for printed propaganda it was obviously very important indeed to influence people who either had votes or could influence voters, whereas the toiling masses were simply viewed as potentially unruly people who must by one means or another be kept under control.

The research carried out for this book has shown that pro-government propaganda during the Walpole period was very well organized. The government's influence in the publishing world was extensive, based not on direct ownership but on the power that came with patronage. In return for considerable financial rewards in the form of artificially inflated sales and/or stipends, publishers, printers, and newspaper proprietors would agree to a significant degree of government supervision.

It was necessary for the government to be generous in such matters because on the open market opposition material had the advantage ("that sells best, that's most against the Law"),[10] although government officials did their best to level the playing field by restricting the circulation of the more extreme opposition productions through sporadic prosecutions and by having material stopped regularly at the post office.

Although a few of the authors willing to write for Walpole were given government pensions, or bounty provided so consistently as to constitute revokable pensions, most of them were either payed a fixed sum for each literary contribution, or were the protégés of individual Old Corps Whig grandees who seem in most cases to have considered that financing one or more authors was part of their service to the party. The fact that so many writers were dependent on pro-government patrons, allowed for a flexible system of political oversight; the weakness of the system resided in its dependance on the political loyalty of the patron himself.

The government's interest in the book trade ensured that there was a publishing network to which writers associated with the Old Corps as well as freelance pro-government authors had access. There were plenty of outlets for the kind of writing they produced. Authors who had suitable literary material to offer could either contact a centrally placed politician or alternatively submit their works directly to the pro-government newspapers or to publishers like James Roberts and be reasonably sure that they would be accepted. Their works—if approved—could then either be included in newspapers or miscellanies or published separately. For material considered suitable for large-scale distribution there was an efficient distribution system capable of providing propaganda free of charge to important individuals both in London and the provinces. As many as 10,000 copies of any given newspaper or pamphlet were bought by the government and distributed gratis through the post office.

The truly impressive part of the propaganda machine is precisely the distribution system. It was designed to reach sympathizers, opponents, and independents alike. Representatives of specific powerful groups were targeted—especially those who through their influence in the local communities could provide a vital link between the periphery and the great world of London (the clergy, election managers, Excise officers, etc.). Not unexpectedly, propaganda was sent regularly to Members of Parliament (regardless of party affiliation) and to people working in the offices of the Ministers of State. Single copies were sent to named individuals active not only within politics, but within finance, the law, the Royal Court.

In a recent article about the structure of the Whig party under Queen Anne, Clyve Jones has shown how political information traveled from a central nucleus of powerful politicians to their supporters around the country. Important matters of policy could be, if not discussed, at least imparted at "major conferences on party strategy between parliamentary session, either at race meetings at Newmarket (a favourite haunt) or in various country houses of the Junto lords themselves or their associates," with special meetings being called to deal with political emergencies. One can begin to see the contours of a system in which the people who participated at these meetings were expected to pass on relevant information to their own protégés, friends, and supporters in their local communities through more or less informal meetings. These individuals again might be at the head of their own small groups.[11] Printed propaganda could be said to follow the same basic fan vault pattern, working its way from the center out to the localities. Produced in London, large numbers of newspapers and pamphlets and perhaps other suitable works destined for the provinces were divided into small packets and sent to specific individuals who through their work or through their association with the government could be counted on to redistribute the material to people that in their opinion ought to be kept regularly informed about pro-government policies. In determining their own distribution lists they could draw on their specialized knowledge of the local communities of which they were part. Lord Hervey, for instance, seems to have supplied his protégé Conyers Middleton with both printed propaganda and information of a political nature, with Middleton acting informally as the head of a small group of pro-government Whigs in Cambridge. The antiquary William Cole was one of those who went to drink "*Tea* and *Coffee* with him *4* or *5 Times* in the *Week* generally, where there used to be a great *Mixture* of the *best Company* in the *University*."[12]

The pro-government propaganda effort seems to have been slow to get off the ground, and it is probably fair to say that in the beginning it was largely defensive, its main goal to respond to and help diffuse opposition attacks. Over the years, however, pro-government writers learned to take the initiative and gradually developed their own fund of themes, symbols, and stock metaphors easily distinguishable from those used by the opposition. On either side of the political divide there was almost a standard formula for how to write propaganda. This is proved by the facility with which Thomas Cooke, James Ralph, Defoe (father and son), Thomas Gordon, and others wrote alternately for the government and the opposition and the ease with which each side produced works in political disguise. With a misleading implied political provenance, such works were designed to be insinuated into the publishing network of the opposite side in order to put across some subversive point or other.

Walpole himself claimed not to spend much time on the journals, but averred that "if the want of wit, learning, good manners, and truth, is the proper object of contempt and ridicule, the writers in the opposition seem to me to have a much better title than those for the Government."[13] Although—generally speaking—pro-government authors were far more competent than Pope, Swift, and others gave them credit for, it has to be admitted that Walpole did not command the support of any writer of a stature comparable to that of—say—Alexander Pope. The authors who benefited financially from an association with the government were not all second rate, however. Joseph Mitchell, Thomas Cooke, Leonard Welsted, Thomas Newcomb, and others certainly were, but to offset them there were authors like Sir Richard Steele, Daniel Defoe, and Edward Young and—after 1741—possibly Henry Fielding.

The truth is that pro-government writers had much to contend with. They were under pressure to write about topical issues in prescribed ways, and in Paul Langford's word "topicality millitates against excellence." Also they were expected to write about the excellence of the status quo and to advocate moderation in politics—hardly the most exciting of themes.[14]

Defending the establishment becomes glamorous only when it is under serious threat, but during Walpole's term in office there were no Jacobite risings. It has been claimed that Walpole exaggerated the Jacobite threat and made it into a regular feature in pro-government propaganda because this represented an easy way of discrediting not only the Tories but the opposition Whigs who were in league with them. It was also calculated to make the Old Corps Whigs close ranks because an enemy is an important part of any propaganda campaign. Perhaps we will never know whether the Jacobite threat was exaggerated on purpose or not, but in either case the periodicity of the attacks would have been extremely important. Some modern historians give the impression that after the Hanoverian Succession, Jacobitism was eradicated at a stroke and the Tories proscribed from power with immediate and irrevocable effect. In fact many Old Corps Whigs—misguidedly or not—seem to have seen the attempt to root out Jacobites and Tories from places of power as an on-going process of subjection that had to be eternally renewed. However, in playing the Jacobite card, pro-government writers were hampered by the need to portray the supporters of James III as a relatively small and insignificant—albeit sinister—group.

The problem with the Walpole administration was that it was too pragmatic, too down-to-earth to serve as an absolute ideal to pit against the charges leveled at it by the opposition. The panegyrics which proclaimed Walpole as a paragon of virtue would not have convinced even Walpole's mother, had she been alive. Writers associated with the government were far more successful in their satirical attacks on the opposition, consistently reducing the actions of individual opposition politicians—especially the older generation of "Patriot" Whigs who had once been allies—to the level of personal frustrations and ambitions, in direct contradiction to their own claims that they were activated by nothing but the most high-minded ideals.

In their satirical attacks on their opponents, however, pro-government authors often refrained from constructing a conventional positive Old Corps Whig standard against which the opposition could be weighed and found wanting. Instead they tend to describe their own number as superior to their opponents only in the consistency of their political actions and opinions and in their refusal to be hypocritical about their motives. This resulted in a kind of satire that is sometimes quite startling in its worldliness—depressing or refreshing, all depending on one's point of view.

If pro-government satire was uniformly cynical about the motives of opposition politicians, it should be remembered that their views were later proved to have been basically correct. When Walpole was forced to resign, William Pulteney and Lord Carteret were bought off by a peerage and a place in the ministry respectively, and places of power or lucre for their closest supporters. Their apostacy allowed the Old Corps to remain in power and to continue to govern the country along familiar lines.

Jeremy Black has stated that "It is sometimes claimed that the Walpole ministry failed to get the better of the public debate with the Opposition, but in 1735–1736 this was far from clear."[15] Possibly this could be extended to more of the period. The basic strategy of the pro-government propagandists was to make the Old Corps join ranks, while driving wedges between the various groups in opposition by creating bad blood between them or by fostering already existing wounds. By presenting the major groups in the opposition as incompatible they tried to render ludicrous the cooperation between Tories (variously described as Jacobites or country bumpkins) and dissident Whigs (on the whole reduced to selfish and hypocritical apostates from true Whiggery with a predilection for high-sounding verbiage).

The measure of pro-government success can be gauged by the fact that long before Walpole was forced out of office, many opposition politicians had started to question the motives of Lord Carteret and William Pulteney and their followers. Up to a point this distrust can, of course, be explained by the personalities and actions of Pulteney and Carteret and their supporters. Probably, however, the progovernment campaign against the members of this particular group contributed considerably. The strategy of creating dissension between the various groups within the opposition was basically successful.

Pro-government writers were not so successful in their attack on what they saw as the immorality of much opposition satire. The point they wished to make was understandable: Walpole and other politicians were routinely accused of every kind of corruption and the most heinous crimes, without any evidence ever being advanced to substantiate these allegations. However, by protesting against this practice, government writers laid themselves open to charges of being humorlessly opposed to innocent mirth and enjoyment. It is this whole debate about the morality or immorality of satire that is implicit in Pope's lines in the first "Epilogue to the Satires:"

> P. See Sir ROBERT!—hum—
> And never laugh—for all my life to come?[16]

It is in such passages that one can see how profound an effect the agon between pro-government and opposition writers had on all the authors of the period, the major ones included. In their works Pope, Swift, Fielding, and others can be seen to be responding to and implicitly arguing against pro-government propaganda. But this is something that has not really been taken sufficiently into account. Pope and Swift, particularly, have been so effective in establishing the myth that Walpole's writers are not even worth examining that the shear *volume* of government propaganda, and its consequent importance as a factor in the consciousness of the period, has simply become more or less invisible to us. Yet this is the sea, as it were, in which Pope, Swift, Fielding, and others had perforce to swim, and whose currents they can often be seen to be resisting: where that is not understood, the motives, meanings, and implications of much in their writings tend also to be ignored.

Notes

When giving the dates of letters the new year has been taken as commencing on 1 January and not on 25 March.

Preface and Acknowledgments

1. *A Further Report from the Committee of Secrecy, Appointed to Enquire into the Conduct of Robert, Earl of Orford; during the Last Ten Years of his being First Commissioner of the Treasury, and Chancellor and Under-Treasurer of His Majesty's Exchequer* (London: printed for T. Leech, 1742), chart placed between pp. 128 and 129.

2. *London Newspapers in the Age of Walpole: A Study of the Origins of the Modern English Press* (London and Toronto: Associated University Presses, 1987).

3. James Alan Downie, *Robert Harley and the Press* (Cambridge: Cambridge University Press, 1979); Tomas W. Perry, *Public Opinion, Propaganda and Politics in Eighteenth-Century England: A Study of the Jew Bill of 1753*, Harvard Historical Monographs 51 (Cambridge, Massachusetts: Harvard University Press, 1962).

4. Bertrand A. Goldgar, *Walpole and the Wits: The Relation of Politics to Literature, 1722–1742* (Lincoln: University of Nebraska Press, 1976), in which the emphasis is on opposition wits.

5. "The Works of Sir Charles Hanbury Williams" (Ph.D. diss., Cambridge University, 1988).

6. See, for instance, Simon Varey, "*The Craftsman* 1726–1752: an Historical and Critical Account" (Ph.D. diss., Cambridge University, 1977).

7. James Alan Downie, "The Development of the Political Press," in Clyve Jones, ed., *Britain in the First Age of Party 1680–1750: Essays Presented to Geoffrey Holmes* (London and Ronceverte: Hambledon Press, 1987), 118–19, 121–23.

Introduction

1. British Library (hereafter BL), Holland House Papers (hereafter HHP), Additional Manuscript (hereafter Add. MS), 51396, fol. 84r (Hervey to Henry Fox, 25 January 1733).

2. Charles Macklin's *A Will and No Will*, acted at Drury Lane in 1746, and edited by Richard W. Bevis in *Eighteenth Century Drama: Afterpieces*, paperback edition (London, Oxford, New York: Oxford University Press, 1970), 59 and note.

3. *Memoirs of Vicountess Sundon, Mistress of the Robes to Queen Caroline, Consort of George II; Including Letters from the most Celebrated Persons of her*

Time, ed. Mrs Thomson, 2 vols (London: Henry Colburn, 1847), 1: 150–51 (Lady Pomfret to Mrs Clayton, later Viscountess Sundon, 6 May 1728).

4. John Nichols, *The History and Antiquities of the County of Leicester*, 4 vols (London: printed by and for John Nichols, 1795), vol. 2, part 1: 260. On the other hand the government supporter Francis Hare was allegedly responsible for "A noted Sermon preached on the 30th of *January* on this Text, *Woe be unto them that are given to Change*," see Paul Whitehead, *The State Dunces: Inscrib'd to Mr. Pope* (London: printed for J. Dickenson, 1733), 12 n.

5. Judith Colton, "Merlin's Cave and Queen Caroline: Garden Art as Political Propaganda," *Eighteenth-Century Studies* 10, no. 1 (Fall 1976): 6–7. Similarly, Queen Caroline attempted to make certain ideological statements in the Gardens at Richmond (11–20).

6. *The Correspondence of Richard Steele*, ed. Rae Blanchard (Oxford: Oxford University Press, 1941), 166 (21 September 1721), quoted in John Clyde Loftis, *The Politics of Drama in Augustan England* (Oxford: Clarendon Press, 1963), 67.

7. *Boswell's Life of Johnson*, ed. George Birckbeck Hill, revised and enlarged by L. F. Powell, 6 vols (Oxford: Clarendon Press, 1934–50), 2: 348 and n. 2.

8. Both Maynard Mack and Howard Erskine-Hill have written pioneering works on political allusions in Alexander Pope's poems: *The Garden and the City: Retirement and Politics in the Later Poetry of Pope* (Toronto: University of Toronto Press, 1969) and *The Social Milieu of Alexander Pope: Lives, Example and the Poetic Response* (New Haven and London: Yale University Press, 1975) respectively. Brean S. Hammond has tried to chart Lord Bolingbroke's influence on Pope, political or otherwise in *Pope and Bolingbroke: A Study of Friendship and Influence* (Columbia: University of Missouri Press, 1984). In his Ph.D. dissertation "*The Craftsman* 1726–1752," Simon Varey has analyzed the contents of the opposition newspaper the *Craftsman*, identifying recurring themes, symbols, and imagery.

9. Herbert M. Atherton, *Political Prints in the Age of Hogarth: A Study of the Ideographic Representation of Politics* (Oxford: Clarendon Press, 1974), 192.

10. Atherton, 192–93.

11. He was not at that point as fat as he was later to become, but even so no lightweight. According to William Coxe, Walpole started to become extremely corpulent and unwieldy, after 1725 (*Memoirs of the Life and Administration of Sir Robert Walpole*, 3 vols [London: printed for T. Cadell, Junior and W. Davies, 1798], 1: 755).

12. Jerry C. Beasley, "Portraits of a Monster: Robert Walpole and Early English Prose Fiction," *Eighteenth-Century Studies* 14, no. 4 (Summer 1981): 419; Vincent Carretta, *The Snarling Muse: Verbal and Visual Political Satire from Pope to Churchill* (Philadelphia: University of Pennsylvania Press, 1983), 42.

13. Paul Langford, *Walpole and the Robinocracy* in *The English Satirical Print 1600–1832* (Cambridge, UK: Chadwyck-Healey, 1986), 26.

14. Jeremy Black, "Party Strife and the Augustan Press," *Publishing History* 23 (1988): 101.

15. Coxe, 1: 760–61.

16. *Correspondence of Steele*, 102 (Steele to Lord Clare [later Duke of Newcastle], 25 May 1715).

17. Isaac Kramnick, *Bolingbroke and his Circle: The Politics of Nostalgia in the Age of Walpole* (Cambridge, Massachusetts: Harvard University Press, 1968), 189. That Defoe was preparing people for the sweeping measures the Government might have to introduce should the plague in Marseille spread to England, is dis-

puted by Stephen Brown who sees Defoe as subverting in *A Journal of the Plague Year* the political message he was propounding in his pamphlet *Due Preparations for the Coming Plague*, "Making History Novel: Defoe's *Due Preparations* and *A Journey of the Plague Year*," *Dalhousie Review* 67, no. 2/3 (1987): 193.

18. W. B. Coley, "Henry Fielding and the Two Walpoles," *Philological Quarterly* 45, no. 1 (January 1966): 161; Martin C. Battestin with Ruth R. Battestin, *Henry Fielding: A Life*, paperback edition (London and New York: Routledge, 1989), 78–79.

19. Harris, *Newspapers*, 71.

20. For a recent evaluation of "Cato's Letters" see Shelley Burtt, *Virtue Transformed: Political Argument in England, 1688–1740* (Cambridge, UK: Cambridge University Press, 1992).

21. See, for instance, K. T. Winkler who, in "The Forces of the Market and the London Newspaper in the First Half of the Eighteenth Century," *Journal of Periodical and Newspaper History* 4, no. 2 (1988), claims that certain Jacobite material introduced into *Mist's Weekly Journal* "had much more to do with the pressure of competition in the market for invectives than with Jacobite agitation" (24).

22. *The Senator*, 28 May 1728 (no. 32): 2; A. S. Collins, *Authorship in the Days of Johnson: Being the Relation between Author, Patron, Publisher and Public 1726–1780* (Clifton: Augustus M. Kelley, 1973), 58; BL, Newcastle correspondence (hereafter NC), Add. MS, 32687, fol. 524r ("John Smith" to Newcastle, no date, hereafter ND).

23. Cambridge University Library (hereafter CUL), Cholmondeley (Houghton) Correspondence (hereafter Ch [H] Corr.), 3116 (essay enclosed in letter from Cave to Walpole, 12 January 1741). The Cholmondeley (Houghton) *Papers* are referred to as Ch (H) Papers. I am grateful to the Syndics of Cambridge University Library for permission to quote from these and other manuscripts.

CHAPTER 1: THE POLITICAL CLIMATE

1. Harris, *Newspapers*, 19–20. As late as in 1743 the printer Daniel Pratt claimed in a petition to Newcastle that the printers of unstamped newspapers had established "a Bank, to maintain such of their hawkers that are or may be putt [sic] in prison for selling the same," and provided a list of eight unstamped newspapers (29, 28).

2. Charles Bechdolt Realey, *The Early Opposition to Sir Robert Walpole, Bulletin of University of Kansas* 32, no. 8, as part of *Humanistic Studies* 4, nos. 2 and 3 (Lawrence: University of Kansas Department of Journalism Press, 1931), 19, 103–54.

3. Loftis, 73; Kenneth Myron Greene, "Sir Robert Walpole and Literary Patronage" (Ph.D. diss., Columbia University, 1964), 50; David Harrison Stevens, *Party Politics and English Journalism, 1702–1742* (Chicago: private edition of dissertation distributed by the University of Chicago Libraries, 1916), 88.

4. Greene, 129; BL, Add. MS, 36772, fol. 193r (Thomas Burnet to George Duckett, ND, annotated "1718"). In another letter Burnet explained that "the Government have sett the Author upon it" and that he himself was "one of a Club that revise every one before they go to the Press" (BL, Add. MS, 36772, fol. 183r–v [Burnet to Duckett, 6 April 1718]).

5. Realey, 153.

6. B. W. Last, *Politics and Letters in the Age of Walpole*, paperback edition

(Newcastle: Avero, 1987), 80; *The Correspondence of Jonathan Swift*, ed. H. Williams, 5 vols (Oxford: Clarendon Press, 1963–65), 3: 267 (Swift to Gay, 26 February 1728), quoted in J. A. Downie, "Walpole, 'the Poet's Foe' " in *Britain in the Age of Walpole*, ed. Jeremy Black (London and Basingstoke: MacMillan, 1984), 181; Quentin Skinner, "The Principles and Practice of Opposition: The Case of Bolingbroke versus Walpole," in *Historical Perspectives: Studies in English Thought and Society in Honour of J. H. Plumb*, ed. Neil McKendrick (London: Europa Publications, 1974), 95.

7. Langford, 22; Loftis, 94. At the same time the coronation ceremony was represented at another theater, and a pro-government writer commented: "To have seen upon *one* Theatre, the greatest CEREMONIAL in the World *Ape'd* by *Vagrants* and *Beggars*, as they are justly stiled by the Laws of the Land; and on the *other*, the MINISTERS of our most August *Monarch*, and those whom he has invested with Posts of the greatest Office and Trust, ridiculed under the prime Characters of a *Thief-Catcher*, a *Jaylor*, and a *Highwayman*," *The Twickenham Hotch-Potch, For the Use of the Rev. Dr. Swift, Alexander Pope, Esq; and Company. Being a Sequel to the Beggars Opera*, marked as "Written by Caleb D'Anvers" but clearly a pro-government production (London: printed for J. Roberts, 1728), i–ii.

8. Langford, 21–22.

9. In *Miscellaneous Poems by Several Hands*, ed. James Ralph (London: printed by C. Ackers, for W. Meadows, J. Batley, T. Cox, S. Billingsley, R. Hett, and J. Gray, 1729), 246–50; William King, *Political and Literary Anecdotes of His Own Time* (London: John Murray, 1819), 151; *Biographia Dramatica; or, A Companion to the Playhouse*, compiled by David Erskine Baker and continued by Isaac Reed and later by Steven Jones, 3 vols, vol. 1 in two parts (London: Longman, 1812), vol. 1, part 1: 120.

10. [John Mottley], "A Complete List of all the English Dramatic Poets and of all the Plays ever Printed in the English Language, to the Present Year M,DCC,XL-VII," appended to T. Whincop, *Scanderbeg: or, Love and Liberty. A Tragedy* (London: printed for W. Reeve, 1747), 260; *Biographia Dramatica*, 3: 338 and vol. 1, part 2: 495; James Miller, *Harlequin Horace: or, The Art of Modern Poetry* (London: printed for Lawton Gilliver, 1731); *Timoleon. A Tragedy. As it is Acted at the Theatre-Royal, by His Majesty's Servants* (London: printed for J. Watts, 1730). Christine Gerrard sees *Timoleon* as "oppositional" and "one of the first Patriot dramas," *The Patriot Opposition to Walpole: Politics, Poetry, and National Myth 1725–1742* (Oxford: Clarendon Press, 1994), 211 n., 108, 55.

CHAPTER 2: DEALING WITH THE OPPOSITION

1. Public Record Office (hereafter PRO), State Papers Domestic (hereafter SPD), George II, vol. 36/26, part 2, fol. 4 (letter from Philip Yorke, 26 March 1732), quoted in Stevens, 129.

2. See, for instance, *Calendar of Treasury Books and Papers, 1735–1738*, ed. William A. Shaw (London: Her Majesty's Stationary Office, 1900), 257, 279, referred to in Harris, *Newspapers*, 136. The suggestion was originally made by Anthony Cracherode, Solicitor to the Treasury, in a letter to Lord Townshend (PRO, SPD, 35/31, fol. 25r [7 April 1722]).

3. On one occasion, for example, the Envoy Extraordinary to Holland was asked to find out where a pamphlet was being printed and "prevent the printing of

it, and even to seize the copy and the whole impression, if the Government will assist you in it." It was taken for granted that the pamphlet must be "certainly a most virulent one, for the printers here, who print the worst of their scandal, would not venture upon this," Jeremy Black, "In Search of a Scandalous Pamphlet: Sir Robert Walpole and the Attempt to Suppress the Publication of Opposition Literature in the United Provinces," *Publishing History* 25 (1989): 6.

4. Harris, *Newspapers*, 151–54.

5. BL, Hardwicke Papers, Add. MS, 36137, fol. 265r–v (Charles Delafaye to Lord Hardwicke, 15 September 1729). See also PRO, SPD, 36/15, fol. 62, "The Examination of Richard Francklin of the Parish of St Pauls [sic] Covent Garden Bookseller."

6. PRO, SPD, 35/117, fol. 266, quoted in G. A. Cranfield, *The Development of the Provincial Newspaper 1700–1760* (Oxford: Clarendon Press, 1962), 145. See also letter from Philip Yorke to Newcastle (16 September 1729), about the risk involved in prosecuting the printer of the *Craftsman* (PRO, SPD, 36/15, fol. 63).

7. BL, NC, Add. MS, 32687, fol. 514r (to Newcastle, annotated September 1732).

8. BL, NC, Add. MS, 32687, fol. 525r ("John Smith" to Newcastle, annotated 13 October 1732).

9. *Memoirs of Viscountess Sundon*, 2: 192–93 (Hoadley to Charlotte Clayton, ND).

10. Harris, *Newspapers*, 147; G. A. Cranfield, *The Development of the Provincial Newspaper*, 150.

11. BL, NC, Add. MS, 32689, fol. 58r–v (Paxton to Newcastle, 29 November 1733); *A Report from the Committee of Secrecy, Appointed to Enquire into the Conduct of Robert Earl of Orford, during the Last Ten Years of his being First Commissioner of the Treasury, and Chancellor and Under-Treasurer of His Majesty's Exchequer* (London: printed for Thomas Cox, Charles Bathurst and John Pemberton, 1742), 4.

12. Philip Woodfine, "Government Harassment of the Press in the Late 1730s," *Journal of Newspaper and Periodical History* 5, no. 2 (Spring 1989): 20; Jeremy Black, "An Underrated Journalist: Nathaniel Mist and the Opposition Press during the Whig Ascendency," *Journal of Newspaper and Periodical History* 5, no. 2 (1989): 38.

13. Paul Chamberlayne, *A Full Answer to that Scandalous Libel, the Free Briton of July 1. That was Pretended to be Written by one Francis Walshingham Esq; alias Ar——n——ld, Clerk* (London: printed for the author, and sold by the booksellers of London and Westminster, 1731), 45–46.

14. CUL, Ch (H) Corr., 3253 (ND). Giffard could possibly have been referring to the theater in Drury Lane where he obtained a sixth share in 1733, see *Letters by Several Eminent Persons Deceased. Including the Correspondence of John Hughes, Esq. . . .* , ed. John Duncombe, 3 vols (London: printed for J. Johnson, 1773), 2: 148 n.

15. Tom Davies, *The Characters of George the First, Queen Caroline, Sir Robert Walpole . . . Reviewed with Royal and Noble Anecdotes* (London: printed for T. Davies and T. Cadell, 1777), 22, quoted in Thomas Lockwood, "Fielding and the Licensing Act," *Huntingdon Library Quarterly* 50, no. 4 (Autumn 1987): 385; Maynard Mack, *Alexander Pope: A Life* (New Haven: Yale University Press in association with W.W. Norton, 1985), 746–49, 922 n.; Thomas Hinde, *Tales from the Pump Room; Nine Hundred Years of Bath: the Place, its People and its Gossip* (London: Victor Gollancz, 1988), 138.

16. *Of True Greatness: An Epistle to the Right Honourable George Dodington, Esq.* (London: printed for C. Corbet, 1741), 4.

17. *The Letters of Daniel Defoe*, ed. George Harris Healey (Oxford: Clarendon Press, 1955), 451–52 (Defoe to Charles De La Faye [sic], 26 April 1718). See Paul Chapman, "Jacobite Political Argument in England, 1714–1766," (Ph.D. diss., Cambridge University, 1984), 34.

18. BL, NC, Add. MS, 32692, fol. 454r (Benjamin Norton Defoe to Newcastle, 11 November 1739).

CHAPTER 3: THE PRO-GOVERNMENT PUBLISHING NETWORK

1. Harris, *Newspapers*, 113; Lord Chesterfield, *Characters of Eminent Personages of His Own Time* (London: printed for William Flexney, 1777), 20.

2. *Memoirs of Viscountess Sundon*, 2: 156 (the Bishop of Killala to Charlotte Clayton, 9 November 1731).

3. CUL, Ch (H) Papers, bundle 75, item 20 (ND).

4. John Nichols, *Illustrations of the Literary History of the Eighteenth Century. Consisting of Authentic Memoirs and Original Letters of Eminent Persons; and Intended as a Sequel to the Literary Anecdotes*, 8 vols (London: printed for the author by Nichols, Son, and Bentley, 1817–1858), facsimile edition (New York: Kraus Reprint & AMS Press, 1966), 2: 617 (Theobald to Warburton, December 1730); *Memoirs of Viscountess Sundon*, 2: 241 (Tyrconnel to Charlotte Clayton, 8 November 1730).

5. Timothy J. Viator, "Theobald's Preface to Richard II, and the Possible Closing of Lincoln's Inn Fields in 1719," *Restoration and 18th Century Theatre Research*, 2d series, 3, no. 1 (Summer 1988): 32; BL, HHP, Add. MS, 51388, fol. 117v (Henry Legge to Henry Fox, 12 May NS 1748); Basil Williams, "The Duke of Newcastle and the Election of 1734," *English Historical Review* 12 (1987): 488.

6. John Nichols, *Literary Anecdotes of the Eighteenth Century*, 9 vols (London: printed for the author by Nichols, Son, and Bentley, 1812–1815), facsimile edition (New York: Kraus Reprint Corporation and AMS Press, Inc., 1966), 1: 288–312; Michael Treadwell, "London Trade Publishers 1675–1750," *The Library*, Sixth Series, 4, no. 2 (June 1982): 108; Harris, *Newspapers*, 88.

7. CUL, Ch (H) Papers, bundle 75, item 11 (ND).

8. CUL, Ch (H) Corr., 1508 (intercepted letter from W. Morrice to Bishop Atterbury (?), 2 January 1728); CUL, Ch (H) Papers, bundle 75, item 15 ("Memorial from J. Peele," ND); *A Dictionary of the Printers and Booksellers who were at Work in England, Scotland and Ireland from 1668–1725*, ed. H. R. Plomer (Oxford: Oxford University Press for the Bibliographical Society, 1922), 315; PRO, SPD, Regencies (letter from Charles Delafaye, 13 September 1723), quoted in Laurence Hanson, *Government and the Press, 1695–1763*, lithographical reprint of the 1936 edition (Oxford: Clarendon Press, 1967), 108.

9. Harris, *Newspapers*, 88–89, quoting *Daily Journal*, 13 April 1733 and 8 October 1733. Harris suggests that Wilkins's standing on the *London Journal* may have been "more secure and that, as a leading proprietor of long standing, he was able to resist any attempt to dislodge him at this stage" (89).

10. *Literary Anecdotes*, 2: 26–27 n.; Harris, *Newspapers*, 117.

11. Nichols, *Literary Anecdotes*, 3: 737 n.; Treadwell, 110.

12. Hanson, 106–8.

13. *Further Report*, Appendix no. 13, chart between pp. 128 and 129.

14. Charles Knight, *The Old Printer and the Modern Press* (London: B. Murray, 1854).

15. *Verres and his Scribblers; A Satire in Three Cantos. To which is added an Examen of the Piece, and a Key to the Characters and Obscure Passages* (London: printed for C. Browne, 1732), 18, quoted in Michael Harris, "Journalism as a Profession or Trade in the Eighteenth Century," in *Author-Publisher Relations During the Eighteenth and Nineteenth Centuries*, ed. Robin Myers and Michael Harris (Oxford: the Polytechnic Press, 1982), 52.

16. Jeremy Black, "Flying a Kite: The Political Impact of the Eighteenth-Century British Press," *Journal of Periodical and Newspaper History* 1, no. 2 (Spring 1985): 13.

17. Winkler, 34–35, n. 30; Harris, *Newspapers*, 77.

18. *The Opinions of Sarah Duchess-Dowager of Marlborough. Published from Original MSS* (No place of publication, no publisher, 1788), 68, 101–2.

19. Oldmixon, *Memoirs of the Press, Historical and Political, For Thirty Years Past, From 1710 to 1740* (London: printed for T. Cox, 1742), 19.

20. Cranfield, *The Development of the Provincial Newspaper*, 125–26.

21. Harris, *Newspapers*, 116.

22. PRO, SPD, George I, 30/5, fols 12, 34, quoted by Hanson, 107, 108.

23. Harris, *Newspapers*, 116–17; Hanson, 110–11, 114.

24. 24 May 1728 (no. 31).

25. *A Further Report*, Appendix 13, chart between pp. 128 and 129.

26. Harris, *Newspapers*, 123–24; Henry Fielding, *The Adventures of Joseph Andrews*, ed. L. Rice-Oxley (London: Oxford University Press, 1973), 194. Proof, if any is needed, that the *London Journal* and the *Daily Gazetteer* continued to cooperate after the latter was supposed to have supplanted the three biggest pro-government papers, is supplied by the journalist Ralph Courteville's assertion that a letter of his for the *Daily Gazetteer* had made its appearance in the *London Journal* instead (CUL, Ch (H) Corr., 1789 [Couteville to Walpole, ND]).

27. Harris, *Newspapers*, 117.

28. Harris, *Newspapers*, 70–71; Winkler, 27.

29. Leonard Howard, *A Collection of State Papers, from the Original Manuscripts of Several Princes and Great Personages in the Two Last Centuries; with some Curious and Scarce Tracts, and Pieces of Antiquity, Modern Letters, &c on Several Important Subjects*, 2 vols (London: printed for the author, 1756), 605–7.

30. Harris, *Newspapers*, 119; BL, NC, Add. MS, 32691, fols 390r–391r (Benjamin Norton Defoe to Newcastle, 2 October 1738).

31. Harris, *Newspapers*, 47. This is clear from the many marked copies that have found their way into various libraries. The Lewis Walpole Library (hereafter LWL), for instance, has several poems written by Sir Charles Hanbury Williams and marked "Tom's Coffee House," see David F. Foxon, *English Verse 1701–1750: A Catalogue of Separately Printed Poems with Notes on Contemporary Collected Editions*, 2 vols (London: Cambridge University Press, 1975), 1: 898. The LWL classmarks are 63 v. 4 nos. 18 and 20, and 762 T59 no. 2. Poems marked Tom's Coffee House in the British Library include William Parratt, *An Ode, to the Right Honourable Sir Robert Walpole on His Majesty's Birth-Day October the 30th, 1739* (London: printed for C. Corbet, 1739), see Foxon, 1: 556.

32. *The Letters of William Shenstone*, ed. Duncan Mallam (Minneapolis: University of Minnesota Press, 1939), 19 (Shenstone to Richard Graves, [soon after 13 February 1741]). Michael Foss, *The Age of Patronage: The Arts in Society 1660–1750* (London: Hamish Hamilton, 1971), 146; Linda Colley, "The Loyal Brother-

hood and the Cocoa Tree: The London Organization of the Tory Party, 1727–1760," *The Historical Journal* 20, no. 1 (1977), 77–95.

33. BL, Add. MS, 32458, fol. 6v (Hervey to Middleton, 22 October 1737).

34. BL, Add. MS, 32458, fol. 11v (Middleton to Hervey, 25 October 1737) and fol. 13r (Middleton to Hervey, 3 November 1737).

35. BL, Add. MS, 32458, fol. 15r–v (Hervey to Middleton, 8 November 1737). See also fol. 79r (Middleton to Hervey, 15 February 1739); Shenstone, *Letters,* 17 (Shenstone to Richard Jago, 6 February [1741]). The stream of information went both ways. Middleton could give Hervey an idea of what Whigs in the provinces were thinking, remarking on the subject of relations with Spain, for instance, "the point of *no search* seems to be ye voice of the nation & not of a party, wth which ye Ministry must either comply or expect no quiet" (BL, Add. MS, 32458, fol. 83r [March 1739]).

36. Kenneth Ellis, *The Post Office in the Eighteenth Century: A Study in Administrative History* (London: Oxford University Press, 1958), viii, 47; Lord Bolingbroke, *Contributions to the Craftsman,* ed. Simon Varey (Oxford: Clarendon Press, 1982), xiv.

37. Ellis, 32.

38. CUL, Ch (H) Papers, bundle 75, item 6. Out of a total of 10,000 copies of William Arnall's pamphlet *Opposition no Proof of Patriotism: With Some Observations and Advice Concerning Party-Writings* (London: printed for J. Roberts, 1735), 3,000 were sent to the post office (CUL, Ch (H) Papers, bundle 75, item 10/1). Although this seems to have been a fairly standard number of copies to be sent directly to the post office, there were variations. In 1735, 3,300 copies of Sir Robert Walpole's pamphlet *Some Considerations Concerning the Publick Funds, the Publick Revenues, and the Annual Supplies, Granted by Parliament. Occasion'd by a Late Pamphlet, Intitled, An Enquiry into the Conduct of our Domestic Affairs, from the Year 1721, to Christmas 1733* (London: printed for J. Roberts, 1735) were sent through that channel, although the total number of copies dispersed was a little lower than usual (9,817). The same bill features 9,797 copies of *The Grand Accuser the Greatest of all Criminals* (London: printed for J. Roberts, 1735), whereof the normal number of 3,000 copies was sent to the post office (CUL, Ch [H] Papers, bundle 75, item 11).

39. Exactly 3,000 copies of each were sent to the post office; the discrepancy in numbers occurs in the category of copies marked down for "the Collectors of the Customs, the Collectors of the Excise, the Clergy, the Peers, Members of ye House of Commons, & several other Persons of Distinction in Town and Country," see CUL, Ch (H) Papers, bundle 75, item 6.

40. CUL, Ch (H) Papers, bundle 75, items 12 and 13.

41. *The Dictionary of National Biography,* ed. Leslie Stephen and Sidney Lee, 63 vols (Oxford: Oxford University Press, 1885–1900), 17: 570.

42. Romney Sedgwick, *The House of Commons 1715–1754,* 2 vols (London: Her Majesty's Stationary Office, 1970), 2: 509–10; *The Eighteenth Century Short Title Catalogue* on CD-ROM.

43. John M. Beattie, *The English Court in the Reign of George I* (Cambridge, UK: Cambridge University Press, 1967), 33 n; Sedgwick, 2: 473.

44. The Duke of Newcastle as Secretary of State for the Southern Department and Lord Harrington as Secretary of State for the Northern Department between them were responsible for domestic affairs. On 6 March and 13 March respectively the two offices received 400 copies each, and this came in addition to the copies received earlier by Newcastle and Harrington (twelve each) and their staff: the two

Under Secretaries in Newcastle's office, Andrew Stone and John Couraud (six each); the Under Secretary in Harrington's office, Edward Weston (six copies), the other Under Secretary (George Tilson) having recently withdrawn without a replacement being appointed before May; the chief clerks, John Wace (Harrington's office) and Daniel Prevereau in Newcastle's office (six copies each); the clerks (three copies for each). The decipherers Dr Edward Willes—the future Bishop of Bath and Wells—and Anthony Corbiere, also had three copies each. These individuals have been identified by consulting J. C. Sainty, *Office-Holders in Modern Britain II: Officials of the Secretaries of State 1660–1782* (London: Athlone Press, 1973).

45. See BL, Althorp MS, E5, unpaginated, letters from Delafaye to Pointz (26 January 1729, 24 March 1730, 2 April 1730).

46. In addition John Hill, Esq, who was Commissioner of the Customs (see William Oldys, *A Literary Antiquary: Memoirs of William Oldys, Esq. Norroy King-at-Arms. Together with his Diary, Choice Notes from his Adversaria, and an Account of the London Libraries*, reprinted from *Notes and Queries*, [by J. Yeowell] [London, 1862], xviii–xix) is specifically mentioned as the recipient of twelve copies.

47. Chris Cook and John Stevenson, *British Historical Facts, 1688–1760* (London: Macmillan, 1988), 96, 98.

48. The Attorney General (Sir Dudley Rider) and the Solicitor General (John Strange), for example. See Dan Pickrill, *Ministers of the Crown* (London, Boston and Henley: Routledge & Kegan Paul, 1981), 109, 111.

49. Sir John Eyles was Postmaster General, but as an alderman and a former Lord Mayor of the City of London, he was also extremely powerful in financial circles with his strong family connections in the City. One assumes that both he and his brother Sir Joseph Eyles received their copies because of their City connections. Sir Joseph's major appointments were all in the past but he remained an alderman and was a Turkey merchant, with extensive commercial interests in the Mediterranean, with close financial links with the government, both financially and politically. Another prominent City figure, Sir Robert Baylis, received 12 copies. It is perhaps significant that the Eyles brothers and Sir Robert Baylis—all known as staunch supporters of Walpole—had only a few days earlier tried to stop a petition from the City which reflected negatively on the Convention with Spain, see Alfred James Henderson, *London and the National Government, 1721–1742: A Study of City Politics and the Walpole Administration, Perspectives in European History* 7 (Philadelphia: Porcupine Press, 1975), 188 and n. 35.

50. The following named individuals have not been properly identified. Apart from the two first men on the list, they received only one copy each:
Richard Arnold, Esq (3)
William Blair, Esq (6)
Mr. Brewer
Mr. Walters (Peter Walter?)
Dr. Andrews (Trinity College, Dublin?)
Dr. Bettesworth (Cambridge University?)
Mr. Gideon (financier?)
Mr. Janssen
Mr. Dickens
Mr. Tho. Ward (Housekeeper of Parliament?)
Mr. Cole (Parliamentary solicitor?)
Mr. Ridge

Mr. Wm. Mount
Mr. James Round
Revd Mr. Finch

51. See Cook, *British Historical Facts*, 63, and *Authentic Memoirs of the Life of Richard Mead, M.D.* (London: printed for J. Whiston and B. White, 1755), 18, 21–22; BL, NC, Add. MS, 32691, fol. 317r (Henry Pelham to Newcastle, 5 September 1738); Plumb, 2: 256 n, 320 n.

52. See Stevens, 119.

53. Ray A. Kelch, *Newcastle, a Duke without Money: Thomas Pelham-Holles 1693–1768* (London: Routledge & Kegan Paul, 1974), 117, 123. For evidence of Colliers' election activities, see BL, NC, Add. MS, 32689, fol. 3r–v (Collier to Newcastle, 1 November 1733).

54. BL, NC, Add. MS, 32691, fol. 97r (Collier to Thomas Pelham, 28 March 1738).

55. Harris, *Newspapers*, 45; Kelch, 123–24.

56. Basil Williams, 476–77.

57. *The Manuscripts of the Earl of Carlisle, Preserved at Castle Howard, Historical Manuscript Commission, 15th Report, Appendix, Part VI* (London: Her Majesty's Stationery Office, 1897), 118 (26 May 1733), 141 (26 October 1734), 145 (16 January 1735), quoted in Hanson, 110.

CHAPTER 4: PRO-GOVERNMENT WRITERS: HIRELINGS,
VOLUNTEERS, AND "BUREAUCRATS"

1. James Ralph, *The Case of Authors by Profession or Trade, Stated with Regard to Booksellers, the Stage, and the Public* (London: printed for R. Griffiths, 1758), 20.

2. Oldmixon, 3; [Eustace Budgell], *Verres and his Scribblers*, 70; *The Dunciad*, in *The Works of Alexander Pope*, ed. William Lisle Bowles, 10 vols, second enlarged edition (London: printed for J. Johnson and others, 1806), 5: 182 n.

3. *Tit for Tat. Or an Answer to the Epistle to a Nobleman* (London: printed for T. Cooper, 1734), 8.

4. *Ballads and Songs Loyal to the Hanoverian Succession (1703–1761)*, ed. John J. McAleer, *Augustan Reprint Society Publication* 96 (Los Angeles: William Andrews Clark Memorial Library, University of California, Los Angeles, 1962), iii; Mable Hessler Cable, "The Idea of the Patriot King in the Propaganda of the Opposition to Walpole, 1735–1739," *Philological Quarterly* 18, no. 4 (1939): 123–24, n. 18; *Anecdotes, Observations and Characters of Books and Men Collected from the Conversation of Mr. Pope and Other Eminent Persons of his Time by the Reverend Joseph Spence*, ed. Bonamy Dobrée (London and Fontwell: Centaur Press, 1964), 137.

5. Harris, *Newspapers*, 110; R. S. Crane and F. B. Kaye with the assistance of M. E. Prior, *A Census of British Newspapers and Periodicals 1620–1800*, new edition (London: Holland Press, 1979), 85; *Free Briton*, 27 August 1730 (no. 39).

6. Battestin, 57, 59.

7. Greene, 54. See Foxon, 1: 796–97.

8. Newcomb mentions specifically "a most signall [sic] instance" of Newcastle's "generous favour," received in return for "a little humerous [sic] ode" ad-

dressed to his patron (BL, NC, Add. MS, 32948, fol. 381r [Newcomb to Newcastle, 25 May 1763]).

9. CUL, Ch (H) Corr., 1507 (Madden to Walpole, September no year [hereafter NY]). See George Lyttleton, *An Epistle to Mr. Pope, from a Young Gentleman at Rome* (London: no imprint 1730).

10. CUL, Ch (H) Corr., 2306, fols 1r, 2r (Arnall to Walpole, 10 August 1734); *The Free Briton* (21 October 1731); Hanson, 113.

11. Edinburgh University Library, La.II.451/2, manuscript Life of Joseph Mitchell, written by John Mitchell, Joseph Mitchell's nephew, fols 367r, 368v.

12. *Notes and Queries* 41, part 2 (1791): 1091.

13. BL, NC, Add. MS, 32691, fol. 390r (2 October 1738); K. L. Joshi, "*The London Journal*, 1719–1738," *Journal of the University of Bombay*, new series, 9 (1940): 55. The letter (PRO, SPD, George I, 35/30, fol. 42) is quoted on p. 51.

14. CUL, Ch (H) Papers, bundle 73, item 21 (ND) and Ch (H) Corr., 3353 (ND); Spence, *Anecdotes*, 109 n.

15. *A Master-Key to Popery: In Five Parts* . . . (London: printed for J. Stephens and sold by A. Bettesworth, etc., 1725); William Stevens Perry, *Historical Collections Relating to the American Colonial Church*, 5 vols (no imprint: 1870–78), vol. 1, *Virginia*, 360–61 (Gavin to the Bishop of London, 5 August 1738); CUL, Ch (H) Papers, bundle 73, item 29 (Gavin to Walpole, 12 September 1734).

16. Sedgwick, 2: 567–68; John Nichols, *Illustrations*, 2: 191 n., 192 n. Sedgwick, 1: 501.

17. Nichols, *Illustrations*, 2: 189 n.; Edinburgh University Library, La.II.451/2, Life of Joseph Mitchell, fol. 368r–v.

18. *Gentleman's Magazine* 62, part 1 (1792): 29; National Library of Scotland, MS 23.3.26, fol. 73r–v (Peele to Lindsay, 31 January 1748); *Dictionary of National Biography*, 4: 1272; Shenstone, *Letters,* 16–17 (Shenstone to Richard Jago, 6 February [1741]); *The Yale Edition of Horace Walpole's Correspondence*, ed. Wilmarth Sheldon Lewis, 48 vols (New Haven: Yale University Press, 1937–83), 16: 21 (Walpole to Henry Zouch, 21 October 1758); *Dunces out of State. A Poem. Addressed to Mr. Pope* ([London, no imprint] 1733). See MS annotation in CUL copy (classmark: 7720.b.20/8).

19. BL, NC, Add. MS, 32697, fols 78r (Willoughby de Broke to Newcastle, 26 May NY) and 138r (Willoughby de Broke to Newcastle, 1 June NY). The money was duly sent, see fol. 291r (Willoughby de Broke to Newcastle, 8 July [1741]).

20. *Memoirs of Viscountess Sundon*, 1: 108.

21. In 1733 Malachi Postlethwayt complained to Walpole that he had not been recompensed "for the Labour of two years, & great Expences, besides the hindrance of seeking preferment in a different Channel." Although he had "long sollicited" [sic] and relied on Walpole's "promises," his hopes of providing for his younger brother by procuring a proctorship for his cousin had come to nothing. Like so many others he had trusted Walpole's reputation, "Twas from that nobel Spirit of Gratitude & Good-Will towards your Friends, confess'd by all, that I was induc'd to risque so much time and money in your Honour's Service." Although deeply disappointed, he still continued to produce pamphlets for Walpole, "tho at the greatest Expence of time and money," making it indirectly clear that if no post was forthcoming for his brother he must reconsider his situation (CUL, Ch [H] Corr., 2069, 1 November 1733). Two years later he was busy soliciting Walpole for the place of Secretary to Sir Everard Fawkener for his brother ("a Word from you will fix it in his Favor"), and he continued to keep the "Prime Minister" informed of the projects on which the two of them were busy (CUL, Ch [H] Corr., 2202 [10 June 1734] and 2459 [4 August 1735]).

22. CUL, Ch (H) Corr. 2776 (Arthur Collins to Walpole, 10 June 1738); *Observations on a Pamphlet, intituled [sic], An Answer to One Part of a Late Infamous Libel, in a Letter to Mr. P.* (London: printed for James Roberts, 1731), 20.

23. BL, NC, Add. MS, 32692, fols 251r-255v (William Bryan to Newcastle, 24 August 1739).

24. James Ralph, *Case of Authors*, 38; CUL, Ch (H) Corr., 1931 (Arnall to Walpole, 6 December 1732); BL, Egerton MS, 1956, fol. 65v (Theobald to Warburton, 18 October 1735).

25. BL, NC, Add. MS, 32691, fol. 390r (Norton Defoe to Newcastle, 2 October 1738).

26. CUL, Ch (H) Corr., 2909 (Malachi Postlethwayt to Walpole, 31 June 1739) and 1965 (Arnall to Walpole, 12 April 1733) and 2069 (Malachi Postlethwayt to Walpole, 1 November 1733), in which Postlethwayt wrote: "if after all my labour and Expense I am to pass disregarded, I shall sustain an irreparable prejudice."

27. Nichols, *Illustrations*, 2: 617 (Theobald to Warburton, December 1730).

28. Greene, 124, 190; *Gentleman's Magazine* 62, part 1 (1792): 315; Howard, *Letters*, 2: 698–99. James Pitt was at Norwich in 1742, but at that time he was 64 years old; CUL, Ch (H) Corr., 2912 (Lyons to Walpole, 16 August 1739).

29. Davies, 23–24 n. Davies gives the wrong date (1735) and the wrong title. The poem in question was probably *They are not* (London: printed for James Roberts, 1740). It went through three editions and was once pirated, see Foxon, 1: 791–92.

30. Oldmixon, 1, 3–4, 13, 52–57, 47, 48, 60.

31. Greene, 43; BL, NC, Add. MS, 32863, fol. 453r (Courteville to Newcastle, 22 March 1756); Harris, *Newspapers*, 107.

32. Coxe, 1: 760; Dr. Samuel Johnson, *An Account of the Life of Mr Richard Savage, Son of the Earl Rivers*, 2nd edition (London: printed for E. Cave, 1748), 98–100; PRO, the Lowther Accounts, class marks T38.233–238.

33. *Further Report*, Appendix 13, chart between pp. 128 and 129.

34. "A Familiar Epistle" in *A Familiar Epistle to the Right Honourable Sir Robert Walpole; Concerning Poets, Poverty, Promises, Places &c. To Which are Added Congratulatory Verses upon His Taking Possession . . . of the New House . . . in St. James's Park* (London: printed for Alexander Cruden, 1735), 7.

35. PRO, Lowther Accounts, T38.233–238.

36. CUL, Ch (H) Corr., 1925 (Mitchell to Walpole, 2 December 1732); Hanson, 95–96.

37. Nichols, *Illustrations*, 2. 745–46 n.; *Works of Pope*, ed. Bowles, 5: 189 n.

38. CUL, Ch (H) Corr., 3231 (Courteville to Walpole, ND).

39. *Biographia Dramatica*, vol 1, part 2, 520.

40. CUL, Ch (H) Corr., 2232 (1 July 1734).

41. BL, NC, Add. MS, 32697, fol. 308r (Oldmixon to Newcastle, 14 July 1741).

42. The problem with people like Benjamin Norton Defoe was that a gift was no sooner received than it was forgotten. In 1736, for instance, he had obtained 50 pounds as bounty, see *Calendar of Treasury Books and Papers, 1735–1738*, lxx.

43. *Correspondence of Steele*, 102 (25 May 1715) and 105 (19 July 1715).

44. CUL, Ch (H) Corr., 3178 [May 1744].

45. *Report*, 1, 7; Horace Walpole, *Correspondence*, 17: 502 (Walpole to Sir Horace Mann, 21 July 1742 OS).

46. Robert Wodrow, *Analecta: or, Materials for the History of Remarkable Providences; Mostly Relating to Scotch Ministers and Christians*, 4 vols (Edinburgh: printed for the Maitland Club, 1842–1843), 3: 432.

47. Synopsis of Robert Halsband, "Literary Patronage in Eighteenth-Century England" in *Expression, Communication and Experience in Literature and Language: Proceedings of the XII Congress of the International Federation for Modern Languages and Literatures Held at Cambridge University, 20 to 26 August 1972,* ed. Ronald G. Popperwell (London: The Modern Humanities Research Association, 1973), 187.

48. Thomas Murray, *The Literary History of Gallaway* (Edinburgh: Waugh & Innes, and London: Ogle, Duncan & Co., 1822), 47; CUL, Ch (H) Corr., 2480 (Buckley to Walpole, 15 September 1735). Buckley reminded Walpole that having applied to have the duty on paper subtracted, Walpole had obtained the king's prior consent, but on the day when it was due to be discussed in Parliament, Walpole sent for Buckley and told him he must desist, probably because it would create a precedent and/or provoke protests.

49. BL, Add. MS, 32458, fol. 49r (Hervey to Middleton, 29 August 1738) and fol. 81r (Hervey to Middleton, 24 February 1739) and fol. 83r (Middleton to Hervey, 1 March 1739).

50. See BL, Add. MS, 32458, fols 88r (Middleton to Hervey, 13 March 1739), 93r (Middleton to Hervey, 18 March 1739), 95r (Middleton to Hervey, 20 March 1739), 106r (Middleton to Hervey, 6 April 1739).

51. BL, Add. MS, 32458, fols 100r (Hervey to Middleton, 27 March 1739), 68r (Hervey to Middleton, 9 December 1738), 96r (Hervey to Middleton, 22 March 1739), 136r (Hervey to Middleton, 18 December 1739).

52. BL, Add. MS, 32458, fol. 100r (Hervey to Middleton, 27 March 1739).

53. BL, Add. MS, 32458, fols 174r (Hervey to Middleton, 27 December 1740), 159r (Hervey to Middleton, 24 June 1740), and Add. MS, 32457, fol. 143v (Middleton to Warburton, 27 October 1739); Dr. Johnson, *Savage,* 134; *Biographia Dramatica,* vol 1, part 2: 530.

54. Hanson, 12; *Memoirs of Viscountess Sundon,* 1: 196 (Alured Clarke to Charlotte Clayton, 4 October 1730) and 1: 190 (Alured Clarke to Clayton, 19 September 1730).

55. *A Sick-Bed Soliloquy to an Empty Purse: in Latin and English Verse . . . To which is added a Curse upon Punch; In Imitation of the third Epode of Horace* (London: printed for the author and sold by W. Mears, [1735]), 7, 13.

56. Oldmixon, 60, 61.

57. *A Short History of a Ten Years Negociation between a Prime Minister and a Private Gentleman,* second edition (London: printed for John Millan and sold at the pamphlet shops in London and Westminster, 1738), 34, 31.

58. Stevens, 96; Foss, 141–42.

59. John Perceval, Lord Egmont, *Manuscripts of the Earl of Egmont. Diary of Viscount Perceval, afterwards First Earl of Egmont,* ed. R. A. Roberts, Historical Manuscripts Commission 63, 3 vols (London: His Majesty's Stationary Office, 1920–23), 1: 144 (21 November 1733), as quoted by Harris, *Newspapers,* 102; Oldys, xviii–xix.

60. *Literary Anecdotes,* 5: 408.

61. BL, Add. MS, 32457, fol. 95r (Middleton to Minshull, ND).

62. *Memoirs of Viscountess Sundon,* 1: 190–91 (Alured Clarke to Charlotte Clayton, 19 September 1730).

63. Dr. Johnson, *Savage,* 64.

64. Howard, *Letters,* 2: 598 (Anthony Henley to Cooke, 17 November 1733); Mitchell, "Postscript," in *Poems on Several Occasions,* 2 vols (London: printed for the author and sold by L. Gilliver, 1729), 2: 384–85.

65. *Dictionary of National Biography*, 18: 1079; Foss, 143.

66. Sir Alexander Brand, *A True Collection on the Several Birthdays of His Majesty King George, and of their Royal Highnesses the Prince and Princess of Wales from the 1st of March 1724–5, to the 1st of March 1727* (no imprint), 1, 6–8, with notes.

67. CUL, Ch (H) Corr., 1931 (Arnall to Walpole, 6 December 1732).

68. CUL, Ch (H) Papers, bundle 73, item 21, ND; CUL, Ch (H) Corr., 1791 (ND, but annotated "1725–1730"); Mitchell, "To the Right Honourable Sir Robert Walpole, Knight of the Most Noble Order of the Garter, &c. In Imitation of Horace's Ninth Epistle," in *Poems*, 2: 363.

69. CUL, Ch (H) Corr., 1585 (Budgell to Walpole, ND, annotated "1728"); *The First Epistle of the First Book of Horace Imitated* (London: printed for J. Roberts, 1738), 6; *Dictionary of National Biography*, 21: 1285. Turner used the same theme in *An Epistle to Dr. Young* (London: printed for W. Mears, 1734).

> Rare *Virtue*, who forsook the Town with You,
> Is here much *talk'd of*, tho' she *visits* Few:
> Where exil'd *Truth*'s so utterly resign'd,
> None boast to *know* her, and none hope to *find*.
> With Thee she dwelt, long plum'd Thy daring Pen,
> Design'd its Course, and scourg'd the Sons of Men:
> *Vice*, then in Darkness sculk'd, far fittest Place;
> Now *stalks* broad Day, and *stares* you in the Face.
>
> (1–2)

70. CUL, Ch (H) Corr., 3047 (3 January 1740). During the Whig Schism Thomas Burnet wrote to his friend George Duckett, denying the authorship to a pamphlet attack on Walpole: "I would not be the Tool of any Ministry in abusing any person, that had not personally injured me, as Mr Walpole never did." (BL, Add. MS, 36772, fol. 169 [14 September 1717]). And again: "I must not suffer such a blemish to be thrown upon my Character, as if I was capable of abusing any man in print, that had done me no injury" (BL, Add. MS, 36772, fol. 142r [ND, annotated "bef. Nov 1717"]).

71. CUL, Ch (H) Corr., 1801 (ND, annotated "c. 1730").

72. Coxe, 1: 761.

73. Michael Harris, "Journalism as a Profession or Trade," 54–55. The Roman Catholic Martin, with whom Walpole opened a correspondence, mentioned in one of his letters one Courteville. Walpole answered that he knew the man and wanted Martin to "explain himself upon that subject" (Coxe, 3: 142).

74. BL, NC, Add. MS, 32692, fol. 454r (Defoe to Newcastle, 11 November 1739); CUL, Ch (H) Corr., 1700 (Defoe to Walpole, 25 March 1730); *The Letters of Daniel Defoe*, 454–55 (Defoe to Baker, 12 August 1730).

75. Dr. Johnson, *Savage*, 15–16, 44, 62, 78–79, 69, 88–89, 108.

76. *Biographia Dramatica*, vol 1, part 2: 519.

77. Harris, *Newspapers*, 101; CUL, Ch (H) Corr., 1446 (Robert Whatley to Walpole, ND), and 3231 (Courteville to Walpole, 4 October, NY).

78. Lord Hardwicke, *Walpoliana* (London, no imprint, 1783), quoted in Black, "In Search of a Scandalous Pamphlet," 5.

79. *Correspondence of Steele*, 176 (Steele to Walpole, 20 May 1722).

80. CUL, Ch (H) Corr., 1837 (Welsted to Walpole, 27 March 1731).

81. CUL, Ch (H) Corr., 1965 (12 April 1733).

82. CUL, Ch (H) Corr., 1965 (Arnall to Walpole, 12 April 1733).

83. CUL, Ch (H) Corr., 2712 (Defoe to Walpole, 11 October 1737).

84. Harris, *Newspapers*, 102.

85. CUL, Ch (H) Corr., 945 (J. C. to Walpole, 4 April 1721) and 1606 (Thomas Digges to Walpole, 14 April 1729).

86. *Catalogue of Prints and Drawings in the British Museum*, Division I, *Political and Personal Satires*, 3 vols (London: Chiswick Press, 1870–77), vol. 3, part 1: 384–86, print no. 2491.

87. *Manners: A Satire* (London: printed for R. Dodsley, 1739), 15.

88. *Report*, 6, 3, 7, 1–2; BL, NC, Add. MS, 32689, fol. 58r (Paxton to Newcastle, 29 November 1733); For Michael Harris's conclusions about Gordon and Paxton, see *Newspapers*, 103–4.

89. Hanson, 113–14; National Library of Scotland, MS 23.3.26, fol. 63v (Gordon to Patrick Lindsay, 1 July 1740).

90. National Library of Scotland, MS 23.3.26, fol. 66v (Gordon to Lindsay, 4 July 1741). I am grateful to the Trustees of the National Library of Scotland for permission to quote from this and other manuscripts.

91. National Library of Scotland, MS 23.3.26, fol. 63r (Gordon to Lindsay, 1 July 1740).

92. Urstad, 137–56.

93. George Bubb Dodington seems to have been active in press matters for Walpole. On 13 March 1726 A.B. wrote to Dodington submitting an essay for the *Plain Dealer*. If the essay was found acceptable, the author was willing to send one every week "to be corrected, or ye Paper to be no longer continu'd." Dodington must have consulted Walpole since the letter is to be found among Sir Robert's personal papers: CUL, Ch (H) Corr., 1407. *The Plain Dealer* was published by Aaron Hill, William Bond and others 1724–1725, so this must have represented an attempt on A.B.'s part to revive the journal (see Crane and Kaye, *Census of Newspapers*, 89). At that time Dodington was a Lord of the Treasury, and a poet of occasional verse. I think it highly unlikely, however, that Walpole would have reposed sufficient trust in Dodington to put him in sole charge of the press. Dodington already had a reputation for being a political weathercock and was the first to desert Walpole when it looked as if Spencer Compton might succeed him on the accession of George II. Thereafter Dodington continued "acting with Walpole in public and abusing him in private" but did not defect properly until 1740 (Sedgewick, 1: 500–503).

94. Sedgwick, 2: 567–68; *Dictionary of National Biography*, 21: 1248; Horace Walpole, *Correspondence*, 30, Appendix 3 "Walpole's Account of Sir Charles Hanbury Williams," 314; Richard Foster Jones, *Lewis Theobald: His Contribution to English Scholarship with Some Unpublished Letters* (New York: Columbia University Press, 1919), 310 (Theobald to Warburton, 10 January 1733); CUL, Ch (H) Corr., 3089 (James Ruffhead to Walpole, 15 February 1740).

95. *The Muse in Distress: A Poem. Occasion'd by the Present State of Poetry; Humbly Address'd to the Right Honourable Sir William Yonge* (London: printed for T. Cooper, 1733), 16, 15; John, Lord Hervey, *Some Material towards Memoirs of the Reign of George II*, ed. R. Sedgwick, 3 vols (London, 1931), 1: 35–37.

96. BL, NC, Add. MS, 32691, fol. 378v (Welsted to Newcastle, 26 September 1738) and fol. 317r (Henry Pelham to Newcastle, 5 September 1738).

97. Sir Joseph Maubey's notes on the life of his friend Thomas Cooke, *Gentleman's Magazine* 61, part 2 (1791): 1090–91, 10902. For the whole account, see *Gentleman's Magazine* 61, part 2 (1791): 1090–94, 1178–85; 62, part 1 (1792): 26–32, 214–21, 313–16; 62, part 2 (1797): 566–67; Nichols, *Illustrations*, 2: 198 and n. (Warburton to Concanen, 2 January 1726–27), 748, 326 n.

98. BL, HHP, Add. MS, 51403, fol. 84r (Harris to Fox, 29 March 1751); Ellis, 129.

99. CUL, Ch (H) Corr., 2389 (John Ker to Walpole, ND, annotated "c. 1734"). This poem can probably be identified as the anonymous *The Cause of Liberty. Addressed to the British Senate* (London: printed by and for J. Chrichley, 1734), see Foxon, 1: 111.

100. CUL, Ch (H) Corr., 3047 (Samuel Madden to Walpole, 3 January 1740).

101. CUL, Ch (H) Corr., 3340 (E.J. to Walpole, 21 April NY).

102. BL, NC, Add. MS, 32687, fol. 514r ("John Smith" to Newcastle, ND, annotated "Sept 1732"); Harris, *Newspapers*, 101, 102. James Pitt, for example, was directly employed by the printer Wilkins (99).

103. Oldmixon, 35, 39; *Memoirs of Viscountess Sundon*, 2: 209–10 (William Somerville to Charlotte Clayton, 7 July 1733), 2: 213, and 2: 275–76 (William Somerville to Charlotte Clayton, 30 September 1734).

104. BL, NC, Add. MS, 32689, fol. 531r (Conybeare to Newcastle, 31 December 1734).

105. CUL, Ch (H) Corr., 1997 (Cooke to Walpole, 10 June 1733) and 2624 (Jos. Nicoll to Walpole, 17 September 1736).

106. CUL, Ch (H) Corr., 3116 (12 January 1741).

107. CUL, Ch (H) Corr., 3082a (10 February 1741). Dicey had written since 1736 under the pseudonym Creolius, see CUL, Ch (H) Corr., 2965 (Dicey to Walpole, 18 September 1740).

108. CUL, Ch (H) Corr., 2484 (Adlam to Walpole, 8 October 1735).

109. CUL, Ch (H) Corr., 2486 (10 October 1735).

110. CUL, Ch (H) Corr., 2487 (Paxton to Walpole, 11 October 1735) and 3205 (Arnall to Walpole, 11 October [1735]) and 2493 (Arnall to Walpole, 23 October 1735).

111. CUL, Ch (H) Corr., 2493 (Arnall to Walpole, 23 October 1735).

112. CUL, Ch (H) Corr., 2504 (Arnall to Walpole, 20 November 1735).

113. CUL, Ch (H) Corr., 2504 (20 November 1735).

114. Samuel Madden, for example, thought that it might be considered "improper" for him as a clergyman to write for a political newspaper, CUL, Ch (H) Corr., 1507 (Madden to Walpole, September NY).

115. CUL, Ch (H) Corr., 2069 (Malachi Postlethwayt to Walpole, 1 November 1733).

116. LWL, Sir Charles Hanbury Williams Archives (hereafter HWA) 68 - 10928, fol. 43r (Wyndham to Williams, 9 July 1745).

117. CUL, Ch (H) Corr., 1931 (Arnall to Walpole, 6 December 1732).

118. BL, Sloane MS, 4052, fol. 77r (Cooke to Sloane, 2 March 1731).

119. Nichols, *Illustrations*, 8: 575; BL, HHP, Add. MS, 51391, fol. 29r (Williams to Fox, ND [but after 14 September 1746]).

120. *Catalogue of Prints, Division I,* part 2: 736, print no. 1867.

121. Loftis, 114; *Notes and Queries*, Third Series, 2: 401–2; *As Much as May be Publish'd of a Letter from the B- of R-ch-r to Mr. P. To which is added, The Several Advertisement for which Mr. Wilkins was assaulted at the Crown-Tavern in Smithfield* (London: printed for A. Moore, 1728), 17–20. The attack on William Wilkins was also reported in *The Senator*, no. 22 (23 April 1728). In Richard Savage's *Author to Lett*, edited by James Sutherland (Los Angeles: William Andrews Clark Memorial Library, 1960), *The Augustan Reprint Society* 84, Iskariot Hackney claimed to have aided "a certain Right Honourable *Didapper Knight* of the *BATHos*" [Sir William Yonge] in writing this advertisement, "for which our printer underwent the Discipline of the Cane" (6–7).

122. Treadwell, 125.
123. *Political Ballads Illustrating the Administration of Sir Robert Walpole*, ed. Milton Percival, *Oxford Historical and Literary Studies* 8 (Oxford: Clarendon Press, 1916), xxx.
124. BL, HHP, Add. MS, 51396, fol. 118r (Hervey to Henry Fox, 14 February 1734).
125. LWL, HWA, 48 - 10914, fol. 91r (Fox to Williams, 18 July 1744).

CHAPTER 5: PROPAGANDA—EIGHTEENTH-CENTURY STYLE

Mitchell, "Congratulatory Verses to the Right Honourable Sir Robert Walpole upon his taking Possession, as First Commissioner of the Treasury, of the New House Adjacent thereto in St. James's Park, in September 1735," in *A Familiar Epistle to the Right Honourable Sir Robert Walpole; Concerning Poets, Poverty, Promises, Places & c. To Which are Added Congratulatory Verses upon His Taking Possession, as First Commissioner of the Treasury, of the New House adjacent thereto in St. James's Park* (London: printed for Alexander Cruden, 1735), 14–15.
1. T. N. Corns, W. A. Speck and J. A. Downie, "Archetypal Mystification: Polemic and Reality in English Political Literature, 1640–1750," *Eighteenth Century Life* 7, no. 3 (May 1982): 1.
2. *Observations on a Pamphlet*, 19.
3. CUL, Ch (H) Corr., 1997 (Cooke to Walpole, 10 June 1733).
4. Sedgwick, 2: 48–49, 550–52.
5. Oldmixon, 50–51.
6. H. T. Dickinson, *Liberty and Property: Political Ideology in Eighteenth-Century Britain*, paperback edition (London: Methuen, 1979); BL, Hardwicke MSS, Add. MS, 35586, fol. 263r (Somerset to Hardwicke, 24 July 1740).

CHAPTER 6: THE RATIONALE BEHIND WALPOLE'S PROPAGANDA EFFORT

1. Lyons, *The Danverian History of the Affairs of Europe, for the Memorable Year 1731* (London: printed for James Robert, 1732), 3–4, 6.
2. *Opinions of Lady Marlborough*, 68.
3. Oldmixon, 19; The Centre for Kentish Studies, U269 C148/2, quoted in Jeremy Black, "Flying a Kite," 14. This document belongs to the Trustees of the Knole Estates.
4. The idea was certainly not new. Between 1643 and 1646 a periodical publication was issued called *The Scottish Dove* and the issue for 22–29 December 1643 reads: *The Scottish Dove, Sent out, and Returning; Bringing Intelligence from their Armies, and makes some Relations of other Observable Passages of both Kingdoms, for Information and Instruction. As an Antidote against the Poisoned Insinuations of Mercurius Aulicus, and the Errours of other Intelligencers* (London: printed for Laurence Chapman, 1643).
5. "Modern Characters," in *A Hue and Cry after Part of a Pack of Hounds, Which Broke out of Their Kennel in Westminster. To which is added, Modern Characters, By another Hand* (London: printed for F. Style, 1739), 28.

6. BL, NC, Add. MS, 32688, fol. 393r (T. Curteis to Newcastle, 15 September 1733).

7. BL, HHP, Add. MS, 51390, fol. 134v (21 October 1743).

8. Oldmixon, 20; BL, HHP, Add. MS, 51396, fols 23r (Winnington to Fox, 20 March [1729]), 24v (Winnington to Fox, 27 March 1729).

9. *Memoirs of the Times, In a Letter to a Friend in the Country. Containing an Account of, and Reflections on Some Late Remarkable Occurences* (London: printed for Anne Dodd, 1737), 3.

10. *Pro and Con* (London: printed for James Roberts, 1741), 3.

11. "Sir Robert Walpole's Newspapers 1722–1742: Propaganda and Politics in the Age of Whig Supremacy" (Ph.D. diss., Cambridge University, 1991).

12. *A Further Report*, Appendix 13, chart between pp. 128 and 129.

13. Howard, *Letters*, 2: 605–6.

14. *Opposition No Proof of Patriotism*, 3–4.

15. *The False Patriot. An Epistle to Mr. Pope* (London: printed for James Roberts, 1734), 8–9.

16. *The False Patriot*, 9.

17. *The Senator*, 16 February 1728 (no. 3).

18. CUL, Ch (H) Corr., 1507 (Madden to Walpole, September NY).

19. Robert L. Haig, *The Gazetteer 1735–1797: A Study in the Eighteenth-Century English Newspapers* (Carbondale: Southern Illinois Press, 1960), 5; Greene, 193–94.

20. Foxon, 2: 172.

21. CUL, Ch (H) Papers, bundle 73, item 15.

22. BL, HHP, Add. MS, 51396, fol. 109r (Hervey to Fox, 31 January 1734).

23. CUL, Ch (H) Corr., 3047 (Madden to Walpole, 3 January 1740).

24. *Dictionary of National Biography*, 14: 863; Loftis, 123 and n. 1. In, for instance, *The Citizen's Procession: or, The Smugler's Success and the Patriots Disappointment. Being an Excellent New Ballad on the Excise-Bill* (London: printed for Ann Dodd, 1733), the Lord Mayor is called "a true *Perkin's* Man" (6).

25. Nichols, *Literary Anecdotes*, 2: 31–32 nn. and 2: 700 nn.; *Themistocles, the Lover of his Country* (Dublin: printed by S. Powell for George Risk, George Ewing and William Smith, 1729); CUL, Ch (H) Corr., 1507 (Madden to Walpole, September NY).

26. Oldys, 31; BL, Add. MS, 32458, fols 6v, 7r (Hervey to Middleton, 22 October 1737) and 8r (Hervey to Middleton, September [corrected to October] 1737).

27. Corns, "Archetypal Mystification," 2; BL, NC, Add. MS, 32692, fol. 300r (Hardwicke to Newcastle, 14 September 1739).

28. CUL, Ch (H) Corr., 3231 (Courteville to Walpole, 14 October NY). The letter from Arnall to Walpole (3 December 1732) has been published in *The Works of Pope*, ed. Bowles, 5: 188–89.

29. CUL, Ch (H) Papers, bundle 75, item 6.

30. Defoe, *The Conduct of Robert Walpole, Esq.; from the Beginning of the Reign of Her Late Majesty Queen Anne, to the Present Time* (London: printed for T. Warner, 1717), 40.

31. BL, NC, Add. MS, 32694, fol. 360r (John Willer to Sir Charles Wager, 29 July 1740).

32. BL, Add. MS, 32457, fol. 132r (Middleton to Warburton, 5 August 1738).

33. *High Boys up go We! Or, A Rod for Somebody. An Excellent New Ballad, Occasion'd by a Late Poem, entitled, An Ode to Mankind. by Timothy Scribble Esq.* (London: printed for J. Roberts, 1741), 4.

34. *A Letter from Mr. Cibber to Mr. Pope, Inquiring into the Motives that might Induce him in his Satyrical Works, to be so Frequently Fond of Mr. Cibber's Name* (London: printed and sold by W. Lewis, 1742), 59–60.

35. Percival, xxxii.

36. *The Art of Poetry* (London: printed for Robert Dodsley, 1741), 11.

37. McAleer, *Ballads and Songs,* ii; BL, NC, Add. MS, 32692, fols 251r-251v (William Bryan to Newcastle, 24 August 1739); McAleer, iv.

38. BL, HHP, Add. MS, 51396, fol. 9r (Winnington to Fox, 18 January [1729]).

39. Coxe, 1: 758.

40. Suffolk Record Office, Bury St Edmunds Branch, Hervey MS, 941/47/18, Verses on lovers' quarrels by Fox, Yonge, Williams, and Winnington, annotated by Hervey.

41. BL, HHP, Add. MS, 51396, fol. 108r (Hervey to Fox, 31 January 1734).

42. Lord Ilchester and Mrs Langford-Brooke, *Sir Charles Hanbury Williams: Poet, Wit and Diplomatist* (London: Thornton Butterworth, 1929), 120.

43. King, 99.

44. "Epilogue to Julius Caesar," in *A Miscellaneous Collection of Original Poems, Consisting of Odes, Epistles, Translations, &c. Written Chiefly on Political and Moral Subjects. To which are added, Occasional Letters and Essays, Formerly Published in Defence of the Present Government and Administration* (London: printed by J. Wilson, 1740), 129–32.

45. Percival, xvii.

46. *The Senator,* no. 10 (12 March 1728).

47. Richard Deacon, *The Truth Twisters. Disinformation: The Making and Spreading of Official Distortions, Half-truths and Lies* (London and Sydney: Futura Publications, 1988), 7, 9, 11.

48. *Catalogue of Prints, Division I,* vol. 2: 790 (print no. 1927).

49. *Daily Gazetteer,* 30 June 1735 (no. 1), quoted in Haig, 5.

50. *A Dialogue between an Oak and an Orange-tree* (London: printed for James Roberts, 1716), 9–10, 7, 8.

51. *Biographia Dramatica,* vol 1, part 2: 403.

Chapter 7: A Nation Truly Fortunate

BL, NC, Add. MS, 32992, fol. 294r (Thomas Newcomb to Newcastle, 24 September NY).

1. See Corns, "Archetypal Mystification"; Cooke, *Tales, Epistles, Odes, Fables, &c. with Translations from Homer and Other Ancient Authors. To which are added Proposals for Perfecting the English Language* (London: printed for T. Green, 1729), 195. This book contains—in Thomas Cooke's own words—"all that I desire to be called mine of original Poetry; all which I have hitherto wrote," so there can be little doubt that Cooke was indeed the author; "To the Earl of Bath; Imitated from Catullus," in *The Works, of the Right Honourable Sir Chas. Hanbury Williams,* 3 vols (London: Edward Jeffery and Son, 1822), 1: 176–77.

2. Duncombe, *Collection of Letters,* xv.

3. *Catalogue of Prints, Division I,* part 2: 578; Christine Gerrard, 235. Nor was this practice limited to printed matter: At Newby Hall in Yorkshire there is a statue which originally represented the Polish king Jean Sobieski riding rough-shod over a Turk, but was brought to England in the late 17th century and changed to represent Charles II trampling on Oliver Cromwell.

4. See, for instance, the first page of "Satire I," in *The Poetical Works of the Rev. Dr. E. Young*, ed. C. Cook, 2 vols (London: C. Cooke, NY), 2: 35.

5. Satire VII, *Works*, 2: 57.

6. "To his Royal Highness the Prince of Wales, On his Birth-Day, Octob. 30th. 1726," in Sir Alexander Brand, *A True Collection of Poems*, 8.

7. *Verses to the Lord Carteret, Occasioned by the Recent Conspiracy* (London: printed for Jacob Tonson, 1722), 4, 3.

8. *An Epistle to the Right Honourable Sir Robert Walpole* (London: printed for J. Walthoe, 1730), 7.

9. Thomas Newcomb, "An Ode to his Grace the Duke of Richmond, Occasioned by Some Fine Italian Paintings at Goodwood," in *A Miscellaneous Collection*, 41–43.

10. Linda Colley, *Britons: Forging the Nation 1707–1837* (New Haven and London: Yale University Press, 1992), 30–32.

11. Spiltimber, *The Statesman: A Poem. Humbly Inscrib'd to the Right Honourable Sir Robert Walpole* (London: published by Charles Corbett, 1740), 8.

12. Ashley Cowper, *The Norfolk Poetical Miscellany. To which are added Some Select Essays and Letters in Prose, Never Printed Before*, 2 vols (London: printed for the author and sold by J. Stagg, 1744), 1: 90.

13. "Prologue the Third (to Penelope)" in *Mr. Cooke's Original Poems, with Imitations and Translations of Several Select Passages of the Antients [sic], in Four Parts: To which are added Proposals for Perfecting the English Language* (London: printed for T. Jackson and C. Bathurst, 1742), 161; "London, an Ode" was printed in Thomas Cooke, *Poems on Affairs of State, Collected from the Daily, Evening, and Weekly, Papers: To which is Added the History of the Traytors Edric the Father, and Edric the Son, and of the Settlement of the Danes on the English Throne. Dedicated to Henry St. John Esqr, Late Lord Viscount Bolingbroke* (London: printed for J. Roberts, 1733), 5–7.

14. BL, Althorp MS, E5, unpaginated (Delafaye to Stephen Poyntz, 3 February 1729); Hildebrand Jacob, *Patriotic Love; An Ode. Chiefly Occasioned by Some Late Acts of Parliament: and Humbly Inscribed to the True Friend of his Country* (London: printed for W. Lewis, 1737); Joseph Mitchell, "Poltis King of Thrace; or the Peace-Keeper: A Tale from Plutarch: Address'd to the Powers of Europe, in the Year 1726," in *Poems*, 2: 124. The poem was published separately in Dublin in 1726 (see Foxon, 1: 468).

15. William Parrat, *Carmen Seculare For the Year 1733. To the King on His Going to Hanover* (London: printed: and sold by J. Roberts, 1735), 9; "To Her Royal Highness, the Princess of Wales, On her Birth-Day, March 1st, 1727," in Sir Alexander Brand, *A True Collection of Poems*, 9.

16. *An Epistle to the Right Honourable Sir Robert Walpole; Occasion'd by the Writings of the Craftsman, and the Late Peace Concluded with Spain* (London: printed for James Roberts, 1730), 16.

CHAPTER 8: "O FAV'RITE SON OF HEAV'N": AN ALTERNATIVE IMAGE OF WALPOLE

Joseph Mitchell, "Congratulatory Verses" in *A Familiar Epistle*, 13.

1. *Dawley, D'Anvers, and Fog's Triumph; or, the Downfall of Belzabub, Bell, and the Dragon: A New Ballad* (London: printed for J. Roberts, 1734), 6. See also

"The Tinker Turn'd Politician; or, Caleb's Metamorphosis" in W. Walker Wilkins, *Political Ballads of the Seventeenth and Eighteenth Centuries*, 2 vols (London: Longman, Green, Longman, and Roberts, 1860) 252–58 (fourteen verses of this poem were printed in the *Daily Gazetteer*, 5 March 1741):

> 'Twas wrong in Sir Robert to suffer our foe,
> A gale from the west, a whole summer to blow;
> That he kept not the winds, like the Senate, in pay,
> To drive both the fleet and Sir John from Torbay.
>
> Derry down, &c. (257)

2. *An Epistle to Walpole; Occasion'd by the Writings of the Craftsman*, 9.

3. Langford, 27. The opposition sometimes sought to deny that there had ever been a defeat on his part at Cartagena (220). See also *An Epistle to Walpole; Occasion'd by the Writings of the Craftsman*:

> Our Fleets in Danger, proving thee unkind
> Not to rebuke the Storm, and calm the Wind;
> A Statesman's Duty sure, when Tempests rise,
> To save our Navies, and command the Skies. (4)

4. Paul Sawyer, "The Popularity of Pantomime on the London Stage, 1720–1760," in *Restoration and 18th Century Theatre Research* 5, no. 2 (1990): 13.

5. "The Memorial: An Ode (Being the last Poetical Petition) to the Right Honourable Sir Robert Walpole, Knight of the Most Noble Order of the Garter," in *Poems*, 2: 53–54; Percival, v.

6. *Verses Addressed to the Right Honourable Sir Robert Walpole, On her Majesty's being Constituted Regent of Great Britain* (London: printed for T. Read, 1729), 5.

7. *An Epistle to the Right Honourable Sir Robert Walpole* (London: printed for W. Mears, 1728), 8; *The Opinions of Lady Marlborough*, 101–2.

8. William Musgrave, *Genuine Memoirs of the Life and Character of Sir Robert Walpole, And of the Family of the Walpole's, From their first Settling in England, before the Conquest, to the Present Times: Containing Several Curious Facts, and Pieces of History Hitherto Unknown*, in 2 parts (London: printed for E. Curll, 1732), part 1, ii.

9. *The Art of Poetry*, 8.

10. Spiltimber, *The Statesman*, 3; *An Epistle to the Right Honourable Robert Walpole, Esq; Upon His Majesty's Arrival* (London: printed for Jacob Tonson, 1723), 6.

11. *A Congratulatory Poem; Humbly Inscribed to the Right Honourable Sir Robert Walpole, On the Conclusion of the Convention between their Majesties of Great-Britain and Spain* (London, printed for J. Brett, 1739), 8; Spiltimber, *The Statesman*, 20; Mitchell, *Poems*, 2: 32.

12. Hildebrand Jacob, *Patriotic Love*, 6, 5; *An Epistle to the Right Honourable Sir Robert Walpole* (London: printed for W. Mears, 1728), 7.

13. The *Gentleman's Magazine*, 8: 653 (December, 1738).

14. "Congratulatory Verses," in *A Familiar Epistle*, 16. See also *An Epistle to Walpole; Occasion'd by the Writings of the Craftsman*:

> Like the strong Rock, that views beneath its Side
> The Billow broke, that strove its Top to hide;

Above the Waters, proud its Height to show,
The Surges dash'd, and dying all below. (9)

15. P. 16.

16. *Pro and Con*, 5. See, for instance, Joseph Mitchell, "The Sine-Cure" in *Poems*, 2: 11, and "The Promotion: A Third Poetical Petition to the Right Honourable Robert Walpole, Esq; for the Office and Importance of Secretary of State for Scotland," in *Poems*, 2: 32.

17. *The Monument: or, The Muse's Motion to the Right Honourable Sir Robert Walpole, Knight of the most Noble Order of the Garter, Upon Occasion of the Death of Sir Richard Steele, Knt.* (London: printed for James Roberts, 1729), 4.

18. *The Statesman's Mirrour, or, Friendly Advice to a Certain Great Minister to Retire from Court. A Poem* (London: printed for J. Huggonson. 1741), 5, 6, 8–9.

19. "To the Right Honourable Sir Robert Walpole with the *Manners of the Age*," in *Miscellaneous Collection*, 139–40.

20. See Shelley Burtt, 15–38.

21. Skinner, 126.

22. King, 44 and Coxe, 1: 757.

23. Burtt, 10. See, however, Lord Hervey's assertion in *Observations on a Pamphlet*: "I believe I may venture to say, this is almost the only Court, the only Reign, in which no one single Instance was ever pretended to be given, of Solicitation made or Favour shown, by the Force of Money" (22–23).

24. Hanson, 107, 108.

25. Howard, *Letters*, 2: 700 (Pitt to Cooke, 14 November 1742).

26. *What of That! Occasion'd by a Pamphlet, intitled, Are These Things So ? And, in Answer, Yes, They Are* (London: printed for T. Cooper, 1740), 7; Mitchell, "Congratulatory Verses," in *A Familiar Epistle*, 14.

27. *Seasonable Admonitions. A Satire. Most Humbly Address'd to the Right Honourable ****** ******** (London: printed for J. Roberts, 1740), 4. For the authorship to this poem, see CUL, Ch (H) Corr., 3089 (James Ruffhead to Walpole, 15 February 1740).

28. "To a Right Honourable Grumbletonian," in *Poems*, 2: 299–302.

29. *A Letter from Mr. Congreve to the Right Honourable the Lord Viscount Cobham* (London: printed for A. Dodd and E. Nutt, 1729), 6.

30. *Poems*, 2: 322–23.

31. Percival, 105–7; *The New Dozen at Westminster; Or Caleb's Good Men, and True* (London: printed for A. Moore, [1729]), 4, 5.

32. J. H. Plumb, *Sir Robert Walpole*, 2 vols, Vol. 1: *The Making of a Statesman* (London: The Cresset Press, 1956), Vol. 2: *The King's Minister* (London: Allen Lane the Penguin Press, 1960), 2: 216; BL, HHP, Add. MS, 51396, fol. 65r (Hervey to Fox, 13 September 1731); *The Opinions of Lady Marlborough*, 15–16.

33. She spoke of her son-in-law the Duke of Montagu's post as Master of the Grand Wardrobe "which I got him for life, and which I was assured by a very understanding man, he would farm of him, and give him £ 8000 a year" (*The Opinions of Lady Marlborough*, 59).

34. *A Touch of the Times. A New Ballad. To the Tune of, Oh!* London is a Fine Town (London: printed for T. Cooper, 1740); Percival, 135.

35. *Analecta*, 3: 228.

36. See, for instance, B. W. Last's assertion that Walpole was "self-made, without a particular social order or tradition behind him" (1).

37. Percival, 1.

38. Charles Beckingham, *An Ode to the Right Honourable Sir Robert Walpole, Knight of the Most Noble Order of the Garter. On his Installation* (London: printed for and sold by J. Millan, J. Roberts, N. Blandford, A. Dodd, E. Nutt, J. Millar, [1726]), 4.

39. Beckingham, *An Ode to the Right Honourable Sir Robert Walpole*, 3.

40. "The Patriot-Statesman," a panegyrical print on Walpole (Langford, 173); CUL, Ch (H) Corr., 1776 (Arthur Collins to Walpole, 10 June 1738); "An Ode in Imitation of the First Horace. Inscrib'd to the Right Honourable Sir Robert Walpole" in *The Two First Odes of Horace Imitated, With an Introductory Epistle to a Friend* (London: sold by James Roberts, 1738), 5.

41. "Congratulatory Verses," in *A Familiar Epistle*, 13.

42. "Congratulatory Verses," in *A Familiar Epistle*, 15.

43. King, 41.

44. Quoted in F.P.W. Rogers, "The Authorship of 'Four Letters to a Friend in North Britain' and Other Pamphlets Attributed to Robert Walpole," *Bulletin of the Institute of Historical Research*, 44, no. 110 (1971), 236, n. 3; "Walpole's Account of Sir Charles Hanbury Williams," *Correspondence*, 30: 314 (Appendix 3).

45. King, 179; *The Character of Pericles; A Funeral Oration, Sacred to the Memory of a Great Man* (London: printed for M. Cooper, 1745), 5.

46. Quoted in Rogers, "Authorship"; *Some Material towards Memoirs of the Reign of George II*, 1: xlix; Quoted by Jeremy Black in *Robert Walpole & the Nature of Politics in Early Eighteenth Century England*, paperback edition (London, 1990), 34.

47. Kenneth Baker, *The Prime Ministers: An Irreverent Political History of Cartoons* (London: Thames and Hudson, 1995), 27.

48. Dedication to Walpole in *The Fall of Saguntum. A Tragedy* (London: printed for J. Crokatt and T. Wood and sold by J. Roberts, 1727), i, iii.

49. *The Royal Hermitage or Temple of Honour: A Poem to Her Majesty the Queen-Regent. To which is Prefix'd, An Epistle to the Right Honourable Sir Robert Walpole* (London: printed for J. Roberts, 1732), 3, 4.

50. CUL, Ch (H) Corr., 1394a (ND).

51. Eusden, *An Epistle to the Noble, and Right Honourable Sir Robert Walpole* (London: printed, and sold by J. Roberts, 1726); John Withers, *An Epistle to the Right Honourable Robert Walpole, Esq; Upon his Majesty's Arrival.*

52. *The Monument*, 2, 3.

53. Greene, 140; "Congratulatory Verses," in *A Familiar Epistle*, 15.

54. *The Twickenham Hotch-Potch*, ii–vi.

55. *The Free Briton*, 39 (27 August 1730).

56. *London Journal*, 611 (10 April 1731), quoted in Hanson, 112.

57. "Postscript," in *A Familiar Epistle*, 11.

58. Edinburgh University Library, La.II.451/2, fol. 364r, Manuscript Life of Joseph Mitchell by John Graham (30 November 1795) and another Manuscript Life by the same (15 April 1797); *A Familiar Epistle*, 11.

59. "The Shoe-heel: A Rhapsody," in *Poems*, 2: 109–10.

60. Hardwicke, *Walpoliana*, 10; Coxe, 1: 759.

61. Plumb, 2: 112–14.

62. Quoted in Donald J. Greene, "Is there a Tory Prose Style?," *Bulletin of the New York Public Library.*

63. Thomas Cooke, "Verses Occasioned by the Death of Lady Malpas," printed in the *St. James's Evening-Post*, 13 January 1732, and included in *Poems on Affairs of State*, 15–16.

CHAPTER 9: "THE BEST OF PRINCES": THE ROYAL FAMILY
IN PRO-GOVERNMENT WORKS

The Crafts of the Craftsmen; or, A Detection of the Designs of the Coalition: Con-
taining Memoirs of the History of False Patriotism for the Year 1735 (London:
printed for J. Roberts, 1736), 5.

1. Hervey, *Memoirs*, 2: 224.

2. For diametrically opposed views concerning the Tories and Jacobitism see
Eveline Cruickshanks, *Political Untouchables: The Tories and the '45* (London:
Duckworth, 1979) and Linda Colley, *In Defiance of Oligarchy: The Tory Party
1714–60* (Cambridge, UK: Cambridge University Press, 1982).

3. See, for instance, Lady Mary Wortley Montagu's description of George I
("In private Life, he would have been call'd an Honest Blockhead") and the future
George II ("being unhappily under the Direction of a small Understanding was
every day throwing him upon some Indiscretion") and further comments in her
"Account of the Court of George I" in Lady Mary Wortley Montagu, *Essays and
Poems and Simplicity, a Comedy*, eds. Robert Halsband and Isobel Grundy, paper-
back edition (Oxford: Clarendon Press, 1993), 86, 93.

4. *The Letters of Atticus, as Printed in the London Journal, in the Years 1729
and 1730, on Various Subjects* (London: printed by J. Chrichley and sold by J.
Roberts, 1731), 10.

5. *The Conduct of the Opposition, and the Tendency of Modern Patriotism, . . .
Review'd and Examin'd* (London: printed for J. Peele, 1734), 45–46.

6. Lord Hervey, *Observations on the Writings of the Craftsman* (London:
printed for J. Roberts, 1730), 14–15.

7. *An Epistle to Walpole; Occasion'd by the Writings of the Craftsman*, 5.

8. BL, NC, Add. MS, 32689, fol. 45r-v (Delafaye to Newcastle, 12 October
1734).

9. Dickinson, 57–59; "An Epistle to the Right Honourable the Lord Viscount
Cornbury", in *Odes and Epistles* (London: printed for R. Dodsley, 1739), 44. Few
of them would, however, have agreed with Nugent when he—inspired by Bolingbroke's thoughts on the subject of patriotic princes—referred to "Kings, the necessary Curse of Heav'n" (41).

10. "An Essay to Virtue. To the Honourable Philip Yorke, Esq.," in *Poems by
*****, 46.

11. Francis Manning, "The Second Ode to Augustus Cæsar Imitated," in *The
Two First Odes of Horace Imitated*, 11–12.

12. Gerrard, 55; *Timoleon*, dedication and 5, 61–62.

13. Laurence Eusden, "A Poem, On the Happy Succession, and Coronation of
His Present Majesty," in *Three Poems; The First, Sacred to the Immortal Memory
of the Late King; The Second, On the Happy Succession, and Coronation of His
Present Majesty; And a Third Humbly Inscrib'd to the Queen* (London: printed for
James Roberts and sold by R. and J. Dodsley, S. Barker, and G. Woodfall, 1727),
10.

14. *Ratho: A Poem to the King* (London: printed for John Gray, 1728); *Memoirs
of Viscountess Sundon*, 2: 86 and 176 (Wainwright to Charlotte Clayton, 11 April
1731).

15. *A Poem on the Marriage of His Serene Highness the Prince of Orange, with
Anne, Princess-Royal of Great Britain* (no imprint, 1734), 3.

16. *The Gods in Debate: or, No Bribe like Beauty. A New Ballad, on the Prince*

of Orange's Arrival (London: printed for J. Roberts and sold by W. Waring), 4 n, 8.

17. Eusden, "A Poem Sacred to the Immortal Memory of the Late King," in *Three Poems*, 6.

18. *Verses to the Lord Carteret, Occasioned by the Present Conspiracy*, 1.

19. *A Poem to Her Royal Highness the Princess of Wales* (London: printed for J. Walthoe, 1737), 3–4. See also "To the Queen" in R.R. B.D. [Richard Roach], *Carmen Corunarium: or, A Gratulatory Poem on the Coronation of King George II. and Queen Caroline* (London: printed for N. Blandford, 1727), in which the Queen is addressed as "QUEEN, *Bride*, and *Fruitful Mother* All in *One* | Surrounded with your Bright and *Royal Train*" (5).

20. Colley, *Britons*, 202.

21. *An Ode for His Majesty's Birth-day, October 30, 1731* (London: printed for John Watts, 1731), 8.

22. *Ratho*, 25.

23. Mitchell, *The Royal Hermitage*, 7–8, 10.

24. Colley, *Britons*, 200–204; Beattie, 264–68. When the Prince and Princess of Wales set up a theater in their summer abode at Richmond, the king had one erected in the Great Hall at Hampton Court (274).

25. *The Opinions of Lady Marlborough*, 13.

26. *Ratho*, 30; William Dunkin seems to have changed political sides more than once. John Boyle, firth Earl of Orrery (opposition supporter, see *Dictionary of National Biography*, 2: 1019) was so incensed against Dunkin who had flattered him in early productions, but later "abused . . . xtremely, in anonymous Papers, & over hibernian claret" that he wrote on the flyleaf of Dunkin's *Epistola ad Franciscum Bindonem, Arm. cui adjiciuntur quatuor Odae* (Dublin: printed for George Faulkner, 1741), given him by the author (CUL, classmark Hib. 7. 741. 27): "O God! how much more, in general, to thy honour is the brute than the human creation!"

27. *Catalogue of Prints, Division 1*, vol. 3, part 1: xxv11.

28. Jeremy Black, *Robert Walpole*, 63; Louis D. Mitchell, "Command Performances during the Reign of George II," *Restoration and 18th Century Theatre Research* 1, part 1 (1986): 18–33; *Memoirs of Viscountess Sundon*, 2: 224.

29. Charles Carthy, *A Translation of the Second Book of Horace's Epistles, together with Some of the Most Select in the First, with Notes. A Pastoral Courtship, from Theocritus. One Original Poem in English, and a Latin Ode Spoken before the Government on His Majesty's Birth-Day, 1730* (Dublin: printed by Christopher Dickson, 1731), 1 n; *Verses on the Coronation of their Late Majesties King George II. and Queen Caroline, October 11, MDCCXXVII. Spoken by the Scholars of Westminster School . . .* (London: printed for W. Bowyer, 1761), 47.

30. See, for example, Eusden, "A Poem on the Happy Succession," in *Three Poems*, 15–17.

31. See, for instance, George Spiltimber, *To the King on his Majesty's Happy Return. An Ode* (London: printed for Charles Corbett [1740]).

32. BL, NC, Add. MS, 32689, fol. 170r (Lord Somerset to Newcastle, 18 March 1734). See also *Comitia Westmonasteriensium, in Collegio Sti Petri Habita Dei Anniversario Fundatricis suae Reginae Elizabethae Inauguratae Jan. XV.* (London: printed for William Bowyer, 1728).

33. McAleer, iii.

34. *A Poem on His Royal Highness Prince of Wales's Birth-Day* ([?Dublin], 1722); *Verses to the Lord Carteret Occasioned by the Present Conspiracy*, 3, 5;

Thomas Newcomb, "Q. Horatii Flacci ad Curionem Epistola: Or, An Epistle from Horace in Elizium to Curio in England, faithfully translated into English from the Elizian copy," in *Miscellaneous Collection*, 53. See also Newcomb's "The Campaign" (79).

35. Eusden, "A Poem on the Happy Succession," in *Three Poems*, 11.

36. William Bisset, "To the King," in *Verses Compos'd for the Birth-Day of our Most Gracious Queen Caroline: The First Birthday of a Protestant Queen Consort for One Hundred and Ten Years. Repeated the same Day in the Great Drawing-Room before Several of the First Quality* (London: printed for J. Roberts, 1728), 1.

37. Foss, 121; Davies, 10–11; "On the Death of the late Queen Caroline. A Poetical Dialogue between Windsor and Richmond," in *The Norfolk Poetical Miscellany*, 271, 270; Nichols, *Illustrations*, 2: 474.

38. See, for example, "To the Queen," in R.R.B.D. [Richard Roach], *Carmen Coronarium*, 6, and Charles Beckingham, *A Poem on His Most Sacred Majesty King George the IId, His Accession to the Throne. Addressed to the Right Honourable the Earl of Peterborow [sic]* (London: printed by J. Read and sold by T. Warner, [1727], and reprinted in Dublin for J. Gowan, 1727), 1.

39. *Verses on her Majesty's Birth-day* (London: printed for J. Watts, 1728), 4.

40. *The Opinions of Lady Marlborough*, 40.

41. *Reports on the Manuscripts of the Earl of Eglinton . . . C.F. Weston Underwood Esquire . . .* , Historical Manuscript Commission Report on the Manuscripts (London: Eyre & Spottiswoode, 1885), 514 (intercepted letter, Hamilton to "Mr Kelly at Avignon," 14 February 1738) and 513 (copy of intercepted letter from Hamilton to the Duke of Ormonde, 27 January 1738) and 518 (Hamilton to Ormonde, 18 April 1738). These letters are among the Weston MSS.

42. *The Vision. A Poem on the Death of Her Most Gracious Majesty Queen Caroline* (London: printed by Samuel Richardson [see Foxon, 1: 202] for J. Roberts and J. Jackson, 1737), 3, 4, 6–7.

43. *The Dream. A Poem, Sacred to the Blessed and Glorious Memory of her late Majesty Queen Caroline* (London: printed for J. Roberts, 1737), 8, 10, 11–12.

44. Frances Manning, *On the Late Queen's Sickness and Death, an Ode. Address'd to His Grace the Duke of Newcastle, One of His Majesty's Principal Secretary's of State, &c.* (London: printed for T. Cooper, 1738), 15.

45. Beckingham, *A Poem on His Most Sacred Majesty King George the IId, His Accession to the Throne*, 1.

46. Cable, 119–20, 121. This disillusionment he voiced in his *Letter on the Spirit of Patriotism*. In *Letters on the Spirit of Patriotism: On the Idea of a Patriot King: On the State of Parties, at the Accession of King George the First* (London: printed for A. Millar, 1749).

47. Cable, 123. For a thorough analysis of Patriot Opposition writers and their association with Prince Frederick's court, see Garrard.

48. James Weston, *The Assembled Patriots; or, the Meeting of the Parliament. A Poem, Dedicated to His Majesty* (London: printed for T. Dormer, 1732), 9.

49. See, for example, Francis Hawling, "Verses upon the Much-Lamented Death of Her Sacred Majesty Queen Caroline. Humbly Inscrib'd to Her Royal Highness the Princess Amelia," in *A Miscellany of Original Poems on Various Subjects . . . Part I* (London: printed for S. Austen, J. Wood and J. Crockat, [1751]), 19.

50. In *The Two First Odes of Horace Imitated*, 12–15.

CHAPTER 10. THE ATTACK ON THE OPPOSITION

1. Cranfield, *The Development of the Provincial Newspaper*, 125–26, 131.

2. G. A. Cranfield, *The Press and Society: From Caxton to Northcliffe* (London and New York: Longman, 1978), 46.

3. CUL, CH (H) Corr., 1507 (Madden to Walpole, September NY).

4. *Catalogue of Prints, Division 1*, vol. 3, part 1: 369–72 (Print 2479).

5. "The Haughty . . ." from *Sedition and Defamation Display'd in a Letter to the Author of the Craftsman* (London: printed for James Roberts, 1731), 43.

6. *An Epistle to Walpole; Occasion'd by the Writings of the Craftsman*, 3; Nottingham University Library, Ne C 191 (Weston to Newcastle, ND).

7. *The Free Briton*, 14 (5 March 1729).

8. BL, Robinson Papers, Add. MS, 23789, fol. 10v (Charles Delafaye to Sir Thomas Robinson, 27 July/7 August 1733).

9. Arnall, *Opposition no Proof of Patriotism*, 11; *A Faithful Report of a Genuine Debate*, 2.

10. *L[or]d B[olingbro]ke's Speech upon the Convention. To the Tune of A Cobler there was* (London: printed for Jacob Littleton, 1739), 4, 7; *Sir *** Speech upon the Peace. To the Tune of the Abbot of Canterbury* (London: printed for Jacob Lock, 1739).

11. "Congratulatory Verses," in *A Familiar Epistle*, 16.

12. Joseph Mitchell, "Congratulatory Verses," in *A Familiar Epistle*, 16; Verses under the print "The Funeral of Faction" (London: printed for T. Cooper, 1741), reproduced in McAleer, 17.

13. "The Patriot-Statesman," reproduced in Langford, 173.

14. *The Fall of Saguntum*, 41.

15. *Manners: An Epistle to Alexander Pope Esq; and Mr. Whitehead* (London: printed for T. Cooper, 1739), 7. See also James Meredith, *Manners Deciphered: A Reply to Mr. Whitehead, on his Satire Call'd Manners* (London: printed for T. Cooper [1739]).

16. *Verses Addressed to the Right Honourable Sir Robert Walpole, On Her Majesty's being Constituted Regent of Great Britain*, 4.

17. *The False Patriot's Confession; or, B-k's Address to Ambition. In Imitation of the First Ode, of the Fourth Book of Horace* (London: printed for R. Charlton, 1737), 8.

18. CUL, Ch (H) Papers, bundle 75, item 11. The copies were "Furnished for His Majesty's Service" by S. Buckley on 27 May 1735.

19. CUL, Ch (H) Corr., 1507 (Samuel Madden to Walpole, September NY).

20. *A Faithful Report of a Genuine Debate*, 2; Mitchell, "To Aaron Hill, Esq;," *Poems*, 1: 312. That "Mobs are but *Mobs* and always in the *Wrong*" is a commonplace in pro-government works: see *A Poetical Essay on Vulgar Praise and Hate; In which is contain'd, The Character of a Modern Patriot* (London: printed for T. Cooper, 1733), 15.

21. *The Conduct of the Opposition*, 49.

22. *The Citizen's Procession*, 4.

23. *L[or]d B[olingbro]ke's Speech upon the Convention*, 6.

24. *Come on Then.—Occasioned by a Pamphlet Lately Published, Intituled. Have at You All. By the Author of, They Are Not* (London: printed for T. Cooper, 1740), 7.

25. *Opposition No Proof of Patriotism*, 5.

26. Quoted in Michael C. McGee, " 'Not Men, but Measures': The Origins and

Import of an Ideological Principle," *The Quarterly Journal of Speech* 64 (1978): 144.

27. *The Jovial Crew. A Comic-Opera. As it is Acted at the Theatre-Royal in Covent-Garden, by His Majesty's Servants* (London: printed for J. Watts, 1731), 25, 53; *Biographica Dramatica*, 2: 349.

28. The whole print is reproduced in Langford, 204–5.

29. *The Statesman's Mirrour*, 10–11.

30. Newcomb, *The Manners of the Age: in Thirteen Moral Satires. Written with a Design to Expose the Vicious and Irregular Conduct of Both Sexes* (London: printed for Jer. Batley, 1733), 66–67.

31. *The Case of Opposition Stated, Between the Craftsman and the People. Occasioned by his Paper of December the 4th, 1731* (London: printed for J. Roberts, 1731), 33; Mitchell, "The Muse's Commission to Sir R. Walpole," in *Gentleman's Magazine* 2 (1732): 1076; *The Citizen's Procession.*

32. Henry Carey, *The Grumbletonians, or The Dogs Without-Doors. A Tale* (London: printed for J. Peele, 1727), 4.

33. *The Fall of Saguntum*, 21, 31, 38, 69–70.

34. "In Answer to the Craftsman's Three Wills," LWL, HWA, 71 - 11383, fol. 96 (Williams to Lady Frances Williams, 14 January 1735). This poem has never been published but Hanbury Williams wanted his wife to show it to two named individuals.

35. Gerrard, 22; William Speck, " 'Whigs and Tories Dim their Glories': English Political Parties under the First Two Georges," in *The Whig Ascendancy: Colloquies on Hanoverian England*, ed. John Cannon (London: Edward Arnold, 1981), 62.

36. Coxe, 3: 180.

37. Sir Charles Hanbury Williams, "On the Princess going to St. James's in February 1741–2," in *Works*, 1: 242; *The Conduct of the Opposition*, 40; *A Coalition of Patriots Delineated: Or, A Just Display of the Union of Jacobites, Malecontents, Republicans, and False Friends, with an Attainted Old Traitor to Revile the Ministry; Impose upon the People; Set Aside the Succession; and Bring in the Pretender* (London: printed for T. Cooper, 1735), 4, 6–7.

38. *The Faction. A Tale. Humbly Inscrib'd to Messrs. Craftsmen & Compy* (London: James Roberts, 1740), 3, 5, 7, 8, frontispiece.

39. Gerrard, 36; *The Oak and the Dunghill; A Fable* (London: printed: and sold by James Roberts, 1728), 5.

40. Horace Walpole, *Correspondence*, 13: 119 (29 December).

41. *Works*, 1: 26–27, 22, and "An Ode to Viscount Lonsdale," in *Works*, 2: 48.

42. *An Epistle to the Right Honourable Sir Robert Walpole* (London: printed for J. Walthoe, 1726). The 1741 edition was printed for T. Cooper, see Foxon, 1: 191. One might, of course, question whether the poem was generally known to be written by Dodington, since his name does not appear on the title-page. However, Foxon notes that the copies at Leeds University Library (the Brotherton Collection), the British Library, and Yale University Library all have manuscript attributions to Dodington. This is at least highly suggestive (Foxon, 1: 191).

43. Williams, *Works*, 1: 23; Thomas Newcomb, "Librorum Catalogus, &c. A Catalogue of Several Curious and Valuable Pieces (Chiefly Controversial) to be Sold by Auction the 26th Instant, at the Great Auction-room against the Royal Exchange, Cornhill," in *Miscellaneous Collection*, 347.

44. Williams, *Works*, 1: 34–35; Sedgwick, 2: 422–23; Hervey, *Memoirs*, 3: 740.

45. Williams, *Works*, 1: 34–5.
46. Williams, *Works*, 1: 30–36.
47. Williams, *Works*, 1: 20.
48. Williams, *Works*, 1: 69.
49. Williams, *Works*, 1: 28.
50. Williams, "To the Rev. Samuel Hill, Canon of Wells, &c. &c.," in *Works*, 2: 60; *Ratho*, 26.
51. Williams, "An Ode to the Right Honourable the Viscount Lonsdale," *Works*, 2: 53–54.
52. BL, Stowe MS, 308, Remarks written in December 1791 by Horace Walpole in his own hand to Lord Chesterfield's *Characters*; Coxe, 1: 757. For Shippen's political career, see Sedgwick, 2: 422–23.
53. Jeremy Black, *Robert Walpole*, 22.
54. Jenyns, *Poems by *****, 37–38.
55. *Works*, 1: 61–70.
56. BL, HHP, Add. MS, 51390, fol. 4v (Williams to Henry Fox, 28 October 1739); Coxe, 2: 137 (letter from Meadowcourt to Delafaye, 16 April 1733). For Meadowcourt's impeccable Whig credentials, see Duncombe, *Correspondence*, 3: 75–76 n.
57. *Sedition and Defamation Display'd*, 1.
58. The poem—attributed to Lord Hervey—was printed in 1730 by A. Moore, a name David Foxon believes to be fictitious (Foxon, 1: 44 and 2: 172).
59. *The Humble Petition of His Grace Ph[ili]p D[uke] of Wh[arto]n to a Great Man* (London: printed for A. Brooks, 1730), 6–7.
60. *The Humble Petition of His Grace Ph[ili]p D[uke] of Wh[arto]n*, 6–7; Peter Wagner, *Eros Revived: Erotica of the Enlightenment in England and America* (London: Paladin Grafton Books, 1990), 47–86; Loftis, 79.
61. In *Verses Addressed to . . . Walpole, On her Majesty's being Constituted Regent*, 4; In *A Political Conversation Which Lately Happened between a Couple of Stanch Patriots, and a Revolter to the Court-Interest. In which Many Important Points are Canvass'd, the True Designs of Both Parties Open'd, and not a Little Secret History Revealed* (London: printed for T. Cowper, 1733), for instance, Will (William Pulteney) asks Harry (Lord Bolingbroke) to try to look more cheerful in their projected conversation with the independent politician Sir Joseph Jekyll: "Do you not consider that your Gloominess may fix him to t'other Side? Who would rejoin a sinking Party" (8).
62. McAleer, 22.
63. *Memoirs of the Twentieth Century* (London: printed by John Bowyer Nichols etc., 1731), 21, 51–52.
64. Wilkins, 220 n.
65. Percival, 160–61; *The Grand Defeat: or, The Downfall of the S[an]d[on]ian Party* (London: printed in the year 1741), 7.
66. Williams, *Works*, 1: 61–70.
67. *The Case of Opposition Stated*, 18.
68. *A Coalition of Patriots Delineated*, 25.
69. Printed separately in 1733 (no imprint), and reprinted in Wilkins, 243.
70. Dickinson, 16.
71. See, for instance, *The Opinions of Lady Marlborough*, 65.
72. *A Selection from the Papers of the Earls of Marchmont, in the Possession of the Right Honble Sir George Henry Rose. Illustrative of the Events from 1685 to 1750*, ed. G. H. Rose, 3 vols (London: John Murray, 1831), 2: 204 (Bolingbroke to Viscount Polwarth, New-Year's Day, 1740), as cited by Coley, 163.

73. *Notes and Queries*, Third Series, 2: 401.

74. *Sedition and Defamation Display'd*, 5.

75. *Letters of Atticus*, 49–50.

76. *A Coalition of Patriots Delineated*, 11.

77. Thomas Newcomb, "Librorum Catalogus," *Miscellaneous Collection*, 348.

78. Thomas Newcomb, "Librorum Catalogus," *Miscellaneous Collection*, 348.

79. BL, HHP, Add. MS, 51391, fol. 20r (Williams to Fox, Tuesday ND, annotated "? 9 Sept 1746") and BL, NC, Add. MS, 32698, fol. 395r ("Philo-Georgius" to Newcastle, 7 December 1741).

80. Williams, "A Grub upon Bub," *Works*, 1: 27.

81. Williams, *Works*, 2: 93–94 and 1: 69–70.

82. *The Three Politicians: or, A Dialogue in Verse between a Patriot, a Courtier, and their Friend. Concluding with an Exhortation to Admiral Vernon* (London: printed for T. Cooper, 1741).

83. *Memoirs of George II*, 1: 487.

84. Horace Walpole, *Reminiscences Written by Mr. Horace Walpole in 1788 for the Amusement of Miss Mary and Miss Agnes Berry,* ed. Paget Toynby (Oxford: Clarendon Press, 1824), 95.

85. See, for instance, Hervey's comments on the possibility that Carteret might wish to return to the flock, *Memoirs*, 2: 410.

86. Williams, "A New Ode to a Great Number of Great Men, Newly Made," *Works*, 1: 138.

87. Percival, 46.

88. Sedgwick, 2: 375–76.

89. Sedgwick, 2: 375–76; *The Lives of Dr. Edward Pocock . . . Dr. Zachary Pearce . . . Dr. Thomas Newton . . . and of the Rev. Philip Skelton*, 2 vols (London: F.C. & J. Rivington, 1816), 2: 134, 139, 135; BL, HHP, Add. MS, 51427, fol. 33v (A. Pulteney to Lady Caroline Lennox, 18 June 1741); Richard Brinsley Peake, *Memoirs of the Colman Family, Including their Correspondence with the most Distinguished Personages of their Time*, 2 vols (London: Richard Bentley, 1841), 1: 55, 8–9.

90. Davies, 43–44.

91. Davies, 29; "The Patriot-Statesman," in Langford, 173.

92. Ll. 9–12.

93. Horace Walpole to Ailesbury, quoted in *Catalogue of Prints*, 391.

94. LWL, CHW, 67 — 10929, fol. 133v (Harris to Williams, 13 October 1752, N.S.).

95. *A Hue and Cry*, 2–3.

96. "Modern Characters," in *A Hue and Cry*, 28.

97. See Percival, 61.

98. Swithin Adee, *The Craftsman's Apology. Being a Vindication of his Conduct and Writings: In Several Letters to the King* (London: printed for T. Cooper, 1732), 5, 11.

99. *Notes and Queries*, Third Series, 2: 402.

100. *Lord B[olingbrok]e's Speech on the Convention*, 4–7.

101. *The Grand Accuser*, 79–80; *A Letter from Sir Robert Walpole to the Lord Bolingbroke* (Dublin: printed by William Shaw-Anburey, 1727).

102. See *An Elegy on the Much Lamented Death of Harry Gambol, who Dy'd of a Pleuresy, Aug. 31* ([London]: printed for John Nichols [1714]).

103. BL, NC, Add. MS, 32687, fol. 518r ("Smith" to Newcastle, ND).

104. "Vindicta Britannica; an Ode to the Real Patriot: Occasioned by the Declaration of War against Spain," in *Miscellaneous Collection*, 5.

105. *Sedition and Defamation Display'd*, 2–3.

106. *Muse in Distress*, 7; *The Tinker Turn'd Politician*, printed in Wilkins, 258. For an attack on Bolingbroke under the name of D'Anvers see "*Aye* and *No*," in Wilkins, 255–56 n., and for an attack on Pulteney under the same name see "The Patriot at full length; or, an inscription for an obelisk."

107. Mottley, *The Craftsman, or, Weekly Journalist: a Farce* (London: printed for J. Roberts, 1728), 13, 4, 5.

108. Ibid, 14, 17.

109. *A Full and True Account of the Sad and Deplorable Death of Caleb D'Anvers, Esq; Who Dy'd Suddenly* (London: printed and sold by J. Roberts, 1731), 17–19.

110. Weinbrot, "Persius, the Opposition to Walpole, and Pope" in *Eighteenth-Century Satire: Essays on Text and Context from Dryden to Peter Pindar* (Cambridge, UK: Cambridge University Press, 1988), 152; *The Grand Accuser*, 30–31.

111. *Sequel of a Pamphlet Intitled Observations on the Writings of the Craftsman* (London: printed for J. Roberts, 1730), 29.

112. "The History of the Traytors Edric the Father, and Edric the Son, and of the Settlement of the Danes on the English Throne," printed in the *British Journal*, 23 January 1731, and included in *Poems on Affairs of State*, 20–24; *Catalogue of Prints*, vol. 3, part 1: 379–80 (Print no. 2487).

113. See, for instance, the frontispiece to *The Life and Death of Pierce Gaveston, Earl of Cornwall; Grand Favourite, and Prime Minister to that Unfortunate Prince, Edward II. King of England. With Political Remarks, by Way of Caution to all Crowned Heads and Evil Ministers. By a True Patriot* (London: printed for G. Bickham, 1740) described in *Catalogue of Prints*, vol. 3, part 1: 353 (Print no. 2462); "The Patriot-Statesman," in Langford, 173. See also Kramnick, 25.

114. In the pro-government print "The Patriot-Statesman," for instance, a figure representing Walpole is greeted by "mighty Burleigh" as he enters "the temple of Fame," see Langford, 173.

115. Thomas Tickell, *On Her Majesty's Re-Building the Lodgings of the Black Prince, and Henry V, At Queen's-College Oxford* (London: printed for J. Tonson, 1733), 7.

116. Gerrard, 150–84; "On her Majesty's Statue in St. Paul's Church-Yard," in *Miscellaneous Poems by Several Hands*, ed. James Ralph, 340–41.

117. Kramnick, 29.

118. *Manners*, 15.

119. Hinde, *Tales*, 145; Quoted by Skinner, 117, 122.

120. Coxe, 1: 762.

121. *The Senator*, 5 March 1728 (no. 8).

122. Quoted by Percival, xiv.

123. Published in *The London Journal* and *Read's Weekly Journal* on 6 February 1731 and reprinted in Percival, 48–49.

CHAPTER 11: "WIT WITH MALICE"

1. Nichols, *Illustrations*, 1: 602.

2. Lord Ilchester, 112.

3. Howard, *Letters*, 690; Nichols, *Illustrations*, 2: 621 (Theobald to Warburton, 17 November 1731) and 2: 552 (Theobald to Warburton, 10 March 1729);

Memoirs of Viscountess Sundon, 1: 197 (Alured Clarke to Charlotte Clayton, ND); *A Letter from Mr. Cibber to Mr. Pope*, 8.

4. [Matthew Concanen], "From the Whitehall Evening-Post March 21 1728. An Epigram," in *A Compleat Collection of all the Verses, Essays, Letters and Advertisements, which have been Occasioned by the Publication of Three Volumes of Miscellanies, by Pope and Company. To which is Added an Exact List of the Lords, Ladies, Gentlemen and Others, who have been Abused in these Volumes* (London: printed for A. Moore, 1728), 8.

5. Cooke, *Tales, Epistles, Odes, Fables*, 105–15; *Letters of Atticus*, 36, 35; Spence, 163.

6. See Peter Seary, *Lewis Theobald and the Editing of Shakespeare* (Oxford: Clarendon Press, 1990).

7. *Gentleman's Magazine* 61, part 2 (1791): 1092; Nichols, *Illustrations*, 2: 730 and n.

8. *Homerides: or, Homer's First Book Moderniz'd. By Sir Iliad Doggrel* (London: printed for R. Burleigh, 1716); BL, Add. MS, 36772, fol. 121r–v (Thomas Burnet to George Duckett, 1 June 1716).

9. "To the Author of the Dunciad" and "From the British Journal, Nov. 25. 1727" in Concanen, *A Compleat Collection*, v–vi, 4.

10. Bolingbroke, *Contributions to the Craftsman*, viii, xxvi.

11. *Hyp-Doctor*, no. 48 (9 November 1731), quoted in Stevens, 126, n. 23.

12. Erskine-Hill, "Alexander Pope: The Political Poet in His Time," in *Modern Essays on 18th Century Literature*, ed. Leopold Damrosch (New York and Oxford: Oxford University Press, 1988), 133.

13. *The State Dunces*, 3; *Works of Alexander Pope*, ed. Bowles, 5: 247 n. (by Warburton).

14. *Remarks on Homer*, 9, 91.

15. Spence, 167–68.

16. Leman Thomas Rede, *Anecdotes & Biography, Including many Modern Characters in the Circles of the Fashionable and Official Life . . . Alphabetically Arranged* (London: printed by J.W. Meyers for R. Pitheathley, 1799), 338–39. That Pope had refused the visit of the queen was mentioned in contemporary poems, like "To Dr. D—ny, Occasion'd by an Epistle to_____" included in *A Vindication of the Libel on Dr. Delany, And a Certain Great Lord. Together with a Panegyric on Dean Sw—t . . .* (Dublin: reprinted in London, for J. Wilford, 1730):

> Hail! happy *Pope*, whose gen'rous Mind,
> Detesting all the Statesman Kind,
> Contemning *Courts*, at *Courts* unseen,
> Refus'd the Visits of a _____. (14)

17. Davies, 15; *Memoirs of Viscountess Sundon*, 1: 197 (Clarke to Sundon, ND).

18. Spence, 182.

19. John M. Aden, "Pope and Politics: 'The Farce of State,' " in *Alexander Pope*, ed. Peter Dixon, *Writers and their Backgrounds* (London: G. Bell & Sons, 1972), 183 and n. 1; Erskine-Hill, "Alexander Pope: The Political Poet," 128; Greene, 66.

20. James A. Winn, "On Pope, Printers, and Publishers," *Eighteenth-Century Life* 6, no. 2–3 (1981): 94; "Vision and Metamorphosis," 81; Reginald Berry, *A Pope Chronology* (London: Macmillan, 1988), 66, 88.

21. Aden, 194.

22. Erskine-Hill, "Alexander Pope: the Political Poet," 134; E. P. Thomson, *Whigs and Hunters: The Origin of the Black Act* (Harmondsworth: Penguin, 1975), 278–94.

23. Nichols, *Illustrations*, 2: 176 (extract of letter from Warburton to Jortin [? 1749]).

24. Spence, 38.

25. Erskine-Hill, "Alexander Pope: The Political Poet," 137; Alexander Pope, *Poetical Works*, ed. Herbert Davis (Oxford and New York: Oxford University Press, 1978), 357 (ll. 221–24).

26. Ibid., p. 38.

27. Oldys, 31; Newcomb, "An Ode on Similes, on some Late Imitations of Horace", in *Miscellaneous Collection*, 52.

28. Jones, *Theobald*, 150, 305–6 (Theobald to Warburton, 4 July 1732) and 310 (Theobald to Warburton, 10 January 1733). Similarly, although Chisselden helped Theobald with an emendation, the latter had "no Liberty to name him," presumably because he was a friend of Pope's (316 [Theobald to Warburton, 28 July 1733]).

29. Jones, *Theobald*, 298 (Theobald to Warburton, 21 March 1731).

30. Howard, *Letters*, 2: 598 (Antony Henley to Thomas Cooke, 19 August 1733).

31. BL, Add. MS, 32458, fol. 45v (Middleton to Hervey, 30 May 1738).

32. "Modern Characters" in *A Hue and Cry*, 27.

33. *An Epistle from a Nobleman to a Doctor of Divinity* (London: published by James Roberts, 1733), 17–18.

34. *The False Patriot*, 3, 4. Likewise Colley Cibber in *A Letter from Mr. Cibber to Mr. Pope*, accords the highest praise to Pope as a poet, yet attacks his character in no uncertain terms.

35. *Of Good Nature: An Epistle Inscrib'd to His G[rac]e the D[u]ke of C[hando]s* (London: printed by J. Hughs for T. Dormer, 1732), facsimile in *Early Eighteenth-Century Essays on Taste*, introduced by B. Gilmor (Delmar, New York: Scholars' Facsimiles & Reprints, 1972).

36. Thomas Newcomb, "'An Ode on Similes, on Some Late Imitations of Horace," in *Miscellaneous Collection*, 51–52.

37. Welsted, "Of Dulness and Scandal. Occasioned by the Character of Lord Timon. In Mr. Pope's Epistle to the Earl of Burlington," in *The Works, in Verse and Prose, of Leonard Welsted, Esq.*, ed. John Nichols (London: printed by and for the editor, 1787), 198. The poem had been published separately by T. Cooper in 1732 ; *The Muse in Distress*, 12.

38. *The False Patriot*, 11.

39. *Memoirs of Viscountess Sundon*, 1: 197 (Clarke to Charlotte Clayton, ND).

40. *Manners*, 7.

41. *A Hue and Cry*, 27.

42. *A Supplement to One Thousand Seven Hundred and Thirty-Eight. Not Written by Mr. Pope* (London: printed for J. Roberts, 1738), 7–8.

43. "Modern Characters," in *A Hue and Cry*, 27, 28.

44. Concanen, *A Compleat Collection*, 51–52.

45. A comment in a MS catalogue of Edward Hawkins's collection of satirical prints, quoted in *Catalogue of Prints, Division I*, 2: 808 (frontispiece to Print no. 1935, "Ingratitude").

46. *Of Good Nature*, 7, 15.

47. *Of Dulness and Scandall Occasion'd by the Character of Lord Timon, In*

Mr. Pope's Epistle to the Earl of Burlington (London: printed for T. Cooper, 1732). Chandos had been praised in verse long before Pope was accused of satirizing him, however. See Samuel Humphreys, *Cannons. A Poem. Inscrib'd to His Grace the Duke of Chandos* (London: printed for J. Roberts, 1728), in which even Envy is impressed with Cannons despite herself.

48. *An Epistle to the Little Satyrist of Twickenham* (London: printed for J. Wilford, 1733), 6. See also *Malice Defeated. A Pastoral Essay. Occasioned by Mr. Pope's Character of Lord Timon, in his Epistle to the Earl of Burlington, and Mr. Welsted's Answer* (London: printed for J. Millan, 1732).

49. Carretta, 61.

50. Printed in *Works of Pope*, ed. Bowles, 5: 171 n. (14 November 1730).

51. "Vision and Metamorphosis," 105, n. 21, referring to *Works of Pope*, ed. Bowles, 5: xxxiv.

52. Wortley Montagu, "Verses Address'd to the Imitator of the First Satire of the Second Book of Horace," in *Essays and Poems*, 268.

53. "From the Daily Journal, May 11. 1728" in Concanen, *A Compleat Collection*, 51; Wortley Montagu, "Verses Address'd to the Imitator of the First Satire of the Second Book of Horace," in *Essays and Poems*, 268, 270.

54. *Of Good Nature*, 9. See also *A Hue and Cry*.

55. Concanen, *A Miscellany on Taste*, 49.

56. "The English Inscription" of "Inscriptions graven on the Four Sides of the Pedestal, whereon is erected the Busto of Martinus Scriblerus, from which Original the Effigies prefix'd to this Work was [sic] Taken," in *Pope Alexander's Supremacy and Infallibility Examin'd*, vi.

57. Concanen, *A Miscellany on Taste*, title page and print; *Catalogue of Prints, Division 1*, vol. 3, part 1: 392 (Print no. 2498).

58. For the debate on satire, see Goldgar, *Walpole and the Wits*. Dean Thomas Herring's opinion of Pope seems to have been shared by many: "I would fain think as well of Mr. Pope's probity as I do of his ingenuity: but his compliments to Bolingbroke upon topics of behaviour in which he is notoriously infamous, so shock me, that they quite disconcert my good opinion of him. I have bought his works, however, in the pompous edition, and read them with peculiar pleasure. The brightness of his wit, his elegant turns, his raised sentiments in many places, and the musical cadence of his poetry, charm me prodigiously," *Collection of Letters*, ed. John Duncombe, 81–82 (Thomas Herring to William Duncombe, 12 May 1735).

59. "Verses Address'd to the Imitator of the First Satire of the Second Book of Horace," in *Essays and Poems*, 267.

CONCLUSION

1. BL, NC, Add. MS, 32689, fol. 421r (Delafaye to Newcastle, 23 September 1734).

2. BL, NC, Add. MS, 32689, fol. 445r–v (J. Pelham to Newcastle, 5 October 1734). Bolingbroke was "but rarely seen in the publick Rooms" and lived "altogether with his Friend Pope, who accompanyd him hither, and, I suppose, a very few more who think in the same way with him," see BL, NC, Add. MS, 32689, fol. 430r (Delafaye to Newcastle, 28 September 1734).

3. BL, NC, Add. MS, 32689, fol. 455r (J. Pelham to Newcastle, 12 October 1734).

4. BL, Birch Correspondence, Add. MS, 4313, fols 153v–154r (Benjamin Martyn to Birch, 19 October 1747); Chapman, 8.

5. *Historical Manuscripts Commission. Miscellaneous Collections* 8 (Vicountess Irwin to Charles Ingram, 1721), quoted in Mark Blackett-Ord, *Hell-Fire Duke* (Windsor Forest: Kensal Press, 1982), 68.

6. BL, NC, Add. MS, 32690, fol. 354r–v (Duke of Devonshire to Newcastle, 18 September 1737). The Lord Lieutenant promised to leave no stone unturned to bring the culprits to justice, but since Dean Swift was clearly involved, the case seems to have been discreetly dropped ("I believe sufficient Evidence would be difficult to be got . . . they say the Dean is really ill"), see BL, NC, Add. MS, 32690, fol. 356r (Devonshire to Newcastle, 13 September 1737).

7. Percival, 132.

8. Thomas Newcomb, *A Miscellaneous Collection*, 208.

9. *Verses on the Coronation of their Late Majesties*, 67.

10. James Bramston, *The Man of Taste. Occasion'd by an Epistle of Mr. Pope's on that Subject. By the Author of The Art of Politicks* (London: printed by J. Wright for Lawton Gilliver, 1733), 8.

11. Clyve Jones, "The Parliamentary Organization of the Whig Junto in the Reign of Queen Anne: The Evidence of Lord Ossulston's Diary," in *Parliamentary History* 10, no. 1 (1991): 164–82.

12. LWL, Middleton folder, extracts from BL, Cole Manuscripts, Add. MS, 5846, fol. 21r Cole described himself as having "an inviolable attachment to her Majesty, & her Family" (fol. 22).

13. Quoted in Hanson, 69.

14. Really, 12.

15. Jeremy Black, "An Underrated Journalist: Nathaniel Mist," 36.

16. *Works*, ed. H. Davis, 410.

A Select Bibliography

MANUSCRIPT SOURCES

British Library:
Add. MSS 36772, 32457, 32458, 36772.
Althorp MS E5.
Birch Correspondence, Add MS 4313.
Cole Manuscripts, Add. MS 5846.
Egerton MS 1956.
Hardwicke Papers, Add. MSS 35586, 36137.
Holland House Papers, Add. MSS 51388, 51390, 51391, 51396, 51403, 51427.
Newcastle Papers, Add. MSS 32687, 32688, 32689, 32690, 32691, 32692, 32694, 32697, 32698, 32863, 32948, 32992.
Robinson Papers, Add. MS 23789.
Sloane MS 4052.
Stowe MS 308.

Cambridge University Library:
Cholmondeley (Houghton) Correspondence.
Cholmondeley (Houghton) Papers.

Centre for Kentish Studies:
U269 C148/2.

Edinburgh University Library:
La.II.322.
La.II.451/2.

Lewis Walpole Library:
Sir Charles Hanbury Williams Archives.
Middleton Folder, Extracts from the Cole Manuscripts in the British Library.

National Library of Scotland:
MS 23.3.26.

Nottingham University Library:
Ne C 191.

Public Record Office:
State Papers, Domestic. George I and George II.
Lowther accounts (T38.233–238).

Suffolk Record Office:
Hervey MS, 941/47/18.

PRINTED SOURCES

Adee, Swithin. *The Craftsman's Apology. Being a Vindication of his Conduct and Writings: In Several Letters to the King.* London: printed for T. Cooper, 1732.

Aden, John M. "Pope and Politics: 'The Farce of State.' " In *Alexander Pope*, edited by Peter Dixon, 172–99. *Writers and their Backgrounds*. London: G. Bell & Sons, 1972.

Arnall, William. *The Case of Opposition Stated, Between the Craftsman and the People. Occasioned by his Paper of December the 4th, 1731.* London: printed for J. Roberts, 1731.

———. *Opposition no Proof of Patriotism: With Some Observations and Advice Concerning Party-Writings.* London: printed for James Roberts, 1735.

The Art of Poetry. London: printed for Robert Dodsley, 1741.

As Much as May be Publish'd of a Letter from the B- of R-ch-r to Mr. P-. To which is added, The Several Advertisement for which Mr. Wilkins was assaulted at the Crown-Tavern in Smithfield. London: printed for A. Moore, [1728].

Atherton, Herbert M. *Political Prints in the Age of Hogarth: A Study of the Ideographic Representation of Politics.* Oxford: Clarendon Press, 1974.

Authentic Memoirs of the Life of Richard Mead, M.D. London: printed for J. Whiston and B. White, 1755.

Baker, David Erskine, ed. *Biographia Dramatica; or, A Companion to the Playhouse.* Continued by Isaac Reed and later by Steven Jones. 3 vols. London: Longman, 1812.

Baker, Kenneth. *The Prime Ministers: An Irreverent Political History of Cartoons.* London: Thames and Hudson, 1995.

The Barber Turn'd Packer. A New Ballad. To the Tune of Packington's Pound. London: printed for A. Moore, 1730.

Battestin, Martin C. with Ruth R. Battestin. *Henry Fielding: A Life.* Paperback edition. London and New York: Routledge, 1989.

Beasley, Jerry C. "Portraits of a Monster: Robert Walpole and Early English Prose Fiction." *Eighteenth-Century Studies* 14, no. 4 (Summer 1981): 406–31.

Beattie, John M. *The English Court in the Reign of George I.* Cambridge, UK: Cambridge University Press, 1967.

Beckingham, Charles. *An Ode to the Right Honourable Sir Robert Walpole, Knight of the Most Noble Order of the Garter. On his Installation.* London: printed for and sold by J. Millan, J. Roberts, N. Blandford, A. Dodd, E. Nutt, J. Millar, [1726].

———. *A Poem on His Most Sacred Majesty King George the IId, His Accession to the Throne. Addressed to the Right Honourable the Earl of Peterborow [sic].* London: printed by J. Read and sold by T. Warner, [1727]. Reprinted in Dublin for J. Gowan, 1727.

Berry, Reginald. *A Pope Chronology.* London: Macmillan, 1988.

Bisset, William. *Verses Compos'd for the Birth-Day of our Most Gracious Queen Caroline: The First Birthday of a Protestant Queen Consort for One Hundred and Ten Years. Repeated the same Day in the Great Drawing-Room before Several of the First Quality.* London: printed for J. Roberts, 1728.

Black, Jeremy, ed. *Britain in the Age of Walpole.* London and Basingstoke: MacMillan, 1984.

Black, Jeremy. "Flying a Kite: The Political Impact of the Eighteenth-Century British Press." *Journal of Newspaper and Periodical History* 1, no. 2 (Spring 1985): 12–19.

———. "In Search of a Scandalous Pamphlet: Sir Robert Walpole and the Attempt to Suppress the Publication of Opposition Literature in the United Provinces." *Publishing History* 25 (1989): 5–11.

———. "Party Strife and the Augustan Press." *Publishing History* 23 (1988): 101–3.

———. *Robert Walpole & the Nature of Politics in Early Eighteenth-Century England.* Paperback edition. London: MacMillan, 1990.

———. "An Underrated Journalist: Nathaniel Mist and the Opposition Press during the Whig Ascendency." *Journal of Newspaper and Periodical History* 5, no. 2 (1989): 27–41.

Blackett-Ord, Mark. *Hell-Fire Duke.* Windsor Forest: Kensal Press, 1982.

Bolingbroke, Henry St. John, Lord. *Letter on the Spirit of Patriotism.* In *Letters on the Spirit of Patriotism: On the Idea of a Patriot King: On the State of Parties, at the Accession of King George the First.* London: printed for A. Millar, 1749.

———. *Lord Bolingbroke, Contributions to the Craftsman.* Edited by Simon Varey. Oxford: Clarendon Press, 1982.

Boswell, James. *Boswell's Life of Johnson.* Edited by George Birckbeck Hill. Revised and enlarged by L. F. Powell. 6 vols. Oxford: Clarendon Press, 1934–64.

Bramston, James. *The Art of Politicks, in Imitation of Horace's Art of Poetry.* London: printed for Lawton Gilliver, 1729.

Brand, Sir Alexander. *A True Collection on the Several Birthdays of His Majesty King George, and of their Royal Highnesses the Prince and Princess of Wales from the 1st of March 1724–5, to the 1st of March 1727.* No imprint.

Brown, Stephen. "Making History Novel: Defoe's *Due Preparations* and *A Journey of the Plague Year.*" *Dalhousie Review* 67, no. 2/3 (1987): 190–201.

[Budgell, Eustace]. *Verres and his Scribblers; A Satire in Three Cantos. To which is added an Examen of the Piece, and a Key to the Characters and Obscure Passages.* London: printed for C. Browne, 1732.

Burtt, Shelley. *Virtue Transformed: Political Argument in England, 1688–1740.* Cambridge, UK: Cambridge University Press, 1992.

Cable, Mable Hessler. "The Idea of the Patriot King in the Propaganda of the Opposition to Walpole, 1735–1739." *Philological Quarterly* 18, no. 4 (1939): 119–30.

Cannon, John, ed. *The Whig Ascendancy: Colloquies on Hanoverian England.* London: Edward Arnold, 1981.

Carey, Henry. *The Grumbletonians, or The Dogs Without-Doors. A Tale.* London: printed for J. Peele, 1727.

Carretta, Vincent. *The Snarling Muse: Verbal and Visual Political Satire from Pope to Churchill.* Philadelphia: University of Pennsylvania Press, 1983.

Carthy, Charles. *A Translation of the Second Book of Horace's Epistles, together with Some of the Most Select in the First, with Notes. A Pastoral Courtship, from Theocritus. One Original Poem in English, and a Latin Ode Spoken before the Government on his Majesty's Birth-Day, 1730.* Dublin: printed by Christopher Dickson, 1731.

Catalogue of Prints and Drawings in the British Museum. Division I. Political and Personal Satires. 3 vols. London: Chiswick Press, 1870–77.

Chamberlayne, Paul. *A Full Answer to that Scandalous Libel, the Free Briton of July 1. That was Pretended to be Written by one Francis Walshingham Esq; alias Ar—n—ld, Clerk.* London: printed for the author, and sold by the booksellers of London and Westminster, 1731.

Chapman, Paul. "Jacobite Political Argument in England, 1714–1766." Doctoral dissertation, Cambridge University, 1984.

The Character of Pericles; A Funeral Oration, Sacred to the Memory of a Great Man. London: printed for M. Cooper, 1745.

Chesterfield, Philip Dormer Stanhope, Lord. *Characters of Eminent Personages of His Own Time.* London: printed for William Flexney, 1777.

Cibber, Colley. *A Letter from Mr. Cibber to Mr. Pope, Inquiring into the Motives that might Induce him in his Satyrical Works, to be so Frequently Fond of Mr. Cibber's Name.* London: printed and sold by W. Lewis, 1742.

———. *An Ode for His Majesty's Birth-day, October 30, 1731.* London: printed for John Watts, 1731.

———. *Verses on her Majesty's Birth-day.* London: printed for J. Watts, 1728.

The Citizen's Procession: or, The Smugler's Success and the Patriots Disappointment. Being an Excellent New Ballad on the Excise-Bill. London: printed for Ann Dodd, 1733.

A Coalition of Patriots Delineated: Or, A Just Display of the Union of Jacobites, Malecontents, Republicans, and False Friends, with an Attainted Old Traitor, to Revile the Ministry; Impose upon the People; Set Aside the Succession; and Bring in the Pretender. . . . London: printed for T. Cooper, 1735.

Coley, W. B. "Henry Fielding and the Two Walpoles." *Philological Quarterly* 45, no. 1 (January 1966): 157–78.

Colley, Linda. *Britons: Forging the Nation, 1707–1837.* New Haven and London: Yale University Press, 1992.

———. *In Defiance of Oligarchy: The Tory Party, 1714–60.* Cambridge, UK: Cambridge University Press, 1982.

———. "The Loyal Brotherhood and the Cocoa Tree: The London Organization of the Tory Party, 1727–1760." *The Historical Journal* 20, no. 1 (1977): 77–95.

Collins, A. S. *Authorship in the Days of Johnson: Being a Study of the Relation between Author, Patron, Publisher, and Public 1726–1780.* Clifton: Augustus M. Kelley, 1973.

Colton, Judith. "Merlin's Cave and Queen Caroline: Garden Art as Political Propaganda." *Eighteenth-Century Studies* 10, no. 1 (Fall 1976): 1–20.

Come on Then.—Occasioned by a Pamphlet Lately Published, Intituled. Have at You All. By the Author of, They Are Not. London: printed for T. Cooper, 1740.

Comitia Westmonasteriensium, in Collegio Sti Petri Habita Dei Anniversario Fundatricis suae Reginae Elizabethae Inauguratae Jan. XV. London: printed for William Bowyer, 1728.

Concanen, Matthew. *A Compleat Collection of all the Verses, Essays, Letters and Advertisements, which have been Occasioned by the Publication of Three Volumes of Miscellanies, by Pope and Company. To which is Added an Exact List of the Lords, Ladies, Gentlemen and Others, who have been Abused in these Volumes*. London: printed for A. Moore, 1728.

A Congratulatory Poem; Humbly Inscribed to the Right Honourable Sir Robert Walpole, On the Conclusionn of the Convention between their Majesties of Great–Britain and Spain London: printed for J. Brett. 1739.

The Conduct of the Opposition, and the Tendency of Modern Patriotism, . . . Review'd and Examin'd. London: printed for J. Peele, 1734.

Congreve, William. *A Letter from Mr. Congreve to the Right Honourable the Lord Viscount Cobham*. London: printed for A. Dodd and E. Nutt, 1729.

Cook, Chris and John Stevenson. *British Historical Facts, 1688–1760*. London: Macmillan, 1988.

[Cooke, Thomas]. *The Battle of the Poets. An Heroick Poem. In Two Canto's*. London: printed for J. Roberts, 1725.

Cooke, Thomas. *The Letters of Atticus, as Printed in the London Journal, in the Years 1729 and 1730, on Various Subjects*. London: printed by J. Chrichley and sold by J. Roberts, 1731.

———. *Mr. Cooke's Original Poems, with Imitations and Translations of Several Select Passages of the Antients [sic], in Four Parts: To which are added Proposals for Perfecting the English Language*. London: printed for T. Jackson and C. Bathurst, 1742.

———. *Poems on Affairs of State, Collected from the Daily, Evening, and Weekly, Papers: To which is Added the History of the Traytors Edric the Father, and Edric the Son, and of the Settlement of the Danes on the English Throne. Dedicated to Henry St. John Esqr, Late Lord Viscount Bolingbroke*. London: printed for J. Roberts, 1733.

———. *Tales, Epistles, Odes, Fables, &c. with Translations from Homer and Other Ancient Authors. To which are added Proposals for Perfecting the English Language*. London: printed for T. Green, 1729.

Corns, T. N, and W. A. Speck and J. A. Downie. "Archetypal Mystification: Polemic and Reality in English Political Literature, 1640–1750." *Eighteenth Century Life* 7, no. 3 (May 1982): 1–27.

The Countryman's Answer to the Ballad, called, Britannia Excisa. No imprint, 1733.

Cowper, Ashley. *The Faction. A Tale. Humbly Inscrib'd to Messrs. Craftsman and compy. By Timothy Scribble Esq*. London: James Roberts, 1740.

———. *High Boys up go We! Or, A Rod for Somebody. An Excellent New Ballad, Occasion'd by a Late Poem, entitled, An Ode to Mankind. By Timothy Scribble Esq.*. London: printed for J. Roberts, 1741.

———. Ashley. *The Norfolk Poetical Miscellany. To which are added some Select Essays and Letters in Prose. Never Printed before. By the Author of the Progress of Physick*. Edited by "Timothy Scribble" [Ashley Cowper]. 2 vols. London: printed for the author and sold by J. Stagg, 1744.

Coxe, William. *Memoirs of the Life and Administration of Sir Robert Walpole. With Original Correspondence and Authentic Papers never before Published*. 3 vols. London: printed for T. Cadell, Junior and W. Davies, 1798.

The Crafts of the Craftsmen; or, A Detection of the Designs of the Coalition: Containing Memoirs of the History of False Patriotism for the Year 1735. London: printed for J. Roberts, 1736.

Crane, R. S., and F. B. Kaye with the assistance of M. E. Prior, eds. *A Census of British Newspapers and Periodicals 1620–1800.* New edition. London: Holland Press, 1979.

Cranfield, G. A. *The Development of the Provincial Newspaper, 1700–1760.* Oxford: Clarendon Press, 1962.

———. *The Press and Society: From Caxton to Northcliffe.* London and New York: Longman, 1978.

Cruickshanks, Eveline. *Political Untouchables: The Tories and the '45.* London: Duckworth, 1979.

Davies, Tom. *The Characters of George the First, Queen Caroline, Sir Robert Walpole . . . Reviewed. With Royal and Noble Anecdotes. . . .* London: printed for T. Davies and T. Cadell, 1777.

Dawley, D'Anvers, and Fog's Triumph; or, the Downfall of Belzabub, Bell, and the Dragon: A New Ballad. London: printed for J. Roberts, 1734.

Deacon, Richard. *The Truth Twisters. Disinformation: The Making and Spreading of Official Distortions, Half-truths and Lies.* London and Sydney: Futura Publications, 1988.

Defoe, Daniel. *The Conduct of Robert Walpole, Esq.; from the Beginning of the Reign of Her Late Majesty Queen Anne, to the Present Time.* London: printed for T. Warner, 1717.

———. *Due Preparations for the Coming Plague, as well for Soul as Body. Being Some Seasonable Thoughts Upon the Visible Approach of the Present Dreadful Contagion in France. . . .* London: printed for E. Matthews and F. Batley, 1722.

———. *The Letters of Daniel Defoe.* Edited by George Harris Healey. Oxford: Clarendon Press, 1955.

A Dialogue between an Oak and an Orange-tree. London: printed for James Roberts, 1716.

Dickinson, H. T. *Liberty and Property: Political Ideology in Eighteenth-Century Britain.* Paperback edition. London: Methuen, 1979.

The Dictionary of National Biography. Edited by Leslie Stephen and Sidney Lee. 63 vols. Oxford: Oxford University Press, 1885–1900.

Downie, James Alan. "The Development of the Political Press." In *Britain in the First Age of Party 1680–1750: Essays Presented to Geoffrey Holmes.* Edited by Clyve Jones, 111–27. London and Ronceverte: the Hambledon Press, 1987.

———. *Robert Harley and the Press: Propaganda and Public Opinion in the Age of Swift and Defoe.* Cambridge, UK: Cambridge University Press, 1979.

———. "Walpole, 'the Poet's Foe.' " In *Britain in the Age of Walpole.* Edited by Jeremy Black, 171–88. London and Basingstoke: MacMillan, 1984.

The Dream. A Poem, Sacred to the Blessed and Glorious Memory of her late Majesty Queen Caroline. London: printed for J. Roberts, 1737.

Duck, Stephen. *A Poem on the Marriage of His Serene Highness the Prince of Orange, with Anne, Princess-Royal of Great Britain. . . .* No imprint, 1734.

———. *The Vision. A Poem on the Death of Her Most Gracious Majesty Queen Caroline.* London: printed by Samuel Richardson for J. Roberts and J. Jackson, 1737.

Duncombe, John, ed. *Letters by Several Eminent Persons Deceased. Including the Correspondence of John Hughes, Esq. . . .* 3 vols. London: printed for J. Johnson, 1773.

Dunkin. William. *Epistola ad Franciscum Bindonem, Arm. cui adjiciuntur quatuor Odae.* Dublin: printed for George Faulkner, 1741.

Dunkin, William and others. *A Vindication of the Libel on Dr. Delany, And a Certain Great Lord. Together with a Panegyric on Dean Sw—t . . .* Dublin printed, reprinted in London for J. Wilford, 1730.

Egmont, John Perceval, Lord. *Manuscripts of the Earl of Egmont. Diary of Viscount Perceval, afterwards First Earl of Egmont.* Edited by R. A. Roberts. Historical Manuscripts Commission 63, 3 vols. London: His Majesty's Stationary Office, 1920–23.

The Eighteenth Century Short Title Catalogue. On CD-ROM.

An Elegy on the Much Lamented Death of Harry Gambol, who Dy'd of a Pleuresy, Aug. 31. [London]: printed for John Nichols [1714].

Ellis, Kenneth. *The Post Office in the Eighteenth Century: A Study in Administrative History.* London: Oxford University Press, 1958.

An Epistle to the Little Satyrist of Twickenham. London: printed for J. Wilford, 1733.

An Epistle to the Right Honourable Sir Robert Walpole London: printed for J. Walthoe, 1726.

An Epistle to the Right Honourable Sir Robert Walpole. London: printed for W. Mears, 1728.

An Epistle to the Right Honourable Sir Robert Walpole; Occasion'd by the Writings of the Craftsman, and the Late Peace Concluded with Spain. London: printed for James Roberts, 1730.

Erskine-Hill, Howard. "Alexander Pope: The Political Poet in His Time." In *Modern Essays on 18th Century Literature,* edited by Leopold Damrosch, 123–40. New York and Oxford: Oxford University Press, 1988.

———. *The Social Milieu of Alexander Pope: Lives, Examples and the Poetic Response.* New Haven and London: Yale University Press, 1975.

Eusden, Laurence. *An Epistle to the Noble, and Right Honourable Sir Robert Walpole.* London: printed, and sold by J. Roberts, 1726.

———. *Three Poems; The First, Sacred to the Immortal Memory of the Late King; The Second, On the Happy Succession, and Coronation of His Present Majesty; And a Third Humbly Inscrib'd to the Queen.* London: printed for James Roberts and sold by R. and J. Dodsley, S. Barker and G. Woodfall, 1727.

The False Patriot. An Epistle to Mr. Pope. London: printed for James Roberts, 1734.

The False Patriot's Confession; or, B-k's Address to Ambition. In Imitation of the First Ode, of the Fourth Book of Horace. London: printed for R. Charlton, 1737.

Fielding, Henry. *The Adventures of Joseph Andrews.* Edited by L. Rice-Oxley. London: Oxford University Press, 1973.

———. *Of True Greatness: An Epistle to the Right Honourable George Dodington, Esq.* London: printed for C. Corbet, 1741.

Foss, Michael. *The Age of Patronage: The Arts in Society 1660–1750.* London: Hamish Hamilton, 1971.

Foxon, David F. *English Verse 1701–1750: A Catalogue of Separately Printed*

Poems with Notes on Contemporary Collected Editions. 2 vols. London: Cambridge University Press, 1975.

Frowde, Philip. *The Fall of Saguntum. A Tragedy*. London: printed for J. Crokatt and T. Wood and sold by J. Roberts, 1727.

A Full and True Account of the Sad and Deplorable, Death of Caleb D'Anvers, Esq; who Dy'd Suddenly London: printed: and sold by J. Roberts, 1931.

A Further Report from the Committee of Secrecy, Appointed to Enquire into the Conduct of Robert, Earl of Orford; during the Last Ten Years of his being First Commissioner of the Treasury, and Chancellor and Under-Treasurer of His Majesty's Exchequer. London: printed for T. Leech, 1742.

Gavin, Antonio. *A Master-Key to Popery: In Five Parts*. . . . London: printed for J. Stephens and sold by A. Bettesworth, etc., 1725.

Gerrard, Christine. *The Patriot Opposition to Walpole: Politics, Poetry, and National Myth, 1725–1742*. Oxford: Clarendon Press, 1994.

The Gods in Debate: or, No Bribe like Beauty. A New Ballad, on the Prince of Orange's Arrival. London: printed for J. Roberts and sold by W. Waring, [1733].

Goldgar, Bertrand A. *Walpole and the Wits: The Relation of Politics to Literature, 1722–1742*. Lincoln: University of Nebraska Press, 1976.

The Grand Accuser the Greatest of all Criminals. Part I. London: printed for J. Roberts, 1735.

The Grand Defeat: or, The Downfall of the S[an]d[on]ian Party. To the Tune of, Chevy Chase: or God Prosper Long our Noble King, &c.. London: printed in the year 1741.

Greene, Kenneth Myron. "Sir Robert Walpole and Literary Patronage." Doctoral dissertation, Columbia University, 1964.

Robert L. Haig. *The Gazetteer 1735–1797: A Study in the Eighteenth-Century English Newspapers*. Carbondale: South Illinois Press, 1960.

Halsband, Robert. "Literary Patronage in Eighteenth-Century England." Synopsis in *Expression, Communication and Experience in Literature and Language: Proceedings of the XII Congress of the International Federation for Modern Languages and Literatures Held at Cambridge University, 20 to 26 August 1972*, edited by Ronald G. Popperwell, 186–87. London: The Modern Humanities Research Association, 1973.

Hammond, Brean S. *Pope and Bolingbroke: A Study of Friendship and Influence*. Columbia: University of Missouri Press, 1984.

Hanson, Laurence. *Government and the Press, 1695–1763*. Lithographical reprint of the 1936 edition. Oxford: Clarendon Press, 1967.

Hardwicke, Philip Yorke, Lord. *Walpoliana*. London: privately printed, 1781.

Harris, Michael. "Journalism as a Profession or Trade in the Eighteenth Century." In *Author-Publisher Relations During the Eighteenth and Nineteenth Centuries*, edited by Robin Myers and Michael Harris, 37–62. Oxford: the Polytechnic Press, 1982.

———. *London Newspapers in the Age of Walpole: A Study of the Origins of the Modern English Press*. London and Toronto: Associated University Presses, 1987.

Haig, Robert L. *The Gazetteer 1735–1797: A Study in the Eighteenth-Century English Newspapers*. Carbondale: Southern Illinois Press, 1960.

Hawling, Francis. *A Miscellany of Original Poems on Various Subjects . . . Part I.* London: printed for S. Austen, J. Wood, and J. Crockat, [1751].

Henderson, Alfred James. *London and the National Government, 1721–1742: A Study of City Politics and the Walpole Administration. Perspectives in European History* 7. Philadelphia: Porcupine Press, 1975.

Hervey, John, Lord. *An Epistle from a Nobleman to a Doctor of Divinity.* London: published by James Roberts, 1733.

———. *The False Patriot's Confession; or, B-k's Address to Ambition. In Imitation of the First Ode, of the Fourth Book of Horace.* London: printed for R. Charlton, 1737.

———. *Observations on a Pamphlet, intitled, An Answer to One Part of a Late Infamous Libel, in a Letter to Mr. P..* London: printed for James Roberts, 1731.

———. *Observations on the Writings of the Craftsman.* London: printed for J. Roberts, 1730.

———. *Some Material towards Memoirs of the Reign of George II.* Edited by R. Sedgwick. 3 vols. London, 1931.

Hinde, Thomas. *Tales from the Pump Room; Nine Hundred Years of Bath: the Place, its People and its Gossip.* London: Victor Gollancz, 1988.

Howard, Leonard. *A Collection of State Papers, from the Original Manuscripts of Several Princes and Great Personages in the Two Last Centuries; with some Curious and Scarce Tracts, and Pieces of Antiquity, Modern Letters, &c on Several Important Subjects.* 2 vols. London: printed for the author, 1756.

A Hue and Cry after Part of a Pack of Hounds, which Broke out of Their Kennel in Westminster. To which is added, Modern Characters, By another Hand. London: printed for F. Style, 1739.

The Humble Petition of His Grace Ph[ili]p D[uke] of Wh[arto]n to a Great Man. London: printed for A. Brooks, 1730.

Humphreys, Samuel. *Cannons. A Poem. Inscrib'd to His Grace the Duke of Chandos.* London: printed and sold by J. Roberts, 1728.

Ilchester, Lord, and Mrs. Langford-Brooke. *Sir Charles Hanbury Williams: Poet, Wit and Diplomatist.* London: Thornton Butterworth, 1929.

Jacob, Hildebrand. *Patriotic Love; An Ode. Chiefly Occasioned by Some Late Acts of Parliament: and Humbly Inscribed to the True Friend of his Country.* London: printed for W. Lewis, 1737.

Jenyns, Soame. *Poems. By *****.* London: printed for R. Dodsley, 1752.

Johnson, Dr. Samuel. *An Account of the Life of Mr Richard Savage, Son of the Earl Rivers.* Second edition. London: printed for E. Cave, 1748.

Jones, Clyve, ed. *Britain in the First Age of Party, 1680–1750: Essays Presented to Geoffrey Holmes.* London and Ronceverte: the Hambledon Press, 1987.

Jones, Clyve. "The Parliamentary Organization of the Whig Junto in the Reign of Queen Anne: The Evidence of Lord Ossulston's Diary." In *Parliamentary History* 10, part 1 (1991): 164–82.

Jones, Richard Foster. *Lewis Theobald: His Contribution to English Scholarship with Some Unpublished Letters.* New York: Columbia University Press, 1919.

Joshi, K. L. *"The London Journal, 1719–1738."* In *Journal of the University of Bombay. New series.* 9 (1940): 44–51.

Kelch, Ray A. *Newcastle, a Duke without Money: Thomas Pelham-Holles 1693–1768.* London: Routledge & Kegan Paul, 1974.

[Ker, John]. *The Cause of Liberty. Addressed to the British Senate*. London: printed by and for J. Chrichley, 1734.

King, William. *Political and Literary Anecdotes of His Own Time*. London: John Murray, 1819.

Knight, Charles. The Old Printer and the Modern Press. London: J. Murray, 1854.

Kramnick, Isaac. *Bolingbroke and his Circle: The Politics of Nostalgia in the Age of Walpole*. Cambridge, Massachusetts: Harvard University Press, 1968.

Langford, Paul. *Walpole and the Robinocracy*. Cambridge, UK: Chadwyck-Healey, 1986.

Last, B. W. *Politics and Letters in the Age of Walpole*. Paperback edition. Newcastle: Avero, 1987.

A Letter to a Noble Lord: Occasion'd by the Late Publication of the Dunciad Variorum. In *Pope Alexander's Supremacy and Infallibility Examin'd; And the Errors of Scriblerus and His Man William Detected. With the Effigies of His Holiness and His Prime Minister, Curiously Engrav'd in Copper*, 9–18. London: printed for J. Roberts, 1729.

The Lives of Dr. Edward Pocock . . . Dr. Zachary Pearce . . . Dr. Thomas Newton . . . and of the Rev. Philip Skelton. 2 vols. London: F. C. & J. Rivington, 1816.

Lockwood, Thomas. "Fielding and the Licensing Act." *Huntingdon Library Quarterly* 50, no. 4 (Autumn 1987): 379–93.

Loftis, John Clyde. *The Politics of Drama in Augustan England*. Oxford: Clarendon Press, 1963.

L[or]d B[olingbro]ke's Speech upon the Convention. To the Tune of A Cobler there was. London: printed for Jacob Littleton, 1739.

[Lyons, John]. *The Danverian History of the Affairs of Europe, for the Memorable Year 1731*. London: printed for James Robert, 1732.

Lyttelton, George, Lord. *An Epistle to Mr. Pope, from a Young Gentleman at Rome*. London: printed for J. Roberts, 1730.

Mack, Maynard. *Alexander Pope: A Life*. New Haven: Yale University Press in association with W.W. Norton, 1985.

———. *The Garden and the City: Retirement and Politics in the Later Poetry of Pope, 1731–1743*. Toronto: University of Toronto Press, 1969.

Macklin, Charles. *A Will and No Will*. In *Eighteenth Century Drama: Afterpieces*, edited by Richard W. Bevis. Paperback edition. London, Oxford, New York: Oxford University Press, 1970.

Madden, Samuel. *Memoirs of the Twentieth Century*. London: printed by John Bowyer Nichols etc., 1731.

———. *Themistocles, the Lover of his Country*. Dublin: printed by S. Powell for George Risk, George Ewing, and William Smith, 1729.

Malice Defeated. A Pastoral Essay. Occasioned by Mr. Pope's Character of Lord Timon, in his Epistle to the Earl of Burlington, and Mr. Welsted's Answer. London: printed for J. Millan, 1732.

Manners: An Epistle to Alexander Pope Esq; and Mr. Whitehead. London: printed for T. Cooper, 1739.

Manning, Frances. *On the Late Queen's Sickness and Death, an Ode. Address'd to His Grace the Duke of Newcastle, One of His Majesty's Principal Secretary's of State, &c.*. London: printed for T. Cooper, 1738.

————. *The Two First Odes of Horace Imitated. With an Introductory Epistle to a Friend*. London: printed, and sold by James Roberts, 1738.

The Manuscripts of the Earl of Carlisle, Preserved at Castle Howard. Historical Manuscripts Commission. 15th Report. Appendix. Part VI. London: Her Majesty's Stationery Office, 1897.

Martyn, Benjamin. *Timoleon. A Tragedy. As it is Acted at the Theatre-Royal, in Drury-Lane*. Dublin: printed by S. Powell for George Risk, George Ewing, and William Smith, 1731.

Maubey, Sir Joseph. Notes on the life of Thomas Cooke. *Gentleman's Magazine* 61, part 2 (1791): 1090–94, 1178–85; 62, part 1 (1792): 26–32, 214–21, 313–16; 62, part 2 (1792): 566–67.

McAleer, John J., ed. *Ballads and Songs Loyal to the Hanoverian Succession (1703–1761). Augustan Reprint Society Publication* 96. Los Angeles: William Andrews Clark Memorial Library, University of California, Los Angeles, 1962.

McGee, Michael C. "'Not Men, but Measures': The Origins and Import of an Ideological Principle." *The Quarterly Journal of Speech* 64, no. 2 (1978): 141–54.

McKendrick, Neil, ed. *Historical Perspectives: Studies in English Thought and Society in Honour of J. H. Plumb*. London: Europa Publications, 1974.

Memoirs of the Times, In a Letter to a Friend in the Country. Containing an Account of, and Reflections on Some Late Remarkable Occurrences. London: printed for Anne Dodd. 1737.

Memoirs of Vicountess Sundon, Mistress of the Robes to Queen Caroline, Consort of George II; Including Letters from the most Celebrated Persons of her Time. Edited by Mrs Thomson. 2 vols. London: Henry Colburn, 1847.

Meredith, James. *Manners Decypher'd. A Reply to Mr. Whitehead, on his Satire Call'd Manners*. London: printed for T. Cooper, [1739].

Miller, James. *Harlequin Horace: or, The Art of Modern Poetry*. London: printed for Lawton Gilliver, 1731.

Mitchell, Joseph. *A Familiar Epistle to the Right Honourable Sir Robert Walpole; Concerning Poets, Poverty, Promises, Places &c. To Which are Added Congratulatory Verses upon His Taking Possession, as First Commissioner of the Treasury, of the New House adjacent thereto in St. James's Park*. London: printed for Alexander Cruden, 1735.

————. *The Monument: or, The Muse's Motion to the Right Honourable Sir Robert Walpole, Knight of the most Noble Order of the Garter, Upon Occasion of the Death of Sir Richard Steele, Knt.*. London: printed for James Roberts, 1729.

————. *Poems on Several Occasions*. 2 vols. London: printed for the author and sold by L. Gilliver, 1729.

————. *Ratho: A Poem to the King*. London: printed for John Gray, 1728.

————. *The Royal Hermitage or Temple of Honour: A Poem to Her Majesty the Queen-Regent. To which is Prefix'd, An Epistle to the Right Honourable Sir Robert Walpole*. London: printed for J. Roberts, 1732.

————. *A Sick-Bed Soliloquy to an Empty Purse: in Latin and English Verse . . . To which is added a Curse upon Punch; In Imitation of the third Epode of Horace*. London: printed for the author and sold by W. Mears, [1735].

Mitchell, Louis D. "Command Performances during the Reign of George II." *Restoration and 18th Century Theatre Research* 1, no. 1 (1986): 18–33.

Montagu, Lady Mary Wortley. *Essays and Poems and Simplicity, A Comedy*. Edited by Robert Husband and Isobel Grundy. Oxford: Clarendon Press, 1993.

[Mottley, John]. "A Complete List of all the English Dramatic Poets and of all the Plays ever Printed in the English Language, to the Present Year M,DCC,XLVII." Appended to Thomas Whincop. *Scanderbeg: or, Love and Liberty. A Tragedy*. London: printed for W. Reeve, 1747.

Mottley, John. *The Craftsman, or, Weekly Journalist: a Farce*. London: printed for J. Roberts, 1728.

———. *Verses Addressed to the Right Honourable Sir Robert Walpole, On Her Majesty's being Constituted Regent of Great Britain*. London: printed, and sold by T. Read, 1729.

Murray, Thomas. *The Literary History of Gallaway*. Edinburgh: Waugh & Innes, and London: Ogle, Duncan & Co., 1822.

The Muse in Distress: A Poem. Occasion'd by the Present State of Poetry; Humbly Address'd to the Right Honourable Sir William Yonge. London: printed for T. Cooper, 1733.

Musgrave, William. *Genuine Memoirs of the Life and Character of Sir Robert Walpole, And of the Family of the Walpoles, From their first Settling in England, before the Conquest, to the Present Times: Containing Several Curious Facts, and Pieces of History Hitherto Unknown*. In 2 parts. London: printed for E. Curll, 1732.

Myers, Robin and Michael Harris. *Author-Publisher Relations During the Eighteenth and Nineteenth Centuries*. Oxford: Polytechnic Press, 1982.

The New Dozen at Westminster; Or Caleb's Good Men, and True. To the Tune of, Which Nobody Can Deny. London: printed for A. Moore, [1729].

Newcomb, Thomas. *The Manners of the Age: in Thirteen Moral Satires. Written with a Design to Expose the Vicious and Irregular Conduct of Both Sexes*. London: printed for Jer. Batley, 1733.

———. *A Miscellaneous Collection of Original Poems, Consisting of Odes, Epistles, Translations, &c. Written Chiefly on Political and Moral Subjects. To which are added, Occasional Letters and Essays, formerly published in Defence of the present Government and Administration*. London: printed by J. Wilson, 1740.

———. *A Supplement to One Thousand Seven Hundred and Thirty-Eight. Not Written by Mr. Pope*. London: printed for J. Roberts, 1738.

Nichols, John. *The History and Antiquities of the County of Leicester*. 4 vols. London: printed by and for John Nichols, 1795.

———. *Illustrations of the Literary History of the Eighteenth Century. Consisting of Authentic Memoirs and Original Letters of Eminent Persons; and Intended as a Sequel to the Literary Anecdotes*. 8 vols. London: printed for the author by Nichols, Son, and Bentley, 1817–1858. Facsimile edition. New York: Kraus Reprint & AMS Press, 1966.

———. *Literary Anecdotes of the Eighteenth Century*. 9 vols. London: printed for the author by Nichols, Son, and Bentley, 1812–1815. Facsimile edition. New York: Kraus Reprint Corporation and AMS Press, Inc., 1966.

Nugent, Robert. *Odes and Epistles*. London: printed for R. Dodsley, 1739.

The Oak and the Dunghill; A Fable. London: printed, and sold by James Roberts, 1728.

Of Good Nature: An Epistle Inscrib'd to His G[rac]e the D[u]ke of C[hando]s.

London: printed by J. Hughs for T. Dormer, 1732. Facsimile in *Early Eighteenth-Century Essays on Taste*, introduced by B. Gilmor. Delmar, New York: Scholars' Facsimiles & Reprints, 1972.

Oldmixon, John. *Memoirs of the Press, Historical and Political, For Thirty Years Past, From 1710 to 1740*. London: printed for T. Cox, 1742.

Oldys, William. *A Literary Antiquary: Memoirs of William Oldys, Esq. Norroy King-at-Arms. Together with his Diary, Choice Notes from his Adversaria, and an Account of the London Libraries*. Reprinted from *Notes and Queries* [by J. Yeowell]. London, 1862.

The Opinions of Sarah Duchess-Dowager of Marlborough. Published from Original MSS. No imprint, 1788.

On the Jewel in the Tower. London: printed in the year 1712.

Parrat, William. *Carmen Seculare, For the Year 1733. To the King, on His Going to Hanover*. London: printed, and sold by J. Roberts, 1735.

—————. *An Ode, to the Right Honourable Sir Robert Walpole, on his Majesty's Birth-Day, October the 30th, 1739*. London: printed for C. Corbet, 1739.

Peake, Richard Brinsley. *Memoirs of the Colman Family, Including their Correspondence with the most Distinguished Personages of their Time*. 2 vols. London: Richard Bentley, 1841.

Percival, Milton, ed. *Political Ballads Illustrating the Administration of Sir Robert Walpole*. Oxford Historical and Literary Studies 8. Oxford: Clarendon Press, 1916.

Perry, Tomas W. *Public Opinion, Propaganda, and Politics in Eighteenth-Century England: A Study of the Jew Bill of 1753*. Harvard Historical Monographs 51. Cambridge, Massachusetts: Harvard University Press, 1962.

Perry, William Stevens. *Historical Collections Relating to the American Colonial Church*. 5 vols. No imprint: 1870–78. Vol. 1. *Virginia*.

Pickrill, Dan. *Ministers of the Crown*. London, Boston and Henley: Routledge & Kegan Paul, 1981.

Plomer, H. R. *A Dictionary of the Printers and Booksellers who were at Work in England, Scotland and Ireland from 1668–1725*. Oxford: Oxford University Press for the Bibliographical Society, 1922.

Plumb, J. H. *Sir Robert Walpole*. 2 vols. Volume 1: *The Making of a Statesman*. London: The Cresset Press, 1956. Vol 2: *The King's Minister*. London: Allen Lane the Penguin Press, 1960.

A Poem on His Royal Highness Prince of Wales's Birth-Day. [?Dublin], 1922.

A Poem to Her Royal Highness the Princess of Wales. London: printed for J. Walthoe, 1737.

A Poetical Essay on Vulgar Praise and Hate; In which is Contain'd, The Character of a Modern Patriot. London: printed for T. Cooper, 1733.

A Political Conversation Which Lately Happened between a Couple of Stanch Patriots, and a Revolter to the Court-Interest. In which Many Important Points are Canvass'd, the True Designs of Both Parties Open'd, and not a Little Secret History Revealed. London: printed for T Cowper, 1733.

Pope, Alexander. *The Works of Alexander Pope*. Edited by William Lisle Bowles. 10 vols. Second enlarged edition. London: printed for J. Johnson and others, 1806.

―――. *Alexander Pope, Poetical Works*. Edited by Herbert Davis. Oxford and New York: Oxford University Press, 1978.

Pope Alexander's Supremacy and Infallibility Examin'd; And the Errors of Scriblerus and His Man William Detected. With the Effigies of His Holiness and His Prime Minister, Curiously Engrav'd in Copper. London: printed for J. Roberts, 1729.

Pro and Con. London: printed for James Roberts, 1741.

Ralph, James. *The Case of Authors by Profession or Trade, Stated with Regard to Booksellers, the Stage, and the Public*. London: printed for R. Griffiths, 1758.

Ralph, James, ed. *Miscellaneous Poems by Several Hands*. London: printed by C. Ackers, for W. Meadows, J. Batley, T. Cox, S. Billingsley, R. Hett, and J. Gray, 1729.

Realey, Charles Bechdolt. *The Early Opposition to Sir Robert Walpole. Bulletin of University of Kansas* 32. no. 8. Part of *Humanistic Studies* 4, nos. 2 and 3. Lawrence: University of Kansas Department of Journalism Press, 1931.

Rede, Leman Thomas. *Anecdotes & Biography, Including many Modern Characters in the Circles of the Fashionable and Official Life . . . Alphabetically Arranged*. London: printed by J. W. Meyers, for R. Pitkeathley, 1799.

A Report from the Committee of Secrecy, Appointed to Enquire into the Conduct of Robert Earl of Orford, during the Last Ten Years of his being First Commissioner of the Treasury, and Chancellor and Under-Treasurer of His Majesty's Exchequer. London: printed for Thomas Cox, Charles Bathurst, and John Pemberton, 1742.

Reports on the Manuscripts of the Earl of Eglinton . . . C. F. Weston Underwood Esquire. . . . *Historical Manuscripts Commission Report on the Manuscripts*. London: Eyre & Spottiswoode, 1885.

[Roach, Richard]. *Carmen Corunarium: or, A Gratulatory Poem on the Coronation of King George II. and Queen Caroline. By R. R. B. D..* London: printed for N. Blandford, 1727.

Rogers, J. P. W. "The Authorship of *Four* 'Letters to a Friend in North Britain' and Other Pamphlets Attributed to Robert Walpole." *Bulletin of the Institute of Historical Research* 44, no 110 (1971): 229–238.

Rose, G. H., ed. *A Selection from the Papers of the Earls of Marchmont, in the Possession of the Right Honble Sir George Henry Rose. Illustrative of the Events from 1685 to 1750*. 3 vols. London: John Murray, 1831.

[Ruffhead, James]. *Seasonable Admonitions. A Satire. Most Humbly Address'd to the Right Honourable ****** *******.* London: printed for J. Roberts, 1740.

Ryder, Dudley. *The Diary of Dudley Ryder, 1715–1716*. Edited by William Matthews. London: Methuen, [1939].

Sainty, J. C. *Office-Holders in Modern Britain: Officials of the Secretaries of State 1660–1782*. London: Athlone Press, 1973.

Savage, Richard. *Author to Lett*. Edited by James Sutherland. *The Augustan Reprint Society* 84. Los Angeles: William Andrews Clark Memorial Library, 1960.

Sawyer, Paul. "The Popularity of Pantomime on the London Stage, 1720–1760." In *Restoration and 18th Century Theatre Research* 5, no. 2 (1990): 1–16.

The Scottish Dove, Sent out, and Returning; Bringing Intelligence from their Armies, and makes some Relations of other Observable Passages of both Kingdoms, for Information and Instruction. As an Antidote against the Poisoned

Insinuations of Mercurius Aulicus, and the Errours of other Intelligencers. London: printed for Laurence Chapman, 1643.

Seary, Peter. *Lewis Theobald and the Editing of Shakespeare.* Oxford: Clarendon Press, 1990.

Sedgwick, Romney. *The House of Commons 1715–1754.* 2 vols. London: Her Majesty's Stationary Office, 1970.

The Senator. London: printed for James Roberts, 1728.

Sequel of a Pamphlet Intitled Observations on the Writings of the Craftsman. London: printed for J. Roberts, 1730.

Shaw, William A., ed. *Calendar of Treasury Books and Papers, 1735–1738.* London: Her Majesty's Stationary Office, 1900.

Shenstone, William. *Letters of William Shenstone.* Edited by Duncan Mallam. Minneapolis: University of Minnesota Press, 1939.

Sir *** Speech upon the Peace. To the Tune of the Abbot of Canterbury. London: printed for Jacob Lock, 1739.

Skinner, Quentin. "The Principles and Practice of Opposition: The Case of Bolingbroke versus Walpole." In *Historical Perspectives: Studies in English Thought and Society in Honour of J. H. Plumb.* Edited by Neil McKendrick, 93–128. London: Europa Publications, 1974.

Speck, William. "'Whigs and Tories Dim their Glories': English Political Parties under the First Two Georges." In *The Whig Ascendancy: Colloquies on Hanoverian England.* Edited by John Cannon, 51–70. London: Edward Arnold, 1981.

Spence, Joseph. *Anecdotes, Observations and Characters of Books and Men Collected from the Conversation of Mr. Pope and Other Eminent Persons of his Time by the Reverend Joseph Spence.* Edited by Bonamy Dobrée. London and Fontwell: Centaur Press, 1964.

Spiltimber, George. *The Statesman: A Poem. Humbly Inscrib'd to the Right Honourable Sir Robert Walpole.* London: published by Charles Corbett, 1740.

———. *To the King, on his Majesty's Happy Return. An Ode.* London: printed for Charles Corbett [1740].

Squire, Francis. *A Faithful Report of a Genuine Debate Concering the Liberty of the Press, Addressed to a Candidate at the Ensuing Election. . . .* London: printed for J. Roberts, 1740.

The Statesman's Mirrour, or, Friendly Advice to a Certain Great Minister to Retire from Court. A Poem. London: printed for J. Huggonson, 1741.

Steele, Richard. *The Correspondence of Richard Steele.* Edited by Rae Blanchard. Oxford: Oxford University Press, 1941.

Stevens, David Harrison. *Party Politics and English Journalism, 1702–1742.* Chicago: private edition of dissertation distributed by the University of Chicago Libraries, 1916.

Swift, Jonathan. *The Correspondence of Jonathan Swift.* Edited by. H. Williams. 5 vols. Oxford: Clarendon Press, 1963–65.

Targett, Simon. "Sir Robert Walpole's Newspapers 1722–1742: Propaganda and Politics in the Age of Whig Supremacy." Doctoral Dissertation, Cambridge University, 1991.

They Are Not. London: printed for James Roberts, 1740.

Thomson, E. P. *Whigs and Hunters: The Origin of the Black Act*. Harmondsworth: Penguin, 1975.

The Three Politicians: or, A Dialogue in Verse between a Patriot, a Courtier, and their Friend. Concluding with an Exhortation to Admiral Vernon. London: printed for T. Cooper, 1741.

Tickell, Thomas. *On Her Majesty's Re-Building the Lodgings of the Black Prince, and Henry V, At Queen's-College Oxford*. London: printed for J. Tonson, 1733.

Tit for Tat. Or an Answer to the Epistle to a Nobleman. London: printed for T. Cooper, 1734.

A Touch of the Times. A New Ballad. To the Tune of, Oh! London is a Fine Town. London: printed for T. Cooper, 1740.

Treadwell, Michael. "London Trade Publishers 1675–1750." In *The Library*. Sixth Series, 4, no. 2 (June 1982): 99–134.

The True English-Boys Song, to Vernon's Glory. Occasioned by the Birth-Day of that Brave Admiral. To be Sung Round the Bonfires of London and Westminster. To the Tune of, Come Let us Prepare, &c.. No imprint [London, 1741].

Turner, Joseph. *An Epistle to Dr. Young*. London: printed for W. Mears [1734].

———. *The First Epistle of the First Book of Horace Imitated*. London: printed for J. Roberts, 1738.

The Twickenham Hotch-Potch, For the Use of the Rev. Dr. Swift, Alexander Pope, Esq; and Company. Being a Sequel to the Beggars Opera. London: printed for J. Roberts, 1728.

Urstad, Tone Sundt. "The Works of Sir Charles Hanbury Williams." Doctoral dissertation, Cambridge University, 1988.

Varey, Simon. "*The Craftsman* 1726–1752: an Historical and Critical Account." Doctoral dissertation, Cambridge University, 1977.

Verses on the Coronation of their Late Majesties King George II. and Queen Caroline, October 11, MDCCXXVII. Spoken by the Scholars of Westminster School. . . . London: printed for W. Bowyer, 1761.

Verses to the Lord Carteret, Occasioned by the Present Conspiracy. By a Gentleman of Cambridge. London: printed for Jacob Tonson, 1722.

Viator, Timothy J. "Theobald's Preface to Richard II, and the Possible Closing of Lincoln's Inn Fields in 1719." *Restoration and 18th Century Theatre Research*. Second Series, 3, no. 1 (Summer 1988): 30–33.

Wagner, Peter. *Eros Revived: Erotica of the Enlightenment in England and America*. London: Paladin Grafton Books, 1990.

Walpole, Horace. "Account of Sir Charles Hanbury Williams," *The Yale Edition of Horace Walpole's Correspondence*. Edited by Wilmarth Sheldon Lewis. 48 vols. New Haven: Yale University Press, 1937–83. 30: 314 (Appendix 3).

———. *Reminiscences Written by Mr Horace Walpole in 1788 for the Amusement of Miss Mary and Miss Agnes Berry*. Edited by Paget Toynby. Oxford: Clarendon Press, 1824.

———. *The Yale Edition of Horace Walpole's Correspondence*. Edited by Wilmarth Sheldon Lewis. 48 vols. New Haven: Yale University Press, 1937–83.

Walpole, Sir Robert. *A Letter from Sir Robert Walpole to the Lord Bolingbroke*. Dublin: printed for William Anburey, 1727.

———. *Some Considerations Concerning the Publick Funds, the Publick Revenues, and the Annual Supplies, Granted by Parliament. Occasion'd by a Late*

Pamphlet, Intitled, An Enquiry into the Conduct of our Domestic Affairs, from the Year 1721, to Christmas 1733. London, printed for J. Roberts, 1735.

Weinbrot, Howard. "Persius, the Opposition to Walpole, and Pope." In *Eighteenth-Century Satire: Essays on Text and Context from Dryden to Peter Pindar.* Cambridge, UK: Cambridge University Press, 1988.

Welsted, Leonard. *Of Dulness and Scandal. Occasion'd by the Character of Lord Timon. In Mr. Pope's Epistle to the Earl of Burlington.* London, printed for T. Cooper, 1732.

———. *The Works, in Verse and Prose, of Leonard Welsted, Esq..* Edited by John Nichols. London: printed by and for the editor, 1787.

Weston, James. *The Assembled Patriots; or, the Meeting of the Parliament. A Poem, Dedicated to His Majesty.* London: printed for T. Dormer, 1732.

What of That! Occasion'd by a Pamphlet, intitled, Are These Things So ? And, in Answer, Yes, They Are. London: printed for T. Cooper, 1740.

Whatley, Robert. *A Short History of a Ten Years Negociation between a Prime Minister and a Private Gentleman.* Second edition. London, printed for John Millan, 1738.

Whitehead, Paul. *Manners: A Satire.* London: printed for R. Dodsley, 1739.

———. *The State Dunces: Inscrib'd to Mr. Pope.* London: printed for W. Dickenson, 1733.

Wilkins, W. Walker. *Political Ballads of the Seventeenth and Eighteenth Centuries.* 2 vols. London: Longman, Green, Longman, and Roberts, 1860.

Williams, Basil. "The Duke of Newcastle and the Election of 1734." *English Historical Review* 12 (1987): 448–88.

Williams, Sir Charles Hanbury. *The Works, of the Right Honourable Sir Chas. Hanbury Williams.* 3 vols. London: Edward Jeffery and Son, 1822.

Willoughby de Broke, Richard Verney, Lord. *Dunces out of State. A Poem. Addressed to Mr. Pope.* No imprint. [London], 1733.

Winkler, K. T. "The Forces of the Market and the London Newspaper in the First Half of the Eighteenth Century." *Journal of Newspaper and Periodical History* 4, no. 2 (1988): 22–35.

Winn, James A. "On Pope, Printers, and Publishers." *Eighteenth-Century Life* 6, no. 2–3 (1981): 93–102.

Withers, John. *An Epistle to the Right Honourable Robert Walpole, Esq; Upon His Majesty's Arrival.* London: printed for Jacob Tonson, 1723.

Wodrow, Robert. *Analecta: or, Materials for the History of Remarkable Providences; Mostly Relating to Scotch Ministers and Christians.* 4 vols. Edinburgh: printed for the Maitland Club, 1842–1843.

Woodfine, Philip. "Government Harassment of the Press in the Late 1730s." *Journal of Newspaper and Periodical History* 5, no. 2 (Spring 1989): 20–34.

Yonge, Sir William, Matthew Concanen, and Edward Roome. *The Jovial Crew. A Comic-Opera. As it is Acted at the Theatre-Royal in Covent-Garden, by His Majesty's Servants.* London: printed for J. Watts, 1731.

Yonge, Sir William. *Sedition and Defamation Display'd in a Letter to the Author of the Craftsman.* London: printed for James Roberts, 1731.

Young, Edward. *The Poetical Works of the Rev. Dr. E. Young.* Edited by C. Cook. 2 vols. London: C. Cook, NY.

Index